DEVELOPING KNOWLEDGE-BASED SYSTEMS USING VP-EXPERT®

Macmillan Publishing Company
New York

Maxwell Macmillan Canada
Toronto

Maxwell Macmillan International
New York Oxford Singapore Sydney

DEDICATION

For all students of knowledge-based (expert) systems, especially those whose work is represented in this book.

Editor: Ed Moura
Production Editor: JoEllen Gohr
Art Coordinator: Peter A. Robison
Cover Designer: Robert Vega
Production Buyer: Patricia A. Tonneman

This book was set in New Baskerville by Carlisle Communications, Ltd., and was printed and bound by Semline, Inc., a Quebecor America Book Group Company. The cover was printed by Phoenix Color Corp.

Macmillan Publishing Company
866 Third Avenue
New York, New York 10022

Macmillan Publishing Company is part of the Maxwell Communication Group of Companies.

Maxwell Macmillan Canada, Inc.
1200 Eglinton Avenue East, Suite 200
Don Mills, Ontario M3C 3NI

Library of Congress Cataloging-in-Publication Data

Dologite, D. G. (Dorothy G.)
Developing knowledge-based systems using VP-Expert / D.G. Dologite.
p. cm.
Includes bibliographical references and index.
ISBN 0-02-381886-7
1. Expert systems (Computer science) 2. VP-expert (Computer program) I. Title.
QA76.76.E95D65 1993
006.3′3—dc20 92-9340
CIP

Printing: 1 2 3 4 5 6 7 8 9 Year: 3 4 5 6

PREFACE

A major problem faced by students and managers interested in expert system, also called knowledge-based system (KBS), development is the lack of complete working examples of such systems. Such examples are needed both to stimulate and to guide broader development of such systems. This book is designed to help overcome that problem.

Part One contains a step-by-step tutorial on developing expert systems using the VP-Expert development shell. Part Two contains descriptions of 12 prototype knowledge-based systems. All are actual working prototypes and are given on the disk accompanying the book. The disk also contains the VP-Expert system development shell that enables running the systems, as well as printing out their knowledge bases for further study. Instructions to install the disk are found in Chapter 7, "Installation." The disk is usable on IBM PC and compatible microcomputers.

The book can be used in several ways. First, it is a useful supplemental text for learning and teaching KBS development to Computer Information System majors in school. It is now used in this way, for example, in courses taught using the author's text *Developing Knowledge-Based Systems: An Introduction to Expert Systems,* published by Macmillan (1992). Second, it can be used as a basic text in school courses designed to teach KBS development to general business non-computer-major students in undergraduate and graduate programs, as well as in one-week seminars aimed at non-computer-trained executives who wish to learn how to develop knowledge-based systems. Third, it can be used as a supplemental text for any college course that uses KBS learning exercises, such as in a business policy course.

Knowledge-based systems for management decision making are decision support systems for managers. As such, they are best developed by (or with the close cooperation of) experts—the managers. Field studies confirm that these decision support systems are often developed by managers or those working for managers, and not by computer technicians.[1] This book is designed to assist managers in developing knowledge-based (expert) systems that will aid them in doing their jobs.

Such development efforts are still in their early stages in business. They will not be widespread until two things happen:

1. More managers become skilled in developing these systems, or at least in developing small prototypes of these systems.
2. More models (actual systems) are created to help guide and stimulate managers in their development efforts.

Books like this one, and courses and training seminars based on them, can assist managers in developing these skills and in providing models of basic prototype systems in various decision-making areas.

This work is only a small beginning, however. Building a base of working systems will take many years of hard work.[2] The task involves defining thousands and thousands of routine decisions that managers make in performing their everyday jobs. Only when this base has been developed and made widely available will there be a sound basis for creating more complex management decision support systems using knowledge bases.

Another school of researchers and practitioners is working on developing these more complex systems, many of them based on larger mathematical models of how managers think and decide. This work is important over the longer term. In the meantime, however, other individuals must get on with the business of making systems that work, helping managers learn how to create and use these systems, providing working managers with examples of these systems, and generally putting the expertise that is currently available in the area to work today. That is the business of this book.

All systems described in this book were prepared under the direction of, and with the participation of, the author. The individual systems and the names of those who worked on them are identified in the acknowledgments section.

The systems described in this book grew out of a research project begun in 1985 by the Strategic Management Research Institute's Center of Knowledge-based Systems for Business. The project has focused on creating knowledge-based systems based on a wide range of cognitive models of strategic, and other types of management decisions, developed through research at the institute. The project also involves developing a variety of computer and non-computer methods and techniques for assisting both technical and non-technical managers and individuals to do decision modelling and KBS development.

This book presents work from the project concerning (1) the KBS development methodology that has evolved from this work (in Part One) and (2) some sample prototype systems developed using the methodology (in Part Two). So far, more than 200 non-technical and technical business managers, most of them working full-time during the project, developed over 160 KBS prototype systems, many in conjunction with MBA courses. Based on replies to a survey of this test group, 28 percent of the survey respondents reported their knowledge-based systems were used at work, 21 percent reportedly received promotions, pay raises, or new jobs based on their KBS development work, and 12 percent reported their work led to participation in other KBS development projects at work. Ninety-five percent of the survey respondents reported that their work on the KBS development project led to a substantial increase in their job knowledge or performance.

ACKNOWLEDGMENTS

Appreciation is extended to:

■ The developers, who worked under the direction and supervision of the author, for contributing their prototype knowledge-based systems to this project, especially:

Developer	For Prototype System
Maria Aguilar and Denise Donovan	Nonprofit Organization Loan Advisor
Anthony Cantarella	Local-Area Network Client Screening Advisor
Daniel Dubinsky	Computer File Fixer Expert System
Sheng Guo	Student Financial Aid Advisor
Vantanee Hoontrakul	Foreign Tourism Authority Travel Assistant—For Thailand
Rajive Jain	Motorcycle Troubleshooting Advisor
Laura Lucchesi	Personal Computer Diagnosis and Repair Assistant
Jason Oliviera	Computer Job Scheduler Assistant
Hiren Patel	Small Business Acquisition Advisor
Robert Pfeffer	Juvenile Delinquent Disposition Advisory System
Toby Shatzoff	College Major Advisor
Tai-Min Wan-Bok-Nale	Job Applicant Screening Assistant

■ Dr. Robert J. Mockler of St. John's University and John Merseburg, developers of many of the prototype knowledge-based systems used in the Chapter 1 exercises of this book.

■ Robert S. Pfeffer for his professional efforts in developing the software and material for Chapter 6.

■ The reviewers of the tutorial part of this book, whose thoughtful comments proved invaluable: Paul Alpar, Tel Aviv University, Israel; Alan Brody, consultant; Carl Clavadetscher, California Polytechnic State University; David Doss, Illinois State University; William Ferns, City University of New York–Baruch College; Brian Forst, George Washington University; Shohreh Hashemi, University of Houston; B. Loerinc Helft, City University of New York–Baruch College; Michael Pazzani, University of California, Irvine; and John Sviolka, Harvard University.

■ Wordtech Systems, Inc., for the use of the VP-Expert development shell software (runtime version and educational version); to Ward Systems Group, Inc., for the use of the runtime version of Neuroshell software included with this book; and Cimflex Teknowledge Corp. for use of the M.1 expert system development shell software.

■ Nancy Ward, who provided not only computer technical expertise to refine the systems presented in this book, but also editorial and production expertise to prepare all aspects of this book for publication. Special thanks go to Mark Aune and Bruce Daniels for their help in preparing the draft for publication.

■ The Macmillan Publishing staff who provided support and guidance for this book project, especially Vern Anthony, Peggy Jacobs, and Ed Moura. Thanks also go to Linda Ludewig and JoEllen Gohr for production support, Jeff Smith for work on the software accompanying this book, Peter Robison for work on the graphics, and Dave Boelio for taking an early interest in the project.

REFERENCES

1. For example, see Peter G. W. Keen, "Value Analysis: Justifying Decision Support Systems," *MIS Quarterly* 5(1) (March 1981), reprinted in *Decision Support Systems*, edited by Ralph H. Sprague, Jr. and Hugh J. Watson, Englewood Cliffs, NJ: Prentice-Hall, 1986 (pp. 48–64), p. 53.
2. For example, Professor Daniel Dennett of Tufts University, quoted in *Time*, cover story, March 23, 1988, p. 63.

ABOUT THE AUTHOR

Dr. Dorothy G. Dologite is a Professor of Computer Information Systems at Baruch College, City University of New York. Her research efforts focus on human factors issues of user-developed knowledge-based systems. She has written nine books and many articles related to computer information systems as well as knowledge-based system development, training, and implementation. She has over 15 years of direct computer industry experience, including positions with computer hardware manufacturing and software development firms.

CONTENTS

THE MACMILLAN SERIES IN INFORMATION TECHNOLOGY

BIDGOLI	*Information Systems Literacy and Software Productivity Tools: DOS, WordPerfect, Lotus 1-2-3 and dBASE III Plus,* 0-02-309421-4, 1991 *Information Systems Literacy and Software Productivity Tools: DOS, WordStar, Lotus 1-2-3, and dBASE III Plus,* 0-02-309431-1, 1991 *Information Systems Literacy and Software Productivity Tools: Introductory Concepts,* 0-02-309474-5, 1991 *Information Systems Literacy and Software Productivity Tools: DOS,* 0-02-309427-3, 1991 *Information Systems Literacy and Software Productivty Tools: dBASE III Plus,* 0-02-309428-1, 1991 *Information Systems Literacy and Software Productivity Tools: WordPerfect 5.1,* 0-02-309429-X, 1991 *Information Systems Literacy and Software Productivity Tools: Goldspread,* 0-02-309461-3, 1991 *Information Systems Literacy and Software Productivity Tools: WordStar 5.5,* 0-02-309451-6, 1991 *Information Systems Literacy and Software Productivity Tools: QuattroPro,* 0-02-309455-9, 1991 *Information Systems Literacy and Software Productivity Tools: IBM Basic,* 0-02-309465-6, 1991
DOLOGITE	*Developing Knowledge-Based Systems Using VP-Expert,* 0-02-381886-7, 1993
DUGGAL	*Business Programming Using dBASE IV: A Structured Approach to Systems Development,* 0-02-330588-6, 1992
ELIASON	*Online Business Computer Applications, Third Edition,* 0-02-332481-3, 1991
ERICKSON/ VONK	*Easy PageMaker: A Guide to Learning PageMaker for the IBM PC,* 0-675-21305-3, 1991 *Easy PageMaker: A Guide to Learning PageMaker for the Macintosh Featuring Version 4.0,* 0-675-21382-7, 1992
HOBART/ OCTERNAUD SYTSMA	*Hands-On Computing Using DOS,* 0-675-22386-5, 1991 *Hands-On Computing Using Procomm,* 0-675-22368-7, 1991 *Hands-On Computing Using Microsoft Word,* 0-675-22370-9, 1991 *Hands-On Computing Using WordStar 5.5,* 0-675-22372-5, 1991 *Hands-On Computing Using WordPerfect 5.1,* 0-675-22374-1, 1991 *Hands-On Computing Using FoxPro,* 0-675-22376-8, 1991 *Hands-On Computing Using Paradox 3,* 0-675-22378-4, 1991 *Hands-On Computing Using dBASE IV,* 0-675-22384-9, 1991 *Hands-On Computing Using Lotus 1-2-3, Release 2.2,* 0-675-22380-6, 1991
INGALSBE	*Business Applications Software for IBM and Compatible Microcomputers: Alternate Edition with WordStar 5.5, dBASE III+, and Lotus 1-2-3 (with Software Disks),* 0-675-22389-X, 1991 *FoxPro for IBM and Compatible Microcomputers (with Software Disk),* 0-675-22394-6, 1991

	Using Computers and Application Software, Second Edition, 0-02-359640-6, 1992 *Computing Fundamentals: Concepts and Applications Software,* 0-02-359712-7, 1992 *Application Software Fundamentals,* 0-02-359702-X, 1992
KROENKE	*Database Processing: Fundamentals, Design, Implementation, Fourth Edition,* 0-02-366875-X, 1992
LAUDON/ LAUDON	*Management Information Systems: A Contemporary Perspective, Second Edition,* 0-02-368101-2, 1991
MARTIN, M.	*Analysis and Design of Business Information Systems,* 0-675-20852-1, 1991
MARTIN/ DEHAYES/ HOFFER/ PERKINS	*Managing Information Technology: What Managers Need to Know,* 0-02-328231-2, 1991
McLEOD	*Management Information Systems, Fifth Edition,* 0-02-379481-X, 1992
MOCKLER	*Computer Software to Support Strategic Management Decision Making,* 0-02-381895-6, 1992 *Developing Knowledge-Based Systems Using an Expert System Shell,* 0-02-381875-1, 1992
MOCKLER/ DOLOGITE	*Knowledge-Based Systems: An Introduction to Expert Systems,* 0-02-381897-2, 1992
NEWCOMER	*Select . . . SQL: The Relational Database Language,* 0-02-386693-4, 1992
OLSON/ COURTNEY	*Decision Support Models and Expert Systems,* 0-02-389340-0, 1992
ORMAN	*Elements of Information Systems: Components and Architecture,* 0-02-389475-X, 1991
RAMOS/ SCHROEDER/ SIMPSON	*Data Communication and Networking Using Novell Netware,* 0-02-407791-7, 1992
REGAN/ O'CONNOR	*End-User Information Systems,* 0-02-399163-1, 1992
ROCHE	*Managing Information Technology in Multinational Corporations,* 0-02-402690-5, 1992
ROWE	*Business Telecommunications, Second Edition,* 0-02-404104-1, 1991
SALKIND	*Applying Macintosh: Solutions, Ideas, and Tools,* 0-675-22133-1, 1992
SCHROEDER/ RAMOS	*Introduction to Microsoft Works: A Problem Solving Approach,* 0-02-408015-2, 1991 *Introduction to Microsoft Works: A Problem Solving Approach, Macintosh Version,* 0-02-407771-2, 1992
SPRANKLE	*Problem Solving and Programming Concepts, Second Edition,* 0-02-415340-0, 1992
SZYMANSKI/ SZYMANSKI/ MORRIS/ PULSCHEN	*Introduction to Computers and Information Systems, Second Edition,* 0-675-21272-3, 1991 *Introduction to Computers and Information Systems with Hands-On Software Tutorials,* 0-675-22184-6, 1991 *Computers and Applications Software, Second Editon,* 0-675-21269-3, 1991
TRAUTH/ KAHN/ WARDEN	*Information Literacy: An Introduction to Information Systems,* 0-675-20843-6, 1991
TURBAN	*Expert Systems and Applied Artificial Intelligence,* 0-02-421665-8, 1992
WENIG	*Introduction to C.A.S.E. Technology Using the Visible Analyst Workbench,* 0-675-21367-3, 1991

1

INTRODUCTION

The objective of this chapter is to provide an introduction to expert systems, also called knowledge-based systems, and how they are developed. Many of the topics presented here are covered in more detail in Part One of this book (Chapters 2 through 7).

Topics discussed in this first chapter are

- Some basic definitions
- Evolution of knowledge-based systems
- Components of a knowledge-based system
- Selecting an area for KBS development
- Basic KBS development activities
- Guidelines for the development process

SOME BASIC DEFINITIONS

As shown in Figure 1–1, knowledge-based systems are a branch of the computer science discipline known as artificial intelligence (AI). **Artificial intelligence** is the capability of a device, such as a computer, to perform functions or tasks that would be regarded as intelligent if they were observed in humans.

A **knowledge-based system (KBS)** is a computer system that attempts to replicate functions performed by a human being. Knowledge-based systems are used to capture, magnify, and distribute access to judgment. Typically, they enable a user to consult a computer system as they would an expert advisor to diagnose a problem or determine how to solve a problem, do a task, or make a decision. For example, human experts make decisions about to whom to give bank loans or what steps to take to fix a turbine engine malfunction. They also assist and train others to perform tasks, such as adjusting temperature controls in a manufacturing plant. Knowledge-based systems can do these intelligent activities.

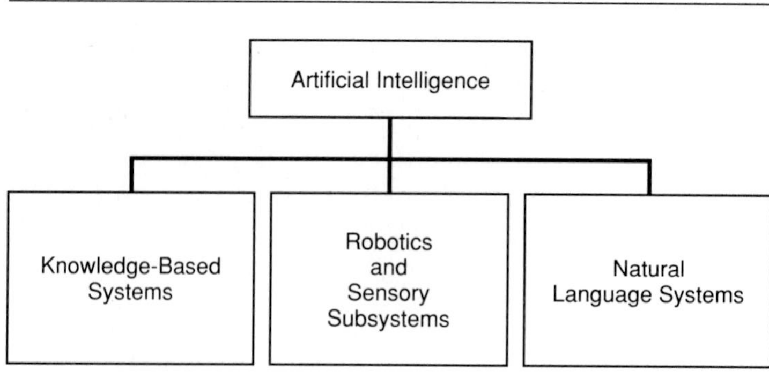

Figure 1–1. Branches of Artificial Intelligence

Like a human expert, a knowledge-based system can extract additional information from a user by asking questions related to the problem during a consultation. It can also answer questions asked by a user about why certain information is needed. An expert system can make a final recommendation to a user and can explain the reasoning steps followed to reach that conclusion.

Expert system is a common expression used to describe this type of computer system. A more technically correct term for most of these systems, as well as those described in this book, is *knowledge-based system* (or *KBS*). Because both terms are often used in the computer field, they are used synonymously in this book. Where the term *expert* is used in relation to the KBS development situations in this book, it is meant in a relative sense. It refers to persons who do their jobs very well or professionally. The actual job can range from order entry clerk, to troubleshooting repairperson, to product planner, to production or operations manager, to strategy developer. The absolute importance of the decision, problem, or task is not what makes it "expert."

EVOLUTION OF KNOWLEDGE-BASED SYSTEMS

The earliest knowledge-based systems were developed in computer science laboratories at universities and supported areas such as medicine, chemistry, engineering, geology, and manufacturing. In the 1980s, KBS development began to take a new direction. Considerable progress was made in developing systems for business applications. Systems started to appear in business areas such as taxation and auditing, banking and commercial financing, strategic planning, insurance underwriting, and stock trading, among other fields.

Businesses discovered the importance of preserving the knowledge of their "experts," whether they be a top-notch investment advisor at a bank or a lead locomotive engine troubleshooter for an electrical engineering firm. Knowledge-based systems serve as repositories of this important corporate asset: the expertise of their employees.

Among the benefits of expert systems found in a study by Feigenbaum et al.[1] are

- They act as intellectual assistants for decision makers and problem solvers.
- They improve the consistency and quality of work because the expert system manages large bodies of knowledge more thoroughly and consistently than people can.

- They can speed professional work by at least a factor of 10.
- They have extraordinarily high return-on-investment percentages.
- They are able to capture company knowledge for use and training by current and future generations of employees, and, in some cases, for sale to customers and others.

Organizations of all types are attempting to broaden their knowledge resources through knowledge-based systems. For example, a Credit Authorizer's Assistant at American Express helps authorizers determine whether to approve customer purchase transactions. This system is used 24 hours a day by some 300 credit authorizers and has increased the number of transactions that can be handled while decreasing losses due to bad judgments. In addition, the time needed to make an authorization decision is reduced, which has resulted in better service to customers.

As another example, Motorola's Expert-Tek system aids in the diagnosis and repair of computers and helps plan for customer service needs. Use of this system has led to quicker response time and resolution of customer problems over the phone.

Figure 1–2 lists commercial KBS applications. These systems range from providing help in capital or personal investment planning to troubleshooting telephone circuit breakdowns.

Many computer industry observers believe that in the future, knowledge-based systems will be built into or integrated with most computer programs. These enhancements will be used to help users navigate new programs without the use of guidebooks. Also, they will add intelligence to programs. This promises to simplify use and improve performance of future computer programs.

While there will always be a need for some stand-alone knowledge-based systems, the bulk of these systems in the future will probably integrate in some way with conventional computer systems and processes already in place or under development. In this sense, it is useful to think of knowledge-based systems and related artificial intelligence as a group of techniques that have applications in many different areas.[2]

For example, knowledge-based systems are sometimes used as so-called "front-ends" to database management systems.[3] They help simplify user inquiries about the data stored in the database management system. They also can help to analyze, or filter for other uses, data in database management systems. The sample prototype systems in this book provide several examples of KBS integration, especially with database management systems.

Different Kinds of Knowledge-based Systems

Knowledge-based systems are sometimes classified by their application areas, such as medicine or chemistry. They also can be classified by the generic problem areas they are concerned with, such as those given in Figure 1–3. These generic categories range from the well-defined, such as diagnosis, monitoring, and debugging, to less-defined areas, such as planning, design, and interpretation. This kind of classification system helps potential users determine if their own problem is appropriate for knowledge-based system technology.

COMPONENTS OF A KNOWLEGE-BASED SYSTEM

A knowledge-based system has three main parts, which are identified in Figure 1–4: the knowledge base, an inference engine, and an explanation facility. The

Figure 1–2. Commercial KBS Applications

ACE (AT&T) provides trouble-shooting reports and analyses for telephone cable maintenance

AS/ASQ (Arthur Young) helps in auditing procedures

AUDITOR (U. of Illinois) selects auditing procedures for the verification of a firm's accounts receivable

AUTHORIZER'S ASSISTANT (American Express) helps in fighting credit card fraud

BUSINESS PLAN (Sterling Wentworth Corp.) advises self-employed professionals and business owners about all aspects of financial planning

CASH VALUE (Heuros Ltd.) provides capital projects planning

COMPASS (GTE Corp.) troubleshoots telephone circuit breakdowns

CONCEPT (Tyashare) produces models of consumer markets

DELTA (GE) helps diagnose and repair diesel electric locomotives

DRILLING ADVISOR (Teknowledge) advises drilling rig supervisors on ways to avoid problems related to drilling and sticking

EDP AUDITOR (Brigham Young and U. of Florida) assists auditors in working with advanced electronic data processing systems

EXPERTAX (Coopers & Lybrand) provides tax accounting advice

FIN PLAN (Wright Patterson Air Force Base) provides personal financial planning

FINANCIAL ADVISOR (Palladian) gives financial advice on projects, products, and mergers and acquisitions

FOLIO (Stanford) helps portfolio managers determine client investment goals and selects portfolios that best meet those needs

GENESIS (IntelliCorp) assists genetic engineers in analyzing DNA molecules

INTELLIGENT SECRETARY (Nippon T&T) manages the schedules of personnel in a company

MORTGAGE LOAN ANALYZER (Arthur Andersen) assists underwriters in making approval decisions on residential mortgage loans

PERSONAL FINANCIAL PLANNER (A.D. Little) prepares total financial plans for individuals with incomes of $25K-100K

PLANPOWER (Applied Expert Systems) gives professional financial planning advice

(R1)XCON (Digital Equipment Corp/Carnegie-Mellon) configures computer systems to meet individual customer specifications

STRATEGIC MANAGEMENT OF TECHNOLOGY (A.D. Little) assists in the planning of research and development investments for key corporate technologies

SYNTELLIGENCE has an expert system to advise insurance underwriters in evaluating commercial risk

TAXADVISOR (U. of Illinois) provides estate planning tax advice

TICOM (U. of Minnesota) models a computer company's internal control systems

TRADER'S ASSISTANT (A.D. Little) assists securities traders in assessing the state of the stock market

XSEL (Digital Equipment) acts as an expert selling assistant to assist DEC salespersons

knowledge base is a collection of information, or expert knowledge, about some specific area or field. This knowledge is often composed of both facts, such as those found in manuals and textbooks, and heuristics, or "rules of thumb," that a human expert uses to do a task or make a decision. In some cases, heuristics represent years of judgment and experience that are the essence of a human expert. **Knowledge engineers** are computer specialists with skills to mine heuristics out from human experts and transfer them into a computerized knowledge base.

Heuristics often end up as "rules" in the knowledge base. For example, the expert system XCON and its related systems at Digital Equipment Corporation contain over 10,000 rules to help configure a minicomputer system. The rules determine what computer parts work together that fulfill a customer's order and

Figure 1–3. Generic Categories of Expert System Applications

Category	Problem Addressed	Types of Systems
Diagnosis	Infers system malfunctions from observations	Medical, electronic, financial analysis, auditing, machine repair
Monitoring	Compares observations in order to identify variations	Management control, nuclear power plant regulation
Debugging	Prescribes remedies for malfunctions	Computer software
Repair	Executes a plan to administer a prescribed remedy	Automobile, computer, telephone
Instruction	Diagnoses, debugs, and corrects student behavior	Tutorial, remedial
Control	Interprets, predicts, repairs, and monitors system behaviors	Air traffic control, battle management, manufacturing process control
Prediction	Infers likely consequences of given situations	Weather forecasting, crop estimation, financial forecasting
Interpretation	Infers situation descriptions from sensor data	Speech understanding, image analysis, surveillance, mapping
Design	Configures objects within situation constraints	Circuit layout, budgeting, automatic program generation
Planning	Develops guidelines for action	Strategic planning, process scheduling, military planning
Classification	Prescribes categories for given sets of criteria	Planning, scheduling, layout, remedial, auditing, forecasting

what engineering constraints and specifications apply to the order. A simplified example of a rule might be: For every five part X's ordered, the customer will also need one part Y.

This kind of information is important to a knowledge base, particularly in a case like Digital, where company policy is to give each customer exactly what is wanted. Customers can order computer equipment in any possible configuration to meet specific needs. The complexity of the problem is compounded by the extensive product line offered by Digital and the continual number of new products made available by the company. The enormous number of possible combinations rapidly translates into a vast knowledge-based system with many rules.

Rules are the most commonly used way to represent knowledge in a KBS. Another is *objects*, or *frames*, among other options. Because all of the sample systems discussed in this book are represented in rules, other knowledge representation methods are not discussed here.

The second main part of a knowledge-based system is the **inference engine,** which is the program that makes the system work. An inference engine handles the logic processing inside a knowledge-based system. For example, the inference engine knows when and how to retrieve rules from the knowledge base and when and how to ask a user a question.

Although inference engines for knowledge-based systems can be created from scratch by programmers, today a majority of knowledge-based systems are being developed using a packaged "shell" with built-in inference engines. Shells are discussed in the following section.

Figure 1–4. Essential Components of a Knowledge-based System

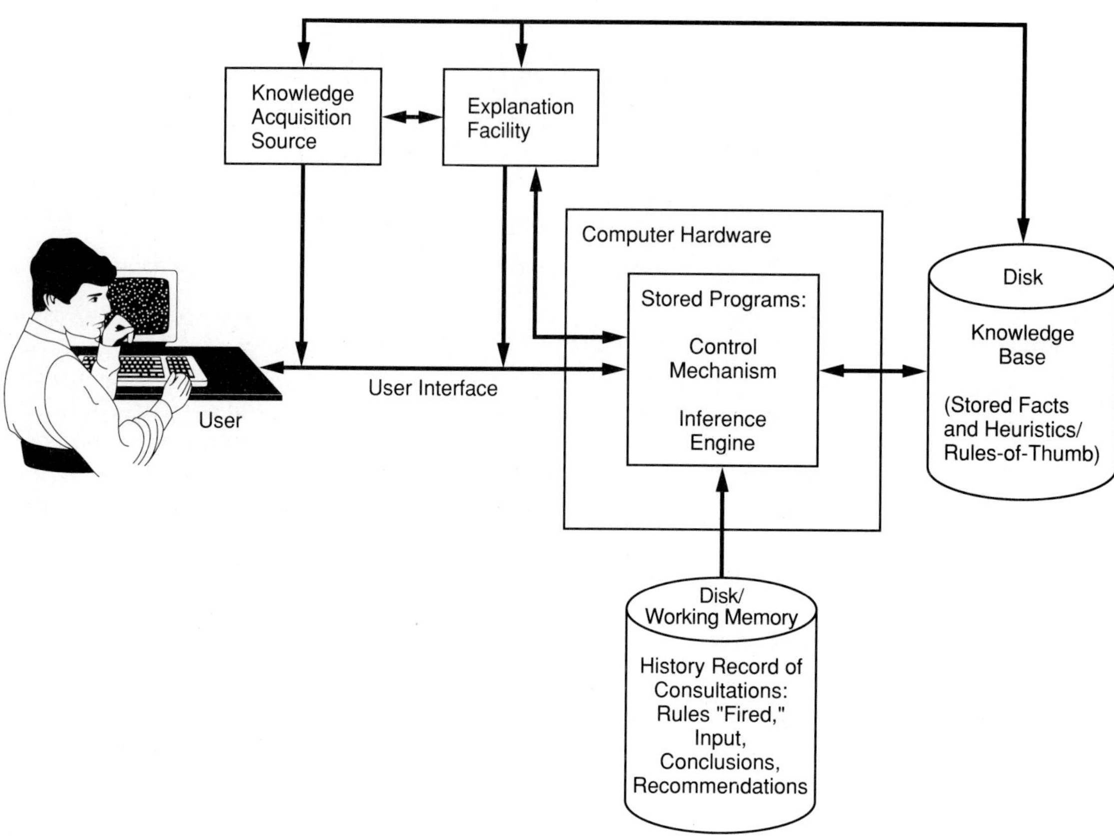

The final component of a knowledge-based system is an explanation facility. For moral, ethical, and legal reasons, a professional is unlikely to accept the advice of a knowledge-based system unless the system's logic and chain of reasoning can be reviewed. An **explanation facility** stores a history file, during a user consultation, of the rules that contribute to a conclusion. The system uses this history file to report exactly how it arrived at a given conclusion or line of reasoning.

Shell Packages

To simplify creating a KBS, developers often use **shell packages.** These packages contain an inference engine but no knowledge base. The knowledge base can be entered by a knowledge engineer or, in some cases, directly by the user.

Shell packages are the predominant way to develop knowledge-based systems on microcomputers. They are especially good for developing small systems that test the feasibility and soundness of proposed larger systems before expensive development efforts are undertaken. Such smaller developmental test systems are called **prototype** systems.

A microcomputer shell package called VP-Expert is the knowledge-based system development tool used in this book. The tutorial in Part One "walks through" the building of a prototype knowledge-based system. Part Two describes 12 prototype systems developed with the VP-Expert shell. Both the VP-

Expert shell (an educational version) and the prototype systems are available on a disk that accompanies this book.

Role and Importance of Prototyping

Since knowledge-based systems are relatively new and costly to develop, it is usually prudent to develop one in stages, starting with small prototypes of the actual system. This enables testing and refining the basic structure and concept of the system, as well as specific parts of the system, before committing substantial resources to its development. It also helps developers become familiar with KBS technology before undertaking larger, more costly systems. Sometimes prototypes are developed of different segments or modules of a system as the overall system is incrementally created.

In prototype development, an effort is made to select only the most critical factors and to show only their most basic relationships. This helps test the underlying structure and concept of the system. For this reason, most prototype systems cannot be expected to capture all the rich complexities involved in the actual situation. That is the function of later, more advanced versions of the system.

Although often crude first efforts, prototypes serve several useful purposes:

- They provide a preliminary analysis of the situation. Since they isolate the essence of the structure and concept of the system, they give the developer and users a chance to evaluate the overall approach before getting too deeply into the system development.
- They enable creating initial systems quickly. Producing a working system helps sustain the interest of experts and whets the developer's appetite for expanding and enhancing the system.
- They encourage building a system in a modular, incremental way that is well coordinated. In larger projects, this enables using a development team while still maintaining the integrity of the unified, overall system.
- They are often a useful tool for quickly eliciting knowledge from experts.

In addition to its practical value in actual situations, prototype development is also an important learning and teaching tool. It introduces a manager or potential manager to knowledge-based systems and to expert system shells in a very compact and efficient way. Another benefit is that prototyping can often lead to smaller working systems that are immediately useful on the job.

SELECTING AN AREA FOR KBS DEVELOPMENT

Sometimes selection of a decision, problem, or task for knowledge-based system development is easy. For example, a diagnostic KBS to help service staff troubleshoot problems in communications equipment can readily be applied to this technology: The troubleshooting task is a structured one with a finite number of well-defined solutions. The task occurs in steps, where each step reduces the possible causes of the equipment problem.

But many decisions and problems are not as suitable for KBS development. Selecting applicable areas for KBS development begins with an examination of needs, including examining answers to questions such as these:

- Is human expertise scarce?
- Is the human expertise in danger of being lost?

- Is the human expertise expensive in relation to a job's value to the company?
- Is the expertise needed in a number of locations?
- Do the job requirements, such as speed and precision, exceed the capacity of normally available experts?

If it is determined that a need exists that can benefit from the development of a computerized system, the next step is to examine the feasibility of the proposed knowledge-based system project. For a KBS project to be feasible, the answer should be "yes" to most of the following questions:

- Do recognized experts exist?
- Can experts do the task better than amateurs and can their skills be taught to others?
- Do experts agree on solutions to the problem or decision?
- Does the task require reason and informed judgments, as opposed to just common sense?
- Can experts articulate their methods or does the expertise exist in books and manuals?
- Is the task well understood?
- Is the task of manageable size?
- Are typical example cases or situations readily available for testing the validity of a computerized system?

If a proposed project is considered to be feasible, the developer should then determine the risks inherent in a proposed system development project. A prototype system is included on the diskette accompanying this book to help evaluate the risks of a KBS project. The prototype, named RISK.KBS, considers some of the factors of project risk assessment. It can be run by following the instructions given in Figure 3–2, "Procedure for Running a Consultation."

BASIC KBS DEVELOPMENT ACTIVITIES

Knowledge-based systems are developed by

- Analyzing, or decomposing, the situation under study and evaluating relationships
- Reformulating or reconceptualizing the model or representation of the decision situation under study in order to put it into a computer-usable format
- Putting the decision onto the computer

This cyclical process of analyzing and reformulating the decision situation under study and transforming it into a computer-compatible knowledge base is diagrammed in Figure 1–5.

The *analysis phase* requires breaking the situation down into its smallest components. Even a seemingly simple decision, such as whether or not to proceed with a small KBS development project, requires considerable imaginative thinking to recreate potential future circumstances that might be encountered.

For someone not trained or naturally skilled in this kind of forward thinking, it is often difficult to specify

- Every step involved in making a decision
- Each piece of information needed
- The many alternative decision paths the mind pursues in the decision process

Figure 1–5. Formulation and Reformulation of a KBS

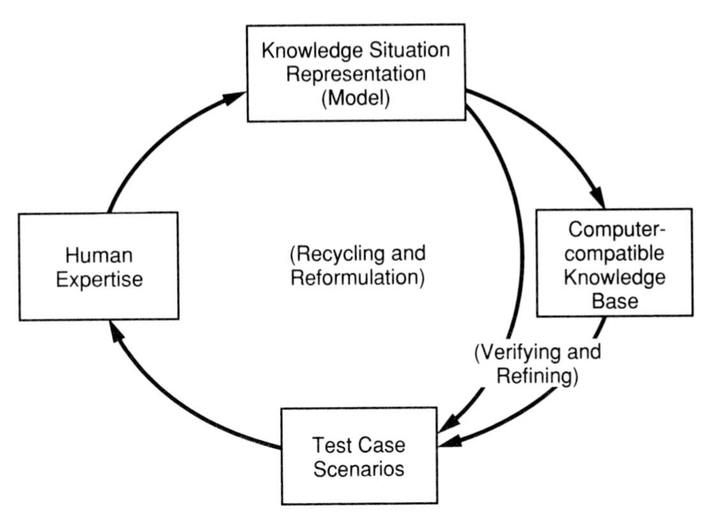

It has been said that a good journalist or story writer is best trained for this analysis and evaluation phase of a knowledge-based system's development. This is because, in a sense, one is writing "an accurate story" or *scenario* of how a situation works.

During the early phases of the development process, the situation under study is explored from a variety of viewpoints. Key terms or key situation factors are defined. For example, if the situation involves a computer configuration decision, terms such as *configuration, computer, components, central processing unit,* and *connectors* would have to be understood and defined. In an automotive diagnostic situation, terms such as *fuel injector, carburetor,* and *spark plug* would be defined. In a marketing management decision situation, terms such as *customer demographics, market mix,* and *media* would need defining.

As the situation analysis phase continues, some sense of the structure of the knowledge segments within the area of expertise under study, sometimes called the **knowledge domain,** or *problem space,* begins to emerge.

As the structure emerges, diagrams are often constructed to get a more precise picture of how the decision is made or the task is carried out. This is variously called the *situation reconceptualization* or *representation* phase. Figure 1–6 gives an example of such a diagram. The decision situation represented in the figure is a preliminary review of the suitability of a proposed KBS project. The decision involves estimating the level of risk or chances for success of a proposed KBS development project.

This example is from an early development phase of a small *concept-testing* prototype KBS. It is called "concept testing" because, during the reconceptualization phase, one is often not sure if the initial situation diagram is an accurate model or representation of the actual situation under study.

An outline for a report made about this structured analysis and reformulation approach is given in Figure 1–7. Such a report can be prepared by the system developer, whether a knowledge engineer or a knowledge domain expert, and is a useful tool in KBS training development programs.

Not all knowledge-based systems are expert-driven systems developed by the expert themselves. Some development situations involve the interaction of knowledge engineers with computer technical personnel, as well as interaction with an expert or experts. The process outlined in Figure 1–8 is typical of the

Figure 1–6. Decision Situation Diagram: Estimating KBS Project Proposal Level of Risk (Initial Prototype Phase)

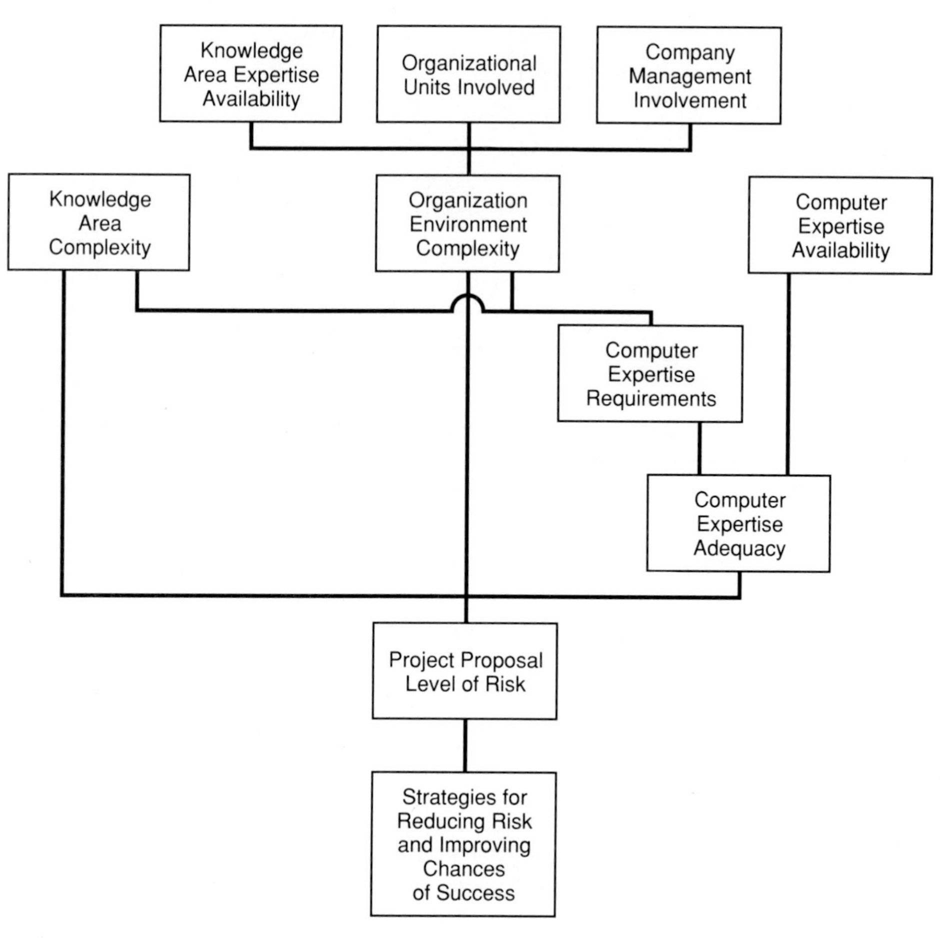

development steps followed when a knowledge engineer is involved in developing a KBS.

GUIDELINES FOR THE DEVELOPMENT PROCESS

There are a variety of ways to diagram or structure a decision situation or knowledge domain. Finding the *best* modelling format is not the goal. Finding a reasonably good one that makes subsequent modelling phases easier *is*, provided that the model used is an accurate representation of the actual situation under study.

The sample prototype systems in Part Two of this book offer many examples of diagrams that evolved over many iterations to help describe the decision making, or reasoning process, in the knowledge domain under study.

Generally speaking, it is best to focus on the most typical situations during the early phases of the study. Exceptional cases should be avoided until reasonably good diagrams or models of the situation have been developed. Trying to incorporate all the nuances of the task into these early models often impedes

Figure 1–7. Topic Outline for a Report Summarizing the Situation Analysis and Reformulation for a Proposed KBS

A. Studying the Overall Situation: Understanding the Expert's Domain

Selecting a decision area to work on
Probing how the situation works
Describing how decisions are made
Narrowing the focus of the study
Getting more specific and defining interrelationships
(This section is needed only in larger development projects.)

B. Studying the Situation to Be Prototyped

The precise decision area under study, including the possible recommendations to be made.
The knowledge segments and the decision processes involved in each phase of the process, including a decision situation diagram showing factors influencing each phase of the decision process
The specific questions which need answering in order to obtain information about the factors needed to make a recommendation
Detailed explanations of the recommendations and the reasoning processes determining them
An example scenario of how a typical decision is made

At each of these phases, *when probing, when getting more specific,* and *when studying the situation to be prototyped,* always

- Write and review a specific example (scenario) of a typical decision situation
- Draw a generalized model (or diagram) of it
- Review additional test or typical cases (scenarios) and revise the diagrams

Figure 1–8. Overview of Development Process Involving a Knowledge Engineer and Expert

■ Expert observation	Watch the expert solving real problems at work.
■ Problem analysis	Explore the kinds of data, knowledge, and procedures needed to solve problems in the expert's area.
■ Problem description	Have the expert describe a typical problem for each category of solution in the expert's area.
■ Problem refinement	Present the expert with a series of realistic problems to solve, probing for the rationale behind the reasoning steps.
■ System development and refinement	Once a description of how the expert works has been developed, have the expert give you a series of problems to solve using the decision steps developed from earlier interviews.
■ System testing	Have the expert examine and critique a prototype system's performance.
■ System validation	Present the cases solved by both the expert and the prototype system to other outside experts.

progress. The initial prototype systems are generally designed to handle only the most typical situations.

The general objective of an initial prototype is to replicate or emulate a composite description of how one pretty good expert might make a decision reasonably well. In major systems, this replication often is arrived at through a compromise, based on the judgments of a variety of experts in the field, after considering

- The ways different experts actually work
- The best way to do the task or decision making theoretically
- The technical limitations inherent in the expert system shells and hardware used to computerize the system

ABOUT THIS BOOK

The next chapter begins Part One of this book (Chapters 2 through 7). Part One is a tutorial to create a knowledge-based system. It "walks through" the development of a sample system used by a Health Maintenance Organization, or HMO. HMOs are an alternative to more common fee-for-service medical facilities. They provide medical services to members for a prepaid fee.

The sample system is created with the VP-Expert development shell software package. The tutorial begins with a simple system. Subsequent chapters build on this preliminary system, adding enhancements such as spreadsheet and database integration, improved user interface, and graphics capabilities.

All of the knowledge base system files discussed in the tutorial are provided on a diskette accompanying this book. The systems can be run on the computer as they are discussed in the tutorial. This provides firsthand illustrations of how a knowledge-based system prototype is developed and incrementally improved.

The completed sample KBS prototypes in Part Two (Chapters 8 through 10) provide many examples of how to use the techniques discussed in the earlier tutorial chapters. They are grouped into three categories according to system complexity: beginner, intermediate, and advanced knowledge-based systems. They also provide an idea of the range of different applications that can benefit from knowledge-based system technology. Hopefully they will inspire others to build on this foundation and create new applications relevant to other experiences or interests that could benefit from knowledge-based system technology.

All systems discussed in Part Two are provided on the diskette that accompanies this book. They can be run by following the instructions in Figure 3–2, "Procedure for Running a Consultation."

REVIEW QUESTIONS

1. What is an expert, or knowledge-based, system?
2. What is artificial intelligence?
3. Discuss some benefits of expert systems.
4. Name several commercial knowledge-based systems.
5. Describe the three main parts of a knowledge-based system.

6. What is the role of knowledge engineers in knowledge-based system development?
7. Describe the predominant method of developing knowledge-based systems on microcomputers.
8. Why are prototypes developed for larger systems? What are some of the benefits of prototypes?
9. What are the steps to select an area for KBS development?
10. Identify the three basic activities of KBS development.
11. What is the general objective of an initial prototype KBS?

EXERCISES

1. The disk accompanying this book contains a number of knowledge-based systems. One of them is a VP-Expert automated travel information system. This prototype KBS is designed to help customers in a Thailand tourism office decide on a suitable vacation destination, based on the customer's preferred vacation activity, means of transportation, and lifestyle. A full discussion of this KBS is given in Chapter 9.

   Following the instructions for running a VP-Expert consultation in Figure 3–2 of this book ("Procedure for Running a Consultation"), run the tourism KBS, which has the filename TAT.KBS. Record your answers to questions asked, as well as the recommendation given.
2. The CAREER.KBS is written to run with the M.1 expert system development shell. It is designed to assist users in deciding if they would make successful entrepreneurs. Follow the directions below for using M.1 to run a consultation of the CAREER.KBS system.
   a. Load the M.1 expert system shell program from the C:>, A:>, or other DOS prompt by typing "start" and pressing the Enter key. (Note: M.1 program shell and data (.KBS) files must be on the *same* disk drive.)
   b. The M1> prompt appears on the screen. To load the desired KBS file, type

      M1>load filename.extension (hit Enter key)

      Example:

      M1>load career.kbs (hit Enter key)

      where filename.extension represents the full DOS name of the M.1 .KBS file you wish to run. Press the Enter key. Loading the file can take from one to five minutes.
   c. Once the file is finished loading, the M1> prompt reappears. Type "go" and press the Enter key.
   d. Then follow the instructions on the screen to run the knowledge-based system consultation. The prompt that appears on screen during the consultation is the >> prompt.
   e. To exit M.1 and go back to DOS, type "exit" or "quit" at the M1> prompt or >> prompt and press the Enter key.

   The knowledge base for this system is stored as a text, or ASCII, file. Print out the knowledge base for this KBS using your word processor or the DOS PRINT command (see Chapter 7) to study its rules and questions.

3. The disk accompanying this book contains two versions of the project risk evaluation KBS mentioned in this chapter. They are named RISK.KBS (VP-Expert version) and KBS-EVAL.KBS (M.1 version) in the disk files. Following the directions in Exercise 2 for using M.1 and the instructions for running VP-Expert in Figure 3–2 of this book ("Procedure for Running a Consultation"), run a consultation of both systems. Which version do you prefer? Why?
4. A more advanced version of the risk evaluation system is also given on the disk accompanying this book. It was built using the M.1 expert system shell and has the filename RISKEVAL.KBS. Run this system, using the guidelines in Exercise 2, to see how a small system can expand during KBS prototyping iterations.
5. Examine recent issues of expert system periodicals, such as *Expert Systems, AI Expert, PC AI,* and *IEEE Expert,* or other related periodicals of your choice. Find a detailed description of a knowledge-based system. Write a brief report comparing the system to the one you consulted in Exercise 1.
6. Develop a small knowledge base for a system of your own. First write a scenario of how a typical decision is made. Next list the major recommendations that might be made, three or four critical factors affecting the recommendation, and the major questions to ask to obtain information about the critical factors. Use the information collected in the first and second steps to develop a block decision situation diagram, similar to the one in Figure 1–6, that replicates or models the decision area. Consult the M.1 KBS on the disk accompanying this book entitled SCREEN.KBS for guidance on how to accomplish this exercise. Follow the directions in Exercise 2 for using M.1 to run the SCREEN.KBS system.

REFERENCES

1. **Feigenbaum, Edward, Pamela McCorduck, and H. Penny Nii.** *The Rise of the Expert Company.* New York, NY: Time Books, 1988.
2. **Bulkeley, William M.** "Bright Outlook for Artificial Intelligence Yields to Slow Growth and Big Cutbacks." *The Wall Street Journal* (July 5, 1990): B1, B3.
3. **Schur, Stephen.** "The Intelligent Database." *AI Expert* (January 1988): 26–34.

Part One

VP-EXPERT TUTORIAL

2

DEVELOPING A FIRST KNOWLEDGE-BASED SYSTEM

This chapter and the next four are designed to be a tutorial on developing a first knowledge-based system (KBS). The chapters walk through the entire development process, which includes using an expert system shell development tool to put the system on the computer.

This chapter provides an overview of the basic design and development process of a knowledge base. It covers these topics:

- The general business area selected for KBS development
- The development environment
- Steps to develop a first KBS
- Step 1—Isolate the area for KBS development
- Step 2—Target a decision to be prototyped
- Step 3—Create a dependency diagram
- Step 4—Create decision tables
- Step 5—Write IF-THEN rules
- Step 6—Construct the user interface
- Structure of a knowledge base

The general topics covered in the remaining four chapters of the tutorial are

- Entering the first knowledge base into the computer
- Database, spreadsheet, and other knowledge base development techniques
- User-interface improvements to the knowledge base
- Advanced features

They are followed by a chapter that provides a summary reference guide.

THE GENERAL BUSINESS AREA SELECTED FOR KBS DEVELOPMENT

The general area selected for KBS development is health maintenance. The rapid escalation in health-care costs, combined with the increasing competition in the health-care industry, has generated a substantial interest in alternative methods for financing and delivering health-care services. Many forms of delivering medical services have developed to address the rising cost problem. Some are group practices that work on a prepaid, rather than a fee-for-service, basis.

One prominent variation on prepaid service is the health maintenance organization (HMO). HMOs provide medical service to members in return for a prepaid fee. For them to operate profitably, however, they must contain costs.

Generally, HMO organizations have been successful in providing a continuum of care based on their members' needs. These organizations have achieved lower costs through hospitalization rates that are lower than those in the fee-for-service sector. To contain costs further, however, HMOs must ration the availability of ambulatory service. This form of care is used more frequently in prepaid plans than in fee-for-service health plans.

To achieve the goal of assuring that serious health problems obtain priority access to treatment over lower priority cases, the health-care manager, in this example, has arranged to have a KBS assist personnel who make screening decisions. In each situation, the pertinent criteria for qualification for treatment can be incorporated into the KBS. Personnel doing the screening can then quickly run through the approval-checking procedure by answering questions posed by the KBS. The system, in turn, asks follow-up questions based on the answers it receives. A fully developed system would cover all the generalized standards for establishing the appropriate level of service support given the apparent seriousness of an individual's condition.

This HMO screening problem is similar to problems faced by other organizations. For example, knowledge-based systems have been built to successfully support decisions involving screening customer requests for bank loans as well as screening factory employee requests for maintenance services. Even though all screening problems are similar in some fundamental ways, screening HMO service requests has unique requirements, because health-threatening, and even life-threatening, factors may arise.

The application of KBS technology to the HMO problem provides the following potential benefits:

- The KBS provides for a consistent level of screening service to be delivered, regardless of who is on duty.
- The KBS makes possible decision making by personnel who were previously unauthorized to make decisions.
- The KBS ensures that screening decisions are always made using the same set of criteria. The possibility of inappropriate concerns (for example, a client's race, sex, political affiliation) are eliminated, and, in the event of a dispute, the criteria by which a particular decision was made can be proven.
- The KBS can be used to train screening personnel, which frees more experienced staff for other duties.
- The KBS can be replicated and used wherever members are serviced, assuring the organization of a consistent level of service.
- The KBS can easily be changed to reflect new or revised screening policies and then quickly replicated and distributed to implement the change uniformly throughout the organization without incurring personnel retraining expenses.

These benefits are similar to those claimed by most organizations where KBS technology has been successfully applied to solve business problems.

THE DEVELOPMENT ENVIRONMENT

For this development exercise, no previous background in computer system design or development is assumed.

The VP-Expert shell, or software development tool, is used throughout this tutorial. It is a rule-based expert system shell that runs on an IBM Personal Computer or compatible machine. A general familiarity with this IBM-PC and its DOS operating system is assumed.

The software links with Lotus 1-2-3 spreadsheet files and dBASE III Plus database files. A working familiarity with these two software packages is assumed in the later sections of the tutorial. Such linkage features are commonplace on modern shell development tools. They enable users to build knowledge-based systems that add value to already developed computer-based files and systems. These enhanced systems are frequently called **integrated systems.** This tutorial will incrementally develop an "integrated" system from one that begins as a "stand-alone" system. Although the shell used is VP-Expert, the design methodology can be applied to any other shell.

The educational version of the VP-Expert shell is included on a disk that accompanies this book. Also included on the disk are all the knowledge base files created in this tutorial, other files used for end-of-chapter exercises, and files for the sample prototype systems discussed in Part Two of this book.

Instructions for installing the VP-Expert shell software on a computer are provided in the summary reference guide of Chapter 7. Also provided is a summary of all the software keywords and other features discussed in this tutorial.

The following sections describe how an initial KBS prototype to test concepts for one segment of an HMO service screening assistant is developed.

STEPS TO DEVELOP A FIRST KBS

The procedure to develop a first KBS is given in Figure 2–1.

The example given in Figure 2–2 is a block diagram for a hypothetical HMO. As is evident from the figure, the focus for the prototype is the HMO facility-management service function.

STEP 1—ISOLATE THE AREA FOR KBS DEVELOPMENT

Although the block diagram of the area under study for this tutorial is compacted into the single Figure 2–2, many actual development cases require several layers of graphic description to move from a broad industry perspective to isolate the functional area selected for prototype development.

Many opportunities for KBS development exist in most organizations. Usually, one area will be isolated for an initial concept-testing, or prototyping, phase. In the HMO example, the member service function is selected for study because of its strategic importance to the success of the organization.

Figure 2–1.

Steps to Develop a First KBS

Steps	Action
1	Create a block diagram of the area under study. It should indicate the sub-area selected for initial KBS prototype development. (See example in Figure 2–2.)
2	Create a block diagram of the exact decision situation to be prototyped. It should indicate the critical factors necessary to make a recommendation. (See example in Figure 2–3.)
3	Convert the final block diagram into a dependency diagram. It should indicate all input questions, rules, values, and recommendations made by the KBS prototype. (See example in Figure 2–4.)
4	Create decision tables for all triangles on the dependency diagram. (See examples in Figures 2–5, 2–7, 2–9.)
5	Convert the reduced decision table to IF-THEN rules. (See examples in Figures 2–6, 2–8, 2–10.)
6	Construct the user interface segments of the KBS. These are the parts a user sees when running a consultation. It usually consists of the opening and closing messages for the consultation session, as well as the questions asked during the session. (See example in Figure 2–15.)
7	Using a word processor or an expert system shell "editor," type the elements that constitute the "knowledge base" into a computer file. (See example in Figure 2–15.)
8	Run a trial consultation. (See example in Figure 2–14.) If errors prevent a smooth run, "debug" the errors using the Editor. (See procedure in Figure 3–8.) This "debugging" process often takes several iterations to rid the file of all latent "bugs." This is normal.

In the sample case, the KBS solution developed will be concerned more with illustrating concepts in an incremental learning process than with providing a comprehensive solution to any real problem. For this reason, selected features of the system are isolated for examination while others are intentionally ignored, although they would not be treated so in a fully developed actual case. Nonetheless, the potential of the sample KBS to evolve into a more comprehensive system that further helps to streamline the service function through a link to the member database, as well as a link to a service-control spreadsheet, will be covered.

STEP 2—TARGET A DECISION TO BE PROTOTYPED

Once an area, such as HMO service, is isolated for study, then the precise opportunity or problem in the area is targeted for the KBS application. In the sample case, the initial intent is to build a stand-alone KBS to assist personnel who screen clients on entering the HMO facility. Clients routinely require medical support for new cases or follow-up cases. While some clients require infor-

Figure 2–2. (a) Block Diagram of the Area under Study; (b) Focus of Concept-testing Initial Prototype Knowledge-based System

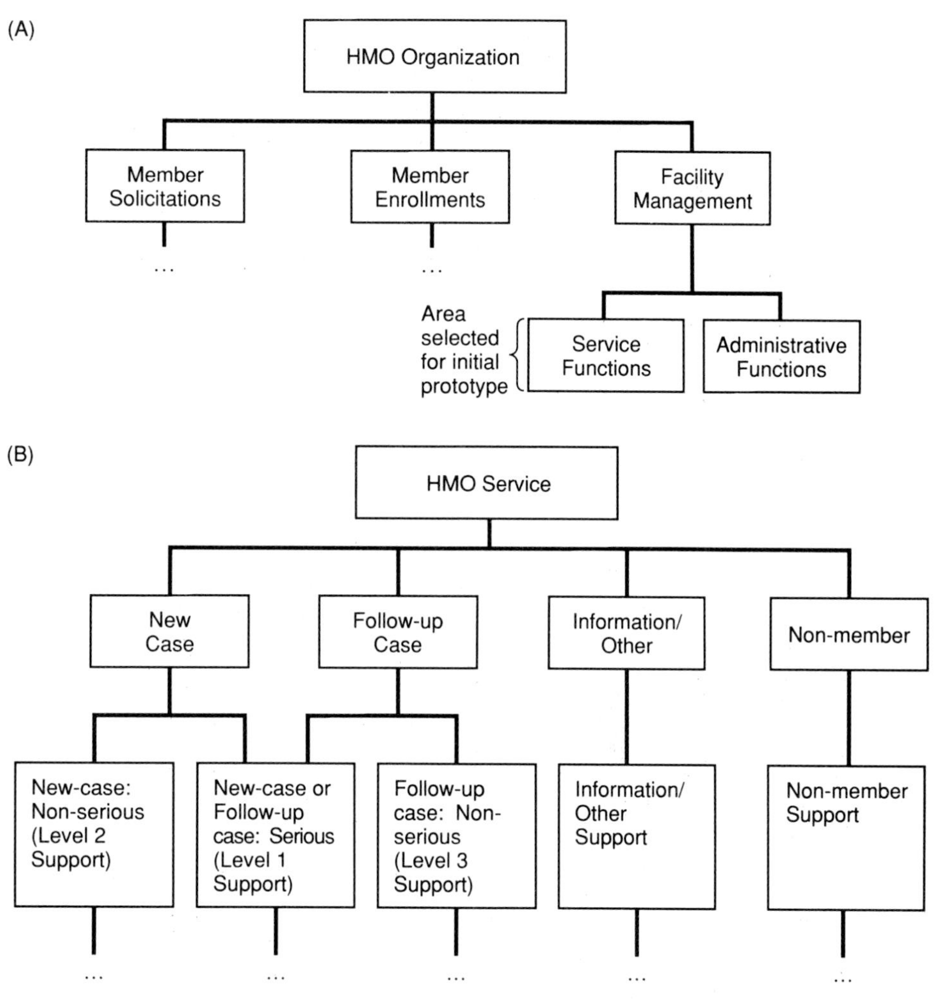

mation or other services, non-members are prime candidates for HMO membership solicitation.

The block diagram in Figure 2–3 helps to define the critical factors in the target decision area to be prototyped. The three critical screening factors selected for this first-effort KBS are the following:

- *HMO status:* Is the client entitled to member service? Two items influence the answer: a client's declaration of membership followed by a verification check of the member's identification number in a control book. (Later, an automatic link to the HMO member database file will make the manual phase obsolete.)
- *Reason:* What is the reason for coming to the HMO facility? Is this a new case, a follow-up case, information-seeking, or "other" visit?
- *Problem:* How serious is the client's current condition? Two items can influence the answer. Are an abnormal temperature or other symptoms present that would require primary-care service?

Figure 2–3. Block Diagram of the Decision Situation to Be Prototyped: HMO Service Screening Assistant (Initial Prototype)

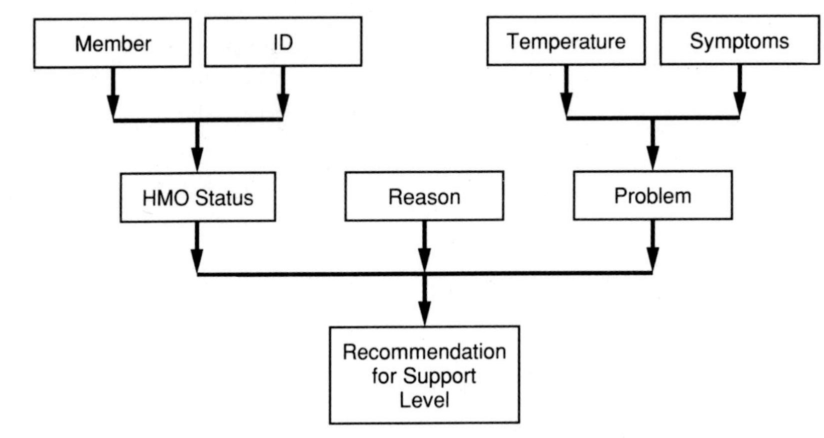

Depending on the answers received, the client would be offered service as follows:

- Level 1 support—for members with serious cases
- Level 2 support—for members with non-serious new cases
- Level 3 support—for members with non-serious follow-up cases
- Information or "other" services support for members
- Non-member support services

The requirements of this sample case are necessarily simplified to allow focusing on situations that illustrate features of the software development shell.

STEP 3—CREATE A DEPENDENCY DIAGRAM

Step 3 in the KBS development process is the transformation of the block diagram from Step 2 into a dependency diagram, as shown in Figure 2–4. A **dependency diagram** indicates the relationships (dependencies) among critical factors, input questions, rules, values, and recommendations made by the KBS prototype. It is a complete graphic statement of the KBS. It serves as the paper model for how to write or code the actual knowledge base.

To begin creating the dependency diagram, it helps to turn the final Step 2 block diagram horizontally. This makes apparent the relation between the block diagram prepared in Step 2 and the result desired in Step 3. To create the Step 3 diagram, begin by drawing boxes with triangles appended for any critical factors identified in Step 2. In the sample case, these factors are member status, reason, and problem. Because "reason" feeds directly into the final recommendation, the intermediate box can be deleted from the dependency diagram. Then on straight lines coming into the triangles, write a word or phrase that best describes the item that will influence the outcome of the critical factor. This item will be called a "variable." Under the line write all the possible values that the variable can have. Also, write names for the values that the critical factor itself can have under each box that represents a critical factor. Do the same for the recommendation box.

At this point, it is customary to label the triangles from right to left with numbers to identify their future status as KBS rule sets. Begin with the one final large triangle that links all the input lines at the concluding recommendation box (see Figure 2–4).

This seemingly mundane modelling forces an evaluation of each piece of the KBS puzzle. The evaluation often causes the modelling process to be repeated over several iterations (with journeys back to Step 2) to model a correct solution. This is normal. The act of putting lines and words on paper and seeing the result causes the critical and creative processes to flow. Usually, after several passes a credible dependency diagram evolves.

In actual practice, there commonly is a hierarchically linked set of dependency diagrams. The one shown in Figure 2–4 would merely represent the highest-level diagram.

STEP 4—CREATE DECISION TABLES

Creating a decision table, such as the one shown in Figure 2–5, for each triangle on the dependency diagram is the final major modelling step. The **decision table** is necessary to show the interrelationships of values to the outcome of any intermediate phase or final recommendation of the KBS.

Preparing a decision table is a straightforward process, as is evident from comparing Figures 2–5, 2–7, and 2–9. The process begins by planning the number of rows necessary for the table. This can be determined by listing all the factors, now called *conditions,* that come into the triangle under consideration. In Figure 2–5, the decision table plan is for the final rule set, which concerns three conditions, each of which can take a number of different values. Member status, the first condition, can take only two values; it is either ok or not ok. Such information comes from the dependency diagram and is easily mapped onto the decision table plan.

Figure 2–4. Dependency Diagram

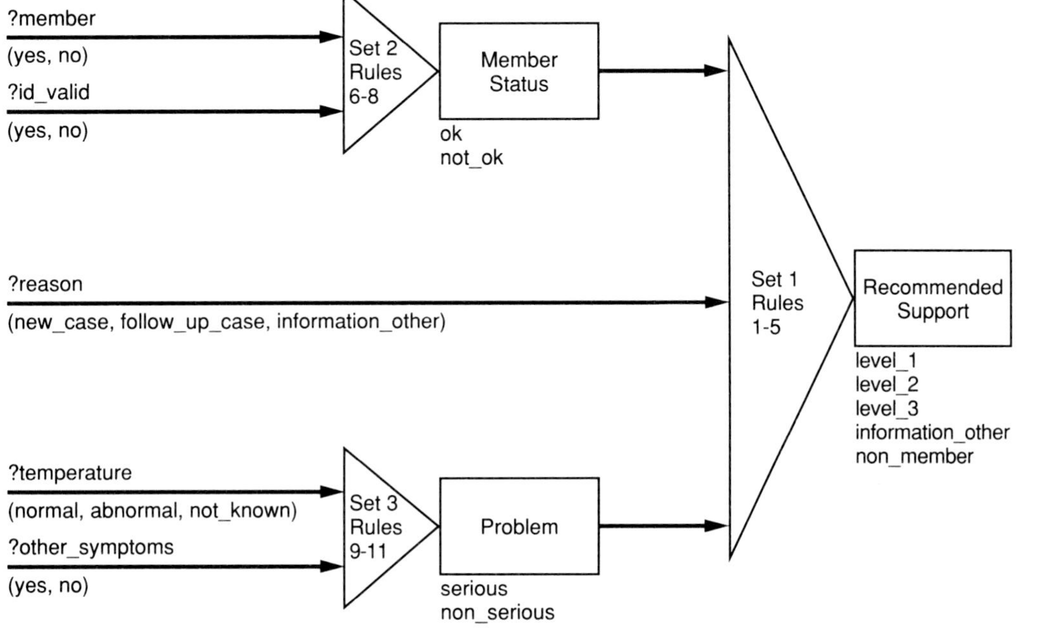

Figure 2–5. Decision Table for Final Rule Set

Step 1: Plan

		Number of Values
Conditions:	Member_status (ok, not_ok)	= 2
	Reason (new_case, follow_up_case, information_other)	= 3
	Problem (serious, non_serious)	= 2

Row = 2 × 3 × 2 = 12 ←

Step 2: Completed Decision Table

Rule	Member Status	Reason	Problem	Concluding Recommendation for Support Level
A 1	ok	new_case	serious	level_1
A 2	ok	new_case	non_serious	level_2
A 3	ok	follow_up_case	serious	level_1
A 4	ok	follow_up_case	non_serious	level_3
A 5	ok	information_other	serious	information_other
A 6	ok	information_other	non_serious	information_other
A 7	not_ok	new_case	serious	non_member
A 8	not_ok	new_case	non_serious	non_member
A 9	not_ok	follow_up_case	serious	non_member
A 10	not_ok	follow_up_case	non_serious	non_member
A 11	not_ok	information_other	serious	non_member
A 12	not_ok	information_other	non_serious	non_member
	↑ 2 cut	↑ 3 cut	↑ 2 cut	

Step 3: Reduced Decision Table

Rule	Member Status	Reason	Problem	Concluding Recommendation for Support Level
B 1	ok	new_case	serious	level_1
B 2	ok	new_case	non_serious	level_2
B 3	ok	follow_up_case	serious	level_1
B 4	ok	follow_up_case	non_serious	level_3
B 5	ok	information_other	—	information_other
B 6	not_ok	—	—	non_member

After all the conditions and values are listed, the number of rows for the decision table can be determined. In this case, there will be 12 rows: two possibilities for "member status," times three possibilities for "reason," times two possibilities for "problem." This calculated number represents all the possible combinations of conditions that can occur at this decision point in the KBS.

The 12 rows are arranged as shown in the completed decision table of Figure 2–5. Creating this table begins by drawing an empty table shell consisting only of row numbers, which will become rule numbers in the knowledge base, and column labels. Column labels are the condition names, and a heading is added for an extra column to identify the possible outcome of each combination of values. This modelling approach allows all combinations of the values of different conditions to be evaluated.

To simplify filling the values into each cell of the table, it helps to draw horizontal dividing lines between rows. The place to draw a dividing line is determined by the number of values from the earlier planning stage. For example, the first condition, member status, has only two possible values. So the first dividing line splits the rows in half (a *2 cut*) between rows 6 and 7. Each half is now a separate whole to be taken into consideration when dividing the rows for the second condition.

The second condition, reason, has three possible values, so a *3 cut* division is appropriate. This 3 cut must now be done twice, once over the top half of rows and once again over the bottom half of rows.

The final condition, problem, requires a 2 cut and calls for treating each of six subdivisions as a whole. So the last horizontal lines split each pair of rows.

Values are next placed into this divided shell of empty cells. As evident from the member status column, the value "ok" is repeated over half the cells and "not ok" is repeated over the other half. Moving right one column, the three values for the second condition are repeated over both halves of the originally divided table. Moving right one more column, it remains to iterate the two values associated with the last condition over each pair of rows.

With all the cells filled in, it now remains to evaluate each combination of values and write the outcome value in the last column. There is no easy formula for doing this. It requires scrutinizing each row, or example case, evaluating all the values listed, and having an expert determine what would be concluded from the evidence given. An evaluation of the first four rows could be read as follows:

1. If member status is ok and reason is a new case, and the problem is serious, then the person should be assigned level 1 support (level 1 is for members with serious problems.)
2. If member status is ok and reason is a new case, and the problem is non-serious, then the person should be assigned level 2 support (level 2 is for members with new cases who do not have serious problems.)
3. If member status is ok and reason is a follow-up case, and the problem is serious, then the person should be assigned level 1 support (level 1 is for members with serious problems.)
4. If member status is ok and reason is a follow-up case, and the problem is non-serious, then the person should be assigned level 3 support (level 3 is for members with follow-up cases who do not have serious problems.)

Reducing a Decision Table

To continue an evaluation of the next row, it quickly becomes obvious that some conditions are meaningless in certain contexts. This is cause for reducing the completed decision table.

In row A5, the case evaluated is a member who requires information or other non-medical service. There is no reason to consider whether there is a medical problem, or its seriousness. In this case, an **indifference symbol**, the hyphen, can be used to indicate that the condition does not have any bearing on the evaluation. Its effect is to collapse rules A5 and A6 into the single rule B5.

Likewise, once it is determined that a case involves a non-member, nothing else is relevant. All non-members are assigned to a special non-member support category. The result is that rules A7 to A12 can be collapsed into the single rule B6.

The final reduced decision table is the last part of Figure 2–5. Figures 2–7 and 2–9 should be examined to see how the same pattern just described is applied to different situations that map dependency diagram triangles into final reduced decision tables.

The decision table format used here is a variation of traditional decision table structure and is adapted to facilitate rule-based modelling. In a traditional decision table, rules would be defined by the columns.

STEP 5 — WRITE IF-THEN RULES

Writing rules for the knowledge base is an easy exercise at this point in the development process. Usually, every rule in the reduced decision table is converted into an IF-THEN rule, as shown in Figures 2–6, 2–8, and 2–10.

The structure and syntax of a rule is given in Figure 2–11. Basically, a rule begins with the keyword IF followed by the conditions evaluated. A series of conditions can be linked by the logical operators AND and OR. AND means that conditions on both sides of the AND must be true in order for the rule to pass or "fire." OR means that one or both conditions must be true.

The first rule in Figure 2–6 illustrates the use of both AND and OR. The use of OR allows combining rules B1 and B3, which explains why the reduced decision table calls for six rules and the conversion process yielded only five rules for the first rule set. A similar use of OR in Rule 11, shown in Figure 2–10, explains why the four-rule reduced decision table in Figure 2–9 yielded only three rules.

If all the conditions in a rule are true, the THEN clause, or conclusion, of a rule is fired. It causes the variable named on the left side of the equal sign in the THEN clause to be assigned the value of the variable on the right side of the equal sign.

For example, look at this simple rule:

```
RULE 6
    IF member = yes and
       valid_id = yes
    THEN member_status = ok;
```

This rule says, in effect, "IF, during a consultation, the value of the variable 'member' is found to be 'yes,' AND the value of the variable 'valid_id' is found to be 'yes,' THEN the variable 'member_status' should be assigned the value 'ok.'"

Rules for naming variables and values, as well as the rule name itself, are identified in Figure 2–12. Because it is not permissible to use keywords as variable or rule names, a list of keywords is given in Figure 2–13 for reference purposes.

Following the THEN conclusion, the ELSE keyword and alternate conclusions can optionally be added to a rule. When present in a rule it says, in effect, "If the premise stated in the rule is known *not* to be true, do this." For example, consider this rule:

Figure 2–6. Convert Decision Table to Rules—Final Rule Set

```
RULE 1
     IF member_status = ok and
        reason = new_case or
        reason = follow_up_case and
        problem = serious
     THEN support = level_1;

RULE 2
     IF member_status = ok and
        reason = new_case and
        problem = non_serious
     THEN support = level_2;

RULE 3
     IF member_status = ok and
        reason = follow_up_case and
        problem = non_serious
     THEN support = level_3;

RULE 4
     IF member_status = ok and
        reason = information_other
     THEN support = information_other;

RULE 5
     IF member_status = not_ok
     THEN support = non_member;
```

```
RULE to_avoid
     IF member = yes and
        valid_id = yes
     THEN member_status = ok
     ELSE member_status = not_ok;
```

This rule suffices to express the entire reduced decision table in Figure 2–7. The rule states that IF a person is a member with a valid ID number, THEN this person's member status is good, otherwise it is not. This is a form of default reasoning provided by the ELSE clause. One reason ELSE is rarely used in this tutorial is that it makes the conditions for the alternative conclusion implicit rather than explicit. Another reason is that it may cause an illogical questioning sequence in a user consultation.

For example, the above rule conditions are tested in sequential order, and in this case, assume that a user is screening a person who is not an HMO member. Since the rule does not conclude after a "no" response to member, it continues to evaluate the next condition and asks if the same person has a valid ID number! The only way to avoid this illogical situation is to make the negative condition explicit with a separate rule, for example:

```
RULE 8
     IF member = no
     THEN member_status = not_ok;
```

Because this negative condition is handled in a separate rule, it requires that Rules 6 and 7 be explicit, as shown in Figure 2–8.

Figure 2–7. Decision Table for Rule Set 2

Step 1: Plan

		Number of Values
Conditions:	Member (yes, no)	= 2
	Valid_ID (yes, no)	= 2
Rows = 2 x 2 = 4 ←		

Step 2: Completed Decision Table

Rule	Member	Valid_ID	Member Status
A 1	yes	yes	ok
A 2	yes	no	not_ok
A 3	no	yes	not_ok
A 4	no	no	not_ok
	↑ 2 cut	↑ 2 cut	

Step 3: Reduced Decision Table

Rule	Member	Valid_ID	Member Status
B 1	yes	yes	ok
B 2	—	no	not_ok
B 3	no	—	not_ok

Figure 2–8. Convert Decision Table to Rules—Rule Set 2

```
RULE 6
     IF member = yes and
        valid_id = yes
     THEN member_status = ok;

RULE 7
     IF member = yes and
        valid_id = no
     THEN member_status = not_ok;

RULE 8
     IF member = no
     THEN member_status = not_ok;
```

A good rule of thumb for a first KBS effort is to write one rule for every row on the reduced decision table. As experience is gained, shortcuts can be explored for increasing the efficiency of writing rules and running a knowledge base consultation.

STEP 6—CONSTRUCT THE USER INTERFACE

Once the IF-THEN rules are written, the **user interface** elements of the knowledge base need to be constructed, as identified in Figure 2–14. In this case, the user interface refers to all the parts a user actually will see and interface with when running the KBS in a consultation session. At a minimum, this consists of the opening and closing messages and the questions posed during the consultation session.

Figure 2–9. Decision Table for Rule Set 3

Step 1: Plan

		Number of Values
Conditions:	Temperature (normal, abnormal, not_known)	= 3
	Other_symptoms (yes, no)	= 2

Rows = 3 × 2 = 6 ←

Step 2: Completed Decision Table

Rule	Temperature	Other Symptoms	Problem
A 1	normal	yes	serious
A 2	normal	no	non_serious
A 3	abnormal	yes	serious
A 4	abnormal	no	serious
A 5	not_known	yes	serious
A 6	not_known	no	serious

↑ 3 cut ↑ 2 cut

Step 3: Reduced Decision Table

Rule	Temperature	Other Symptoms	Problem
B 1	normal	yes	serious
B 2	normal	no	non_serious
B 3	abnormal	—	serious
B 4	not_known	—	serious

Human factor considerations come into play as the KBS developer constructs appropriate questions for each question mark on the dependency diagram. There is a fine art to posing questions in a way that elicits the input desired. Often questions are rewritten several times until they seem right. Even after they seem right, they must be tested in live consultation sessions.

Writing the actual questions on paper often crystalizes one's thinking about the overall design of the KBS. It is not unusual to find some questions superfluous and others missing. This sends the developer back to earlier steps in the development process to rethink and retool the KBS design. Designing and developing a KBS is essentially an iterative process. The developer moves back and forth among the various steps in the development process to incrementally improve the design. The design is the creative part of the job. Converting the design to knowledge base code is mechanical.

Figure 2–10. Convert Decision Table to Rules—Rule Set 3

```
RULE 9
     IF temperature = normal and
        other_symptoms = yes
     THEN problem = serious;

RULE 10
     IF temperature = normal and
        other_symptoms = no
     THEN problem = non_serious;

RULE 11
     IF temperature = abnormal or
        temperature = not_ known
     THEN problem = serious;
```

Figure 2–11.

Rule Structure for VP-Expert

RULE label	The keyword RULE followed by a label.
IF	Identifies the beginning of the RULE condition(s).
THEN	Identifies the beginning of the RULE conclusion.
ELSE	Used optionally to identify the beginning of an alternative conclusion of a RULE.
BECAUSE	Used optionally to offer an explanation of the meaning of the premise, conclusions, and alternate conclusions of the RULE.

A RULE must end with a semicolon.
Conditions can be combined in rules using the logical operators:

AND	Both conditions must be met for the rule to be "true" and, therefore, "pass." Up to 20 conditions using AND can be combined in one rule.
OR	One or both conditions must be true. Using OR with AND in a rule limits the number of conditions that can be combined to 10.

Figure 2–12.

Variable and Rule Names in VP-Expert

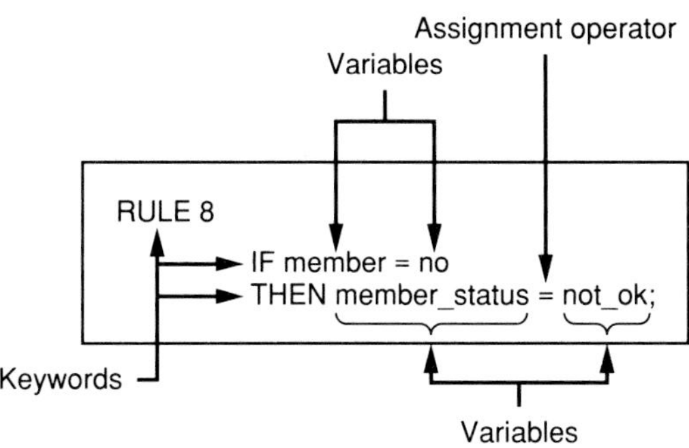

Variable Names

- Variable names must begin with a letter.
- Each variable name must be unique.
- Variable names and values are restricted to 40 characters, which can include letters (upper or lower case), numbers, and the following special characters: _ $ ^ ¦ %
- Spaces are not allowed in variable names or values. Instead of spaces, use the underline character (for example, member_status).
- Keywords cannot be used as variable names. If they are, errors may occur when the consultation is executed. Keywords can, however, be included within variable names. For example, color cannot be used as a variable name, because COLOR is a keyword. But the_color is a perfectly legal variable name. A complete list of keywords is provided in Figure 2–13.
- Most variables can be assigned values of no more than 40 characters.

Rule Names

- Rule names (or labels) generally follow the same naming conventions as variables (given above), except that a rule name can begin with a number.
- Each rule name must be unique.

For example, consider the question: "What is the reason for coming to the HMO facility?" The developer tested the term *purpose* in place of *reason* and tried variations such as "What is the reason the person came to the HMO facility?" Often, there is no guidance for what works in a given situation except trial and error.

Coding the questions into the knowledge base requires using two new keywords:

- ASK, which is used to query the user for values to be assigned to a variable when there are no value assignments in the rules
- CHOICES, which is used in conjunction with the ASK keyword to present a number of allowable values that can be assigned to the requested variable

Figure 2–13.

Knowledge Base Keywords

Note: Keywords are used in the construction of a knowledge base. They include the words that begin every line (clause or statement), special words used in rule construction, and other words reserved for special use in the knowledge base.

@ABS	BUTTON	ENDOFF	HYPERTEXT	PLURAL	*THEN
@ACOS	CALL	EXECUTE	*IF	POP	TMODE
@ASIN	CCALL	FDISPLAY	INDEX	PRINTOFF	TRACK
@ATAN	CHAIN	FILL	LBUTTON	PRINTON	TRUTHTHRESH
@COS	*CHOICES	*FIND	LENGTH	PSET	UNKNOWN
@EXP	CHR	FIXED	LINETO	PUT	VGAUGE
@LOG	CLOSE	FOR	LOADFACTS	PWKS	WCLOSE
@SIN	CLROFF	FORMAT	LOCATE	RECEIVE	WFORMAT
@SQRT	CLRON	FORMFIELD	MENU	RECORD_NUM	WHENEVER
@TAN	CLS	GBCOLOR	MENU_SIZE	RECTANGLE	WHILEKNOWN
*ACTIONS	COLOR	GCLS	METER	REPORT	WHILETRUE
ACTIVE	COLUMN	GCOLOR	MOUSEOFF	RESET	WKS
ALL	COUNT	GDISPLAY	MOUSEON	ROW	WOPEN
*AND	CURR	GET	MOUSEX	*RULE	WORKON
APPEND	DBFORM	GETCH	MOUSEY	RUNTIME	WORKSHEET
*ASK	*DISPLAY	GETMOUSE	MOVETO	SAVEFACTS	
AUTOQUERY	EJECT	GLOCATE	MRESET	SCI	
BCALL	ELLIPSE	GMODE	NAMED	SHIP	
BECAUSE	ELSE	HGAUGE	*OR	SHOWTEXT	
BKCOLOR	END	HOTREGION	PDISPLAY	SORT	

*The most critical VP-Expert keywords are discussed in this chapter.

Figure 2–14. Example of How a User Interfaces with a KBS During a Consultation Session

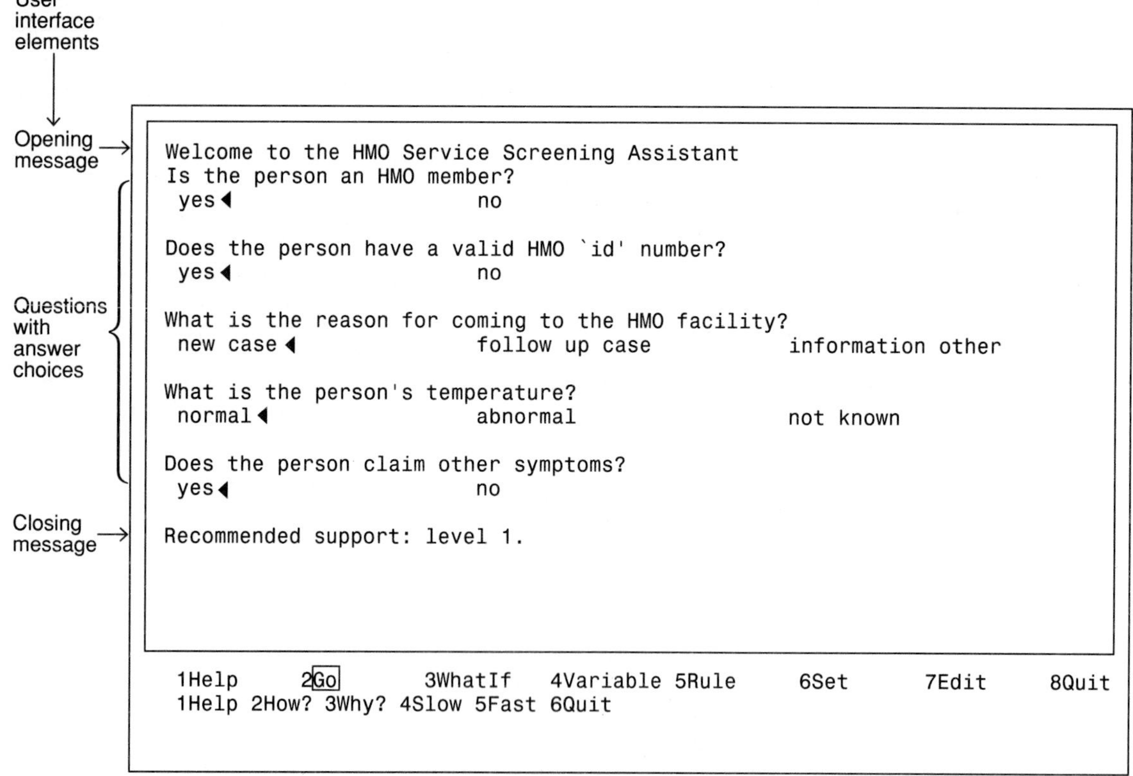

Examples of how the ASK and CHOICES keywords are used with questions in the knowledge base can be found in Figure 2–15. Typically, the user questions are found at the end of the knowledge base in a separate Questions Block.

The last user interface element to be considered appears in the Actions Block, which is located at the beginning of the knowledge base. For this example, it consists of a line that serves as an opening message and another line that concludes the consultation. The keyword DISPLAY causes these messages to appear on the user's screen during a consultation. The text of the concluding message includes the variable name "support" surrounded by curly brackets. The curly brackets are symbols that cause replacement of the enclosed variable name with its value whenever the accompanying text is displayed. Such a replacement is illustrated in Figure 2–14, where level 1 is the support recommended for the person screened.

Much can be done to improve this user interface. Such improvements will be the main topic of Chapter 5.

STRUCTURE OF A KNOWLEDGE BASE

Figure 2–15 shows the overall structure of a knowledge base, which consists of three basic parts:

- Actions Block
- Rules Block
- Questions Block

The keyword ACTIONS identifies the beginning of an **Actions Block.** It sets the agenda for a consultation. In this case, it DISPLAYS the opening message, then sets out to FIND a value for the goal variable in this consultation, and concludes by reporting to the user what it finds in a concluding message. This set of only three procedural instructions drives the entire consultation. It says, in effect, "First do this, then do this, then do this," and so on sequentially through each line in the Actions Block.

An Actions Block typically contains at least one FIND keyword. It is the critical keyword in this KBS because it causes control to be transferred to the Rules Block during the consultation. The expertise contained in the Rules and Questions Block of the knowledge base then is used to solve the problem of the consultation. In this case, it is to find an appropriate level of support to recommend for the person being screened.

Once a value is known for the variable "support," control is returned to the Actions Block. When the final instruction in the Actions Block has been executed to completion, the consultation is finished.

REVIEW QUESTIONS

1. What are the eight major steps in developing a KBS?
2. What occurs during Steps 1 and 2?
3. How does one progress from Step 2 to Step 3?
4. What is the reason for creating dependency diagrams?
5. Why are decision tables created?

Figure 2–15. Structure of a Knowledge Base and Printout of the Complete First Knowledge Base File

Structure of a Knowledge Base ↓

Note: The name of this knowledge base file on the Sample Files disk is HMO.KBS or HMORUN. KBS

ACTIONS Block

```
ACTIONS
     DISPLAY "Welcome to the HMO Service Screening Assistant"
     FIND support
     DISPLAY "Recommended support: {support}."
;
```

RULES Block

```
RULE 1
     IF member_status = ok and
        reason = new_case or
        reason = follow_up_case and
        problem = serious
     THEN support = level_1;

RULE 2
     IF member_status = ok and
        reason = new_case and
        problem = non_serious
     THEN support = level_2;

RULE 3
     IF member_status = ok and
        reason = follow_up_case and
        problem = non_serious
     THEN support = level_3;

RULE 4
     IF member_status = ok and
        reason = information_other
     THEN support = information_other;

RULE 5
     IF member_status = not_ok
     THEN support = non_member;

RULE 6
     IF member = yes and
        valid_id = yes
     THEN member_status = ok;
```

6. What occurs during the preparation phase of Step 4, creating decision tables?
7. How is the decision table actually laid out?
8. How is the decision table actually filled in?
9. Why is it that frequently there are fewer IF-THEN rules than combinations of outcomes in the decision table?
10. What are the major considerations in completing Step 6, constructing the user interface?
11. Describe the structure of a knowledge base.

```
RULE 7
     IF member = yes and
        valid_id = no
     THEN member_status = not_ok;

RULE 8
     IF member = no
     THEN member_status = not_ok;

RULE 9
     IF temperature = normal and
        other_symptoms = yes
     THEN problem = serious;

RULE 10
     IF temperature = normal and
        other_symptoms = no
     THEN problem = non_serious;

RULE 11
     IF temperatue = abnormal or
        temperature = not_known
     THEN problem = serious;

ASK member: "Is the person an HMO member?";
CHOICES member: yes, no;

ASK valid_id: "Does the person have a valid HMO `id' number?";
CHOICES valid_id: yes, no;

ASK reason: "What is the reason for coming to the HMO facility?";
CHOICES reason: new_case, follow_up_case, information_other;

ASK temperature: "What is the person's temperature?";
CHOICES temperature: normal, abnormal, not_known;

ASK other_symptoms:  "Does the person claim other symptoms?";
CHOICES other_symptoms: yes, no;
```

QUESTIONS Block

EXERCISES

1. This exercise concerns the mechanics of running a consultation. Run a consultation with the knowledge base HMORUN.KBS from the Sample Files disk.
   a. Use the "Procedure for Running a Consultation," given in Figure 3–2, to run the consultation.
   b. Use Figure 2–14 as a guide for response entries, which should be as follows:

Response	*Keys to Press to Indicate Response*
yes	(Enter, End)
yes	(Enter, End)
new case	(Enter, End)
normal	(Enter, End)
yes	(Enter, End)

c. Run another consultation and enter different responses.
d. Compare and record the results observed from the two consultations.

2. This exercise continues to explore the mechanics of running a KBS. Run a consultation with the knowledge base TAXGUIDE.KBS from the Sample Files disk.
   a. Use the "Procedure for Running a Consultation," given in Figure 3–2, to run the consultation.
   b. Run another consultation entering different responses.
   c. Compare and record the results observed from the two consultations.
3. This exercise looks at an "industrial strength" KBS. Run a consultation with the knowledge base DEPENDEN.KBS from the Sample Files disk.
   a. Because this knowledge base exceeds the limits of the educational version of VP-Expert, it is stored in a special file DEPENDEN.KMP. It has a special .KMP (versus a .KBS) filename extension. To run this knowledge base, start at the DOS prompt. For example, if your Sample Files disk is in the A drive, type

```
A>VPXRUN DEPENDEN
```

   Notice that the filename extension is *not* entered.
   b. Run another consultation entering different responses.
   c. Compare and record the results observed from the two consultations.
   d. Examine this knowledge base by getting a printout from the normal .KBS file (DEPENDEN.KBS, which is also on the Sample Files disk). Follow the instructions for "Printing the Sample Files," found in the summary reference guide in Chapter 7.
4. For this exercise concerning the mechanics of diagramming, assume that four (instead of three) critical factors determine the recommendation made in the HMO Service Screening Assistant KBS.
   a. Redraw Figure 2–3 and position a blank box to indicate the influence of a fourth critical factor on the recommendation made.
   b. Assume that two items influence the outcome of the fourth critical factor. Refine the above block diagram to illustrate this hierarchical linkage.
   c. Redraw the dependency diagram in Figure 2–4 to position the addition of the fourth critical factor.
   d. Revise Step 1 in Figure 2–5, "Decision Table for Final Rule Set," to show the influence of a fourth critical factor with two values.
   e. Revise Step 2 in Figure 2–5, the "Completed Decision Table," to show the influence of a fourth critical factor with two values. Label the actual data elements Value 1 and Value 2 for the fourth critical factor in your decision table. Leave the recommendation area blank.
5. This exercise concerns the mechanics of creating a decision table. Prepare a decision table for one rule set of a knowledge base that determines pricing from two conditions:

   - Quantity ordered is greater than the discount quantity (yes, no)
   - Customer is a wholesaler (yes, no)

A discount is given only to wholesalers who order in quantities greater than the discount quantity. Use Figure 2–5 as a guide for doing the three steps of this exercise to plan, complete, and reduce the decision table.

6. This exercise concerns the conversion of a decision table into rules. Convert the reduced decision table from Exercise 5 into rules. Use Figures 2–11 and 2–12 for guidance concerning rule structure and naming conventions.
7. This exercise explores the construction of the user interface questions. Write the questions and answer choices that would be appropriate for the scenario given in Exercise 5.
8. Build a knowledge-based system of your own design that progressively develops through Steps 1–6 described in Figure 2–1. Expect to throw out and redo the work from one or more steps. This is normal, because development involves an iterative process of backing up one or more steps, improving your design, and then moving ahead again.

3

ENTERING THE FIRST KNOWLEDGE BASE INTO THE COMPUTER

This chapter discusses the concluding steps and related background material in the basic knowledge base design and development process that began in Chapter 2.

After all elements of the knowledge base are defined, the knowledge base must be entered, or typed, into the computer and saved as a knowledge base file on a disk. This working disk file is then available for use as often as desired for consultation sessions.

The chapter covers these areas:

- Step 7—Enter the knowledge base into the computer
- Step 8—Run a trial consultation
- How the inference engine works
- An example of backward chaining
- Using the Editor
- Basics of debugging
- The developer's toolkit—more on debugging
- The user's options—more on running a consultation

STEP 7—ENTER THE KNOWLEDGE BASE INTO THE COMPUTER

To type the knowledge base into the computer, a developer can use a favorite word processor. Alternatively, a developer can type the knowledge base into the computer using the word processor built into the expert system shell software. The built-in word processor is called an *Editor* or *Editor and debugger.*

Figure 3–1 identifies the Editor as one of several components in the expert system shell software. Usually it is the main component used to develop a new KBS.

Follow this procedure for entering the knowledge base into the computer:

1. Type the knowledge base into a computer file using the Editor.
2. Run a trial consultation. It is normal to expect errors or "bugs" because of typing mistakes or logic errors.

Figure 3–1. Expert System Shell Components

Source: Adapted from Bruce G. Buchanan. From a presentation made at the First Artificial Intelligence Satellite Symposium, sponsored by Texas Instruments, Nov. 23, 1985.

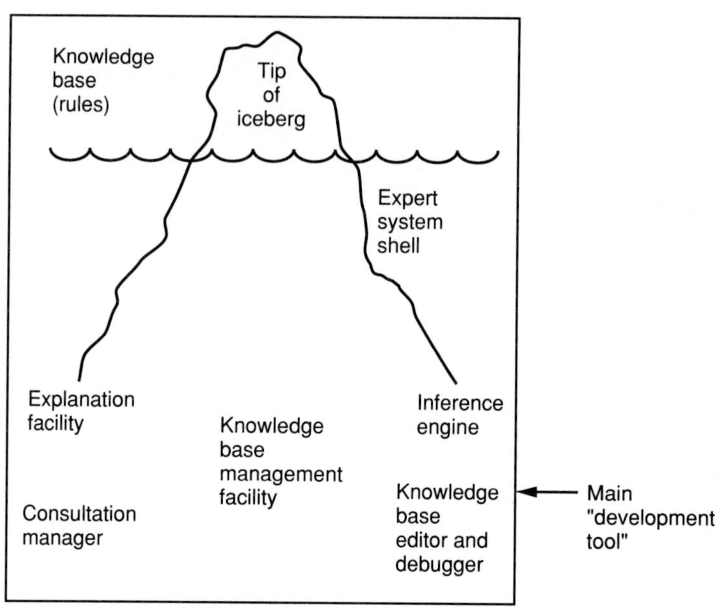

Figure 3–2.

Procedure for Running a Consultation

The following instructions are written to guide a user, who is sitting at a microcomputer, to run the HMO Service Screening Assistant sample system. (Computer set-up requirements are available in Chapter 7, "Summary Reference Guide".)

1. Load the expert shell program from the C:>, A:> or other system prompt by typing VPX and pressing the Enter key.

   An opening copyright screen appears with the following Main Menu at the bottom of the screen.

Main Menu (first line)

Lightbar over the "Consult" menu option

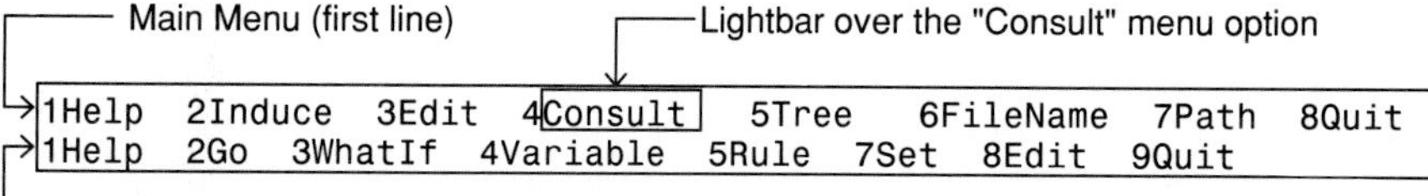

Submenu for the item highlighted on the first line ("Consult" in this example)

2. Use the right arrow key to move the lightbar to Path and press Enter. A message appears on the screen asking "What is the pathname?" If your Sample Files Disk (or other working disk) is in drive A, type A: or if it is in drive B, type B:. Press Enter. (Note: This step is normally done only once at the start of a session.)

3. Use the right arrow key to move the lightbar to FileName and press Enter. A message appears on the screen asking "What is the name of the knowledge base you want to use?" A list of existing knowledge base files is presented. To choose from this list, move the lightbar to a desired filename (using the arrow keys) and press Enter. To run the first sample system, select the HMORUN.KBS filename. The Main Menu reappears. (Note: This step has to be done only once if repeated consultations are desired using the same knowledge base file.)

3. Return to the Editor to correct the errors. This process is called *debugging* the file or system.
4. Run another trial consultation.
5. Repeat Steps 3 and 4 until a clean consultation run is achieved.

Learning to use the Editor of any shell, like learning to use a new word processor, is a tedious, time-consuming task. But it usually is necessary to facilitate the debugging process. A brief tutorial for using the VP-Expert Editor is presented later in this chapter.

STEP 8—RUN A TRIAL CONSULTATION

Running a trial consultation, such as the example given in Figure 2–14, is a normal part of the KBS development process. It is often repeated many times to completely debug a new knowledge base.

New KBS developers find that understanding knowledge-based systems is aided by running consultations with preexisting knowledge-based systems. Since the KBS shown in Figure 2–15 is available on the Sample Files disk that accom-

Note: There are four ways to make a menu selection:

- Use the right and left arrow keys to move the lightbar to a desired choice, then press Enter.
- Press the number associated with a desired choice
- Press the first letter of a desired choice.
- Press the function key corresponding to the menu number (for example, for menu choice 1, press F1).

4. Press Enter to select Consult from the Main Menu. The message "Loading File..." appears on a blank screen. If you are running the consultation shown in Figure 2-14, the message "a:/hmorun.kbs loaded" appears at the upper left corner of the consultation screen, and the following Consult Menu appears at the bottom of the screen:

Consult Menu

```
1Help  2Go     3WhatIf  4Variable   5Rule  6Set  7Edit  8Quit
1Help  2How?  3Why?  4Slow   5Fast  6Quit
```

Using one of the menu selection methods described in the accompanying box, choose Go to begin the consultation. (Because the lightbar is already on Go, simply press Enter.)

For the example case, the top of the consultation window should look like Figure 2-14. The lightbar rests over the first answer to the first question.

5. Pressing Enter chooses the highlighted option and automatically places a triangle next to the chosen item. The arrow keys are used to move the lightbar among answer choices. Pressing the End key on the numeric keypad signals the end of an answer.

   Note: To cancel a selection before pressing End, presss the Del key while the lightbar is over the item you wish to "unchoose."

   Use this procedure to answer each question. After the last question, the consultation ends with a recommendation.

6. Select Quit to return to the Main Menu, or Go to run another consultation.

panies this book, the reader may want to explore how a consultation works firsthand. The procedure for doing this is available in Figure 3–2.

(It is highly recommended that a duplicate working copy be made of all original disks supplied with this book. The originals should be stored safely and the working copies used for all exercises. This way, if an exercise disk or file is somehow destroyed, the original is always available to begin again.)

New developers also benefit from an understanding of how the inference engine works during a consultation. The inference engine is the shell component that directs the path or search strategy through the Rules Block of the knowledge base. It is quite different from the sequential process explored earlier for the Actions Block.

HOW THE INFERENCE ENGINE WORKS

The process the inference engine in VP-Expert uses to manipulate the rules during a consultation session is called *backward chaining.* The concept is diagrammed in Figure 3–3 using an abbreviated version of the HMO sample system.

Figure 3–3. A Backward Chaining Example

This is the "goal" variable (it starts the problem-solving process called "backward chaining")

```
ACTIONS
  DISPLAY "Welcome to the HMO Client Screening Assistant"
  FIND support
  DISPLAY "Recommended support: {support}."
;

(A)
RULE 1
  IF member_status = ok and
(B)  reason = new_case                          (C)
  THEN support = level_1;

RULE 2
  IF member = yes and
(D)  valid_id = yes
  THEN member_status = ok;

ASK member:  "Is the person an HMO member?";
CHOICES member: yes, no;

ASK valid_id: "Does the person have a valid HMO `id' number";
CHOICES valid_id: yes, no;

ASK reason:  "What is the reason for coming to the HMO facility?";
CHOICES reason: new_case, follow_up_case, information_other;
```

It starts by knowing the goal variable for which the consultation session must determine a value. The first rule found with the goal in its conclusion causes the conditions of that rule to become sub-goals. All the sub-goals must be determined or known for the THEN part of the rule to fire the goal variable and pass control back to the Actions Block. If at any point a sub-goal cannot be satisfied with another sub-goal in another rule, the inference engine looks for an ASK statement in the Questions Block to obtain the value from the user. If this alternative does not work, the search fails and the consultation aborts.

Backward chaining is characteristic of many rule-based systems as well as artificial intelligence techniques in general. In particular, the rules in the rule base are not processed in a purely sequential order; rather, they are selected based on their relevance to the unique problem at hand.

AN EXAMPLE OF BACKWARD CHAINING

Tracing each step the inference engine takes to satisfy a goal helps to understand how backward chaining works. It also helps show why questions are displayed in a given sequence during a consultation session.

This section will walk through the step-by-step process the inference engine uses to satisfy the goal variable in Figure 3–3.

The inference engine begins by knowing that the goal variable to be satisfied is "support." It then searches for the first rule showing "support" in its THEN conclusion. In the example, it is Rule 1. The value of the variable is "level_1," but it is not yet known. For it to be known, all the IF conditions of Rule 1 also have to be known.

The inference engine backs up to examine all the IF conditions in Rule 1. When it goes to the first IF condition, it finds the variable "member_status" is unknown. So it establishes "member_status" as a sub-goal.

Then the inference engine looks for the first available rule that has the sub-goal "member_status" in its THEN conclusion. In this example, it finds "member_status" in the conclusion to Rule 2. Again, the value of the sub-goal "member_status" is not yet known.

The inference engine must now try to solve or test all the open IF conditions in Rule 2 to fire the rule. To do this, it backs up to examine the first IF condition, "member." Once again, it finds "member" has never been tested. It is an unknown variable that must be set up as a new sub-goal and be resolved before resuming. In this case, although the inference engine first looks for a rule with "member" in its THEN conclusion, it finds none in the example system. At this point its problem-solving strategy is to see if this variable can be found through direct user input. In other words, it looks for an ASK statement, which it finds. So the solution to the IF condition is simply to ask the user consulting the expert system for a direct keyboarded response to a prepared question attached to the variable "member." Once the user inputs a response, "member" becomes the first known sub-goal.

In this example, the inference engine continues to pursue the task of resolving the most recent sub-goal, which is "member_status," by examining the next IF condition in Rule 2. "Valid_id" is not found in the THEN conclusion of any rule. The strategy is, as before, to locate an ASK statement and seek direct user input. Once a user response is obtained to "valid_id," all IF conditions are known and Rule 2 can fire. The inference engine assigns the value "ok" to "member_status" only if the user answers "yes" to both Rule 2 IF conditions. A more complete example would have other rules to handle "no" responses (see Rules 7 and 8 in Figure 2–15).

With the sub-goal "member_status" solved, the inference engine chains back to resolve the second IF condition in Rule 1. The sub-goal "reason" is established and no rule is found that has "reason" in its THEN clause. So the inference engine checks and finds an ASK statement.

Once the user inputs a response, "support" becomes known because all IF conditions in Rule 1 are tested. It then is appropriate to fire the THEN conclusion to Rule 1. The inference engine assigns the value "level_1" to the primary goal variable "support" only if "reason" is "new_case" and "member_status" is "ok."

With a value found for the goal variable, the inference engine returns control to the Actions Block, which continues sequentially through its instructions. In the example, the next instruction generates a screen display of a concluding message, which terminates the user session.

USING THE EDITOR

Using the Editor built into an expert system shell is like using a crude word processor. It has fewer features than a good word processor and can seem awkward at times. Nonetheless, it is important to learn how to use it, especially for debugging purposes.

There is an alternative, but it requires an undesirable tradeoff. It is possible to link VP-Expert to a favorite word processor for entering and debugging a knowledge base. The tradeoff is that if a bug is detected during a trial consultation, no error message is provided about where the error occurred. This rates as a debugging nightmare.

On the other hand, when using the built-in Editor, bugs are identified and located during a consultation. Simply pressing the Enter key switches from the Consult to the Edit mode with the cursor placed in the approximate vicinity of the error that needs fixing. This feature alone seems justification enough to learn how to use the built-in Editor.

A good way to learn the built-in Editor is to enter a first knowledge base that is bug-free and known to run or execute correctly, such as the sample in Figure 2–15. A step-by-step procedure for getting into the Editor to enter the sample, or any other knowledge base, is given in Figure 3–4.

Initially the Editor's screen is blank, but after some typing it should resemble the one shown in Figure 3–5. Typing the knowledge base is very much like typing with a word processor. The basic editing keys, identified in Figure 3–6, are the same.

The knowledge base can be typed in all lowercase letters, including keywords, to simplify typing. It also may be desirable to type the knowledge base in all lowercase letters because they are much easier to read than all uppercase letters. The reason this book has keywords in uppercase letters is for emphasis and to support learning. Only DISPLAY text requires careful attention to mixed uppercase and lowercase letters. DISPLAY text normally is designed to resemble normal text.

The upper right corner of the screen identifies the filename, and the bottom of the screen presents a menu of options. The menu options change when the Alt, Ctrl, or Shift keys are pressed. Some of the more useful key combinations, as well as other editing keys, are listed in Figure 3-7.

Figure 3–4.

Procedure for Entering (or Editing) a Knowledge Base

The following instructions are written to guide a user, who is sitting at a microcomputer, to enter the HMO Service Screening Assistant sample system. (System set-up requirements are available in Chapter 7, "Summary Reference Guide".)

1. Load the program from the C:>, A:> or other system prompt by typing VPX and pressing the Enter key. An opening copyright screen appears with the following Main Menu at the bottom of the screen.

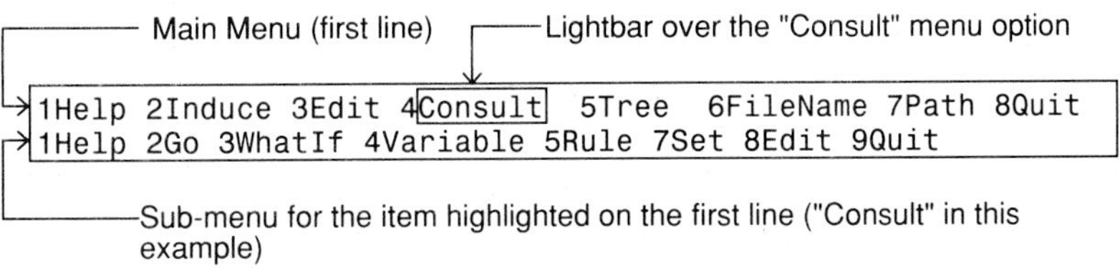

2. Use the right arrow key to move the lightbar to Path and press Enter. A message appears on the screen asking "What is the new pathname?" If your Sample Files disk (or other working disk) is in drive A, type A: or if it is in drive B, type B:. Press Enter. (Note: This step is normally done only once at the start of a session.)

3. Use the right arrow key to move the lightbar to Edit and press Enter. A message appears on the screen . "Choose a file:" with the cursor positioned after the colon. Type a new filename of your choice, such as XHMO, and press Enter. Alternately, use the arrow key to move the lightbar over any existing filename that appears on the screen and press Enter to select it.

4. This opens the Editor, which has a blank screen and a distinctive bottom panel that looks similar to the one in Figure 3-5. The blank screen has the new filename in the upper right corner. A .kbs extension has automatically been added to the filename. If an existing file is selected, it will appear on the screen and look similar to Figure 3-5.

5. Type the knowledge base into the computer. As it is typed, it appears on the screen (see Figure 3-5), just as it would if using a word processor. All the basic editing keys on the computer keyboard (see Figure 3-6) work exactly as they do with a word processor. Other useful editing keys (see Figure 3-7), have to be mastered as needed.

   Note:
   The knowledge base can be typed in all upper-, lower-, or mixed-case characters. A left-pointing triangle, called a hard carriage return symbol, automatically appears at the end of each line and the beginning of blank lines.

6. After completely typing the knowledge base, check it for errors. Then save it by pressing the Alt key and the F6 function key together. At the prompt, "Save as XHMO.KBS (Y or N)?," type Y.

7. When returned to the Main Menu, choose Consult to run a trial consultation. On the top of the three-window consultation screen, similar to the one in Figure 3-9, the message "Loading File..." and "file Loaded" appear. At the bottom of the screen, the lightbar is over Go. Press Enter to select Go.

8. If no errors are present in the knowledge base, it is possible to run a consultation following the "Procedure for Running a Consultation" given in Figure 3-2. If errors are detected, the knowledge base must be "debugged." To debug a knowledge base, follow the "Procedure for Debugging a Knowledge Base" given in Figure 3-8. (Note: During a consultation, compound variables such as "level_1" or "follow_up_case" appear on the screen without the underscore connectives. The underscore connectives always appear during editing sessions.)

Figure 3–5. Using the Editor

Typed (or entered) by the knowledge base developer

Filename extension automatically supplied by the Editor

New filename typed by the developer

```
                                        Editing: New File a:\hmo.kbs

ACTIONS ◄
     DISPLAY "Welcome to the HMO Service Screening Assistant"◄
     FIND support◄
     DISPLAY "Recommended support: {support}."◄
;◄
◄
RULE 1 ◄
     IF member_status = ok and◄
        reason = new_case or◄
        reason = follow_up_case and◄
        problem = serious◄
     THEN support = level_1;◄
◄
RULE 2 ◄
     IF member_status = ok and◄
        reason = new_case and◄
        problem = non_serious ◄
     THEN support = level_2;◄

+ ▲     ▲     ▲     ▲     ▲     ▲     ▲     ▲     ▲     ▲     ▲     ▲     ▲
Insert On    Document Off                        Boldface Off Underline Off
 1Help    2Reform 3TabSet 4Margin 5Center 6     7Bold    8Ulin 9Dcumnt10Print
```

Currently available Editor options which can be selected only by typing the function key corresponding to the number shown. These options change when the Alt, Ctrl, or Shift key is pressed.

Editor status bar (for reference only)

Tab tick marks (Press function key F3 to place a tab or remove an existing tab setting in the column of the cursor's current position.)

Figure 3–6.

Main Editing Keys

The following keys work just as they would in most word processors.

Key	Action
←(Backspace)	Deletes character left of cursor
Del	Deletes character at cursor
↵ (Enter)	At the end of a line, or any entry, creates a hard carriage return.
Esc	Cancels incomplete operations
Ins	Toggles insert mode on and off (for character inserts at the cursor). Inserted text pushes existing text to the right.
↑ ↓ ← →	Arrow keys move the cursor around the screen in the direction of the arrow.
PgDn	Moves cursor to next screen
PgUp	Moves cursor to previous screen
PrtSc	Prints the contents of the screen when pressed with the Shift key
Tab	Moves cursor forward one tab stop

Figure 3–7.

Other Important Editing Keys

Action Desired	Key(s) to use
Help	F1
Tab set	F3
Insert a line	Ctrl Enter
Delete entire line	Ctrl Y
Cursor moves—special:	
Move cursor to the beginning of the line	Home
Move cursor to the end of the line	End
Move cursor to the top of the file	Ctrl PgUp
Move cursor to the bottom of the file	Ctrl PgDn
Move cursor left one word	Ctrl ←
Move cursor right one word	Ctrl →
Block text	
Start block	Ctrl F3
End block	Ctrl F4
Copy block	Ctrl F7
Delete block	Ctrl F8
Cancel block (Use this after Copy block)	Ctrl F5
Move block	Ctrl F6
Recall block	Ctrl F10
Files	
Save file and leave Editor* The previously saved version automatically becomes a backup file (with a filename extension .BAK).	Alt F6
Update file without leaving Editor	Alt F5
Insert existing file, which can be another .KBS or .TXT or other type of file, at the location of the cursor	Alt F4
Abandon file without saving or changing	Alt F8
Print file Pressing F10 calls the Print Menu screen. Press the END key to print the file with the current setting, or change settings and then press END.	F10

*Note: If you save an edited file under a *new* name, always include the drive and path prefix. This avoids saving files on the hard drive that are intended for the floppy disk drive. Also, to make a backup file the first time requires going into DOS to do a, for example, "COPY a: filename b:filename." This establishes the filename on the backup disk. Future saves to the backup disk then can be made using Alt F6.

After the knowledge base is completely typed, it should be checked visually for errors. Some common errors to look for are

- Missing semicolons
- Misspelled keywords
- Illegal characters in rule labels, variable names, or values
- Keywords mistakenly used as variable names

If there appear to be no errors, the knowledge base is ready to be saved according to the instructions found in the procedure for entering (or editing) a knowledge base in Figure 3–4. After the file is saved, the Editor returns control to the Main Menu.

The normal procedure at this point is to see if the file works. This requires running a trial consultation. Generally, the file does not work during the first trial consultation due to commonly overlooked errors.

Figure 3–8.

Procedure for Debugging a Knowledge Base

1. Run a trial consultation by selecting Consult from the Main Menu and Go from the Consult Menu. Alternatively, follow the appropriate steps in "Procedure for Running a Consultation" given in Figure 3–2. This causes the file to be loaded and checked for errors.
2. If there are any mistakes, a message appears that might look something like this:

   Missing ';'
   (Press any key to go on)
   Error in line 20

   This particular message would indicate that line 20 of the knowledge base is missing a semicolon. If such a message appears, press any key to automatically return to the knowledge base in the Editor. The cursor will be placed on (or near) the offending line (which has no line reference number!). If there appears to be no problem with the line the cursor is on, look at the "Quick Checklist" below to see if that helps.

   Note: VP-Expert only makes assumptions about which line contains an error. For example, if a semicolon is omitted at the end of a rule, it may assume that the rule continues past where it should end and not recognize the mistake until it finds a semicolon several lines later. If an error is reported in a line that looks all right, check previous lines for errors. Frequently, the real cause of an error is one or more lines above the line identified with the error message.
3. If the knowledge base is edited correctly, the consultation begins immediately.

Quick Checklist

- Do the Actions Block, each rule, and each statement in the Questions Block end with a semicolon? Are there any additional semicolons out of place? The only place—besides the end of a rule, statement, or Actions Block—that a semicolon can be used is inside the double quotes that surround display text (for example, the text in an ASK statement, DISPLAY clause, etc.)
- Are all keywords spelled correctly (see Figure 2–13)?
- Are there any illegal characters (see Figure 2–12) in rule labels, variable names, or values?
- Are any keywords (see Figure 2–13) mistakenly used as variable names?

BASICS OF DEBUGGING

Cleaning up the errors at this point is commonly called "debugging" the file. A procedure for debugging a knowledge base file is given in Figure 3–8.

When the knowledge base hasn't been edited correctly, the developer is confronted with error messages that appear on the screen. They either pinpoint the problem, such as "Missing ;" or generalize the problem, such as "Syntax error." The message also includes "Error in line (number)," even though the knowledge base has no line numbers! In most cases, this is not a problem, because by pressing any key, the developer is returned to the Editor with the cursor placed on, or near, the line with the problem.

Frequently, the real cause of an error is one or more lines above the line the cursor rests on when the Editor returns from an error message. The shell program only makes assumptions about which line contains the error. For example, if the semicolon is missing from the end of the Actions Block, the program may assume that the Actions Block continues past where it should end. It may not recognize the mistake until it finds the first keyword RULE in the Rules Block.

If the knowledge base is edited correctly, a consultation screen will appear much like the one in Figure 2–14 or 3–9. During development, the consultation screen is usually a three-window screen as shown in Figure 3–9. The screen consists of a reduced consultation window, as compared to the full user-version of the consultation screen shown in Figure 2–14, and the "Rules" and "Facts" windows.

For the developer, the Rules window is a viewport into the inference engine's search strategy. It is a live scrolling record of how the inference engine

Figure 3–9. Consultation Screen for Developers

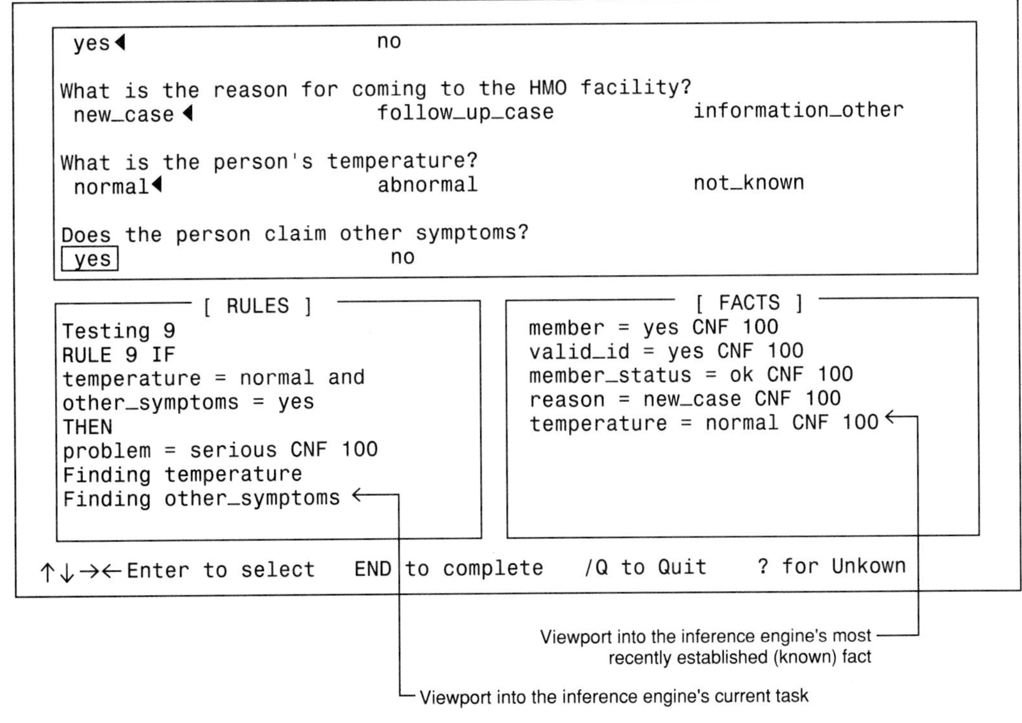

performs its search strategy and what the inference engine is currently doing. Its path of reasoning is made transparent for the developer to observe while a consultation is actually in progress.

The Facts window is a viewport into the system's **working memory** (sometimes called the cache). It identifies the values, both intermediate and final, derived during the course of the consultation. They are expressed in equations like "member = yes CNF 100." A confidence factor of 100 (CNF 100) is given to indicate the degree of certainty, or confidence, that a particular conclusion is valid. More will be said about confidence factors in Chapter 4.

Placing the RUNTIME keyword in a KBS eliminates the two bottom windows. This is usually done before a KBS is delivered to a user.

Figure 3–10. VP-Expert Menu Tree

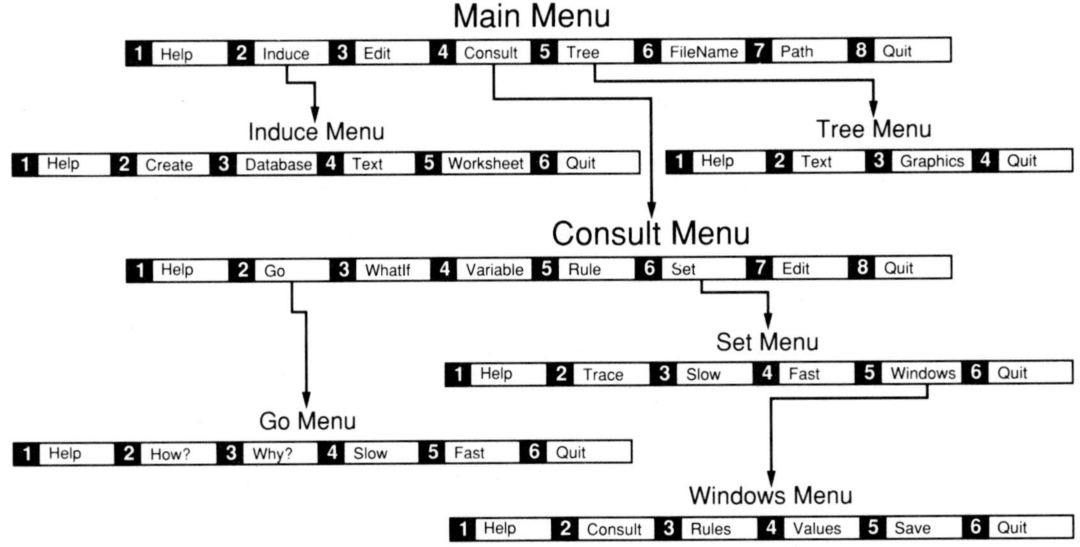

Selecting Menu Options

Menu options can be selected in any one of the following ways:

Type the first letter of the option.

Type the number of the menu option selected or, alternatively, the identically numbered Function Key.

Use the arrow keys to move the lightbar to a menu option and press Enter.

Menu Options Reference

Consult — Permits getting into the Consult submenu in order to begin a consultation.

Create — Brings up the Editor in order to create or edit an induction table. The extension .TBL is assumed.

Edit — Brings up the Editor.

THE DEVELOPER'S TOOLKIT—MORE ON DEBUGGING

Expert system shells generally make a variety of tools available to assist in developing and debugging a knowledge base. Most of those discussed here are available as options selected from various menus. Figure 3–10 illustrates the hierarchy, or tree, of menus in VP-Expert and describes toolkit features in more detail.

The Slow option on the Set Menu, as an example, slows down the execution of the knowledge base so that a developer can more easily follow the activity in the Rules and Facts windows visually during a consultation. Figure 3–11 outlines the procedure to follow to explore this and other options available for developers.

Fast	Undoes the Slow option.
Filename	Loads a knowledge base for consultation or editing.
Go	Begins a consultation.
Graphics	Displays a consultation Trace in tree form.
Help	Allows getting information on menu options.
How?	Used during a consultation to find how a variable value was assigned.
Induce	Creates a knowledge base from a table of examples, a database file, or a worksheet file.
Path	Used to change the default data directory.
Quit	Permits leaving the current menu and going back to the previous menu.
Rule	Allows examining any rule in the knowledge base.
Set	Allows using the Trace, Fast, and Slow menu options.
Slow	Used as a development tool. Slows down the inference engine so that the displayed results can be followed more easily.
Text	1. On the Induce menu: Informs the inference engine that the induction table from which the knowledge base will be induced is contained in a text file with a TBL extension. 2. On the Tree menu: Displays in text form a consultation trace.
Trace	Stores the reasoning strategy that the inference engine uses during a consultation. These results may be examined by using either the Text or the Graphics options found on the Tree menu.
Tree	Enables examining the results of a consultation Trace in either Text or Graphic form.
Variable	Allows examining the values and confidence factors assigned to a variable as a result of a consultation.
WhatIf	Allows seeing the effect of a change in the value of a variable on the results of a consultation.
Why?	Used during a consultation to find out why a particular question is being asked.
Windows	Allows moving or re-sizing the consultation window.

Figure 3–11.

Procedures to Explore Options Useful to Developers

Slow Down a Consultation

1. Choose Consult from the Main Menu, then choose Set to display the Set Menu.
2. Select Slow. Note: Slow affects some computers more than others. If Slow does not slow a consultation enough, repeatedly press the F3 function key. This has a cumulative effect.
3. Choose Quit to return to the Consult Menu.
4. Select Go to begin the consultation. The activity in the Rules and Facts windows should now be slow enough to follow.
5. To return to normal speed, type a slash (/) and choose Fast from the Go Menu. Note: Slow and Fast options appear on the Go Menu as well as the Set Menu. This allows altering consultation speed both prior to and during a consultation.

Trace a Consultation

1. Choose Consult from the Main Menu, then choose Set to display the Set Menu.
2. Select Trace. This displays the message, "The trace is on," indicating that the subsequent consultation will be recorded and sent to a disk file.
3. Choose Quit to return to the Consult Menu.
4. Select Go to begin the consultation.
   After the consultation concludes, to see the result of the Trace:
5. Choose Quit from the Consult Menu, then choose Tree from the Main Menu.
6. Choose Text. This displays a text representation, similar to the one in Figure 3–12, of the previous consultation on the Editor screen.
7. Press Alt and function key F8 to quit the Editor.
   If the computer being used has graphics capability (a CGA, EGA, Hercules monochrome, or compatible graphics board):
8. Choose Graphics from the Tree Menu. A graphics tree appears in the upper left corner of the screen in a highlighted box.
9. Press the spacebar to enlarge the area inside the box, making that portion of the display legible, similar to the example shown in Figure 3–13. Use the arrow keys or the PgUp and PgDn keys to zoom in on other areas of the tree. Press the spacebar again to return to the box on the previous display. Alternatively, the box can be moved with the arrow keys or the PgUp and PgDn keys. By moving in box-size steps, and pressing the spacebar, it is possible to zoom in on any section of the graphic tree for closer examination.
10. Pressing ESC at the first graphics screen with the highlighted box causes a return to the Tree Menu.

Learn "Why?" a Question Is Asked or "How?" a Value Was Assigned to a Variable

1. Choose Go from the Consult Menu and after any question is displayed, type the backslash (/) key.
2. Move the lightbar to Why? and press Enter. The appropriate response is displayed.
3. Press any key to escape. Resume the consultation and answer one or more questions.
4. Type the backslash (/) key.
5. Move the lightbar to How? and press Enter. Make a selection by using the arrow keys to highlight a variable choice. Press Enter. A response identifying how the variable was set is displayed.
6. Press any key to escape.

Explore Alternatives ("WhatIf") or Examine a Rule or Variable

1. Choose WhatIf from the Consult Menu.
2. Choose a variable from the list of variable names presented and press Enter. The appropriate question appears for answering.
3. Select an answer. This may, in some circumstances, cause the consultation to restart. In some cases, the inference engine has all the information it needs to draw a new conclusion. In other cases, the new answer might cause the inference engine to take a new logic path through the rules. This may generate new questions.
4. At the Consult Menu, choose Rule or Variable. Make a selection from the list of rules or variables presented. A response identifying the variable with its value(s) or the rule chosen is displayed.
5. Press any key to escape.

Frequently, a developer has to deal with the problem of a knowledge base that runs, or executes, but seems to contain some logical errors. An aid in this situation is to perform a *trace* on the consultation to see what's going on behind the scenes. The procedure to perform a trace is given in Figure 3–11.

A trace saves the search pattern used by the inference engine to a file with the same name as the knowledge base, but with a TRC file extension. This file can be viewed two ways: as a *text tree* or as a *graphics tree*. Examples of both are shown in Figures 3–12 and 3–13.

The following three options may also help a developer during a debugging session:

- *How?*—describes how a value was assigned to a variable that a developer selects from a list of choices. Responses are because "You said so," or because "Rule X fired," or even "There are no values for that variable."
- *Rule*—allows examining any rules (selected from a list of choices) in the knowledge base
- *Variable*—allows examining the value(s) and confidence factors assigned to any variable (selected from a list of choices) as a result of a consultation

The procedure to use these options is described in Figure 3–11. When these options are used, they all appear in pop-up windows that resemble the examples in Figures 3–14 and 3–15.

Figure 3–12. Text Trace of a Consultation Session

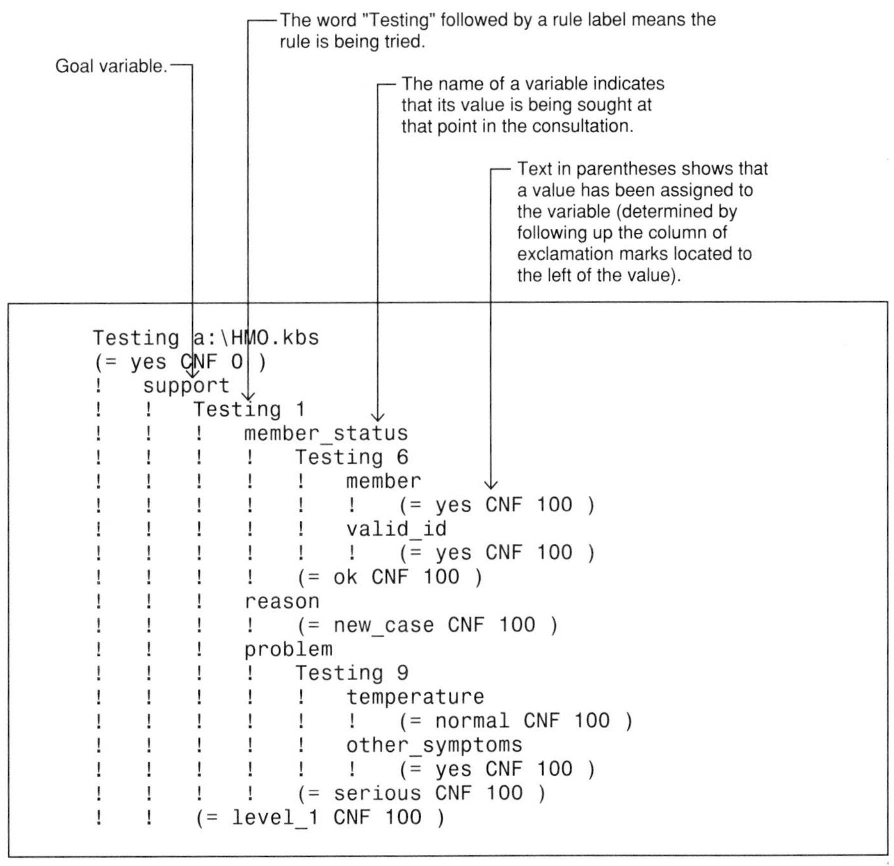

Figure 3–13. Graphic Trace of a Consultation Session

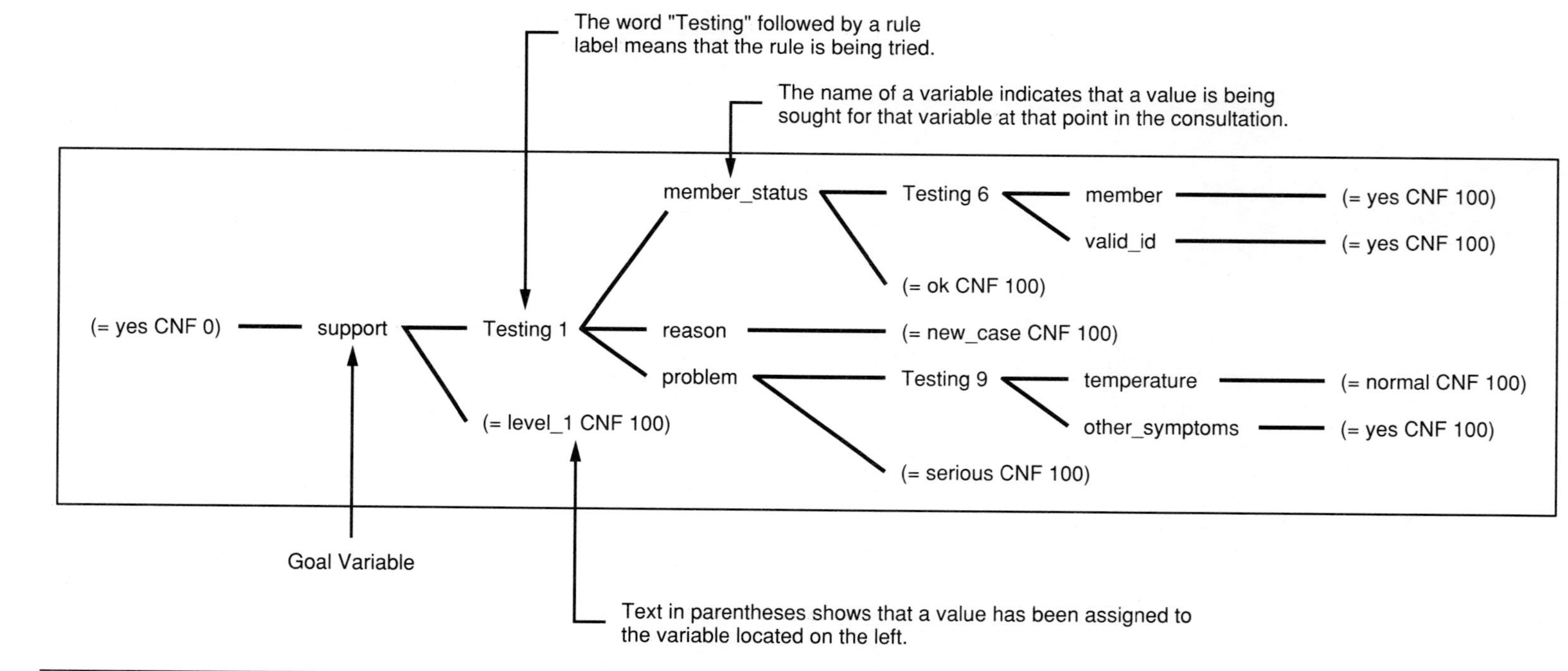

Figure 3–14. The "Why?" Explanation Feature

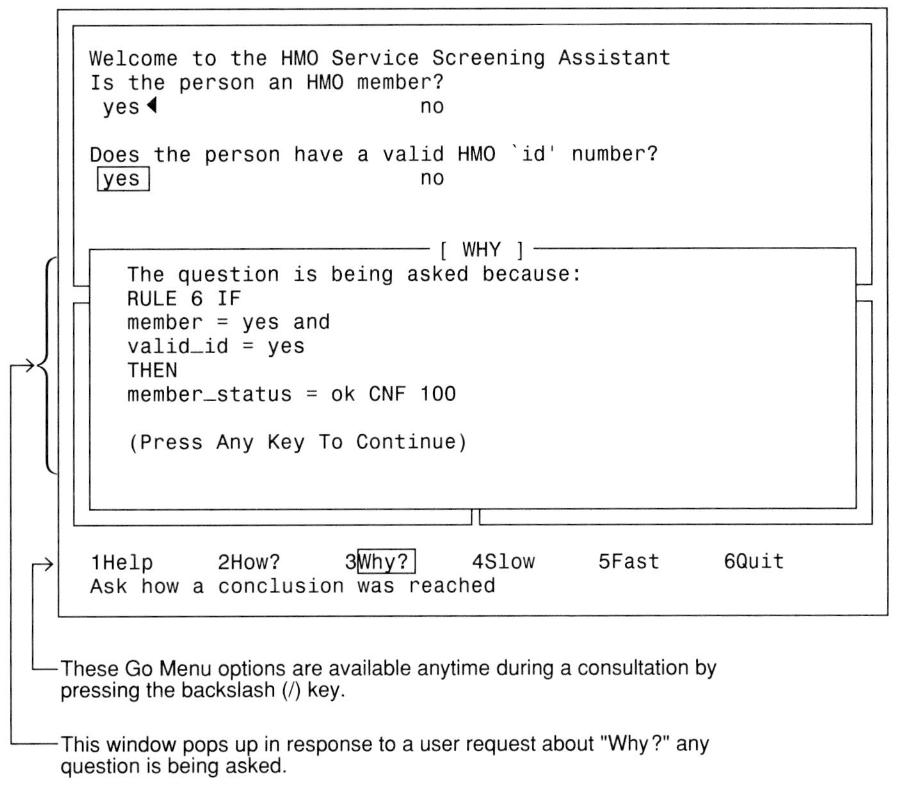

Figure 3–15. Examining "What If" Alternatives

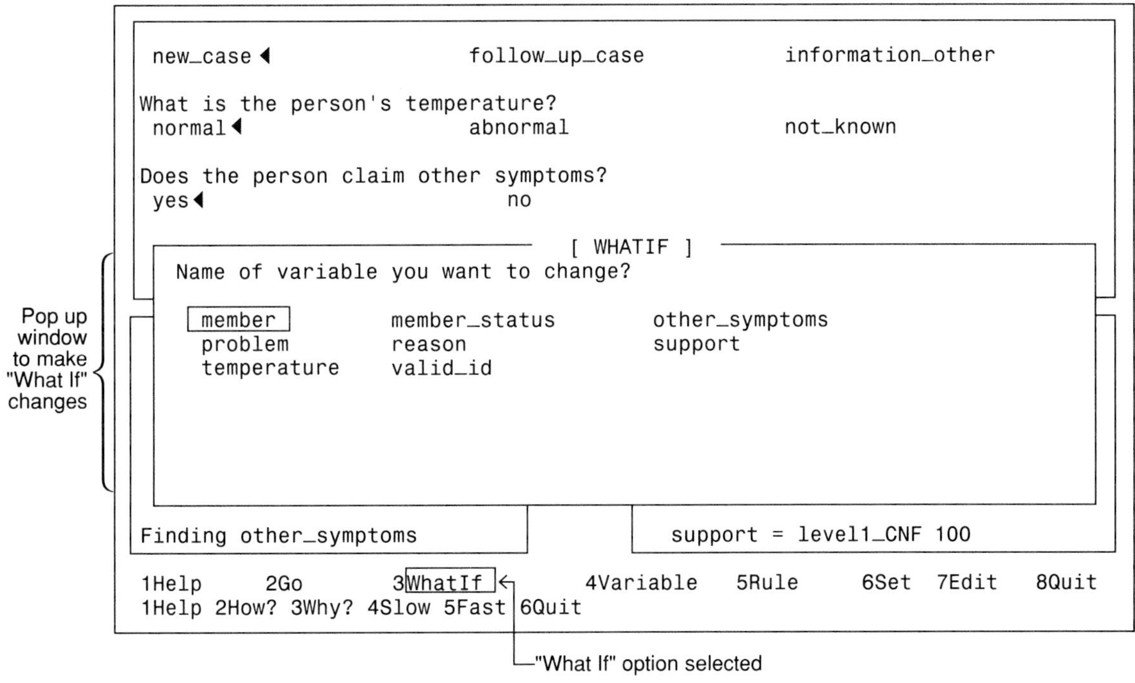

THE USER'S OPTIONS—MORE ON RUNNING A CONSULTATION

Two menu options benefit users who run a consultation as much as they benefit developers. These are the *Why?* and *What If* options.

One of the features of a KBS compared to a conventional computer system is its ability to explain. This feature allows a user, or developer, to stop a consultation anywhere and ask why a question is being asked. Figure 3–11 provides the procedure for exploring this feature. Figure 3–14 illustrates an example of using the Why? feature.

Especially with a KBS designed to assist in managerial decision-making tasks, users often consider it essential to be able to examine and critique how a decision is determined. The built-in Why? feature enables this kind of probing. Chapter 5 discusses a way to improve this explanation facility with the use of the BECAUSE keyword.

Also, if a decision maker is using a KBS to explore various scenarios, as in a strategy-planning KBS, it is valuable to be able to change a variable to see how that change could affect a solution. The What If feature answers questions such as, "What if I had chosen 'No' instead of 'Yes' at the last prompt?" The procedure to use the What If feature is given in Figure 3–11 and illustrated in Figure 3–15.

The options discussed should be sufficient for completing and debugging the sample systems in this tutorial. Detailed documentation is provided in the *VP-Expert Manual*.

REVIEW QUESTIONS

1. How does the inference engine work?
2. What generalizations can be made concerning backward chaining?
3. How does the Editor function in an expert system shell?
4. What are the basics of debugging a knowledge base?
5. What kinds of errors commonly occur in KBS programs?
6. Why does the configuration of the consultation screen sometimes vary between the development and delivery phases?
7. What are the benefits of the Why? and What If options in an expert system shell?
8. What are the reasons for using the How? or Variable options in an expert system shell?

EXERCISES

1. This exercise contrasts the user's and the developer's view of a KBS. Run a consultation with the knowledge base HMORUN.KBS from the Sample Files disk.
   a. Use the "Procedure for Running a Consultation," given in Figure 3–2, to run the consultation.
   b. Run a consultation using the knowledge base HMO.KBS from the Sample Files disk.

c. Compare and record the results observed from the two consultations. Why are they different?

2. To explore working with the Editor, enter the knowledge base from Figure 3–3 into the computer. When asked to "choose a file," enter any 8-digit or less filename, such as MYHMO. Use your own personal disk to save this exercise, which will be referenced as your Exercise disk in future exercises. (It is highly recommended that you have two Exercise disks. One should be the Master disk and the second a duplicate Backup safety disk.)

a. Use the "Procedure for Entering (or Editing) a Knowledge Base," given in Figure 3–4, to key the code into the computer.

b. Run a trial consultation and record the results. Use the "Procedure for Running a Consultation," given in Figure 3–2, to run the consultation.

c. If errors are present, use the "Procedure for Debugging a Knowledge Base," given in Figure 3–8, to make corrections.

d. Repeat Steps b and c until the knowledge base is completely debugged, or error free.

e. Test all possible paths through the knowledge base. Record each test attempted and the result of each.

3. This exercise continues to explore working with the Editor. Make the following changes to the knowledge base created in Exercise 2.

a. Insert a blank line above the keyword ACTIONS and type the keyword RUNTIME; (include the semicolon) on the new first line. Run a trial consultation. Record the results observed.

b. Delete the first line (RUNTIME;). Block all of Rule 2 and move it above Rule 1. Renumber the rules. Run a trial consultation. Record the results observed. Does switching the rules make a difference as to how the knowledge base executes?

c. Print a copy of the knowledge base file. Follow the "Print file" instructions in Figure 3–7.

4. Explore other kinds of options available to developers. Follow the "Procedures to Explore Options Useful to Developers," given in Figure 3–11.

a. Use the knowledge base created in Exercise 2 for exploring options. Record the results observed.

b. Use the HMO.KBS knowledge base from the Sample Files disk. Record the results observed.

5. Use a word processor or the Editor to enter a knowledge base of your own design into the computer file.

a. Run a trial consultation.

b. Debug any errors using the Editor and make another trial run. Repeat this procedure until your new knowledge base is completely debugged.

4

DATABASE, SPREADSHEET, AND OTHER KNOWLEDGE BASE DEVELOPMENT TECHNIQUES

This chapter continues the tutorial that began in Chapter 2 on developing a first knowledge-based system. The chapter moves beyond the basics to cover

- Database integration
- Indirect addressing
- Arithmetic and relational symbols
- RUNTIME keyword
- MENU keyword
- Looping, or iterative processing
- Spreadsheet integration
- Using induction to create a knowledge base
- Confidence factors

To focus learning, each new theme begins by going back to the original simplified knowledge base presented in Figure 2–15. Then incremental changes are discussed as applied to that basic knowledge base.

For examples presented in this chapter, the recommended learning process involves these steps:

1. Run the new knowledge base using the file on the Sample Files disk to see how it works. Use the "Procedure for Running a Consultation" (given in Figure 3–2) to do this.
2. Go back to copy the original simplified knowledge base (HMO.KBS shown in Figure 2–15) and make the incremental changes to it that you will be learning about in this chapter. Use the "Procedure for Entering (or Editing) a Knowledge Base" (given in Figure 3–4) to do this. Match your finished knowledge base with the one on the Sample Files disk. There should be no differences between them. This method always starts with a model that is known to be correct. It provides a goal to aim for during the early phase of learning how to develop a KBS.

If you follow this learning plan, it is ideal to have two blank formatted disks labelled as

1. KBS Exercises—Master
2. KBS Exercises—Backup

The Backup, which is a safety disk, is a copy of the Master disk. The Master should be backed up frequently during and after each development session at the computer. This is always good computing practice to protect against inadvertently erased or damaged disks.

As mentioned earlier, although the software development tool used is the VP-Expert system shell, the themes discussed are applicable to whatever shell is used. Also, only selected keywords and features are covered in this tutorial. It is advisable to consult the *VP-Expert Manual* for additional detail.

DATABASE INTEGRATION

One of the powerful features of today's expert system shells is their ability to integrate with existing database and spreadsheet files. Such files store a vast amount of information that represents, for many organizations, a substantial corporate asset.

Often a KBS can help to leverage use of the information contained in the files. For example, in the HMO case, database information can be imported at the start of the consultation to replace the tedious manual ID-verification task otherwise performed by an HMO service representative.

The first example of this chapter explores *database integration.* Here, the HMO KBS integrates with a MEMBER database file to verify that a client is, in fact, a valid HMO member. This automated check has several benefits:

- Spares the HMO service representative from having to consult a large computer printout of current members
- Makes the operation more efficient and accurate
- Reduces the total time needed to service the HMO client

This KBS application takes the HMO client's "ID" number from the MEMBER database, processes it, and converts it into specific action recommendations. If the client is a valid member, the service representative is informed and prompted to proceed with screening the client. If the client is not validated, the KBS informs the service representative and recommends further action as a "non-member" client. This application is characterized by taking database output as its input, making judgments based on it, and then presenting specific suggestions to the user.

But the application also captures information during processing and updates the database to support management decision making. For example, decisions on how much to charge HMO members for services is based on historical records of services rendered to clients. To automate the maintenance of these important historical records, the KBS updates a member's record each time the screening process results in a validated request for service.

Member Database File

Assume for this example that the HMO organization has a computerized database of member information that includes, among other items, the following:

- Member ID or identification number
- Full name and address

- Type of plan (example: family, individual, co-payment, etc.)
- Plan payor (example: private, company, etc.)
- Original date of membership
- Date of current membership expiration
- Annual service charge
- Payment schedule (example: yearly, monthly, etc.)
- Payment status (example: good, delinquent, etc.)
- Number of requests for service during current year
- Number of requests for service previous year

This administrative information is included in addition to detailed billing and medical history files.

Figure 4–1 shows an extract of this database information and presents it as the MEMBER file. Both the record structure and test records for this file are given. It is on the Sample Files disk as a dBASE file with the .DBF filename extension (MEMBER.DBF).

KBS Link to Database

The knowledge base that links into the MEMBER file to automate member validation is given in Figure 4–2. When the HMO service representative runs a consultation with it, the screen looks like the example in Figure 4–3.

Figure 4–1. MEMBER Database File

Structure for Each Record
in the MEMBER Database File

Field Name	Width	Field Type (Character or Numeric)	Field Description
ID	3	N	ID
P_TYPE	10	C	PlanType(FAM=family; COPAY= co-payment; IND=individual)
LNAME	15	C	Last Name
FNAME	15	C	First Name
REQUESTS	3	N	Requests for service this year

Test Records
(9 test records exist
in the MEMBER database file)

Record Number	ID	P_TYPE	LNAME	FNAME	REQUESTS
1	111	fam	Jones	Irene	12
2	222	ind	Tyson	Christopher	2
3	333	copay	Wong	Swee	4
4	444	fam	Malone	John	10
5	555	copay	Mendez	Nick	7
6	666	copay	Dietz	Elizabeth	1
7	777	ind	Lacy	MaryBeth	5
8	888	fam	Tillman	Bradford	5
9	999	fam	Gilmore	Matthew	2

Figure 4–2. A Knowledge Base with a Link to a Database File

Notes:
. The name of this knowledge base file on the Sample Files disk is HMO.KBS and MEMBER. DBF is the database file.
. The blocked areas indicate changes to the original HMO.KBS file (see Figure 2-15).

```
RUNTIME;
ACTIONS
  DISPLAY "Welcome to the HMO Service Screening Assistant"
  FIND support
  DISPLAY "Recommended support: {support}."
;

RULE 1
      IF member_status = ok and
         reason = new_case or
         reason = follow_up_case and
         problem = serious
      THEN support = level_1;

RULE 2
      IF member_status = ok and
         reason = new_case and
         problem = non_serious
      THEN support = level_2;

RULE 3
      IF member_status = ok and
         reason = follow_up_case and
         problem = non_serious
      THEN support = level_3;

RULE 4
      IF member_status = ok and
         reason = information_other
      THEN support = information_other;

RULE 5
      IF member_status = not_ok
      THEN support = non_member;

RULE 6
      IF member = yes
      THEN member_status = check_valid
         FIND id_number                        !ASK for direct user input
         GET id_number = id, member, ALL !look in database for a match
         RESET member_status;
```

The database link has little effect on the screen that the service representative sees. This is evident from a comparison of Figures 4–3 and 2–14. Formerly, the service representative had to get a client's ID, then walk over to a centrally located computer-printed listing of member information. The result of this manual verification of member status was keyboarded into the KBS. Consultation resumed in cases where a valid ID was found and terminated if the client was found to be invalid.

The new KBS version asks for the client's ID number and instantly returns the message "Member status" is "ok" or "not ok" as appropriate. The status is determined from a database search by the KBS for a record with a matching ID number.

A successful match causes additional database processing that remains invisible to the KBS user. The member record that causes the match is automati-

```
RULE 7
     IF member = no
     THEN member_status = not_ok;

RULE 8
     IF id_number = (id)
     THEN member_status = ok
        DISPLAY "Member status is ok"
        requests = (requests + 1)               !increment requests
        PUT member;                     !update the database record

RULE 9
     IF id_number <> (id)
     THEN member_status = not_ok
        DISPLAY "Member status is not valid.";

RULE 10
     IF temperature = normal and
        other_symptoms = yes
     THEN problem = serious;

RULE 11
     IF temperature = normal and
        other_symptoms = no
     THEN problem = non_serious;

RULE 12
     IF temperature = abnormal or
        temperature = not_known
     THEN problem = serious;

ASK member: "Is the person an HMO member?";
CHOICES member: yes, no;

ASK id_number: "What is the 'id' number?";

ASK reason: "What is the reason for coming to the HMO facility?";
CHOICES reason: new_case, follow_up_case, information_other;

ASK temperature: "What is the person's temperature?";
CHOICES temperature: normal, abnormal, not_known;

ASK other_symptoms:  "Does the person claim other symptoms?";
CHOICES other_symptoms: yes, no;
```

cally updated to reflect an addition to the number of requests for HMO service in the current year. In a more sophisticated system, this update would be more refined to reflect the specific type of service rendered. It could also allow for matching on either ID number or last name.

The GET Keyword

Figure 4–4 provides a summary of GET and other selected keywords used to integrate a KBS with a database file. Figure 4–2 shows how the GET and PUT database keywords are used in practice. In the example, they are used as enhancements to the original KBS which appears in Figure 2–15.

Rule 6 in Figure 4–2 uses the GET keyword to search ALL the records in the MEMBER file for a record whose ID matches the one just entered. The entry

Figure 4–3. Using GET and PUT Keywords to Retrieve and Update a Database Record

This number is used by the GET keyword (in RULE 6) to look for a match in the MEMBER database file.

This message verifies that a matching record is found (see RULE 8). It causes an automatic update of the database record with the PUT keyword (which is not visible to the user). The update adds one to the number of service "requests" in the member's record.

```
Welcome to the HMO Service Screening Assistant
Is the person an HMO member?
[yes] ◄                       no

What is the `id' number?
[666]

Member status is ok
What is the reason for coming to the HMO facility?
[new case] ◄              follow up case          information other

What is the person's temperature?
[normal] ◄                abnormal               not known


Does the person claim other symptoms?
[yes] ◄                   no


Recommended support: level 1.
```

Figure 4–4. Database Access Keywords

Selected Database Keywords

Keyword	Description
ALL	Used with GET and MENU keywords to indicate that no special condition needs to be met when selecting a record.
GET	Used to retrieve values from a database file.
MENU	Used in conjunction with the ASK statement to generate a menu of allowable values that can be assigned to a variable based on the field values of a database file.
PUT	Used to update or change a record in a database file.

Other Related Keywords

Keyword	Description
END	Signals the end of a WHILEKNOWN–END loop. END is the last word of a WHILEKNOWN-END loop.
RESET	Removes any values assigned to the named variable and returns it to the value UNKNOWN. The most frequent use of the RESET keyword is in a WHILEKNOWN–END loop where a variable's value is being repeatedly sought, but where the value must be returned to UNKNOWN before each iteration of the FIND clause.
WHILEKNOWN	All lines appearing between the WHILEKNOWN keyword and the END keyword are repeatedly executed in loop fashion so long as the value of the variable named in the WHILEKNOWN clause has a known value. Once the value of the variable becomes UNKNOWN, the lines contained inside the loop are executed one final time. (A loop can begin with the WHILEKNOWN variable set to UNKNOWN. If the variable is not set to some other value before the END key is reached, however, the loop will terminate.) This WHILEKNOWN-END loop is frequently used with the GET keyword to access records in a database file. (Nested, or loop-within-a-loop, techniques are not supported. Only one WHILEKNOWN-END loop can be active at a time.)

of the current ID is caused by the FIND keyword instruction, which precedes the GET instruction. FIND is used here simply to force the "ASK id_number" statement to solicit keyboarded input.

Figure 4–5 identifies the meaning of each parameter associated with the GET keyword. The first parameter specifies either that ALL records are to be selected, or only those records that match one or more conditions specified. In the example shown, the first parameter is "id_number = id." This specifies the

Figure 4–5. Database Access Examples

GET (Retrieve) Information from a Database File

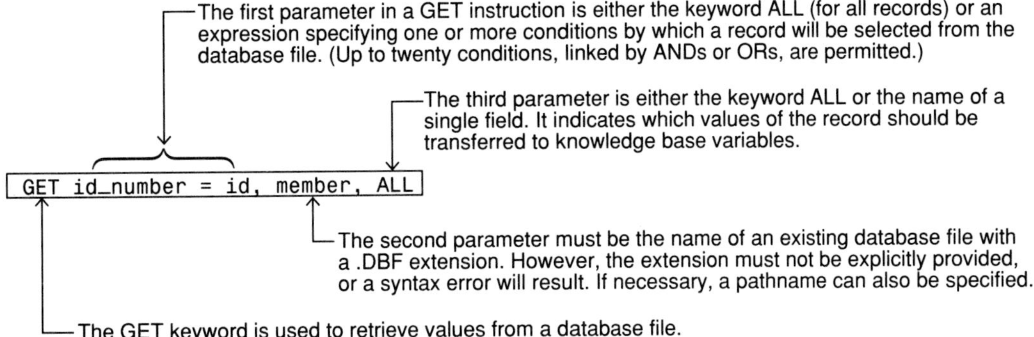

PUT (Write) Information to a Database File

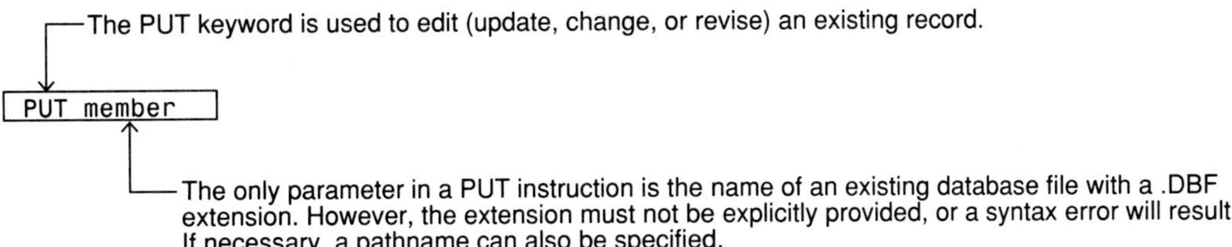

Generate a MENU of Options to Accompany an ASK Question

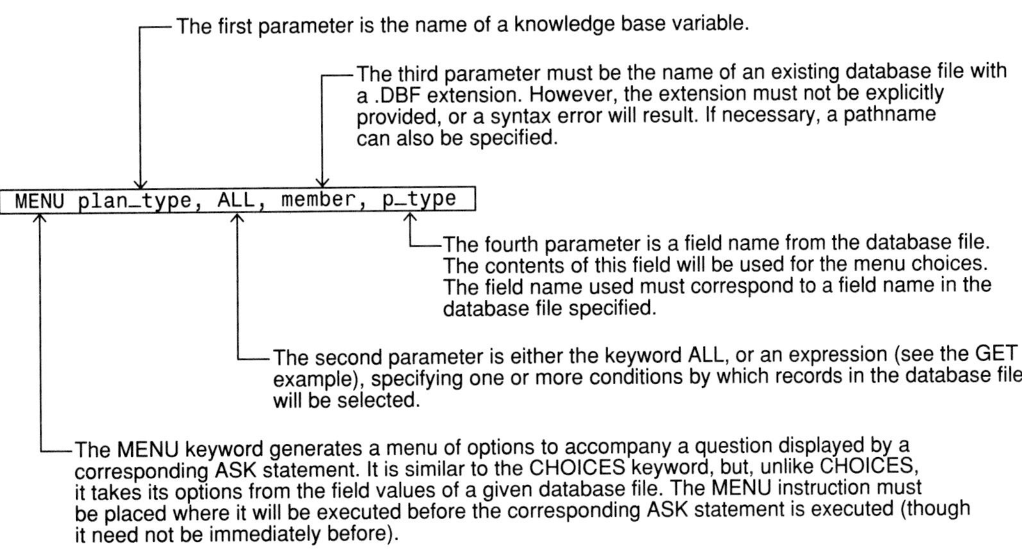

condition for which a record is to be selected from the database file. The consultation screen in Figure 4–3 shows 666 is the "id_number" entered, so a match is expected with record number 6 in the file of test records shown in Figure 4–1.

The second GET parameter identifies the name of the database file to be searched. In this case it is the MEMBER file. It must be a file with a .DBF filename extension. However, the extension must not be explicitly provided, or a syntax error will result. If necessary, a DOS pathname can also be specified with the filename.

The third and final parameter indicates which fields in a record are of interest. Either ALL or one field can be specified. In the example, ALL fields are identified, which is the normal case.

The final instruction in Rule 6 uses the RESET keyword, which automatically changes the value of any variable named to UNKNOWN. In the example, it is necessary to change the variable "member_status" to UNKNOWN to return the inference engine to its normal search path.

The inference engine originally arrived at Rule 6 searching for "member_status" because the first IF condition in Rule 1 sent it there. Rule 6 is the first rule in the knowledge base that has "member_status" in its THEN clause, so the inference engine stops to evaluate all IF conditions in Rule 6 first. The IF part of the rule has only one condition and it requires a keyboarded response to indicate whether a client is an HMO "member." If the response is "yes," the inference engine needs to do a database check. To do this, it is necessary to "skip over" the first THEN clause and get on to the second and third clauses. This is easily done by temporarily filling "member_status" with a "dummy" value. In this case, "member_status" is temporarily set to "check_valid," but could just as well be any other value desired.

Such a temporary procedure forces the inference engine to execute all the instructions after the THEN clause. Once these instructions are executed, it is appropriate to restore the "member_status" variable to UNKNOWN, because it forces further searching to establish its correct value in Rule 7, 8, or 9.

It is interesting to compare the position of rules in Figures 2–15 and 4–2. A comparison highlights the importance of rule placement, or position, in a knowledge base. For example, in Figure 2–15 both "member = yes" conditions appear in Rules 6 and 7 before the single "member = no" condition (Rule 8). Following this pattern, it would seem instinctively right in Figure 4–2 to position Rules 8 and 9, which are logical follow-up questions to "member = yes," right after Rule 6. In practice, however, this placement causes an illogical request for a member's ID, even if the client is not a member! To correct this requires bumping the "member = no" rule to a higher position in the sequential rule order.

Every KBS developer creates techniques to expedite coding a knowledge base. There are usually several solutions that would work equally well to solve any single coding challenge.

To help document new additions to the knowledge base, comments are added to the right of selected program lines. Comments begin with an exclamation mark (!) and may appear anywhere in the knowledge base. The inference engine ignores all text after an exclamation mark.

The PUT Keyword

Rule 8 in Figure 4–2 demonstrates the use of the PUT keyword to update an existing record in a database file. (The term *update* is used interchangeably with the terms *edit, change,* or *revise.*) In this case, the update concerns incrementing by one the number in the REQUESTS field of the member's record. Management policy decisions are based on the data provided by this field, which is a running tally of the number of times a member solicits HMO services in the current year. The PUT instruction that actually causes the HMO member's record to be updated in the database file is straightforward. It includes only two elements: the keyword PUT and the name of the database file. To verify that the update has taken place, it is necessary to go into the dBASE program and check the record in the MEMBER.DBF file.

Before the update takes place, the IF condition in Rule 8 acts as a filter. It allows only certain cases to pass through. The ID number entered must match an ID number in the database.

INDIRECT ADDRESSING

The ID number in the IF clause of Rule 8 is surrounded by parentheses. They indicate to the inference engine that the enclosed item is a variable name whose value must replace the name. To replace the variable name with its value, the inference engine goes into its working memory and makes the replacement itself. Programmers call this *indirect addressing.* It is a technique in which a variable name is used as an indirect way of addressing its value.

This technique is always useful, for example, to display the results of a consultation. Look at the last line of the Actions Block in Figure 4–2. There the value of the variable "support" is displayed when a consultation session terminates.

Figure 4–6 provides examples to show the various ways indirect addressing is useful in knowledge base development. Example 4 is taken from Rule 8 in Figure 4–2. It shows its use in math operations. In this case, the value of the REQUESTS field is incremented by one. After this operation occurs on the right side of the equal sign, the result is assigned to the variable named on the left of the equal sign. In this case, it is the same variable. REQUESTS ends up containing the result of the addition.

Once the addition is done, the updated record is ready to be returned to the MEMBER database file.

Other Applications of Database Linkage

This update example only begins to tap the surface of the potential use of linking a database with a KBS. To extend the present example, assume management wants to know when something is about to go wrong. It would like to embed intelligence in the KBS to flag cases, for example, of members who have an "individual" policy and who exceed, say, five requests for service this year. The KBS could have a rule that watches in the background and when it finds such a case, it could, for example:

- Automatically create a new record of the exception in a special file created for this purpose. (The APPEND command, not covered here, provides for adding records to a database file.)
- Automatically display or print a message about any special processing required. Chapters 5 and 6 describe how a message could be printed, or alternatively, a warning could be displayed in a pop-up window.

This extra embedded intelligence makes the KBS a low-cost diagnostic tool that can make a major contribution to operational control.

Figure 4–6. Indirect Addressing or Referencing the Value of a Variable

The method of indirectly accessing a value by means of a variable name is called "indirect addressing."

Example 1

```
DISPLAY "Recommended support: {support}."
```

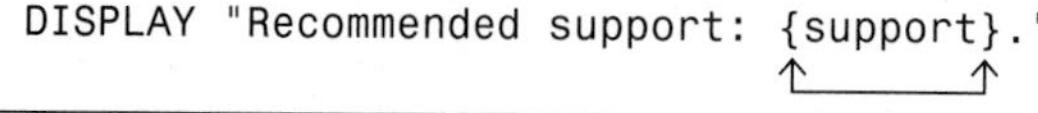

```
Assume:  support = level_1
The displayed result is:
Recommended support:  level 1.
```

Curly brackets mean that the "value" of the named variable should be shown. (Curly brackets are used for indirect addressing in a DISPLAY instruction).

Example 2

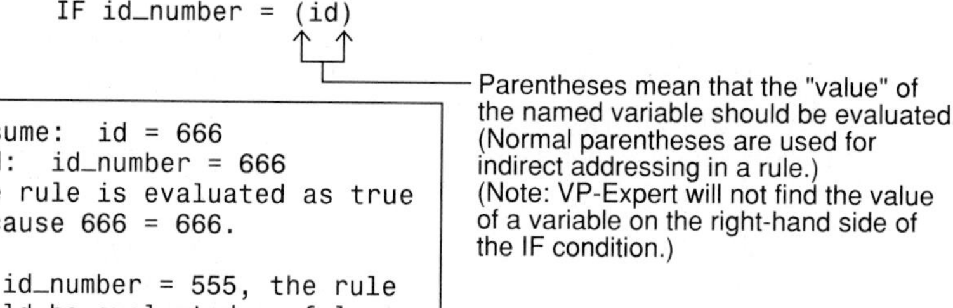

```
IF id_number = (id)
```

Parentheses mean that the "value" of the named variable should be evaluated. (Normal parentheses are used for indirect addressing in a rule.) (Note: VP-Expert will not find the value of a variable on the right-hand side of the IF condition.)

```
Assume:  id = 666
And:  id_number = 666
The rule is evaluated as true
because 666 = 666.

If id_number = 555, the rule
would be evaluated as false.
```

Example 3

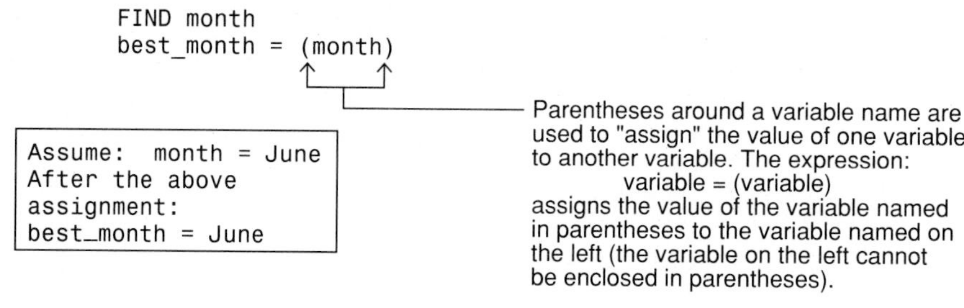

```
FIND month
best_month = (month)
```

Parentheses around a variable name are used to "assign" the value of one variable to another variable. The expression:
variable = (variable)
assigns the value of the variable named in parentheses to the variable named on the left (the variable on the left cannot be enclosed in parentheses).

```
Assume:  month = June
After the above
assignment:
best_month = June
```

Example 4

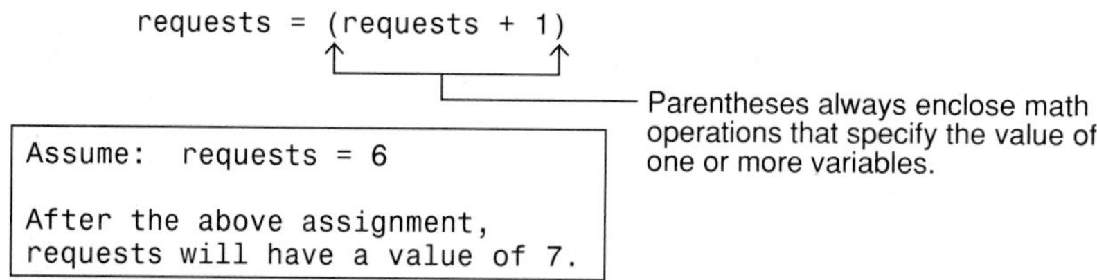

```
requests = (requests + 1)
```

Parentheses always enclose math operations that specify the value of one or more variables.

```
Assume:  requests = 6

After the above assignment,
requests will have a value of 7.
```

ARITHMETIC AND RELATIONAL SYMBOLS

Rules 8 and 9 introduce new arithmetic and relational symbols, which are identified in Figure 4–7. These symbols, also called operators, are the same as those used in almost every modern program coding language.

In the HMO example, the plus sign represents the add operation required in "requests = (requests + 1)." Any arithmetic operation that specifies using the

Figure 4–7. Arithmetic and Relational Symbols (Operators)

Arithmetic Symbols

Symbol	Meaning
+	Used for addition of numbers.
–	Used for subtraction of numbers.
*	Used for multiplication of numbers.
/	Used for division of numbers.

Relational Symbols

Symbol	Meaning
=	Used as the equal-to relation.
>	Used as the greater-than relation.
<	Used as the less-than relation.
>=	Used as the greater-than-or-equal-to relation.
<=	Used as the less-than-or-equal-to relation.
<>	Used as the not-equal-to relation.

value of one or more variables must be enclosed in parentheses, as the example demonstrates.

The IF condition in Rule 9 illustrates the use of the not equal to (<>) relational symbol. It consists of placing a less than (<) symbol next to a greater than (>) symbol.

Rule 9 filters out any case where the database file has no record for a client who claims to be a member. IF the "id number" that the client gives is "not equal to" an ID in the database, then the "member_status" is set to "not_ok." A message is immediately displayed to tell the HMO service representative that the member status is not valid. In this example case, all clients with a "member_status" of "not_ok" are automatically recommended for non-member support.

RUNTIME KEYWORD

The knowledge base in Figure 4–2 begins with the RUNTIME keyword. Placing this keyword in the KBS eliminates the two bottom windows, shown in Figure 3–9, that appear during a consultation. Instead, the consultation window occupies the full screen, as shown in Figure 2–14. This improves the appearance of the system that the user sees.

The RUNTIME keyword should be added to a knowledge base when development is finished and the knowledge base is ready for user, or "runtime," consultations.

MENU KEYWORD

Another keyword used exclusively for database access is MENU. The example in Figure 4–8, which is created only for illustration purposes, demonstrates how MENU is used in practice. This keyword is used in conjunction with the ASK statement to generate a menu of allowable values that can be assigned to a variable. The assignable values are extracted from those found in the actual database records.

Figure 4–8. Using the MENU Keyword and a WHILEKNOWN-END Loop

Note: The name of this knowledge base file on the Sample Files disk is HMODB1.KBS or HMODB1R.KBS and MEMBER.DBF is the database file.

```
ACTIONS
     DISPLAY "This example assists your interrogation of the"
     DISPLAY "MEMBER database file."
     MENU plan_type, ALL, member, p_type
     FIND plan_type
     FIND cut_off
     DISPLAY "The following database records meet your criteria:"
     WHILEKNOWN p_type
          GET plan_type = p_type and cut_off < requests, member, ALL
          RESET message
          FIND message
     END
;

RULE 1
     IF p_type <> unknown
     THEN message = displayed
          DISPLAY "{id}, {p_type}, {lname}, {fname}, {requests}"
     ELSE message = displayed
          DISPLAY "End of file";

ASK plan_type: "What plan type do you want to check?";

ASK cut_off: "If you want only those records with `requests'
above a certain number, please enter the number (or zero).";
```

This knowledge file created this consultation screen:

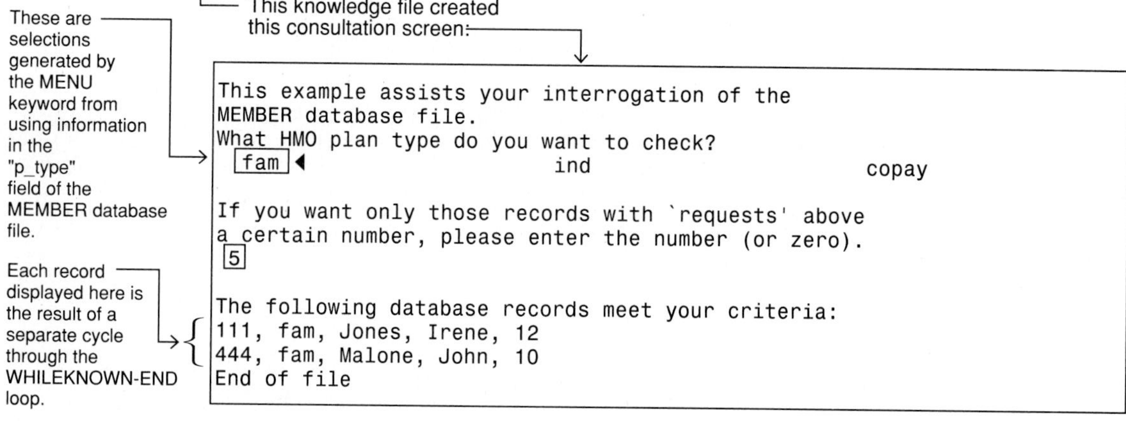

In the example, the database variable of interest is "p_type." Figure 4–1 shows that the MEMBER database file has three unique values repeatedly used in the "p_type" field:

Value	*Meaning*
fam	family plan
ind	individual plan
copay	co-pay plan

In the example, a user selects from this list of plan types to trigger a selective retrieval of database records.

The MENU keyword, in the Actions Block of Figure 4–8, sets up the menu of values that will be called into action when needed. Its three parameters, generally identified in Figure 4–8, are

Parameter	*Meaning*
plan_type	knowledge base variable that will accept all the values from the database variable of interest
plan_type = p_type and cut_off < requests	conditions to preselect records
MEMBER	name of the database file
p_type	field name that contains the values of interest

The next keyword in the Actions Block, after MENU, is "FIND plan_type." Since no rule has "plan_type" in its conclusion, the inference engine automatically looks for user input. The "ASK plan_type" question is not, however, followed by a CHOICES keyword. Instead, the ASK and MENU keywords are linked by their common variable "plan_type." So the MENU keyword provides the choices this time.

The second FIND keyword in the Actions Block similarly causes the second ASK statement to be activated. The user is asked if database record retrieval should be based on the number of times a member has requested service in the current year. Because a typed response is expected, no CHOICES statement is appropriate here.

LOOPING, OR ITERATIVE PROCESSING

The HMO example in Figure 4–2 works on the assumption that only one database record meets the selection criteria. But what if an application, like the one in Figure 4–8, anticipates several records meeting the selection criteria?

The solution is to use *looping*, or *iterative processing*. This is accomplished with the combination of the WHILEKNOWN and END keywords. They mark the beginning and end, respectively, of a loop that is processed repetitively until some exit condition is reached.

The main reason a loop is required is because the GET keyword retrieves only one database record at a time. To retrieve other records, the GET must be reactivated. Reactivation is normally done inside a WHILEKNOWN-END loop.

The example in Figure 4–8 retrieves decision-making information from the MEMBER database file. It first asks a user what type of plan is of interest. Available member plan types are displayed. After the user makes a selection, an option is presented. The KBS is to select records where members have requested service more than a specific number of times. A list follows of database records that meet the selection criteria entered.

WHILEKNOWN-END Loops

In the example, the WHILEKNOWN-END loop occurs in the Actions Block. Looping can also occur, if an application requires it, in the THEN part of a rule. A limitation is that only one WHILEKNOWN-END loop can be active at a time.

The variable after the keyword WHILEKNOWN performs a role similar to a guard at a gate who checks a pass to see if entry should be allowed. Entry is allowed under two conditions:

- The first time through the loop, no entry variable is checked. This is normal because the first GET call to the database occurs after initial entry to the loop. Once the first record is retrieved, the "entry" variable, which is "p_plan," is a "known variable."
- All other times, entry into the loop is allowed only if the entry variable has a known value. This will be true until the last database record is reached. After the last record is reached, "p_plan" is automatically set to "unknown." The loop logically terminates only after one final pass through the loop after the exit variable is set to "unknown."

Comparing the consultation screen in Figure 4–8 with the MEMBER database records in Figure 4–1 helps to demonstrate how looping works in practice. In the first pass through the loop, the WHILEKNOWN variable is ignored. Then the following sequence occurs:

- GET retrieves the first "Jones" record. It is a "fam" family type, and so matches the entered selection criterion (plan_type = p_type).
- The GET instruction requires a match on another condition. That is, the entered "cut_off" value, 5 in this example, must be less than the value in the requests field of the record. In the Jones case, 5 is less than the number in the requests field, which is 12. The second criterion matches, so the first record passes the GET rule.
- "RESET message" in the WHILEKNOWN-END pair clears the goal variable and "FIND message" activates a jump to the only rule in this example.
- RULE 1 first checks to be sure the end of the file is not reached. The variable "p_type" will be automatically set to "unknown" after the last record is processed.
- If it is not the last record, the "THEN message" is fired. It causes the display of all the values in the Jones record.
- After the display, the inference engine returns to the WHILEKNOWN loop to find the END keyword. Control returns to the top of the loop and the process begins again.

Since only the first record has been processed, there still is a value in "p_type" so the loop begins again. The second time through the loop, the GET statement finds no match of its conditions with record number 2 or 3. Their "p_type" are different. But record number 4 matches the "p_type" as well as the cut_off conditions. So the record is retrieved and the loop repeats, as before.

Recycling occurs with no further successful matches. Although records 8 and 9 pass on the "p_type" condition, they fail on the cut_off criteria. Record 8 has a value of 5 for "requests," which is equal to the cut_off point, not above it, as required. So it is rejected. The AND condition requires both premises to pass.

After the last record, "p_type" automatically becomes "unknown." The loop executes one final time from beginning to end. When the FIND message clause sends the inference engine to Rule 1, the IF condition fails. Finally, "p_type" does, indeed, equal "unknown." This causes the alternate ELSE conclusion to fire. It causes "End of file" to display. It also causes the session to end.

Figure 4–9 illustrates, in skeleton outline form, another WHILEKNOWN-END loop. The only difference between this example and the one in Figure 4–8 is in the GET first parameter. In Figure 4–8, a selection criterion occurs in the

Figure 4–9. Looping, or Iteration, Using the WHILEKNOWN-END Keywords

```
Example:

      .
      .
      .
   --> WHILEKNOWN stock_name
  /      GET all, stock, ALL
 (       RESET response
  \      FIND response
   --- END
      .
      .
      .
     RULE 11
       IF stock_price > (buy_price) and
         stock_price < (10_wk_average)
       THEN response = sell
      .
      .
      .

Sample STOCK Database File:

STOCK NAME    STOCK PRICE   BUY PRICE    10 WK AVERAGE  : Loop Results
                                                        :
   AAA           28.16        24.68          31.14      :<—sell (first loop)
   BBB           16.11        17.24          16.79      :(skip) (second loop)
   CCC           43.62        35.91          45.44      :<—sell (third loop)
                                                        :    end (fourth loop)
```

first parameter of the GET instruction. In Figure 4–9, by contrast, ALL records are retrieved. But a similar selection process occurs in Rule 11. This comparison illustrates alternative ways to accomplish the same thing. The creative developer can find many alternatives, among the options offered, to produce effective applications.

Other Database Applications and Considerations

Figure 4–9 illustrates how a WHILEKNOWN-END loop is the focus of another database-oriented application. It is part of a commodities advisory system that recommends when it is appropriate to sell stock based on "buy-price" and other factors stored in a database. Database information comes from financial data services that transfer the data over communication lines.

Another database-oriented application contains information about factors that go into a decision of whether to grant a customer credit. For each factor in the decision, the file contains a list of all possible values. A numeric weight is stored with each value to indicate its significance in the overall decision-making process. Although this information could have been stored in the form of rules, it was stored in a database file to make the system more efficient and easier to maintain.

In another system, a travel-advisory KBS at a foreign consulate office in the United States, the system's recommendations are stored in a database file. The file contains information about hotels, restaurants, and other facilities in the country, arranged by categories such as luxury, budget, and so forth. Once the KBS evaluates the category of travel desired, along with other preferences, it displays or prints its recommendations of services available. Having the list of hotels and restaurants in a database file enormously simplifies the KBS program. It also allows the consulate to easily add, change, or delete records to keep the KBS's recommendations current. This way, updates never require a single change to a KBS rule.

Many developers can take similar advantage of using database files to enhance KBS projects. In particular, many designs can benefit from narrowing a conclusion to a category or type. This classification can then be used to retrieve more specific detail from records stored in a database file.

SPREADSHEET INTEGRATION

Similar to database integration, spreadsheet integration includes transferring data back and forth between a spreadsheet and a knowledge base. Most modern expert system shells provide links to integrate a knowledge base file with a spreadsheet file. As an example, the VP-Expert shell transfers data with the Lotus 1-2-3, VP-Planner, and Symphony spreadsheet programs.

To explore how spreadsheet integration works, assume that the director of the HMO service facility wants to keep a daily running total of how many clients are serviced, by service type. She wants to be able to look at a simple spreadsheet, such as the one in Figure 4–10, at the end of each day, or at random times throughout the day, to check on case volume. The up-to-the-minute figures enable her to make adjustments in personnel to avoid potential service bottlenecks and to maintain a high level of member-service responsiveness.

Changes would have to be made to the original knowledge base presented in Figure 2–15 to satisfy the director's need for current decision-making information.

Figure 4–10. Sample Spreadsheet

Note: The name of this spreadsheet on the Sample Files disk is SSHMO.WKS.

```
              A                 B        C             D
1     HMO Service Screening Control 3/11/9X
2
3     Service_Type              No_Cases
4
5     level_1                         34
5     level_2                         65
7     level_3                        104
8     information_other               41
9     non_member                      17
10
11
12
```

Figure 4–11 shows the revised knowledge base that integrates with the spreadsheet shown in Figure 4–10. The spreadsheet was prepared using Lotus 1-2-3.

When the knowledge base is run, the user consultation screen remains unchanged from Figure 2–14. The spreadsheet is updated in the background with processing that remains hidden from the user's view. The user will, however, experience a longer delay in processing on some slower computers.

Processing requires that the spreadsheet template be already prepared and ready for update when the knowledge base system is running. A fresh copy of the spreadsheet template, with cells B5 to B9 set to an initial value of zero, is always prepared at the end of one work day in readiness for the next day's processing.

During processing, each time a consultation results in firing a rule that establishes a value for "support," it also triggers a spreadsheet update. The update adds one to the number already accumulated in the spreadsheet cell that corresponds to the "support" type. This immediate updating provides the director with control figures, whenever desired, that are as current as the last update.

The WKS Keyword

As evident from Figure 4–11, the WKS keyword retrieves data from a spreadsheet. It is only one of several keywords, as identified in Figure 4–12, used to access a spreadsheet from the knowledge base.

When the WKS keyword is used, it requires three parameters. They are identified in detail in Figure 4–13. The first is the name of any knowledge base variable that receives the value or values being transferred from the spreadsheet. The second parameter identifies the location of the values in the spreadsheet. The final parameter identifies the spreadsheet filename.

Figure 4–14 shows only two of many variations that the "second," or location, parameter, can take. The first example comes from the knowledge base given in Figure 4–11. It shows the WKS keyword used to transfer the value 34 from the single spreadsheet cell, B5, into the knowledge base variable "old-number." This is the simplest transfer of all.

The second example is for illustration purposes. It shows the WKS keyword used for a more complex transfer of values. In this case, an entire column of values is being transferred from the spreadsheet into the knowledge base variable "cases." Because the column contains five values, the inference engine automatically provides five slots to hold all the values. To keep each value unique, it assigns a so-called "subscript" number to each.

When the WKS keyword retrieves data from more than one cell, such as from a column, range, or row, the values are stored in a so-called "subscripted," or "dimensioned," variable. The programming required to manipulate such a variable is more complex than for one that contains a single value.

In the example in Figure 4–11, after Rule 1 fires, the THEN part of the rule has several tasks to do. First, the WKS keyword activates the transfer of the value from spreadsheet cell B5. It is loaded into the knowledge base variable "old_number." Next, a calculation must be performed. It involves adding one to the value in the variable "old_number." Since the old value is 34, the addition sums to 35. This result is assigned to the variable "new_number." In this case, the "equal" sign is read as an "assignment" symbol. It assigns the value on the right of the equal sign to the variable on the left side. Any arithmetic operation is always performed before an assignment takes place.

After the arithmetic, the next step is to transfer the new number back to the spreadsheet.

Figure 4–11. Knowledge Base File with a Link to a Spreadsheet

Notes:
. The name of this knowledge base file on the Sample Files disk is HMOSS.KBS and SSHMO. WKS is the spreadsheet file.
. The blocked areas indicate changes to the original HMO.KBS file (see Figure 2-15).

```
RUNTIME;
ACTIONS
     DISPLAY "Welcome to the HMO Service Screening Assistant"
     WFORMAT fixed, 0               !format PWKS values without decimal places
     FIND support
     DISPLAY "Recommended support: {support}."
;

RULE 1
     IF member_status = ok and
        reason = new_case or
        reason = follow_up_case and
        problem = serious
     THEN support = level_1
        WKS old_number, B5, SSHMO          !transfer the value of spreadsheet
                                     !cell B5 into the variable "old_number"
        new_number = (old_number + 1)               !add 1 to the old number
        PWKS new_number, B5, SSHMO;                 !put the new number back

RULE 2
     IF member_status = ok and
        reason = new_case and
        problem = non_serious
     THEN support = level_2
        WKS old_number, B6, SSHMO
        new_number = (old_number + 1)
        PWKS new_number, B6, SSHMO;

RULE 3
     IF member_status = ok and
     reason = follow_up_case and
     problem = non_serious
     THEN support = level_3
     WKS old_number, B7, SSHMO
     new_number = (old_number + 1)
     PWKS new_number, B7, SSHMO;

RULE 4
     IF member_status = ok and
        reason = information_other
     THEN support = information_other
        WKS old_number, B8, SSHMO
        new_number = (old_number + 1)
        PWKS new_number, B8, SSHMO;
```

The PWKS Keyword

The PWKS keyword does the job of transferring the value 35 from the knowledge base to the spreadsheet. The PWKS keyword requires the same three parameters as the WKS keyword. In this HMO example, the PWKS parameters attached to Rule 1 have the following meaning:

1. "New_number" is the knowledge base variable that contains the value 35.
2. "B5" is the spreadsheet cell where the value stored in "new_number" will be sent.
3. "HMOSS" is the name of the spreadsheet file.

```
RULE 5
     IF member_status = not_ok
     THEN support = non_member
        WKS old_number, B9, SSHMO
        new_number = (old_number + 1)
        PWKS new_number, B9, SSHMO;

RULE 6
     IF member = yes and
        valid_id = yes
     THEN member_status = ok;

RULE 7
     IF member = yes and
        valid_id = no
     THEN member_status = not_ok;

RULE 8
     IF member = no
     THEN member_status = not_ok;

RULE 9
     IF temperature = normal and
        other_symptoms = yes
     THEN problem = serious;

RULE 10
     IF temperature = normal and
        other_symptoms = no
     THEN problem = non_serious;

RULE 11
     IF temperature = abnormal or
        temperature = not_known
     THEN problem = serious;

ASK member: "Is the person an HMO member?";
CHOICES member: yes, no;

ASK valid_id: "Does the person have a valid HMO `id' number?";
CHOICES valid_id: yes, no;

ASK reason: "What is the reason for coming to the HMO facility?";
CHOICES reason: new_case, follow_up_case, information_other;

ASK temperature: "What is the person's temperature?";
CHOICES temperature: normal, abnormal, not_known;

ASK other_symptoms:  "Does the person claim other symptoms?";
CHOICES other_symptoms: yes, no;
```

The PWKS instruction ends the three-part sequence added to the conclusion of Rules 1 to 5. The sequence consists of these steps:

- First, retrieve a value from the spreadsheet cell where the "service type" corresponds to the "support" type in the knowledge base rule.
- Second, add one to the value just retrieved.
- Third, replace or update the value in the same spreadsheet cell with the new incremented value.

Figure 4–12. Selected Spreadsheet Access Keywords

Selected Spreadsheet Keywords

Keyword	Description
COLUMN	Used with the WKS or PWKS keywords to identify a column location in a spreadsheet.
NAMED	Used with the WKS or PWKS keywords to identify a cell range in a spreadsheet.
PWKS	Used to transfer values from a knowledge base variable into a spreadsheet.
ROW	Used with the WKS or PWKS keywords to identify a row location in a spreadsheet.
WFORMAT	Defines the cell format for numeric values that will be transferred to a spreadsheet with the PWKS keyword.
WKS	Used to transfer values from a spreadsheet into a knowledge base variable.

Figure 4–13. WKS and PWKS Keywords for Spreadsheet Access

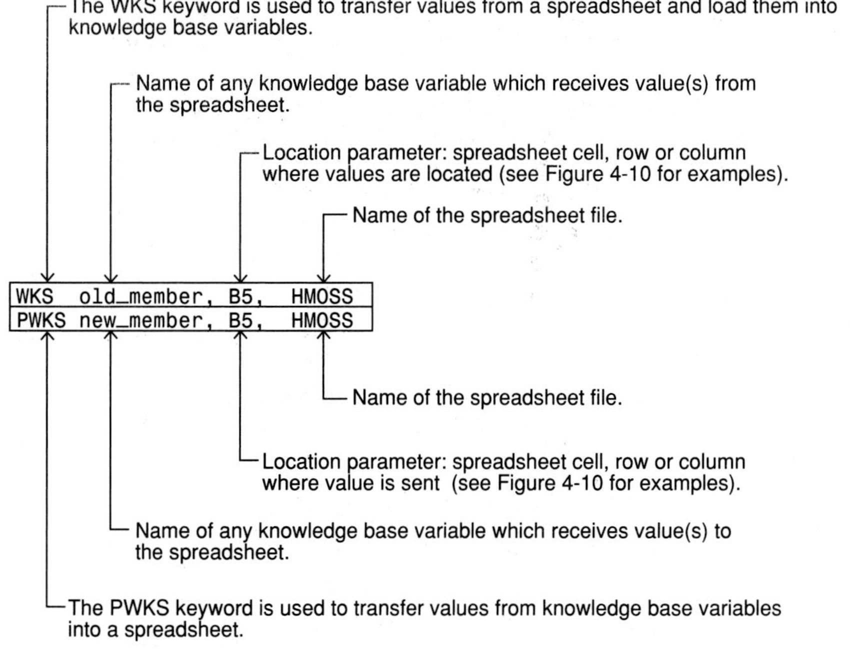

The WFORMAT Keyword

The WFORMAT keyword defines the format for numeric values that are transferred to target cells in a spreadsheet with the PWKS keyword. In the HMO example, the WFORMAT keyword appears in the Actions Block, where it defines the format desired, before rule processing begins. WFORMAT can appear, however, anywhere in a knowledge base before the PWKS instruction.

Figure 4–14. The Location Parameter in WKS and PWKS Keywords

When the WKS or PWKS keywords are used, the second parameter is a location parameter. It can reference a spreadsheet cell, row, column, or range. Examples of reference to both a single cell and a column follow:

Single Cell

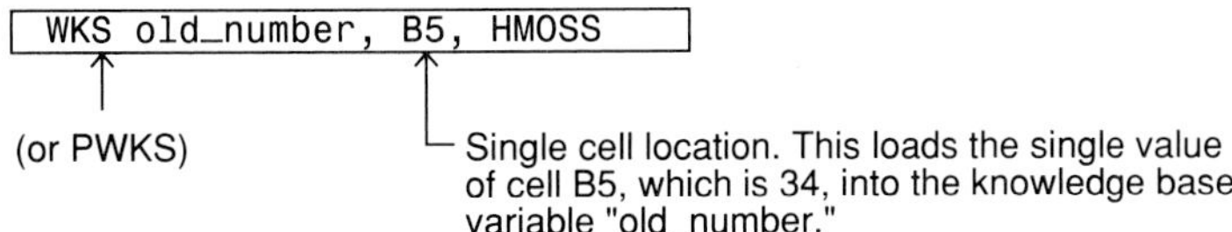

Column

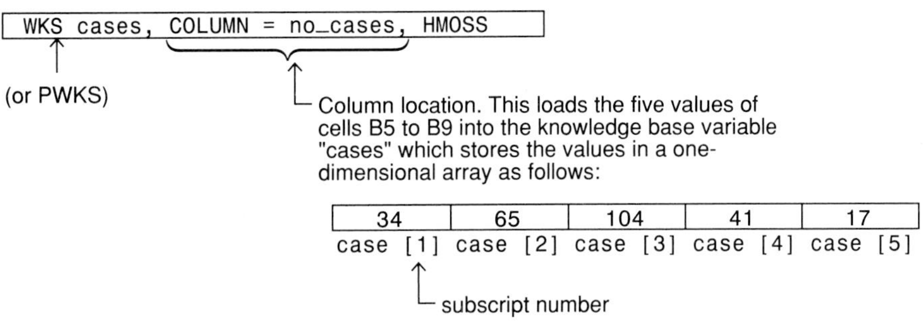

The WFORMAT keyword requires two parameters. The first parameter defines the data format that will be assigned to values transferred to the spreadsheet. There are three possible numeric formats:

Numeric Data Format	*Meaning*
FIXED	fixed decimal point format
CURR	currency format
SCI	scientific format

The second parameter indicates the number of places behind the decimal point. Two examples of its use are

Example	*Stored in Spreadsheet*
WFORMAT FIXED, 0	35
WFORMAT CURR, 2	$35.00

To examine spreadsheet updates made by a knowledge base, it is necessary to

- Activate the spreadsheet program, such as Lotus 1-2-3
- Retrieve the spreadsheet, such as SSHMO.WKS

The SSHMO.WKS spreadsheet should have an accurate count of any consultations processed.

Spreadsheet Considerations

Spreadsheet integration includes several considerations that can make it more problematical than database integration. For example, VP-Expert supports the older Lotus 1-2-3 Version 1A spreadsheet WKS filename extension. Later Lotus versions have a WK1 filename extension. In order to be usable, WK1 filename extensions must be renamed (during a spreadsheet/File, Save operation, or with the DOS rename command). It is possible to retrieve and view or check the renamed file, however, with the later Lotus version programs.

Two other considerations follow:

- The "at" symbol (@) must be used for indirect addressing. For example:

```
cell = B5
WKS new_number, @call, SSHMO
```

  This technique could be used to develop a more streamlined code in the HMO example.
- Blank spreadsheet cells can cause potential assignment errors in the knowledge base. For example, if columns are being read and one column has a blank cell while the other columns contain values, the values would not end up in the correct relationship. Cells can be given a value of zero or the value of a space, but they must have a value.

Other considerations apply to importing and exporting more than one spreadsheet value at a time. Information on this and other spreadsheet uses are contained in Chapter 6, Advanced Features, as well as the *VP-Expert Manual.*

USING INDUCTION TO CREATE A KNOWLEDGE BASE

One simple way of constructing a small knowledge-based system is to represent the expert's knowledge in a table of examples, much like the one shown in Figure 4–15. The example cases can come from a text, database, or spreadsheet file. Once the example cases are recorded in a file, the file can be processed through a so-called "induction algorithm." This processing automatically converts the examples into a working minimal knowledge base.

Absolutely no program coding is required to get results such as the knowledge base shown in Figure 4–16.

Figure 4–15. Creating an Induction Table

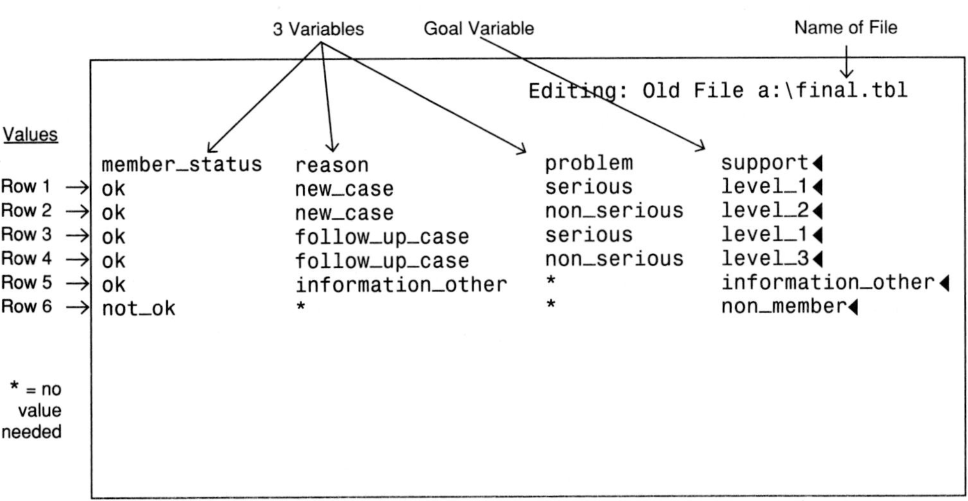

Note: The name of this file on the Sample Files disk is FINAL.TBL.

Figure 4–16. A Minimal "Induced" Knowledge Base (No Programming)

Comparisons with the FINAL.TBL file in Figure 4-15

Notes:
. The name of this knowledge base file on the Sample Files disk is HMOIND.KBS.
. This KBS file was created without programming using the FINAL.TBL file and the "Induce" Main Menu option.

```
               ACTIONS
Goal                   FIND support
variable               DISPLAY "The value of support is {support}";

Row 1      ->  RULE 0
               IF      member_status=ok AND
                       reason=new_case AND
                       problem=serious
               THEN    support=level_1;

Row 2      ->  RULE 1
               IF      member_status=ok AND
                       reason=new_case AND
                       problem=non_serious
               THEN    support=level_2;

Row 3      ->  RULE 2
               IF      member_status=ok AND
                       reason=new_case AND
                       problem=serious
               THEN    support=level_1;

Row 4      ->  RULE 3
               IF      member_status=ok AND
                       reason=new_case AND
                       problem=non_serious
               THEN    support=level_3;

Row 5      ->  RULE 4
               IF      member_status=ok AND
                       reason=information_other
               THEN    support=information_other;

Row 6      ->  RULE 5
               IF      member_status=not_ok
               THEN    support=non_member;

Variable 1 ->  ASK member_status: "What is the value of member_status?";
               CHOICES member_status: ok,not_ok;

Variable 2 ->  ASK reason: "What is the value of reason?";
               CHOICES reason: new_case,follow_up_case,information_other;

Variable 3 ->  ASK problem: "What is the value of problem?";
               CHOICES problem: serious,non_serious;
```

Usually, a consultation session with an "induced" knowledge base is very crude, or user "unfriendly," as the example in Figure 4–17 demonstrates.

Some expert system shells, such as 1st CLASS, are optimized **induction systems.** They are designed to take a file of examples and produce a working knowledge base from the file without any programming.

A file of examples consists of rows, similar to those in Figure 4–15. Each row is one example case with the outcome at the end of the row. The case in each row is described by values that are carefully aligned under column headings.

After inducing a knowledge base from the example cases, a shell like 1st CLASS might ignore some columns determined to be unnecessary to reach a

Figure 4–17. Consultation Screen from "Induced" Knowledge Base

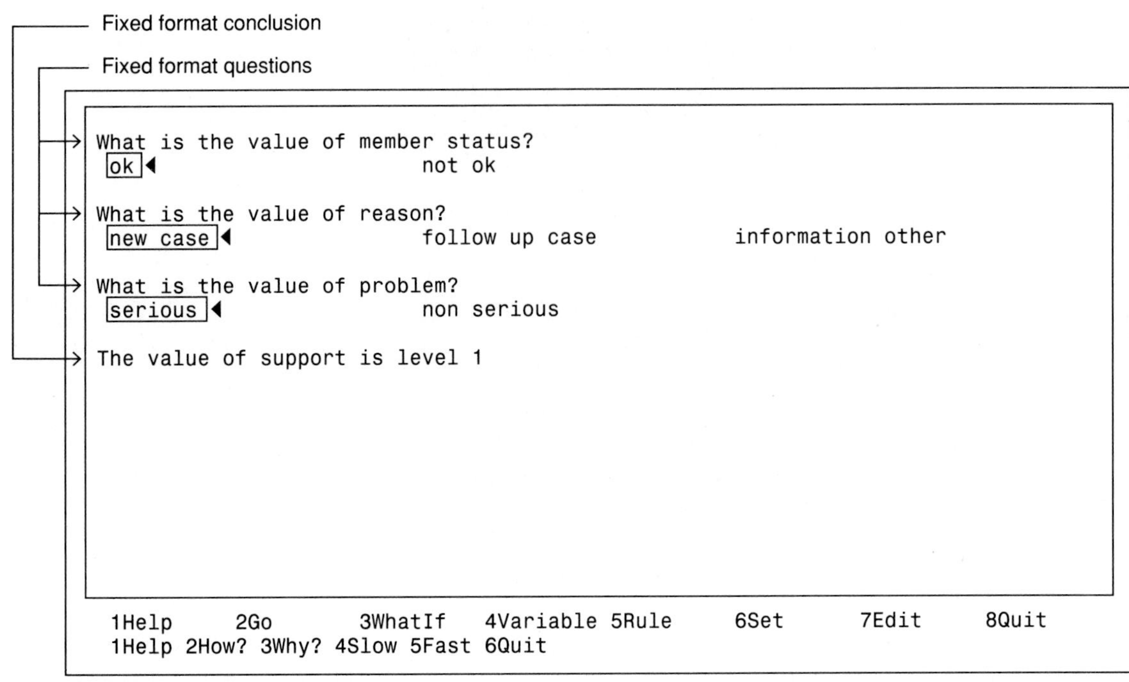

conclusion. This kind of optimization may mean that only two questions are necessary to determine a solution instead of three or more. Also, the columns of values might be reordered into a different sequence determined to be the most efficient to reach a specific recommendation. Such an "induction" system, or shell, is an ideal KBS prototyping tool.

The Induce Option

In a less robust way, the Induce option in the VP-Expert system shell can induce a simple knowledge base from a table of examples. Since no optimization occurs, all columns of values remain in the order given and every row becomes one rule in the knowledge base. In effect, the result is more realistically approached as a syntactic transformation of a set of examples into a set of rules. A one-for-one conversion of rows to rules takes place. The procedure to follow to use the Induce option in VP-Expert is given in Figure 4–18.

Once a KBS problem has been modeled using decision tables, such as the HMO example in Figure 2–5, it can be converted into rules in a straightforward fashion using the Induce option on VP-Expert's Main Menu. This is one use of the Induce option, since a one-for-one syntactic transformation of the decision table into rules is required.

Even though the HMO example consists of three decision tables (Figures 2–5, 2–7, and 2–9), for the sake of demonstrating use of the Induce option, it temporarily will be assumed to consist of only one decision table. That will be the decision table in Figure 2–5.

Step 1: Create an Induction Table or File. The decision table in Figure 2–5 first must be entered into an induction table or file with a .TBL extension. The

Figure 4–18.

Procedure to Create a Table File and "Induce" a Knowledge Base

The following instructions are written to guide a user, who is sitting at a microcomputer, to create a table file and use it to "induce" a minimal knowledge base. The example aims to create the table file (FINAL) shown in Figure 4–15, and the knowledge base (HMOIND) shown in Figure 4–16.

Keystrokes	Action
i	To select Induce from the Main Menu
c	To select Create from the Induce Menu
FINAL	To enter the table filename
	A blank editing screen appears with the filename in the upper right corner. Type the table columns as shown in Figure 4–15.
Alt-F6	To save the completed table file as FINAL.TBL
y	Yes, to confirm. This returns the Induce Menu.
t	To indicate a "text" file will be used to induce a knowledge base file
Enter	To select the filename FINAL.TBL (which will be under the lightbar)
HMOIND	To enter the filename for the knowledge base when asked to "Choose a file:"
	The knowledge base is created instantly and invisibly in the background and the Induce Menu appears again.
q	To "quit" the Induce Menu and return to the Main Menu
e	To enter the "edit" screen to view the "induced" knowledge base file
Alt-F8	To exit the edit screen
y	Yes, to confirm the exit without saving the file (it is already saved) and to return to the Main Menu
c	To select "consult" to run a consultation
g	To select "go"

detailed procedure for doing this is given in Figure 3–4. Essentially, it consists of going into the Editor, or any word processor that outputs an ASCII text file, and typing the table with the following considerations:

- The top row will become the variable names in the resulting knowledge base.
- The last column will become the conclusion for each rule.
- A star or asterisk symbol (*) represents a "don't care" situation where no specific value is needed.

The completed table should look like the example in Figure 4–15.

From a review of the Induce Menu options in Figure 3–10, it is evident that three kinds of files are acceptable. This HMO example uses the Text option to create a file with a .TBL extension from scratch. Other options allow inducing a knowledge base from

- A database file with a .DBF filename extension
- A spreadsheet file with a .WKS filename extension

Many organizations have database and spreadsheet files that contain information used for decision making. Sales information, customer information, employee data, and similar kinds of information traditionally are stored in such files. With the Induce feature, files can easily be transformed into knowledge bases that can leverage their decision-making value.

To use the records and fields of an existing database as an induction table, several changes must typically be made, such as:

1. Fields that are not relevant in decision making must be eliminated from the database.
2. A column will usually have to be added at the extreme right of the file. This column contains data representing the conclusion or decision indicated for each row of "decision-making" data.
3. Fields containing additional relevant data may need to be added.

Similar changes are necessary to make a spreadsheet file usable as an induction table. Tables created with spreadsheets also have a few restrictions that do not apply to text or database tables, such as:

1. A spreadsheet must contain a blank row under the column headings.
2. There can be no blank cells in columns.
3. There can be no blank rows above or to the left of the table.

Any knowledge base created from any induction table is only as good as the data from which it was induced. In other words, if crucial decision-making factors are absent from the induction table, then the resulting knowledge base will be of questionable value.

Step 2: Induce the Knowledge Base File. After the "induction table" is available in a file, the second step is simple. It requires providing a name for the new knowledge base file. The knowledge base is created instantly and invisibly in the background. In the HMO case, the induced knowledge base file will look like the one in Figure 4–16.

The transformation that occurs can be made visible by viewing the induced knowledge base file using the Editor. The screen shows the following characteristics:

- The heading of the last table column is taken as the goal variable used for the FIND keyword in the Actions Block. It is also used to display a message at the end of the consultation session.
- Each table row becomes one rule. Rules start with zero and appear slightly different from the style conventions used for other knowledge bases in this tutorial.
- An ASK statement is generated for all IF condition variables. The values in the corresponding CHOICES statements come from reading down the columns with the appropriate heading.

This "induction" technique creates a minimal rule base, which usually must be modified for appearance or functionality. The consultation screen as shown in Figure 4–17, for example, could use upgrading to appear more user-friendly. The fixed format questions and concluding display are minimally acceptable. In addition, the known rules for determining "member_status" and "problem" must be added, and the ASK/CHOICES statements for these variables removed. This rule base then would be functionally equivalent to the one shown in Figure 2–15.

Limitations of the Induce Option. Caution is urged in using the Induce feature. It may not be as useful as it may appear on first glance. One limitation is that it can generate rules only from a single decision table. Since most realistic applications are more complicated than this, other rules need to be added manually to the generated rule base. Once the generated rule base has been modified to add other rules or to change the ASK statements, it cannot be regenerated in its upgraded format from the simpler original decision table.

CONFIDENCE FACTORS

A method normally used to deal with uncertain data in a knowledge base is to use confidence factors. In Figure 4–19, as an example, the THEN clauses of Rules 9, 10, and 11 use confidence factors. They demonstrate varying levels of confidence that the expert has concerning these conclusions.

A **confidence factor** is a number attached to a value that indicates the developer/expert's or user's degree of certainty in the value. In VP-Expert, zero indicates no confidence and 100 indicates total confidence or trust in the value. Other development shells may use different scales, such as −1 to +1 or −100 to +100, among other possibilities.

A confidence factor is not a statistical probability, although it often is referred to as a percentage. It may be based on subjective intuition or objective criteria to represent how sure one is that a value is correct. It can be compared with other confidence factors and used as a guide. If no confidence factor is expressed, the default value of 100 is normally assumed.

The knowledge base in Figure 4–19 gives an example of how confidence factors are used by a developer or expert. By examining the THEN clauses for Rules 9, 10, and 11, it is evident that the developer/expert has varying degrees of confidence in the conclusions reached. On the one hand, an HMO client who claims to have a normal temperature and no other symptoms is considered, with 99 percent confidence (see Rule 10), to be a non-serious case. On the other hand, the developer/expert is less certain that a client who claims to have a normal temperature and other symptoms is a serious case (see Rule 9). The numbers preceded by CNF express the reliability attached to these conclusions.

Figure 4–20 demonstrates the effect on a consultation of these confidence factors, an effect which is mainly invisible to a user. In this case, the HMO service representative indicates that a client reports a normal temperature and the presence of other symptoms. These conditions cause Rule 9 to fire. The conclusion of Rule 9 automatically assigns the "problem" variable a value of "serious" along with a confidence factor (CNF) of 80. This fact is displayed in the lower right FACTS window in Figure 4–20.

The FACTS window shows another item of interest. The CNF from the firing of Rule 9 has a ripple effect. It changes the CNF value for the "support" variable found in Rule 1. Recall that Rule 1 exerts the driving force that causes Rule 9 to fire. Once Rule 9 fires, the final unknown IF condition in Rule 1 is satisfied. The way is then clear to fire Rule 1 itself.

For the purpose of this example, the final recommendation is displayed with a confidence factor. Mechanically this requires including a pound sign (#) inside the curly brackets of the display message, as shown in Figure 4–19.

How Confidence Factors Are Calculated

It is necessary to understand something about how confidence factors are combined and calculated to see how Rule 1 concluded with "support = level 1 CNF 80." For example, reconsider the simpler Rule 9 again. It contains two IF conditions. When one or more AND connectives are used in a rule, the confi-

Figure 4–19. A Knowledge Base with Confidence Factors

Notes:
. The name of this knowledge base file on the Sample Files disk is HMOCNF.KBS.
. The blocked areas indicate changes to the original HMO.KBS file (see Figure 2-15).

```
ACTIONS
     DISPLAY "Welcome to the HMO Service Screening Assistant"
     TRUTHTHRESH = 60
     FIND support
     DISPLAY "Recommended support: {# support}."
;

RULE 1
     IF member_status = ok and
        reason = new_case or
        reason = follow_up_case and
        problem = serious
     THEN support = level_1;

RULE 2
     IF member_status = ok and
        reason = new_case and
        problem = non_serious
     THEN support = level_2;

RULE 3
     IF member_status = ok and
        reason = follow_up_case and
        problem = non_serious
     THEN support = level_3;

RULE 4
     IF member_status = ok and
        reason = information_other
     THEN support = information_other;

RULE 5
     IF member_status = not_ok
     THEN support = non_member;

RULE 6
     IF member = yes and
        valid_id = yes
     THEN member_status = ok;
```

dence factor is calculated by multiplying the *lowest* confidence factor assigned to the conditions being tested times the confidence factor of the rule conclusion. When Rule 9 is evaluated, the so-called Final-CNF is 1.00 (the lowest default condition CNF) times .80 (the conclusion CNF), or 80 percent.

From this example, it is possible to see how Rule 1 concludes with a CNF of 80. Only one of its conditions has a specific CNF assigned during a consultation. It is "problem = serious CNF 80." All other conditions are assigned the default CNF 100 value. So when Rule 1 fires, the so-called Final-CNF is .80 (the lowest condition CNF) times 1.00 (the default conclusion CNF), or 80 percent.

Confidence factor calculations remain the same when users choose, or are invited to enter, confidence factors for any or all CHOICES selections. For example, consider the consultation shown in the second example in Figure 4–21.

Figure 4–19 *continued*

```
RULE 7
     IF member = yes and
        valid_id = no
     THEN member_status = not_ok;

RULE 8
     IF member = no
     THEN member_status = not_ok;

RULE 9
     IF temperature = normal and
        other_symptoms = yes
     THEN problem = serious cnf 80;

RULE 10
     IF temperature = normal and
        other_symptoms = no
     THEN problem = non_serious cnf 99;

RULE 11
     IF temperature = abnormal or
        temperature = not_known
     THEN problem = serious cnf 90;

ASK member: "Is the person an HMO member?";
CHOICES member: yes, no;

ASK valid_id: "Does the person have a valid HMO `id' number?";
CHOICES valid_id: yes, no;

ASK reason: "What is the reason for coming to the HMO facility?";
CHOICES reason: new_case, follow_up_case, information_other;

ASK temperature: "What is the person's temperature?";
CHOICES temperature: normal, abnormal, not_known;

ASK other_symptoms:  "Does the person claim other symptoms?";
CHOICES other_symptoms: yes, no;
```

The procedure used by the HMO service representative to dynamically enter the "user" confidence factors during a consultation is given at the bottom of Figure 4–21. This procedure can be used to experiment not only with the HMOCNF knowledge base, but also with any other knowledge base on the Sample Files disk.

In the hypothetical case shown in Figure 4–21, assume that the HMO service representative learns from a client that he is almost positive, with 90 percent certainty, that his temperature is normal. He also reports he is only 75 percent certain that he has other symptoms, because an allergy problem always seems to interfere with his well-being. These percentages, entered by a user as confidence factors, affect the calculation of the CNF attached to the recommendation made in Figure 4–21.

Figure 4–20. Displaying a Confidence Factor with a Recommendation

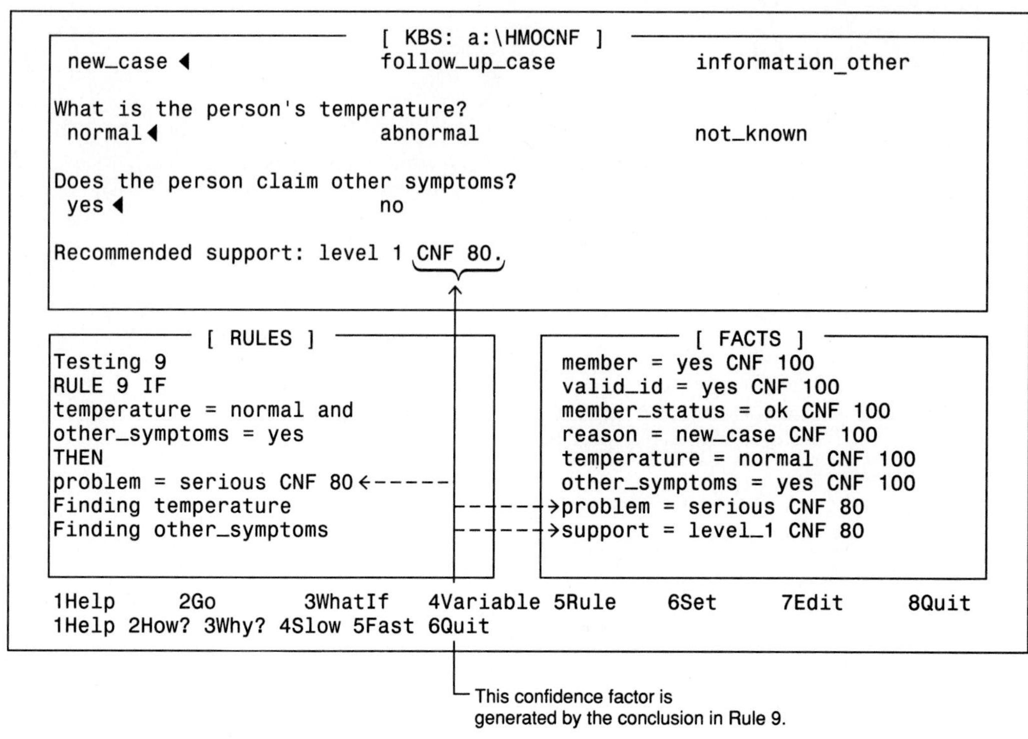

Figure 4–21. User Entry of Confidence Factors

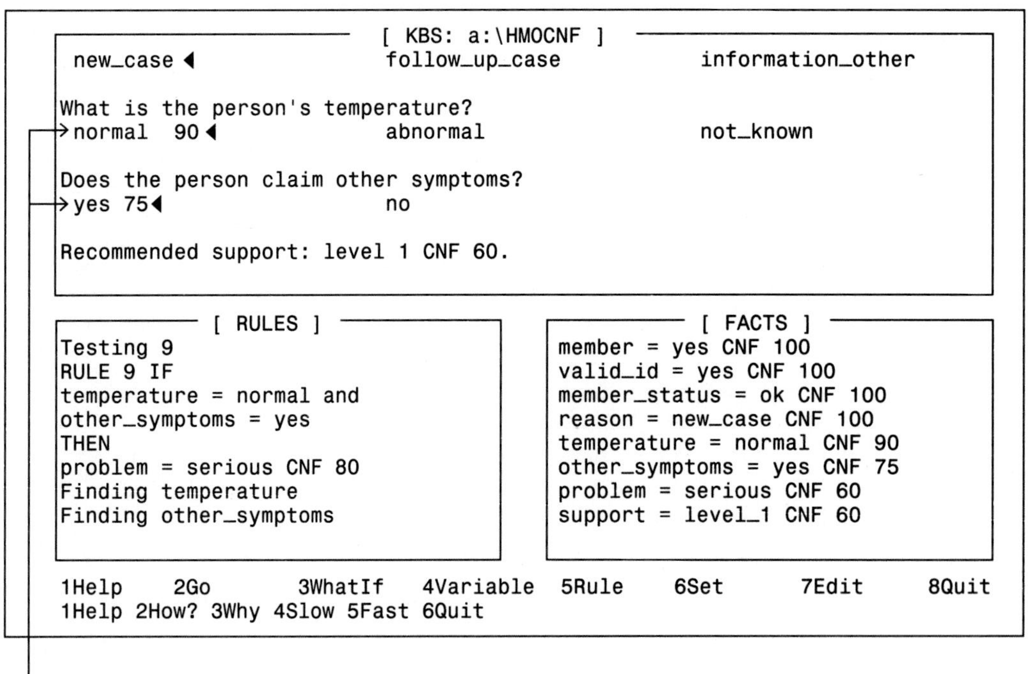

Procedure to enter a confidence factor in response to a question:
1. Move the lightbar to the desired response.
2. Press the HOME key, then type the confidence factor value.
3. Press the ENTER key to continue.

Both Figures 4–20 and 4–21 were produced using the same HMOCNF knowledge base (shown in Figure 4–19).

The calculation to arrive at "problem = serious CNF 60" in Figure 4–21 is straightforward. It involves a rule with two conditions connected by AND. The lowest condition CNF entered is 75. So the Final-CNF is .75 (the lowest condition CNF) times .80 (the conclusion CNF), or 60 percent.

If Rule 9 had an OR connector, and both conditions tested true, a "multiple path formula" would apply as follows:

(Condition 1 CNF + Condition 2 CNF) − (Condition 1 CNF × Condition 2 CNF)
(CNF1) (CNF2) (CNF1) (CNF2)

Then this condition CNF result would be multiplied by the conclusion CNF to get a Final-CNF. The actual calculation would be as follows:

Step 1: Condition CNF = (CNF1+ CNF2) − (CNF1 × CNF2)
= (.90 + .75) − (.90 × .75)
= 1.65 − .68
= .97
Step 2: Conclusion CNF = .80
Step 3: Final-CNF = Condition CNF × Conclusion CNF
= .97 × .80
= .77

By contrast, Rule 1 has an OR in it but it is not calculated with the OR "multiple path rule." The reason is that only one of its OR conditions tests true. Rule 1, therefore, is treated as having only AND connectives.

More complex combinations are possible which result in more complex calculations. The *VP-Expert Manual* contains more information on this.

Truth Threshold

Another method of dealing with uncertain data in a KBS is to set a **truth threshold.** This is a number, supplied by the developer, to determine the minimum confidence factor required for a rule condition to be considered true.

Each expert system shell sets its own default truth threshold. In VP-Expert it is published in various sources as 40 or 50, while the educational version actually tested at 20! In any case, the developer can control the cutoff point with the keyword TRUTHTHRESH. An example of use is the clause "TRUTHTHRESH = 60" shown in the Actions Block in Figure 4–19.

To experiment with its use, try running a trial consultation with the HMOCNF knowledge base. Enter a confidence factor of 50 for the question about temperature, after selecting "normal." Use the procedure found in Figure 4–21 to enter the confidence factor during the consultation. Since 50 is below the boundary that divides a true from a false condition, Rule 9 fails and the consultation aborts. For the rule to pass, both conditions must be true. New rules would be necessary to handle exceptions gracefully and avoid the abrupt termination of the session.

It is also possible to reset TRUTHTHRESH anywhere after the THEN clause within the KBS rules. Such a setting would affect everything that occurs after the rule passes, until another TRUTHTHRESH clause is encountered.

TRUTHTHRESH in no way affects the conclusion of a rule (the THEN or ELSE parts); it only concerns rule conditions or premises (the IF part). Should the confidence factor of a conclusion CNF value fall below the "truth threshold," the rule will not be prevented from passing.

Practical Considerations

Using confidence factors should be approached with caution. Unless carefully planned and tested, they can produce unpredictable results. Also, they often become far more complicated to manage than expected.

In practice, confidence factors are reserved for use in special cases or small segments of larger systems. Rarely are they used throughout a full production KBS.

Interestingly, since no approach has been established as a standard, there are various methods of calculating confidence values. It is up to a developer to determine if the approach used by one expert system shell, as opposed to another, best fits a KBS development project.

REVIEW QUESTIONS

1. What is the importance of database integration with a knowledge-based system?
2. How does a database become mechanically integrated with a KBS?
3. How does a KBS transfer data to a database?
4. What is the purpose of indirect addressing?
5. How is looping, or iterative processing, accomplished?
6. Why is it important to be able to integrate a spreadsheet with a knowledge-based system?
7. How is a spreadsheet mechanically integrated with a KBS?
8. How does a KBS transfer data to a spreadsheet?
9. How are numeric formats handled when transferring data from a KBS to a spreadsheet?
10. How does one use induction to create a knowledge base?
11. What is the meaning of a confidence factor?

EXERCISES

1. This exercise explores KBS and database integration. Run a consultation with the knowledge-base HMODB.KBS from the Sample Files disk. This KBS uses the MEMBER.DBF database file from the Sample Files disk. Enter the following responses:

Response	*Keys to Press to Indicate Response*
yes	(Enter, End)
666	(Enter)
new case	(Enter, End)
normal	(Enter, End)
yes	(Enter, End)

   a. Run a second consultation using 123 as the ID (second) entry.
   b. Compare and record the results observed from the two consultations.

c. If possible, use dBASE III Plus or dBASE IV to add a new record to the MEMBER.DBF database file:

Field	*Entry*
ID	123
P_TYPE	ind
LNAME	Ward
FNAME	Kim
REQUESTS	9

Then repeat Steps 1a and 1b above.

d. Obtain a printout of HMODB.KBS. Identify the code that links HMODB. KBS to the MEMBER database file.

e. Use the printout of HMODB.KBS and identify all examples of

- Indirect addressing
- Arithmetic symbols
- Relational symbols

2. This exercise explores loop processing. Run a consultation with HMODB1.KBS from the Sample Files disk and enter the following responses

fam	(Enter, End)
5	(Enter)

a. Run a second consultation using 0 (numeric zero) as the second entry.
b. Compare and record the results observed from the two consultations.
c. Obtain a printout of HMODB1.KBS. Identify the code that processes each database record through a loop.

3. This exercise explores KBS and spreadsheet integration. Run a consultation with the knowledge base HMOSS.KBS from the Sample Files disk. This KBS uses the SSHMO.WKS spreadsheet file from the Sample Files disk.
a. Observe and record the "support" level recommended.
b. If possible, use Lotus 1-2-3 to view the spreadsheet SSHMO.WKS. Get a "screen dump" of the screen on paper. To do this, first make sure the printer is turned on. While the spreadsheet is displayed on the screen, press the Shift key and Prt Sc key together. Note: Since the file is already saved, it is important to exit the spreadsheet without resaving the file. If it is necessary to save the file, it must be saved with a .WKS (not a .WK1) filename extension.
c. Run a consultation with HMOSS.KBS. Observe and record the "support" level recommended.
d. Use Lotus 1-2-3 to view the spreadsheet SSHMO.WKS. Compare the current screen with the earlier "screen dump" and record the difference observed.
e. Obtain a printout of HMOSS.KBS. Identify the code that links HMOSS.KBS to the SSHMO.WKS spreadsheet file.

4. This exercise examines induction. Use the instructions given in Figure 4–18 ("Procedure to Create a Table File and 'Induce' a Knowledge Base") to:
a. Enter the table from Figure 4–15 with the Editor. Save the completed file as MYFINAL.TBL on your exercise disk. When asked to "Choose a file," enter the filename MYIND. Run a consultation using MYIND.
b. Run a consultation with the knowledge base HMO.KBS. Compare and record the results observed from the consultations with MYIND.KBS and HMO.KBS.
c. Get printouts of MYIND.KBS and HMO.KBS. Compare and record the differences observed.

  d. Use the instructions given in Figure 4–18 to enter a table of your own design and "induce" a knowledge base.

5. This exercise explores confidence factors. Run a consultation with the knowledge base HMOCNF.KBS from the Sample Files disk.

  a. Enter the following responses:

Response	*Keys to Press to Indicate Response*
yes	(Enter, End)
new case	(Enter, End)
normal	(Enter, End)
yes	(Enter, End)

  b. Observe and record the recommendation made as well as the CNF values displayed in the FACTS window.

  c. Write an explanation of how the final confidence factor was calculated.

  d. Run a consultation with the knowledge base HMO.KBS. Repeat Steps 5a and 5b above.

  e. Compare and record the differences observed in the two consultations.

  f. Obtain a printout of HMOCNF.KBS. Identify the code that

- Produces the display of the final recommendation CNF value
- Gives a CNF value to a rule conclusion

6. This exercise continues to explore confidence factors. Run a consultation with the knowledge base HMOCNF.KBS from the Sample Files disk.

  a. Use the instructions given at the bottom of Figure 4–21 to enter the confidence factors shown in the same figure.

  b. Write an explanation as to how the final confidence factor was calculated. Write another explanation of how the final confidence factor would be calculated if Rule 9 separated its IF conditions with an OR instead of an AND, and both conditions tested true.

  c. Copy HMOCNF.KBS to your exercise disk as MYCNF.KBS. Then use MYCNF.KBS and the Editor to change the AND in Rule 9 to an OR. Repeat Step 6a above. Then compare the Final-CNF with the one calculated in 6b above and record the result.

7. This exercise explores truth threshold. Run a consultation with the knowledge base HMOCNF.KBS from the Sample Files disk.

  a. Enter a confidence factor of 50 after "normal" for the question about temperature. Use the instructions found in Figure 4–21 to enter this. Provide an explanation for the results observed in the FACTS window and in the main consultation window.

  b. Run another consultation and enter a confidence factor of 70 after "normal." Provide an explanation for the results observed in the FACTS window and in the main consultation window.

  c. Copy HMOCNF.KBS to your exercise disk as MYCNF1.KBS. Then use MYCNF1.KBS and the Editor to change the TRUTHTHRESH value in the Actions Block. Run trial consultations to observe and record the results of the changes on the Final-CNF.

8. Develop or enhance a knowledge base of your own design that incorporates one or more of the following features:

- Integration with a database
- Integration with a spreadsheet
- Confidence factors

5

USER INTERFACE IMPROVEMENTS TO THE KNOWLEDGE BASE

This chapter continues the tutorial that began in Chapter 2. Its main topics are

- Improving the user interface
- Additional enhancements and keywords
- WHENEVER: forward chaining
- Plural variables
- Chaining knowledge bases

The quality of the user interface, or dialogue between the computer and user during a consultation, can make the difference between whether or not a KBS is actually used in a real-world situation. In many instances, a developer or KBS researcher becomes enamored of the technical capability of the system being developed. Little attention is given to the user interface requirements of the system. This situation is the main cause, some researchers believe, that some knowledge-based systems never make the transition from the research or development laboratory to the real world.

In this chapter, the basic knowledge base file from Chapter 2 (Figure 2–15) is taken through two levels of user interface improvements. First, screen display enhancements are covered, then print enhancements. The final result incorporates some design and layout improvements that begin to be representative of a more "industrial-strength" KBS.

Since working, sophisticated knowledge-based systems are often designed in modules, then linked together, chaining knowledge base files is also covered.

Follow this learning process for the example incrementally developed in this chapter:

1. Run the new knowledge base using the file on the Sample Files disk to see how it works. Use the "Procedure for Running a Consultation" (given in Figure 3–2) to do this.
2. Make a copy of the original knowledge base file HMO.KBS (see Figure 2–15), but give it a new knowledge base filename with an "X" or number or other unique identifier.

3. Make incremental changes to the "X" file until it runs or executes exactly like the finished model file. Use the "Procedure for Entering (or Editing) a Knowledge Base" (given in Figure 3–4) to do this.

As mentioned earlier, while the software development tool used is the VP-Expert system shell, the themes discussed are applicable to whatever shell is used. Also, only selected keywords and features are covered in this tutorial. It is advisable to consult the *VP-Expert Manual* for additional information.

IMPROVING THE USER INTERFACE

Building the user interface of a KBS takes almost as much effort as building the main part of the system. Studies show that developing the user interface for a KBS approximately doubles the resources and time committed to a project. It also increases the coding necessary in the KBS file. This is evident in Figure 5–1. Although the base file is unchanged from Figure 2–15, the additional user interface considerations are responsible for all the added new code.

The crude user interface built into the first KBS effort from Chapter 2 offers many opportunities for improvements. Figure 5–1 is a printout of the revised knowledge base that incorporates user interface improvements. The improvements include

- A new opening screen (see Figure 5–2)
- A new instructions window (see Figure 5–3)
- A new closing screen (see Figure 5–4)

Opening Screen

Figure 5–2 shows the improvements made beginning to appear as soon as a user starts a consultation. The new opening screen is colored with a light blue background that has a visually attractive frame around the opening message. The message now does four things:

- It describes the objective of the consultation.
- It describes how the consultation will work.
- It indicates what kind of closure to expect.
- It puts the user in control to activate the consultation.

These are the kinds of things that a human factors practitioner or researcher would recommend for any well-designed application of KBS technology.

The opening screen was created with the code, shown in Figure 5–1, that begins with the first WOPEN keyword and concludes with the first WCLOSE keyword. As explained in Figure 5–5, the WOPEN keyword creates a window on the consultation screen. Each number following the WOPEN keyword has a special meaning. The numbers are called parameters and their purpose is as follows:

Parameter Number	*Parameter Purpose*
1	number of the window being opened
2 & 3	row and column coordinates of the upper left-hand corner of the window
4	number of rows the window occupies (a number from 2 to 77)
5	number of columns the window should occupy (a number from 2 to 77)
6	color for the background of the window (a number from 0 to 7—see Figure 5–6)

Figure 5–1. First Knowledge Base with an Improved User Interface

Notes:
. The name of this knowledge base file on the Sample Files disk file is HMOUSER.KBS.
. Blocked areas indicate new additions (to HMO.KBS)

```
! HMO Service Screening Assistant
! with an improved user interface
! Saved as HMOUSER.KBS
!**************************************************************************
BKCOLOR = 3;                    !set screen background color to light blue
RUNTIME;                               !eliminate rules and facts windows
ENDOFF;                        !eliminate need to press END after a choice

!============================== Actions Block ===========================
ACTIONS
     WOPEN 1,3,10,13,60,7                          !define opening window 1
     ACTIVE 1                                            !activate window 1
     DISPLAY "

                  HMO Service Screening Assistant

  This consultation assists you to screen a person who
  enters an HMO facility.  It asks a series of questions
  about the person, then recommends a level of support
  appropriate to the person's needs.

  Please press any key to begin the consultation.~

     "
     WCLOSE 1                                              !remove window 1
     WOPEN 1,1,1,5,77,2                              !define instructions w
     ACTIVE 1                                            !activate window 1
     DISPLAY "                       Instructions
          Use the arrow keys to move the lightbar to a desired
          answer choice then press the Enter key."
     WOPEN 2,7,1,14,77,3                     !define consultation window 2
     ACTIVE 2                                            !activate window 2
     FIND support
     WCLOSE 1                                              !remove window 1
     WCLOSE 2                                              !remove window 2
     WOPEN 1,5,13,9,48,7        !define concluding recommendation window 1
     WOPEN 2,6,14,7,46,7            !define window 2 (nested in window 1)


     ACTIVE 2                                            !activate window 2
     LOCATE 1,9                !specify row and column for next display
     DISPLAY "Based on the answers given,
         the recommended support is:
                  {support}.
(Press any key to conclude the consultation.)~"
 :
!============================== Rules Block =============================

RULE 1
     IF member_status = ok and
        reason = new_case or
        reason = follow_up_case and
        problem = serious
     THEN support = level_1;

RULE 2
     IF member_status = ok and
        reason = new_case and
        problem = non_serious
     THEN support = level_2;
```

Figure 5–1 *continued*

```
RULE 3
      IF member_status = ok and
         reason = follow_up_case and
         problem = non_serious
      THEN support = level_3;

RULE 4
      IF member_status = ok and
         reason = information_other
      THEN support = information_other;

RULE 5
      IF member_status = not_ok
      THEN support = non_member;

RULE 6
      IF member = yes and
         valid_id = yes
      THEN member_status = ok
      BECAUSE "Validated members are provided with medical support, while
      non-members are provided with other appropriate support.";

RULE 7
      IF member = yes and
         valid_id = no
      THEN member_status = not_ok;

RULE 8
      IF member = no
      THEN member_status = not_ok;

RULE 9
      IF temperature = normal and
         other_symptoms = yes
      THEN problem = serious
      BECAUSE "The presence of an abnormal temperature or other symptoms
      indicate a serious problem that requires immediate attention.";

RULE 10
      IF temperature = normal and
         other_symptoms = no
      THEN problem = non_serious;

RULE 11
      IF temperature = abnormal or
         temperature = not_known
      THEN problem = serious;

!================================ Questions Block ==========================

ASK member: "Is the person an HMO member?";
CHOICES member: yes, no;

ASK valid_id: "Does the person have a valid HMO `id' number?";
CHOICES valid_id: yes, no;

ASK reason: "What is the reason for coming to the HMO facility?";
CHOICES reason: new_case, follow_up_case, information_other;

ASK temperature: "What is the person's temperature?";
CHOICES temperature: normal, abnormal, not_known;

ASK other_symptoms:  "Does the person claim other symptoms?";
CHOICES other_symptoms: yes, no;
```

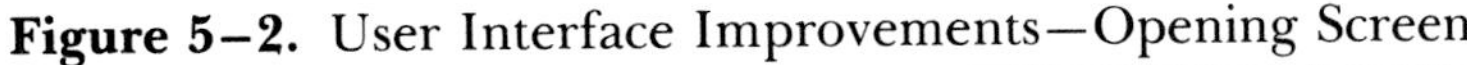

Figure 5–2. User Interface Improvements—Opening Screen

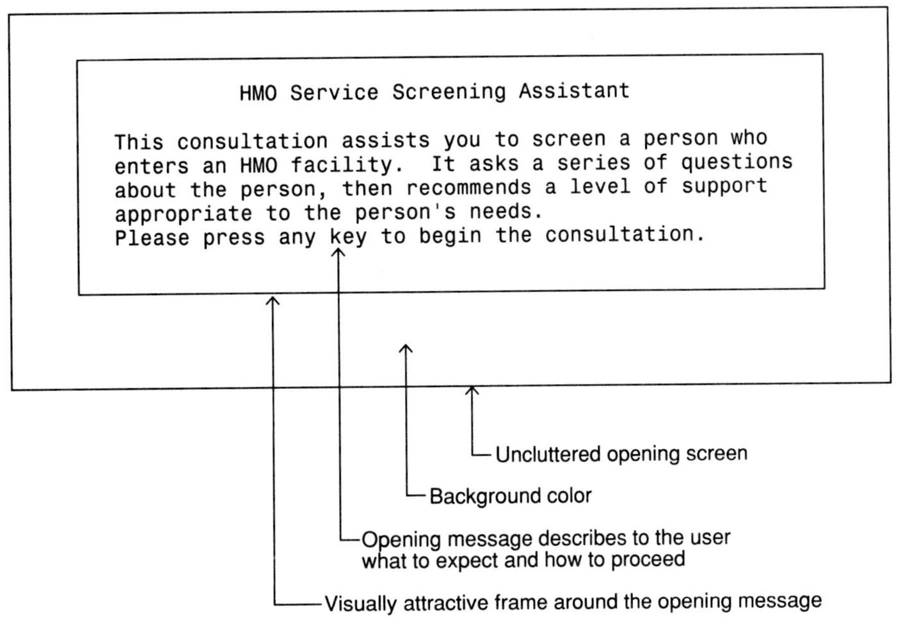

Although WOPEN defines a consultation window, it does not activate it. The keyword ACTIVE (along with a window number) is required to actually place the window image on the screen.

All following DISPLAY text appears in the activated window. Some trial and error is required to discover the best placement of text within a window. Even if the LOCATE keyword is used (see the bottom of the Actions Block in Figure 3–1) to specify row and column placement for text within a window, some experimentation is needed to arrive at a visually pleasing window arrangement.

The tilde character (~) at the end of the DISPLAY message causes the message to pause until the user presses any key. Any number of tildes can be used in the DISPLAY clause.

Instructions Window

Figure 5–3 shows that the user interface design improvements include an "instructions" window. It has a uniquely colored background to set it apart from the main consultation window. This design has the instructions window remain on the screen during the entire consultation.

The instructions convey precise directions to anyone consulting the KBS. Such detailed keystroke-by-keystroke instruction is helpful especially to non-technically oriented computer users. Some users are afraid of making a mistake and "freeze" at the computer keyboard. Simple, clear operating instructions go a long way toward improving a user's comfort level at the computer and with the software.

The instructions window is defined by the second WOPEN keyword in the knowledge base printout shown in Figure 5–1. It is activated just before the full consultation window, which is defined by the third WOPEN keyword on the printout.

Figure 5–3. Instructions Window

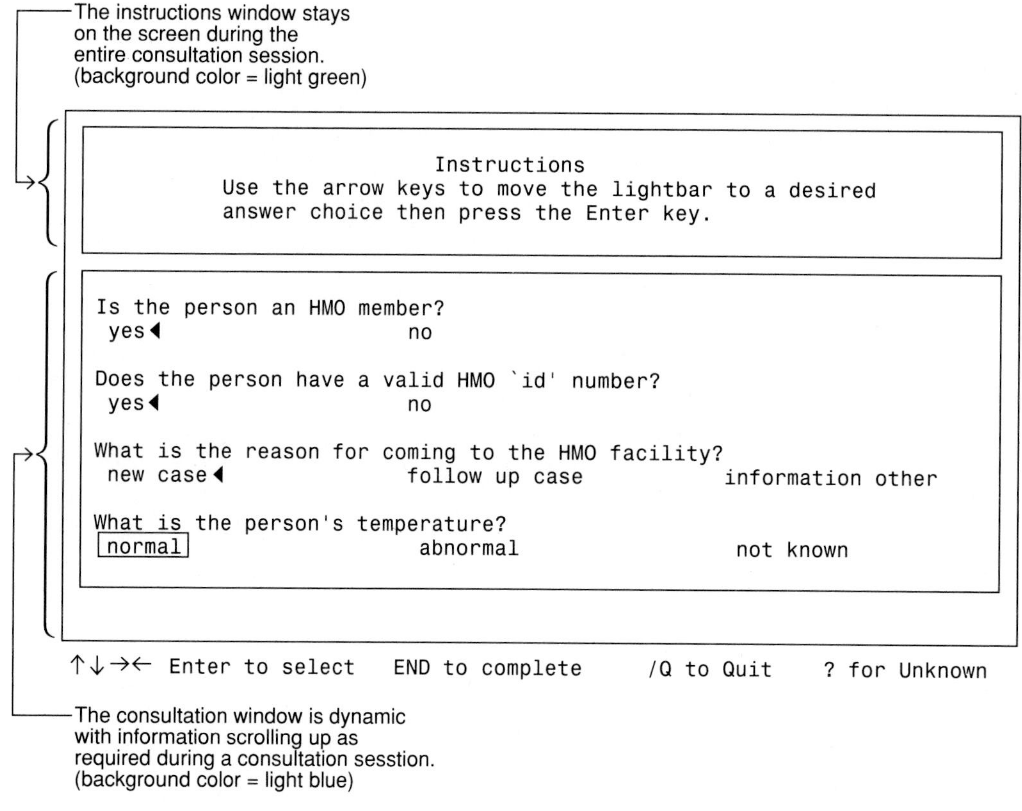

During a user session, if questioning continues beyond the window space available, information scrolls off the top edge of the consultation window section and disappears from the screen. This scrolling technique is common in modern software design.

Another improvement that could be evident to a user during a consultation appears in the Rules Block. It is the addition of BECAUSE text to Rules 7 and 10. BECAUSE is used to provide explanatory text in response to the Why? command given by a user during a consultation. When BECAUSE text is not provided, and a user issues the Why? command, an appropriate IF-THEN rule is displayed. This is far less user-friendly than providing a logical explanation in an idiom that the user understands.

Frequently, developers use the BECAUSE keyword to document the source or reference for a rule. In a KBS that assists tax auditors, for example, a feature similar to BECAUSE is used to document sections of the tax law that influence the expertise in the rule or its conclusion.

Closing Screen

The consultation ends with a simple message in a double frame on an uncluttered screen, as shown in Figure 5–4. The message states that the user's input, or responses, played the key role in arriving at a recommendation. The recommendation itself is highlighted by its presence on a line by itself. Finally,

Figure 5–4. A Nested Window Example—Closing Screen

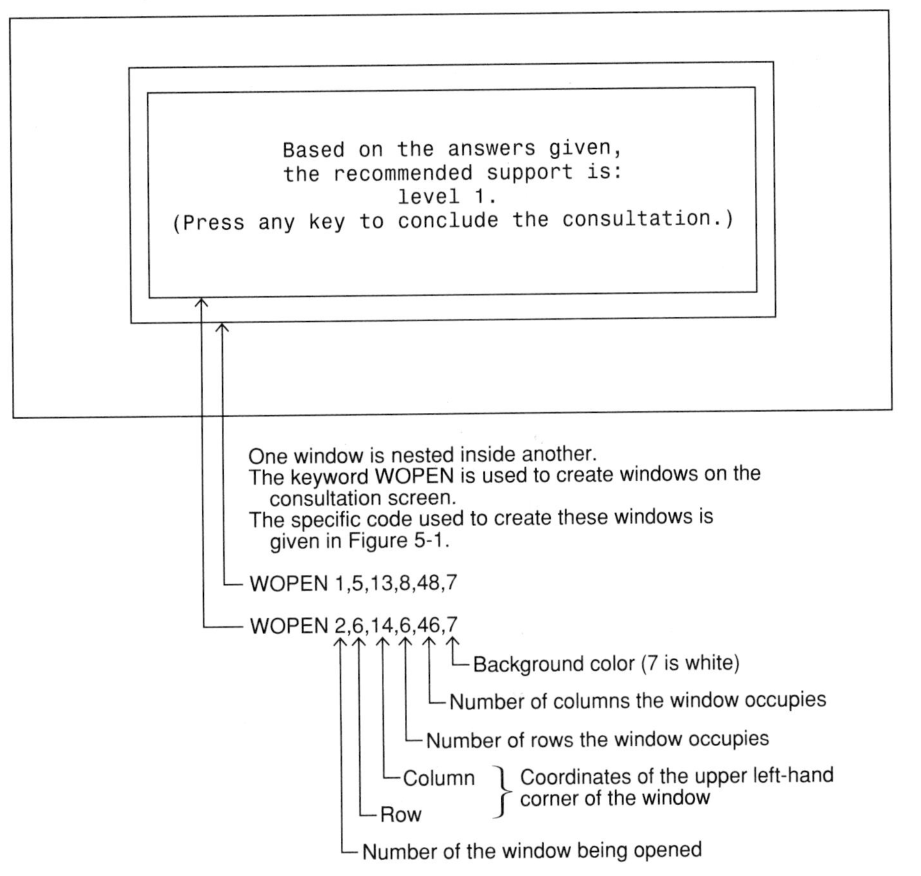

control is returned to the user in the request to "Press any key to conclude the consultation."

The fourth and fifth WOPEN statements in the listing in Figure 5–1 created the double-frame, or nested, windows shown in Figure 5–4. Only the last-defined window, number 2, is activated to DISPLAY the text that follows.

Text is placed inside the display space with the help of the LOCATE keyword. Its parameters are the starting row and column coordinates where text is to be placed inside the window.

Other Improvements

Three other improvements are not as obvious as the windows. They are features introduced with the addition of new keywords:

Keyword	*Action*
BKCOLOR	used to set the background color of the consultation screen (see Figure 5–6)
RUNTIME	eliminates the Rules and Facts windows from the consultation screen
ENDOFF	eliminates the need to hit the End key when finished choosing answers to a question

Figure 5–5.

Creating a Window

WOPEN is used to create a window on the consultation screen. (Note: A knowledge base can contain a maximum of 9 WOPEN windows). It requires six parameters. The meaning of these parameters is as follows:

Parameter Number	Parameter Purpose
1	The number of the window being opened (a number from 1 to 9)
2 & 3	The row and column coordinates of the upper left-hand corner of the window
4	The number of rows the window should occupy (a number from 2 to 77)
5	The number of columns the window should occupy (a number from 2 to 77)
6	The color for the background of the window (a number from 0 to 7)

Each parameter must be typed in the sequence noted, followed by a comma only (no space), as in the following example:

WOPEN 1,5,13,8,48,7

Related Keywords

ACTIVE is used to activate a window. The keyword ACTIVE is followed by a single number from 0 to 9. This is the number of the window inside which the following DISPLAY text is to appear. This number will be the same as the first parameter of the corresponding WOPEN clause, except for the number zero. ACTIVE 0 will cause the text to be DISPLAYed on the default, or regular, Consult (three-window) screen.

LOCATE is used to specify where in the active text window the next executed DISPLAY text should begin. The keyword LOCATE is followed by two number parameters. These are the row and column coordinates inside the designated ACTIVE window where the next DISPLAY text is to begin. (Note: Trial runs are frequently necessary to place text accurately in a window.)

WCLOSE is used to remove text windows created using the WOPEN clause. When a window is removed, the contents of the text window are erased as well. The keyword WCLOSE is followed by a single integer to specify the window number in a previously executed WOPEN instruction.

These keywords normally appear grouped together at the beginning of a knowledge base. Figure 5–7 shows this order in its "Suggested Structure for a Knowledge Base."

During debugging, it is often helpful to disable the RUNTIME feature. The simplest way to do this is to put an exclamation point in front of the keyword. The inference engine ignores any text after an exclamation point. Such text is regarded as comment, or memo, items.

Typically, any text preceded by an exclamation point is a comment by the KBS developer to document what is going on in the knowledge base. The comments are sometimes called **remarks** or **in-program documentation** or internal documentation. These comments help anyone, such as another developer or a user, to understand the knowledge base. They are especially valuable if a KBS prototype is passed on to other developers for full production. Also, they help

Figure 5–6. Color Choices

For Background (BKCOLOR keyword)

Number	Color Represented
0	Black
1	Blue
2	Green
3	Light Blue
4	Red
5	Magenta
6	Brown
7	White

For Text (COLOR keyword)

Number for Normal	Color Represented	Number for Blinking
0	Black	16
1	Blue	17
2	Green	18
3	Cyan	19
4	Red	20
5	Magenta	21
6	Brown	22
7	White	23
8	Gray	24
9	Light Blue	25
10	Light Green	26
11	Light Cyan	27
12	Light Red	28
13	Light Magenta	29
14	Yellow	30
15	Bright White	31

users or others who have the continuing responsibility to maintain or revitalize the knowledge base once it is released from development.

In addition to the comments, physical layout considerations also make the knowledge base easier to understand. All the lines inside the Actions Block are evenly indented, except for DISPLAY text which breaks out of the alignment due to actual screen alignment considerations. Also, horizontal lines separate major segments of the knowledge base. This facilitates focusing on one segment of the knowledge base as a single problem distinct from the rest during debugging sessions.

ADDITIONAL ENHANCEMENTS AND KEYWORDS

As a knowledge base is incrementally improved, physical layout considerations become more important to help keep track of the increasingly refined logic. Consider, for instance, the example in Figure 5–8. The main improvement here

Figure 5–7. Suggested Structure for a Knowledge Base

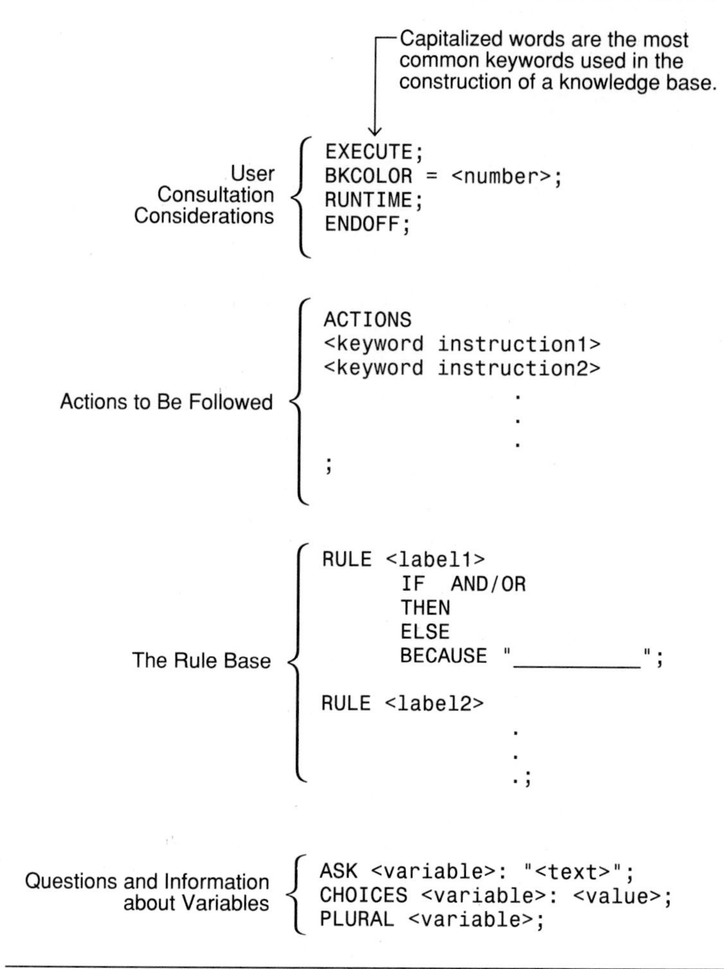

is to customize the recommendations made by the HMO Service Screening Assistant. Figure 5–9 illustrates the main changes made.

An "Authorization Form for Service" is printed on the spot to give to the HMO client. The form contains the available client information, including three new items of interest:

- The client's ID number is used to make an automatic determination of whether the client participates in a co-payment plan and is charged a nominal fee for service. Any HMO member with an ID number greater than 999999, for this example case, is assessed a fixed co-payment fee.
- A specific room-location number tells the client where the required support is administered. There is a different room for each level of service support offered.
- If appropriate, a reminder is printed on the "Authorization Form" that a co-payment charge is to be collected for service.

The blocked areas of the knowledge base printout, shown in Figure 5–8, indicate the exact changes made to implement the improvements. A new rule set is added to customize the concluding messages. Each of the changes is discussed more fully in the following sections.

Figure 5–8. Enhancing the Knowledge Base with Customized Conclusions

Notes:
. The name of this knowledge base file on the Sample Files disk is HMOADD1.KBS.
. Blocked areas indicate new additions (to HMOUSER.KBS)

```
! HMO Service Screening Assistant
! with additional enhancements: customized conclusions
! Saved as HMOADD1.KBS

!*************************************************************************
                                    !set screen background color to light blue
BKCOLOR = 3;                                !eliminate rules and facts windows
RUNTIME;

!============================== Actions Block ============================

ACTIONS
     WOPEN 1,3,10,13,60,7                          !define opening window 1
     ACTIVE 1                                            !activate window 1
     DISPLAY "

              HMO Service Screening Assistant

   This consultation assists you to screen a person who
   enters an HMO facility.  It asks a series of questions
   about the person, then recommends a level of support
   appropriate to the person's needs.

   Please press any key to begin the consultation.~

      "
      WCLOSE 1                                             !remove window 1
      COLOR = 20                  !set following text color to blinking red
      DISPLAY "         CAUTION!"
      COLOR = 4                     !set following text to non-blinking red
      DISPLAY "Please make sure your printer in ON."
      DISPLAY "Press any key to continue.~"
      CLS                                                 !clear the screen
      COLOR = 0                         !set following text to normal black
      WOPEN 1,1,1,6,77,2                       !define instructions window 1
      ACTIVE 1                                            !activate window 1
      DISPLAY "                         Instructions
           Use the arrow keys to move the lightbar to a desired
           answer choice then press Enter key.
           Press the End key to move to the next question."
      WOPEN 2,8,1,13,77,2                      !define consultation window 2
      ACTIVE 2                                            !activate window 2
      FIND support
      FIND message                      !set sub-goal to customize messages
      DISPLAY "Press any key to conclude this consultation.~"
```

Figure 5–8. *continued*

```
;
!============================== Rules Block ==============================

!-------------------- Rule Set 1: Recommendations ----------------------

RULE 1_1                                !number rules to correspond to rule set
     IF member_status = ok and
        reason = new_case or
        reason = follow_up_case and
        problem = serious
     THEN support = level_1
             room = room_201;           !assign a value to a variable

RULE 1_2
     IF member_status = ok and
        reason = new_case and
        problem = non_serious
     THEN support = level_2
             room = room_202;           !assign a value to a variable

RULE 1_3
     IF member_status = ok and
        reason = follow_up_case and
        problem = non_serious
     THEN support = level_3
             room = room_203;           !assign a value to a variable

RULE 1_4
     IF member_status = ok and
        reason = information_other
     THEN support = information_other;

RULE 1_5
     IF member_status = not_ok
     THEN support = non_member;

!-------------------- Rule Set 2: Member Status ------------------------

RULE 2_1
     IF member = yes and
        valid_id = yes
     THEN member_status = ok
        FIND id_number                         !get direct user input
     BECAUSE "Validated members are provided with medical support,
     while non-members are provided with other appropriate support.";

RULE 2_2
     IF member = yes and
        valid_id = no
     THEN member_status = not_ok;

RULE 2_3
     IF member = no
     THEN member_status = not_ok;
```

```
!----------- Rule Set 3: Problem (Determine seriousness) --------------------

RULE 3_1
     IF temperature = normal and
        other_symptoms = yes
     THEN problem = serious
     BECAUSE "The presence of an abnormal temperature or other symptoms
     indicate a serious problem that requires immediate attention.";

RULE 3_2
     IF temperature = normal and
        other_symptoms = no
     THEN problem = non_serious;

RULE 3_3
     IF temperature = abnormal or
        temperature = not_known and
        other_symptoms = yes
     THEN problem = serious
     BECAUSE "The presence of an abnormal temperature or other symptoms
     indicate a serious problem that requires immediate attention.";
```

```
!---------------------- Rule Set 4: Concluding Messages --------------------

RULE message_level123                  !use a meaningful name for a rule label
     IF support = level_1 or
        support = level_2 or
        support = level_3
     THEN message = print_form
        PRINTON                     !send display text to screen and printer
        DISPLAY "Authorization Form For Service - {support}"
        DISPLAY "ID: {id_number}"
        DISPLAY "Reason: {reason}"
        DISPLAY "Self-reported: temperature - {temperature}"
        DISPLAY "               symptoms - {other_symptoms}"
        PRINTOFF                                            !disable printon
        PDISPLAY "Kindly go to {room} for service."          !send text only
                                                                 !to printer
        FIND co_pay                 !set sub-goal to determine co-pay charges
        EJECT                         !move printer paper to top of next page
        DISPLAY ""                                     !display one blank line
        DISPLAY "Please tear the Authorization Form off the printer.";

        RULE check_co_pay           !single rule to determine co-pay charges
             IF id_number > 999999
             THEN co_pay = yes
                  PDISPLAY"(Co-Payment charge of $8.00 made for service.)";

RULE message_non_member
     IF support = non_member
     THEN message = station_Z
        DISPLAY "Appropriate service is available at {message}.";
```

Figure 5–8. *concluded*

```
RULE message_info
     IF support = information_other
     THEN message = station_X
         DISPLAY "Appropriate service is available at {message}.";

!============================ Questions Block =============================

ASK member: "Is the person an HMO member?";
CHOICES member: yes, no;

ASK valid_id: "Does the person have a valid HMO `id' number?";
CHOICES valid_id: yes, no;

ask id_number: "What is the `id' number?";

ASK reason: "What is the reason for coming to the HMO facility?";
CHOICES reason: new_case, follow_up_case, information_other;

ASK temperature: "What is the person's temperature?";
CHOICES temperature: normal, abnormal, not_known;

ASK other_symptoms:  "Does the person claim other symptoms?";
CHOICES other_symptoms: yes, no;
```

To make the growing knowledge base easier to follow, the physical layout has been improved, as has the in-program documentation. For example:

- Rule sets are labeled and separated from each other with horizontal lines. Rule sets one to three contain the same 11 rules shown earlier in Figures 2–15 and 5–1.
- Rule labels have meaningful names or numbers that easily relate a rule to a rule set.
- All instructions that relate to a rule are either: (a) subordinated under the rule that controls execution (see the THEN part of rule message_level123), or (b) set apart in a separate rule set (see Rule Set 4: Concluding Messages).

It is recommended that the reader run a consultation using the file HMOADD1.KBS on the Sample Files disk to examine how the design enhancements described in this section work.

The best way to learn how to use the keywords and features described in this section is to upgrade the base file HMOUSER.KBS to include the enhancements made to HMOADD1.KBS. To do this:

1. Start with the base file, which is HMOUSER.KBS. Make a copy of it and name the copy XHMOADD1.KBS. An example of how this can be done at the DOS prompt is: copy B:HMOUSER.KBS B:XHMOADD1.KBS/V <Enter>.
2. Use the new file (XHMOADD1.KBS) and incrementally add changes until the file runs or executes exactly as the HMOADD1.KBS model.

This procedure is highly recommended to learn each incremental upgrade in this tutorial.

Figure 5–9. Using the PRINTON and PDISPLAY Keywords

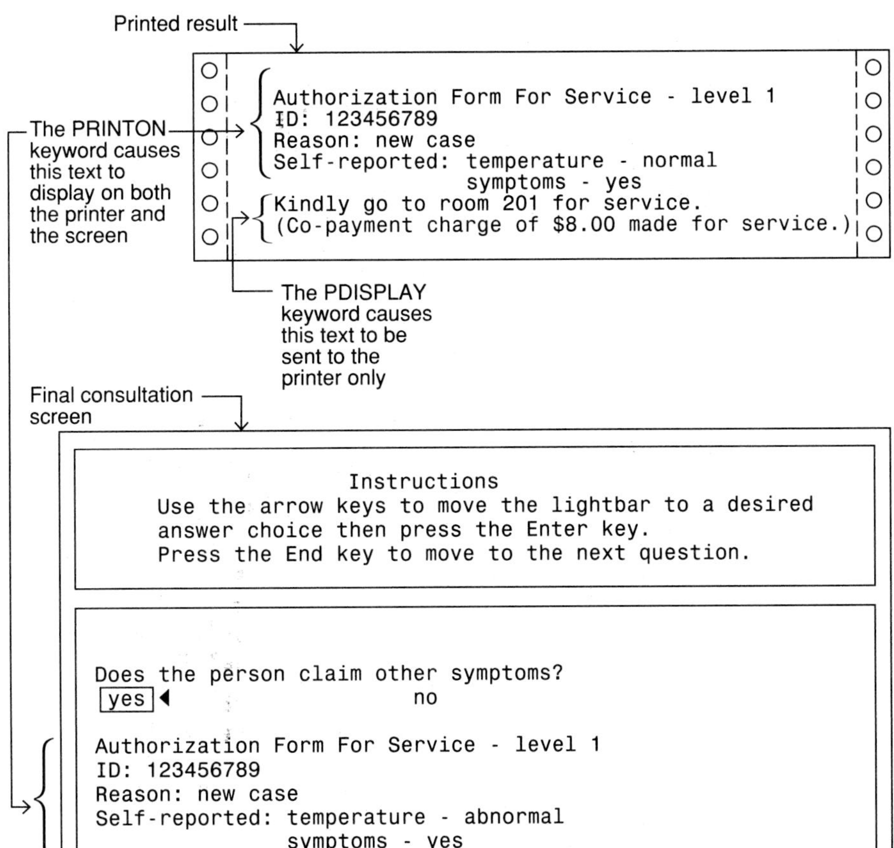

Color Text

The first enhancement shown in the Actions Block of Figure 5–8 is DISPLAY text that not only is differently colored, but also is set to blinking. Figure 5–10 illustrates the effect of this change on the user's consultation screen.

Blinking red text (COLOR = 20), used for the word "CAUTION," alerts a user to the importance of the message that follows. Figure 5–6 shows that the keyword COLOR can be assigned up to 32 numbers (0–31) that give text either normal or blinking color attributes.

After the blinking text, normal red text (COLOR = 4) is used for instructions that tell the user to make sure the printer is turned on and to signal the program to continue. Unlike previously displayed messages, this one repeatedly uses the DISPLAY keyword for each line of text displayed. This alternative way of displaying text often makes it easier to control text placement on the screen. If the printer is not turned on, displays that are directed to the printer will instead be sent to the screen.

Figure 5–10. Using the COLOR Keyword

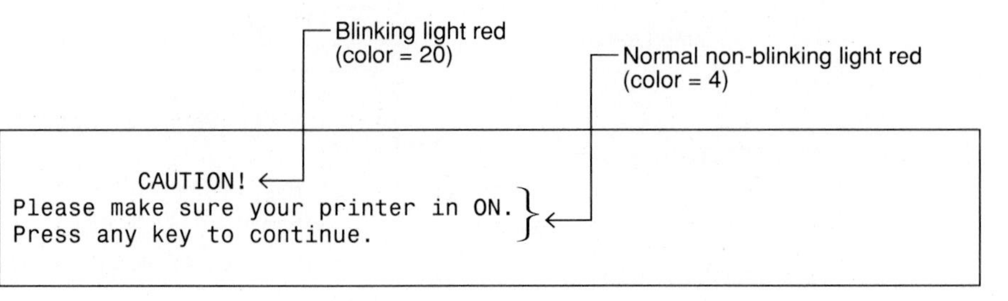

Once the user signals the program to continue, the keyword CLS clears the screen. Text is restored to normal black (COLOR = 0).

Multiple FIND Goals

The Actions Block now has two FIND goals. The first one, FIND support, works exactly as it did in the original HMO example in Figure 2–15. The new one, FIND message, is used to return control to the Rules Block to customize the recommendation from a consultation session. The added "Rule Set 4: Concluding Messages" provides solutions (in the THEN part of the rules) for the goal FIND message. Once these rules serve to customize a conclusion, by either printing or displaying a message, control returns to the Actions Block and the session terminates.

An overview of the three main rules that make up this new rule set follows:

- Rule message_level123 prints the "Authorization Form for Service" shown in Figure 5–9. Only sessions that conclude with a support level of 1, 2, or 3 end with a printed form. The THEN part of the rule uses a dummy word, in this case "print_form," which serves only to send the inference engine to execute all of the remaining instructions below THEN. Technically, the THEN part of the rule does not conclude until the semicolon after the word "printer," about 13 lines below the THEN keyword.

  As evident from the instructions shown, the expanded THEN portion of the rule resembles the type of instructions formerly associated with the Actions Block. This example demonstrates how convenient it is to execute procedural tasks right in the THEN portion of a rule, if appropriate.

  Observe that the THEN portion of this rule also sets up its own sub-goal, FIND co-pay. Since the sub-goal is solved with only one rule, that rule is included and indented right under the controlling rule.
- Rule message_non_member displays a screen message that indicates where appropriate service is available for non-members.
- Rule message_info displays a screen message that indicates where appropriate service is available for members who require information or other non-member services.

Another FIND keyword appears after the THEN clause in Rule 2–1. In this case, FIND is used only to get a direct user response to the new ASK question "What is the 'id' number?" Any number the user enters during the consultation is assigned to the variable "id_number." Because an entry is expected, the ASK question is not followed by a CHOICES keyword.

The ID number is used in "rule check_co_pay" to determine if an HMO member owes a fixed nominal co-payment fee for services. Only members with ID numbers greater than (indicated by the > symbol) 999999 are assessed the fee.

Print Options

The "rule message_level123" uses two print options that are illustrated in Figure 5–9. The first is PRINTON, which is used to send text to both the screen and the printer. All DISPLAY messages following PRINTON go to both devices until a PRINTOFF keyword disables the feature.

In the example, the first five lines of the "Authorization Form" are sent to both the screen and the printer. They include customized data supplied by values in the following variables:

- Support
- ID number
- Reason
- Temperature
- Other-symptoms

A sixth line is sent only to the printer by using the PDISPLAY keyword. The line includes the room number where the HMO client is to go for appropriate service support. The room number is set with a variable assignment appended to Rules 1–1, 1–2, and 1–3.

The PDISPLAY keyword is also used to print a seventh optional line. It alerts a member that a co-payment charge for service is made. Only members who have the co-pay plan see this printed message.

After all information is printed on the "Authorization Form," the EJECT keyword moves the printed paper to the top of the next page. The HMO service representative then sees a reminder message on the screen to tear the form off the printer. The form is given to the HMO client as a formal document to receive the type of service indicated at the location specified. In a real situation, the form would be printed on multi-part paper. One part would serve as a receipt for payment of the service fee. It would include the name and address of the HMO organization, as well as other pertinent information.

WHENEVER: FORWARD CHAINING

Even though backward chaining is the control strategy used by VP-Expert, a WHENEVER rule provides a means for performing forward chaining. Consider the following example:

```
WHENEVER message_non_member
IF support = non_member
THEN DISPLAY "Appropriate service is available at
station Z.";
```

This rule is automatically checked any time the value of the variable named in the IF statement, in this case "support," changes.

This WHENEVER rule provides what is known in artificial intelligence programming as a **demon.** It watches the variable(s) referenced by its IF condition(s) and executes each time the condition(s) evaluates as true. This causes the inference engine to jump out of its backward chaining search strategy and, instead, leap forward to execute the appropriate WHENEVER rule, wherever it appears in the knowledge base. In the example in Figure 5–8, the WHENEVER rule would cause an immediate forward chain to itself the moment the variable "support" is set to "non_member" in Rule 1–5.

One restriction is that a WHENEVER rule cannot have a FIND keyword in its conclusion. This eliminates using it for the first rule in "Rule Set 4: Concluding Messages." It could, however, have been used for the last rule, message_info, of the same rule set.

Unlike standard rules, the WHENEVER rule does not require a typical THEN conclusion of assigning a value to a variable. As the example demonstrates, it is possible to follow the THEN keyword with another keyword. In the example, the DISPLAY keyword follows the THEN clause. The example is saved on the Sample Files disk as filename HMOADD1F.KBS.

PLURAL VARIABLES

The PLURAL keyword identifies "plural variables," or variables that can be assigned multiple values during a consultation, as shown in Figure 5–11. When the inference engine sets out to find values for PLURAL variables, it "assigns" to them as many values as it possibly can before ending the search.

Figure 5–12 illustrates additions to the HMO Service Screening Assistant that show how the PLURAL keyword is used. The example is saved on the Sample Files disk as HMOADD2.KBS. The extension concerns a consultation where the HMO client requires "information" or "other" services. In this case, the system asks "What kind(s) of information is (are) desired?" The service representative could indicate that the client requires information on one or more of the following:

- Individual plan
- Family plan
- Co-pay plan
- Other

Based on the items selected, the system displays where the requested information or service is available. As evident from Figure 5–11, the display of PLURAL variables is limited and somewhat awkward without more extensive programming.

Figure 5–12 shows one FIND keyword added to "RULE message_info" that is used to get direct user input about what kind of information is desired.

Figure 5–11. Using the PLURAL Keyword

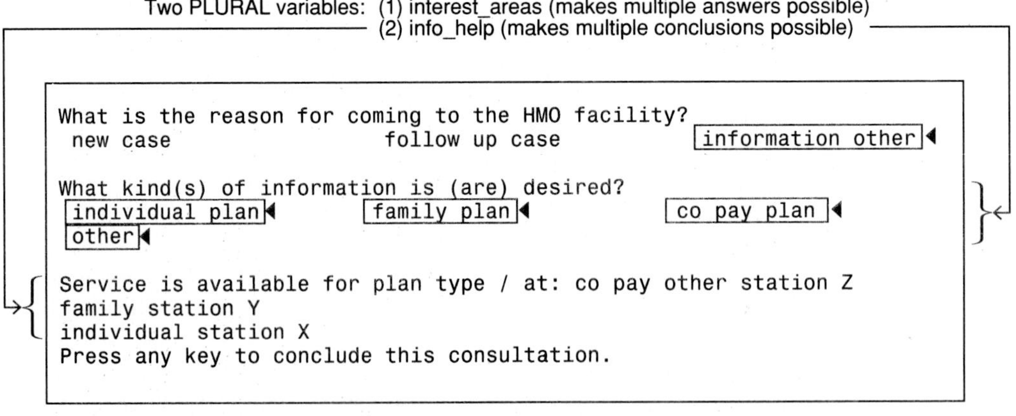

Figure 5–12. Additions to Explore PLURAL Variables

Notes:
. The name of this knowledge base file on the Sample Files disk is HMOADD2.KBS.
. Blocked areas indicate new additions to HMOADD1.KBS. See Figure 5-8 for the parts of this file not shown here.

```
RULE message_info
     IF support = information_other
     THEN message = display_service
        FIND interest_areas                         !get direct user input
        FIND info_help                 !set sub-goal to customize messages
        DISPLAY "Service is available for plan type / at: {info_help}";

!------------------- Rule Set 5: Information Help Messages ---------------

RULE 5-1
     IF interest_areas = individual_plan
     THEN info_help = individual_station_X;

RULE 5-2
     IF interest_areas = family_plan
     THEN info_help = family_station_Y;

RULE 5-3
     IF interest_areas = co_pay_plan or
        interest_areas = other
     THEN info_help = co_pay_other_station_Z;
.
.
.

ASK interest_areas: "What kind(s) of information is (are) desired?";
CHOICES interest_areas: individual_plan, family_plan, co_pay_plan, other;

PLURAL: interest_areas, info_help;
```

This requires the addition of an ASK question to the Questions Block to get a member's "interest_areas." Because one or more CHOICES items can be selected to answer the question, the "interest_areas" variable is declared to be PLURAL. This is done in the last line of code in the knowledge base.

To select more than one item, the user must move the lightbar over a selection and hit the Enter key. After all selections are made, the End key must be pressed. The reminder to press the End key, even after single-valued variables, is coded in the second box in Figure 5–8. This reminder is necessary because the keyword ENDOFF is deleted from this knowledge base. Its absence allows a user to make mistakes or change answers without penalty. Changes are made with the DEL delete key. In some cases, the extra step of having a user hit both the Enter and End keys to record a choice is desirable. In other cases, it can be an annoyance.

A second variable name, "info_help," also appears in the PLURAL statement at the end of the knowledge base. It identifies the PLURAL nature of the FIND sub-goal in "RULE message_info." Any or all of the three rules in Rule Set 5 can satisfy the sub-goal "info_help" through THEN clauses. As evident from Figure 5–11, all these rules can fire for a single consultation, if appropriate.

Figure 5–13 shows an expanded dependency diagram that summarizes all the current changes to the HMO Service Screening Assistant. It shows the "fan

Figure 5–13. Expanded Dependency Diagram

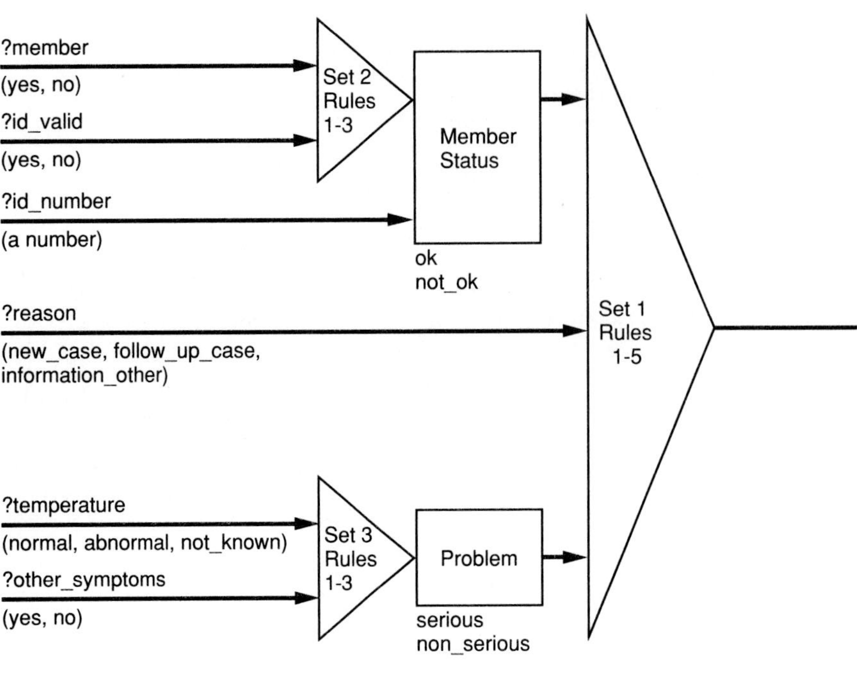

in" to a recommendation and the "fan-out" to a customized conclusion. All information comes from old data, except "interest_areas." Since "interest_areas" comes from direct user input, it is shown with the conventional initial question mark.

CHAINING KNOWLEDGE BASES

If a knowledge base file becomes too large, it runs slowly or not at all when a computer does not have enough memory. One solution is to divide the large file into two or more smaller files. The CHAIN, SAVEFACTS, and LOADFACTS keywords, described in Figure 5–14, enable a KBS developer to *chain* together two or more knowledge bases for use in a single consultation.

The chaining feature encourages the modular development of very large knowledge-based systems. Each module remains a smaller independent subset of the whole KBS. This enables each subset to be designed, coded, and maintained more easily and, if necessary, by different developers.

The educational version of VP-Expert used for this tutorial allows the chaining of only three 16-Kbyte knowledge base files. The regular version is not limited in the size or number of files that can be chained.

In some cases, it may be practical to chain two knowledge bases together to obtain information not available from each knowledge base alone. For example, one investment advisory knowledge base may determine that a client should consider investing in bonds. Another knowledge base may advise a client about which bonds are best to consider. The chained knowledge bases offer a more comprehensive system than either stand-alone KBS.

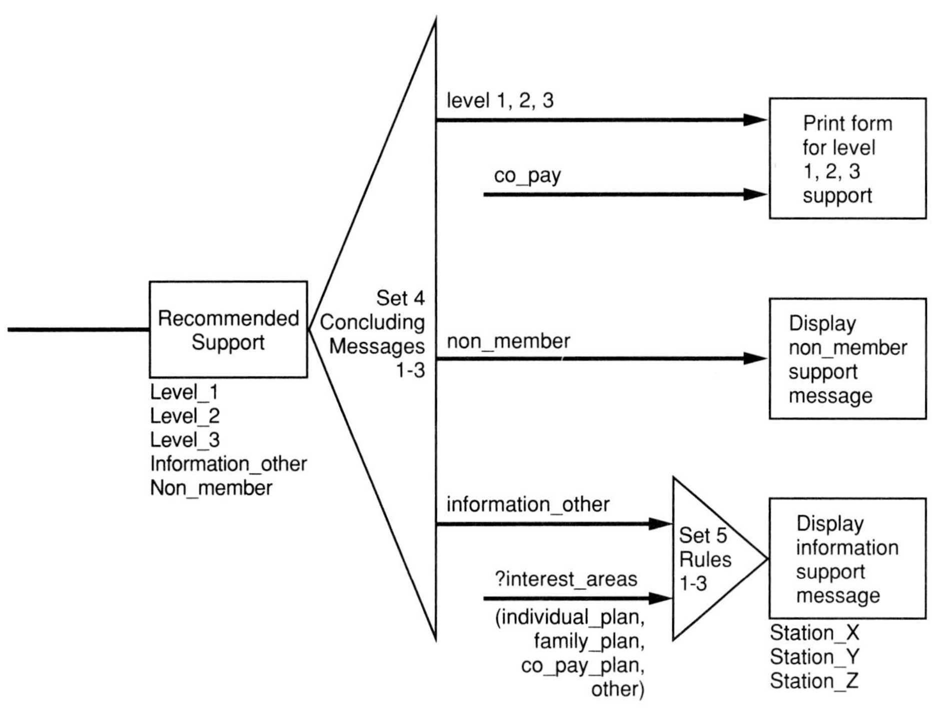

A Chaining Example

To examine how chaining works, the HMOADD2.KBS file is separated into two modules. Each module is a smaller logical segment of the larger KBS. The two modules roughly concern the following logic:

Logic Segment	*Sequence*	*Filename*
FIND support This is the original kernel of the HMO Service Screening Assistant.	1	MODULE1.KBS
FIND message This is the added module that customizes the concluding messages.	2	MODULE2.KBS

For the sake of this example, assume that the two logic segments were created by different developers and it is decided to CHAIN the finished modules together.

As evident in Figure 5–15, the logic embodied in MODULE1.KBS is the opening message and main "FIND support" goal. Most of this code is not shown because it duplicates that shown in Figure 5–8, except for Rule Set 4.

To a user, this KBS produces screens during a consultation that are similar to those in Figures 5–2 and 5–3.

Once a "support" level is known, there is a pause and a screen message indicates "Loading file..." This message is automatically generated by the CHAIN keyword. CHAIN causes the MODULE2 knowledge base file to be loaded for continuing the rest of the consultation. (Although the example does not show it, a pathname can prefix any filename used in the knowledge base. No filename extension is allowed.)

Figure 5–14.

Chaining Keywords

Keyword	Description
CHAIN	Permits the use of knowledge bases that would otherwise be too large to be contained in memory. Also permits the modularization of knowledge bases which makes both troubleshooting and writing effective knowledge bases easier.
SAVEFACTS	Stores the names and values of *all* variables whose values are presently known in the consultation to an ASCII text file with the following format: variable1 = value1 CNF n variable2 = value2 CNF n SAVEFACTS usually is the first step in the process of chaining knowledge base files. SAVEFACTS cannot be used to save *selected* variables. If the text file named in the SAVEFACTS clause already exists, it will be overwritten when SAVEFACTS is executed.
LOADFACTS	Loads the names and values of *all* variables saved by SAVEFACTS into the new knowledge base. (It is not possible to selectively retrieve values from a file created by SAVEFACTS.)

Basic Steps Required in Knowledge Base Chaining

- Use SAVEFACTS to save the known values (facts) from the current consultation. (It is not always necessary to pass information from one knowledge base to another.)
- Use CHAIN to name a new knowledge base file. (The old knowledge base file will be closed, and this file will take its place in the current consultation.)
- Use LOADFACTS to load the values saved by SAVEFACTS into the new knowledge base.

SAVEFACTS and CHAIN should occur in the first knowledge base file. LOADFACTS occurs in the second knowledge base file.

An example of the syntax normally used in transferring knowledge and execution from the first knowledge base is:

```
SAVEFACTS B:tempdata
CHAIN B:module2.kbs
```

The syntax of the second knowledge base is:

```
LOADFACTS B:tempdata
```

Just before the link occurs, the SAVEFACTS keyword stores all known variable values in a temporary file called TEMPDATA. A developer can give the SAVEFACTS file any name desired, as long as it remains within file-naming constraints.

Figure 5–16 gives the listing for the second file, MODULE2.KBS. Its purpose is to produce a concluding message customized by "support" level. To a user, this KBS generates screens during a consultation that are similar to those in Figures 5–9 and 5–11.

Figure 5–15. First of Two Chained Knowledge Bases

Notes:
. The name of this knowledge base file on the Sample Files disk is MODULE1.KBS.
. Blocked areas indicate changes from HMOADD2.KBS.
. The part of the knowledge base file after the "Rules Block" line is not shown here. It matches a similar part already given in Figure 5-8. The only difference is that Rule Set 4 does not appear in this MODULE1.KBS.

```
! HMO Service Screening Assistant
! Chaining Example: This is the first of two linked knowledge base files.
!                   It is saved as MODULE1.KBS.
!                   It saves all names and values of variables in
!                   a SAVEFACTS file called TEMPDATA.
!                   (It links to MODULE2.KBS)

!*************************************************************************

!EXECUTE;                                    !start consultation immediately
      !use exclamation point temporarily to disable execute while debugging
BKCOLOR = 3;                           !set screen background color to light blue
RUNTIME;                                       !eliminate rules and facts windows

!============================== Actions Block ============================

ACTIONS
     WOPEN 1,3,10,13,60,7                          !define opening window 1
     ACTIVE 1                                            !activate window 1
     DISPLAY "

              HMO Service Screening Assistant

   This consultation assists you to screen a person who
   enters an HMO facility.  It asks a series of questions
   about the person, then recommends a level of support
   appropriate to the person's needs.

   Please press any key to begin the consultation.~

      "
     wclose 1                                                !remove window 1
     COLOR = 20                      !set following text color to blinking red
     DISPLAY "        CAUTION!"
     COLOR = 4                         !set following text to non-blinking red
     DISPLAY "Please make sure your printer in ON."
     DISPLAY "Press any key to continue.~"
     CLS                                                     !clear the screen
     COLOR = 0                             !set following text to normal black
     WOPEN 1,1,1,6,77,2                          !define instructions window 1
     ACTIVE 1                                              !activate window 1
     DISPLAY "                                 Instructions
          Use the arrow keys to move the lightbar to a desired
          answer choice then press the Enter key.
          Press the End key to move to the next question."
     WOPEN 2,8,1,13,77,3                         !define consultation window 2
     ACTIVE 2                                              !activate window 2
     FIND support
     SAVEFACTS tempdata                 !save all variable names and values in a
                                            !temporary text file called TEMPDATA
     CHAIN module2                     !link to another .KBS file called MODULE2

;
!============================== Rules Block ==============================
```

(See Figure 5-8 for the code following the Rules Block)

Figure 5–16. Second of Two Chained Knowledge Bases

Notes:
. The name of this knowledge base file on the Sample Files disk is MODULE2.KBS.
. Blocked areas indicate changes from HMOADD2.KBS. In addition, Rule Set numbers are changed.

```
! HMO Service Screening Assistant
! Chaining Example: This is the second of two linked knowledge base files.
!                   It is saved as MODULE2.KBS.
!                   It does not have any variables.
!                   (It links back to MODULE1.KBS.)

!****************************************************************************

!EXECUTE;                                    !start consultation immediately
      !use exclamation point temporarily to disable execute while debugging
BKCOLOR = 3;                           !set screen background color to light blue
RUNTIME;                                     !eliminate rules and facts windows

!============================== Actions Block ==============================

ACTIONS
     LOADFACTS tempdata     !load into memory all variable names and values
                              !stored in the temporary file called TEMPDATA
     COLOR = 0                          !set following text to normal black
     WOPEN 1,1,1,6,77,2                       !define instructions window 1
     ACTIVE 1                                            !activate window 1
     DISPLAY "                          Instructions
          Use the arrow keys to move the lightbar to a desired
          answer choice then press the Enter key.
          Press the End key to move to the next question."
     WOPEN 2,8,1,13,77,3                      !define consultation window 2
     ACTIVE 2                                            !activate window 2
     FIND message                           !set goal to customize messages
     DISPLAY "Press any key to conclude this consultation.~"
     CHAIN module1          !link back to the original MODULE1.KBS to begin
                                  !another consultation session, if desired
;
!============================== Rules Block ==============================

!-------------------- Rule Set 1: Concluding Messages --------------------

RULE message_level123                 !use a meaningful name for a rule label
     IF support = level_1 or
        support = level_2 or
        support = level_3
     THEN message = print_form
        PRINTON                       !send display text to screen and printer
        DISPLAY "Authorization Form For Service - {support}"
        DISPLAY "ID: {id_number}"
        DISPLAY "Reason: {reason}"
        DISPLAY "Self-reported: temperature - {temperature}"
        DISPLAY "              symptoms - {other_symptoms}"!disable printon
        PRINTOFF                                           !send text only
        PDISPLAY "Kindly go to {room} for service."            !to printer
                                   !set sub-goal to determine co-pay charges
        FIND co_pay                 !move printer paper to top of next page
        EJECT                                      !display one blank line
        DISPLAY ""
        DISPLAY "Please tear the Authorization Form off the printer.";
```

Figure 5–16 *continued*

```
          RULE get_co_pay            !single rule to determine co-pay charges
          IF id_number > 999999
          THEN co_pay = yes
               PDISPLAY"(Co-payment charge of $8.00 made for service.)";

RULE message_non_member
     IF support = non_member
     THEN message = station_Z
        DISPLAY "Appropriate service is available at {message}.";

RULE message_info
     IF support = information_other
     THEN message = display_service
        FIND interest_areas                          get direct user input
        FIND info_help                  !set sub-goal to customize messages
        DISPLAY "Service is available for plan type / at: {info_help}";

!------------------- Rule Set 2: Information Help Messages ---------------

RULE 2-1
     IF interest_areas = individual_plan
     THEN info_help = individual_station_X;

RULE 2-2
     IF interest_areas = family_plan
     THEN info_help = family_station_Y;

RULE 2-3
     IF interest_areas = co_pay_plan or
        interest_areas = other
     THEN info_help = co_pay_other_station_Z;

!=========================== Questions Block ============================

ASK interest_areas: "What kind(s) of information is (are) desired?";
CHOICES interest_areas: individual_plan, family_plan, co_pay_plan, other;

PLURAL: interest_areas, info_help;
```

As evident from Figure 5–16, the LOADFACTS keyword is used to load into memory all variable names and values stored in the temporary file TEMP-DATA. Although only one value, for "support," is relevant to MODULE2.KBS, all variables whose values are known and saved at the time the SAVEFACTS keyword is executed are loaded.

In this example, after an appropriate message is displayed or printed, the knowledge base chains back to MODULE1.KBS. This creates a looping action to enable a user to begin another consultation session, if desired. Since the educational version of VP-Expert permits only three links, after the second consultation a warning message appears. It declares that the limits of this version are exceeded, then proceeds to terminate at the DOS prompt. By contrast, a full version of VP-Expert would cycle through the two-part KBS session as often as desired.

Because MODULE2.KBS is an independent module, rule set numbers and rule numbers are changed as appropriate. Rule Sets 1 and 2, for example, were Rule Sets 4 and 5 in the original single HMOADD2.KBS.

Practical Considerations

Chained segments can be linked in the THEN part of a rule as well as in the Actions Block. Consider the following example:

```
IF advice = invest and
   investment = bonds
THEN type = bonds
     CHAIN B:BONDS
```

The THEN part of this rule links directly to the KBS that determines bond investments. If necessary, a SAVEFACTS statement could have captured all known variables before chaining.

It is not necessary in all cases to pass information from one knowledge base to another. An example is given in Figure 5–16. After the end of the consultation session, the CHAIN keyword in the Actions Block returns control to MODULE1.KBS to begin another session, if desired. In this case, there is no need to pass data, so CHAIN is not preceded by a SAVEFACTS keyword.

It is recommended that the EXECUTE keyword be the first keyword in a file to achieve a smooth transition when chaining from one knowledge base to another. But use of this keyword causes a consultation to terminate a session at the DOS prompt, which is very inconvenient when debugging a KBS. Putting an exclamation point in front of EXECUTE conveniently disables it for debugging sessions. The chained KBS files will seem to function just as well with EXECUTE disabled.

Finally, some debugging tips for working with chained KBS files follow:

- First, make a chained module or KBS work independently of all linkages.
- During independent module tests, set up dummy variables and values in the Actions Block, if necessary, to simulate imported SAVEFACTS data.
- Create extra DISPLAY messages that serve as an audit trail to track the progress of execution through difficult or problem code.
- Use the exclamation point to deactivate dummy variables and the EXECUTE keyword during live tests of linkages. Remember to delete dummy variables, extra DISPLAYS, and any exclamation points used only to support debugging sessions after the chained KBS works smoothly.

REVIEW QUESTIONS

1. How much effort and time must be allotted to user interface?
2. What is the importance of the opening message?
3. What is the function of the BECAUSE text in a rule?
4. What is the definition and function of a comment in a knowledge base file?
5. How does the physical layout of the knowledge base assist in understanding the KBS?
6. What is the function of a WHENEVER rule in a backward-chaining KBS?
7. What is the purpose of chaining knowledge bases together in an expert system?

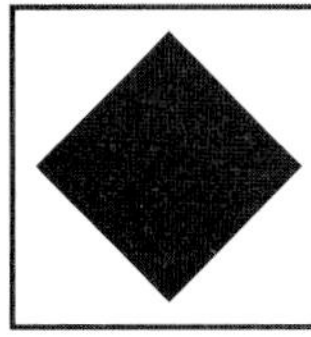

EXERCISES

1. The object of this exercise is to examine how a KBS's user interface can be improved. Run a consultation with the knowledge base HMOUSER.KBS from the Sample Files disk. Then run a consultation with HMORUN.KBS.
   a. Compare and record the differences observed.
   b. When the question appears "Is the person an HMO member?" type the backslash (/) key, move the lightbar to Why? and press Enter. Record the response observed. Press the Escape key to resume the consultation.
2. The goal of this exercise is to explore how to create windows to enhance a KBS's user interface. Copy HMOUSER.KBS from the Sample Files disk to your Exercise disk with

   ```
   A>COPY HMOUSER.KBS B:MYUSER.KBS
   ```

   a. Use the Editor to create changes that produce a double framed window around the opening message of MYUSER.KBS.
   b. Change the background color for the opening message to another color of your choice.
3. This exercise demonstrates how selected changes to a "plain vanilla" KBS can make it more user-friendly. Copy HMORUN.KBS from the Sample Files disk to your Exercise disk with

   ```
   A>COPY HMORUN.KBS  B:XMYUSER.KBS
   ```

   Use the Editor to enter into XMYUSER.KBS the new additions shown in the blocked areas of Figure 5–1. Your completely debugged knowledge base should run just like the model HMOUSER.KBS on the Sample Files disk.
4. This exercise explores printing and other enhancement options. Run a consultation with the knowledge base HMOADD1.KBS from the Sample Files disk. Compare and record the differences between it and HMOUSER.KBS.
5. This exercise demonstrates how to handle a multiple-response question. Run a consultation with the knowledge base HMOADD2.KBS from the Sample Files disk using the following responses:

Response	*Keys to Press to Indicate Response*
yes	(Enter, End)
yes	(Enter, End)
99999	(Enter)
information other	(Enter, End)
family plan	(Enter)
co-pay plan	(Enter, End)

   a. Record the results observed.
   b. Compare your observations with Figure 5–12 and identify which lines of code produced which part of the results observed.
6. This exercise demonstrates the use of chained or linked KBS modules. Run a consultation with the knowledge base MODULE1.KBS from the Sample Files disk. This file will automatically call and use MODULE2.KBS from the Sample Files disk. During the consultation, a temporary file called TEMPDATA is created.
   a. Observe and record the results observed during the transition from MODULE1 to MODULE2.
   b. Obtain a printout of MODULE1.KBS and MODULE2.KBS. Identify the code that processes the linkages.

7. Improve the user interface for a knowledge base of your own design with these features:
   a. An opening message that
      - Describes the objective of the consultation
      - Describes how the consultation will work
      - Indicates what kind of closure to expect
      - Puts the user in control to activate the consultation

   b. An "instructions" window.

6

ADVANCED FEATURES

The focus of this chapter is several advanced features included in the VP-Expert development shell. They are

- Advanced database functions
- Advanced spreadsheet functions
- SORT and POP keywords
- SHIP and RECEIVE keywords
- Graphics capabilities and functions
- BCALL, CALL, and CCALL keywords
- FORMAT keyword

Hands-on examples are included on the Sample Files disk to facilitate understanding these advanced features.

Only selected keywords and features are covered in this chapter. Consult the *VP-Expert Manual* for additional information.

ADVANCED DATABASE FUNCTIONS

Facts used in an expert system often represent data that frequently changes or needs to be modified. The tasks of creating and maintaining large amounts of data often are better handled by database management system software.

For a developer to integrate the dBASE III Plus database management system with a VP-Expert application, it may be necessary to use more advanced functions than those already covered in Chapter 4. The MENU_SIZE, MRESET, CLOSE, and RECORD_NUM keywords represent advanced functions that are used in the example shown in Figure 6–1.

Figure 6–1. MENU_SIZE, MRESET, CLOSE, and RECORD_NUM Keywords Used for Database Integration

Note: The name of this knowledge base file on the Sample Files disk is HMODB1S.KBS and MEMBER.DBF is the database file.

```
RUNTIME;
ACTIONS
     DISPLAY "This example assists your interrogation of the"
     DISPLAY "          MEMBER.DBF database file."
     DISPLAY "                                              "
     DISPLAY "It also demonstrates the use of the MENU SIZE,"
     DISPLAY "MRESET, CLOSE, and RECORD NUM keywords."
     DISPLAY "                                              "
     DISPLAY "        PLEASE PRESS ANY KEY TO BEGIN~"

     MENU plan_type, ALL, member, p_type
     DISPLAY "Please select one of the following {MENU_SIZE} choices...."
     DISPLAY "                                                          "
     FIND plan_type
     FIND cut_off
     MRESET plan_type
     DISPLAY "The following database records meet your criteria:"
     WHILEKNOWN p_type
          GET plan_type = p_type and cut_off < requests, member, ALL
          RESET message
          FIND message
     END
     CLOSE member
;

RULE 1
     IF p_type <> UNKNOWN
     THEN message = displayed
          DISPLAY "Record number {RECORD_NUM} meets your criteria"
          DISPLAY "{id}, {p_type}, {lname}, {fname}, {requests}"
          DISPLAY "                                              "
     ELSE message = displayed
          DISPLAY "                                              "
          DISPLAY "End of file";

ASK plan_type: "What plan type(s) do you want to check?";

ASK cut_off: "If you want only those records with 'requests' above
a certain number, please enter the number (or zero).";

PLURAL: plan_type
```

This KBS file produced this result.

```
This example assists your interrogation of the
          MEMBER.DBF database file.

It also demonstrates the use of the MENU_SIZE,
MRESET, CLOSE, and RECORD_NUM keywords.

         PLEASE PRESS ANY KEY TO BEGIN
Please select one of the following 3 choices....

What plan type(s) do you want to check?
 fam ◄                   ind                        copay

If you want only those records with 'requests' above
a certain number, please enter the number (or zero).
 3

The following database records meet your criteria:
Record number 1 meets your criteria
111, fam, Jones, Irene, 12

Record number 4 meets your criteria
444, fam, Malone, John, 10

Record number 8 meets your criteria
888, fam, Tillman, Bradford, 5

Record number 9 meets your criteria
999, fam, Gilmore, Matthew, 4

End of file
```

MENU_SIZE Keyword

The MENU_SIZE keyword is used to determine the number of options the MENU keyword generates (see Chapter 4). The MENU_SIZE keyword is always used in conjunction with the MENU keyword and is always placed in any program line after the MENU keyword.

In Figure 4–8, the user is asked to select from HMO plan options. In this instance, there are three plan types, but there could be any number. The number of options is retrievable with the MENU_SIZE keyword. In some cases, this number may be useful to an application.

The HMODB1S.KBS example in Figure 6–1 builds on the example in Figure 4–8. In HMODB1S.KBS, the MENU keyword specifies three plan_type options from which the user can choose. The numeric value three (3) is displayed when a DISPLAY clause is executed with the MENU_SIZE keyword.

A developer cannot assign a value to MENU_SIZE because it always contains a count of the current values generated by the MENU keyword.

MRESET Keyword

A large menu created with the MENU keyword requires a great amount of the computer's working memory. If many large menus are created during a single consultation, an "out-of-memory" condition can occur. In general, it is good practice to use the MRESET keyword soon after each MENU keyword to free working memory, as shown in the example given in Figure 6–1. The format of this clause is

```
MRESET variable
```

where the variable is the same as that specified in a previously executed MENU clause.

The MRESET keyword should be placed where it will execute after the menu has been displayed.

CLOSE Keyword

Some KBS designs require accessing data from many different database files. VP-Expert allows a maximum of only six open database .DBF files. When six files are already open and it is necessary to access an additional file, the CLOSE keyword must be used to close one of the currently open .DBF files.

CLOSE can close only one file at a time, as shown in the example in Figure 6–1. Naming more than one .DBF file, or no file, will result in a syntax error. The format to use this keyword is as follows:

```
CLOSE filename
```

A path can optionally be specified using the same format as that used by DOS. This informs VP-Expert where to locate the named file. The default path is the current path where the KBS is running. The filename supplied with CLOSE must be an existing database file with a .DBF extension. However, the extension should not be provided, or a syntax error will result.

The CLOSE keyword should be used after the developer has determined that an open database file is no longer needed. In the HMODB1S.KBS example in Figure 6–1, CLOSE appears near the end of the Actions Block. When executed, the CLOSE keyword resets the record pointer to the top (first record) of the closed database file.

Even though there is a CLOSE keyword, there is no OPEN keyword in VP-Expert. The GET keyword is, in effect, VP-Expert's OPEN keyword.

RECORD_NUM Keyword

In many instances, it is useful for a developer to access the physical record number for a specific record in a dBASE III Plus database file. The RECORD_NUM keyword contains the record number of the last record accessed by a GET statement.

An example of how RECORD_NUM can be used is shown in Figure 6–1. Here, it displays the physical record number of each record that meets the selection criteria. RECORD_NUM might also be used to display the current record number during updates of a database.

It is possible to change the value of RECORD_NUM by assigning it a new value, for example, RECORD_NUM = 28. Such an assignment will not affect the position of the record pointer in the actual database file.

RECORD_NUM can also be used as an important debugging tool in the development of WHILEKNOWN looping constructs associated with dBASE III Plus files. Through the use of this keyword, it is possible to observe if selected records and code are executing properly.

ADVANCED SPREADSHEET FUNCTIONS

Facts used in an expert system can also be obtained from a spreadsheet file. The COLUMN, ROW, and NAMED keywords access data from a spreadsheet. These keywords reduce the task of updating a rule base whenever the size of a spreadsheet is changed. As the spreadsheet grows or shrinks, VP-Expert adjusts automatically to access all the information within the range specified.

For the developer to manipulate data between a Lotus 1-2-3 spreadsheet file and a VP-Expert file, it is necessary to select between two methods of accessing spreadsheet data. The methods are static range accessing and ROW, COLUMN, or NAMED keyword accessing. Both of these methods are discussed in the following sections.

Static Range Accessing

The simplest method of data retrieval from spreadsheets is static range accessing. A *static range* is a rectangular block of one or more spreadsheet cells that a Lotus 1-2-3 user treats as a unit. To specify a group of cells as a range, the user needs to type the cell coordinates of the two most distant cells in the range and separate them with two periods. For example, B4..F4 means cell B4 through F4.

To retrieve values from a range of spreadsheet cells into a KBS, the range can be identified by its top left-hand and bottom right-hand corner cell addresses, separated by two periods (no spaces). Referring to the spreadsheet example SSHMO1.WKS in Figure 6–2, the cell range that contains the necessary data is B5 through B9.

The static range accessing method requires the rule base to be changed if the spreadsheet range becomes larger (or smaller) than the initial range specified.

ROW or COLUMN Keyword Accessing

An alternative method for accessing spreadsheet data is through ROW, COLUMN, or NAMED keywords. Figure 6–2 illustrates the use of the ROW and

COLUMN keywords to access the first spreadsheet in Figure 6–3. (Tests of the NAMED keyword produced unreliable results and so NAMED is not covered here.)

In Lotus, ROW and COLUMN names are useful when referencing a range of data (or even a single cell). For example, if a row with the range B6..H6 contains profit results, the range can be named PROFIT. A developer no longer has to remember cell addresses to access it.

VP-Expert automatically assigns a slot in memory for every element in a ROW or COLUMN range. Every memory slot is assigned a common variable name, with a unique subscript identifier. VP-Expert is unaware of the fact that a range may have grown or shrunk since it was last used. It does not matter. This feature alone often makes it preferable to the static range accessing method of spreadsheet access.

Figure 6–2. Various Methods to Access Spreadsheet Data

Note: The name of this knowledge base file on the Sample Files disk is SSHMO1.KBS and SSHMO1.WKS is the spreadsheet file.

```
RUNTIME;
ACTIONS
     DISPLAY "       This demonstrates Static Range B5..B9 Spreadsheet Access"
     DISPLAY "                  from the spreadsheet SSHMO1.WKS"
     DISPLAY "                                                          "
     WFORMAT FIXED, 0             !format PWKS values without decimal places

          WKS example, B5..B9, SSHMO1        !declare static range B5..B9
          DISPLAY "          January Cases                              "
          DISPLAY "                                                     "
          DISPLAY "          level 1 cases =             {example[1]}"
          DISPLAY "          level 2 cases =             {example[2]}"
          DISPLAY "          level 3 cases =             {example[3]}"
          DISPLAY "          information other cases = {example[4]}"
          DISPLAY "          non member cases =          {example[5]}"
          DISPLAY "                                     "
          DISPLAY "          PLEASE PRESS ANY KEY TO CONTINUE~"
          DISPLAY "                                     "

     DISPLAY "          This demonstrates Named COLUMN Spreadsheet Access"
     DISPLAY "          The COLUMN is named 'month'"
     DISPLAY "                                                          "

     FIND month
          WKS cases, COLUMN = (month), SSHMO1             !declare a COLUMN
          DISPLAY "                {month} Cases                        "
          DISPLAY "                                                     "
          DISPLAY "          level 1 cases =             {cases[1]}"
          DISPLAY "          level 2 cases =             {cases[2]}"
          DISPLAY "          level 3 cases =             {cases[3]}"
          DISPLAY "          information other cases = {cases[4]}"
          DISPLAY "          non member cases =          {cases[5]}"
          DISPLAY "                                     "
          DISPLAY "          PLEASE PRESS ANY KEY TO CONTINUE~"
          DISPLAY "                                     "

     DISPLAY "          This demonstrates Named ROW Spreadsheet Access"
     DISPLAY "          The ROW is named 'level'"
     DISPLAY "                                                          "

     FIND level
          WKS figures, ROW = (level), SSHMO1            !declare a ROW
          DISPLAY " Jan     Feb     Mar"
          DISPLAY "                                          "
          DISPLAY " {figures[1]}     {figures[2]}       {figures[3]}"

ASK month: "For which month do you wish to retrieve case figures?";
CHOICES month: January, February, March;

ASK level: "For which case level do you wish to retrieve figures for?";
CHOICES level: level_1, level_2, level_3, information_other, non_member;
```

This KBS file produced this result.

Figure 6–2. *concluded*

```
        This demonstrates Static Range B5..B9 Spreadsheet Access
                  from the spreadsheet SSHMO1.WKS.

    January Cases

    level 1 cases =            37
    level 2 cases =            65
    level 3 cases =            104
    information other cases =  41
    non member cases =         18

    PLEASE PRESS ANY KEY TO CONTINUE

        This demonstrates Named COLUMN Spreadsheet Access.
        The COLUMN is named 'month.'

For which month do you wish to retrieve case figures?
 January                 February ◄              March

              February Cases

       level 1 cases =            88
       level 2 cases =            309
       level 3 cases =            55
       information other cases =  3
       non member cases =         201

       PLEASE PRESS ANY KEY TO CONTINUE

          This demonstrates Named ROW Spreadsheet Access.
          The ROW is named 'level.'

For which case level do you wish to retrieve figures?
 level 1                 level 2                    level 3
 information other ◄     non member

  Jan    Feb    Mar
  41     3      69
```

Note: Boxes are added for emphasis.

VP-Expert recognizes both specific and indirect addressing to indicate a desired spreadsheet location. Row location in the worksheet is identified using this format:

```
ROW = row_heading_name or
ROW = (variable_name)
```

Column location is identified using this format:

```
COLUMN = column_heading_name or
COLUMN = (variable_name)
```

The value assigned to the variable named in the ROW or COLUMN specification need not be assigned in the Actions Block. It can be assigned in a rule or by the user at an ASK prompt. This must occur, however, before the execution of the WKS keyword, or the WKS clause will not work.

If the parentheses around the variable name are omitted, VP-Expert treats the variable name as a literal ROW or COLUMN heading. In the example

```
WKS the_price, COLUMN = May, PRICE
```

the KBS will look for a COLUMN named "May" in the spreadsheet named PRICE.WKS.

Figure 6–3. Sample Spreadsheets

Spreadsheet Used for Demonstrating ROW and COLUMN Keyword Accessing (SSHMO1.WKS)

	A	B	C	D	E
1	HMO Cases Control	3/30/9X			
2					
3	Case Type	January	February	March	
4					
5	level_1	37	88	66	
6	level_2	65	309	57	
7	level_3	104	55	82	
8	information_other	41	3	69	
9	non_member	18	201	5	
10					
11					

Spreadsheet Used for Demonstrating Subscripting (TEMPRA.WKS)

	A	B	C	D	E	F
1			"Temperature	Record"		
2	==========	==========	==========	==========	==========	==========
3						
4	Patient	Day1	Day2	Day3	Day4	Avg
5						
6	Joseph	101	100	100	99	100
7	Michael	99	100	102	101	100.5
8	Peter	100	100	100	99	99.75
9						
10						
11						

Figure 6–2 illustrates the use of ROW and COLUMN spreadsheet access. Running a consultation of the SSHMO1.KBS displays a prompt and a menu that requires the user to choose a month or level for which to retrieve case figures. The month or level chosen is assigned as the value of the variable. The WKS clause then retrieves the COLUMN or ROW that matches the chosen value and assigns each cell in that COLUMN or ROW as one element of the dimensioned, or subscripted, variable.

Subscripting. It is possible to store multiple values as a one-dimensional array of elements in VP-Expert. In this spreadsheet example, an element represents the value of a single spreadsheet cell. Elements of the dimensioned variable are assigned and identified by a bracketed number (called a *subscript*), corresponding to a position in a column, row, or range from which it was copied. For example, the variable names cost[1], cost[2], and so on would be assigned to the elements of the dimensioned variable cost as follows:

cost

15	25	35	45
cost[1]	cost[2]	cost[3]	cost[4]

Consider the Lotus 1-2-3 spreadsheet for temperature record given at the bottom of Figure 6–3. To obtain the information contained in row 6, the developer could type the statement

```
WKS Joseph_Temp, ROW = Joseph, TEMPRA
```

which would assign the five values from the row labeled Joseph to the dimensioned variable Joseph_Temp as follows:

- Joseph_Temp[1] will correspond to the value contained in row Joseph and column Day1 (101)
- Joseph_Temp[2] will correspond to the value contained in row Joseph and column Day2 (100)
- Joseph_Temp[3] will correspond to the value contained in row Joseph and column Day3 (100)
- Joseph_Temp[4] will correspond to the value contained in row Joseph and column Day4 (99)
- Joseph_Temp[5] will correspond to the value contained in row Joseph and column Avg (100).

Ordering of Subscripts. A matrix of numeric values is read row by row in ascending order from the leftmost to the rightmost column. For example, to access all the values in TEMPRA.WKS starting with row 6 and column B, the subscripts and their respective values would consist of the following:

```
Temps[1] = 101 Temps[6]  =  99   Temps[11] = 100
Temps[2] = 100 Temps[7]  = 100   Temps[12] = 100
Temps[3] = 100 Temps[8]  = 102   Temps[13] = 100
Temps[4] =  99 Temps[9]  = 101   Temps[14] =  99
Temps[5] = 100 Temps[10] = 100.5 Temps[15] =  99.75
```

The SSHMO1.KBS example in Figure 6–2 illustrates the use of subscripting with the COLUMN and ROW keywords.

SORT AND POP KEYWORDS

The SORT and POP keywords add flexibility when using a PLURAL variable (see Chapter 5). Their use is illustrated in Figures 6–4 and 6–5 and described below.

SORT Keyword

The SORT keyword enables a developer, for example, to organize a list of user preferences from most preferable to least preferable. Preference depends on an assigned confidence factor. To do this, a developer must use the PLURAL keyword in the Questions Block of the knowledge base.

The SORT keyword orders the values of a PLURAL variable in descending order of confidence factor. For example, assume the PLURAL variable COMPUTER_STOCKS has been assigned the following values:

```
IBM      CNF 80
DEC      CNF 90
WANG     CNF 70
UNISYS   CNF 85
```

Figure 6–4. Using the SORT Keyword

Note: The name of this knowledge base file on the Sample Files disk is HMOFLU.KBS.

```
ACTIONS
    WOPEN 1,1,1,20,77,3
    ACTIVE 1
    DISPLAY    "
          ** WELCOME TO THE HMO SERVICE FLU SCREENING ASSISTANT **

          Please indicate the patient's symptom, press the HOME key,
          then enter a two-digit distress level factor.  Complete the
          entry by pressing the ENTER and ARROW keys. Repeat the process
          until all of the patient's symptoms are accounted for.  Press
          the END key when finished to continue the consultation.

             This example demonstrates use of the SORT keyword.

                     PRESS ANY KEY TO CONTINUE~
"
 WCLOSE 1
 FIND symptom
 SORT symptom                                   !SORT is used to organize
 FIND temp                                      !a variable in descending
 FIND condition                                 !CNF order
 DISPLAY "The patient's body temperature is {#temp}."  !The # symbol is used to
 DISPLAY "Initial diagnosis: {#condition}."            !display/print a CNF level
;
RULE 1
     IF temp = over_98.6_degrees AND
        symptom = sore_throat OR
        symptom = stomach_ache OR
        symptom = headache OR
        symptom = nausea OR
        symptom = severe_cough OR
        symptom = G_I_discomfort
     THEN condition = Serious
     DISPLAY "{#symptom}.";

RULE 2
     IF temp = over_100_degrees AND
          symptom = sore_throat OR
          symptom = stomache_ache OR
          symptom = headache OR
          symptom = nausea OR
          symptom = severe_cough OR
          symptom = G_I_discomfort
     THEN condition = Very_serious
     DISPLAY "{#symptom}.";

ASK temp: "What is the body temperature of the patient?";
CHOICES temp: over_98.6_degrees, over_100_degrees;

ASK symptom: "What are the patient's symptoms? (rate distress level
             on a scale of 0 to 100)";
CHOICES symptom: sore_throat, stomach_ache, headache, nausea,
                 severe_cough, G_I_discomfort;

PLURAL: symptom;
```

This KBS file produced this result after the opening screen.

```
What are the patient's symptoms? (rate distress level
              on a scale of 0 to 100)
 sore_throat 23 ◄          stomach_ache 89 ◄          headache 67 ◄
 nausea 12 ◄               severe_cough 22 ◄          G_I_discomfort 45 ◄

What is the body temperature of the patient?
 over_98.6_degrees ◄        over_100_degrees


stomach ache CNF 89
headache CNF 67
G I discomfort CNF 45
sore throat CNF 23
severe cough CNF 22
nausea CNF 12.
The patient's body temperature is over 98.6 degrees CNF 100.
Initial diagnosis: Serious CNF 98.
```

Figure 6–5. Using the POP Keyword

Note: The name of this knowledge base file on the Sample Files disk is HMOFLU1.KBS.

```
ACTIONS
     WOPEN 1,1,1,20,77,3
     ACTIVE 1
     DISPLAY  "

         ** WELCOME TO THE HMO SERVICE FLU SCREENING ASSISTANT **

        Please indicate the patient's symptom, press the HOME key,
        then enter a two-digit distress level factor.  Complete
        the entry by pressing the ENTER and ARROW keys.  Repeat the
        process until all of the patient's symptoms are accounted for.
        Press the END key when finished to continue the consultation.

          This example demonstrates use of the POP keyword.

                         PRESS ANY KEY TO CONTINUE~
"
 WCLOSE 1
 FIND symptom
 WHILEKNOWN symptom
     RESET symptom1
     SORT symptom
     POP symptom, symptom1       !POP is used to obtain the top value
                                 !variable in the PLURAL variable 'symptom'
                                 !symptom1 is a variable used to hold the
                                 !top value

     DISPLAY "{#symptom1} is one of the patient's symptoms."
 END
     DISPLAY "End of Patient Symptom list.";

ASK symptom: "What are the patient's symptoms? (rate distress level
                  on a scale of 0 to 100)";
CHOICES symptom: sore_throat, stomach_ache, headache, nausea,
                  severe_cough, G_I_discomfort;

PLURAL: symptom;
```

This KBS file produced this result after the opening screen.

```
What are the patient's symptoms? (rate distress level
              on a scale of 0 to 100)
 sore_throat 67 ◄        stomach_ache 33 ◄        headache 45 ◄
 nausea 75 ◄             severe_cough 25 ◄        G_I_discomfort 15 ◄

 nausea CNF 75 is one of the patient's symptoms.
 sore throat CNF 67 is one of the patient's symptoms.
 headache CNF 45 is one of the patient's symptoms.
 stomach ache CNF 33 is one of the patient's symptoms.
 severe cough CNF 25 is one of the patient's symptoms.
 G I discomfort CNF 15 is one of the patient's symptoms.
 End of Patient Symptom list.
```

The execution of SORT COMPUTER_STOCKS would result in the reorganization of these values as follows:

```
DEC       CNF 90
UNISYS    CNF 85
IBM       CNF 80
WANG      CNF 70
```

The list appears in descending numeric confidence factor (CNF) order with the highest CNF placed at the top of the list, the next highest second on the list, and the value with the lowest CNF at the bottom of the list.

Use of the SORT keyword for a single-valued variable is ignored when the knowledge base is executed. In addition, if a PLURAL variable contains equal confidence factors, the SORT clause has no effect.

The HMOFLU.KBS file in Figure 6–4 gives a simple example that uses the SORT keyword.

POP Keyword

The POP keyword is used to control the individual values of a PLURAL variable. A PLURAL variable stores values in a "stack." A *stack* in this sense means that the last assigned value is at the top of the stack. When the POP keyword is executed, the PLURAL variable's "top value" is obtained from the stack and assigned to the single-valued variable named in the POP clause. The next value in the plural variable stack then moves to the top of the stack. Because each invocation of the POP keyword removes the top variable from the PLURAL variable stack, a WHILEKNOWN-END loop can be used to extract each value from the stack one at a time, as demonstrated in the example given in Figure 6–5.

Consider the following sequence of clauses from the computer stocks example:

```
RESET   PREFERRED_STOCK
SORT    COMPUTER_STOCKS
POP     COMPUTER_STOCKS, PREFERRED_STOCK
```

The value of the variable PREFERRED_STOCK is reset to UNKNOWN, then the values of the PLURAL variable COMPUTER_STOCKS are sorted into descending order by confidence factor. Next, the value on the top of the COMPUTER_STOCKS list, or stack, is removed (or "popped") and assigned to the variable PREFERRED_STOCK. As a result, COMPUTER_STOCKS is now assigned the following list containing only these values:

```
UNISYS   CNF 85
IBM      CNF 80
WANG     CNF 70
```

The value UNISYS CNF 85 now resides on top of the stack. The value of PREFERRED_STOCK is now DEC CNF 90.

In the HMOFLU1.KBS example in Figure 6–5, the user is asked to select symptoms from a list of six possible symptom types. Because symptom is a PLURAL variable, a user can make up to six symptom selections. Each selection is assigned a separate value. After the user presses END to complete the selection process, the selections are SORTed in descending confidence factor order. The POP and DISPLAY clauses in the WHILEKNOWN-END loop display a message for each of the selected symptoms, starting with the last one chosen. Notice that the RESET clause is used here to reset the variable symptom1 to UNKNOWN. Without it, the last value in the stack would be repeatedly displayed in an endless loop.

If the first variable named in a POP clause is not named in a PLURAL statement, or has no value assigned to it, the POP clause is ignored. In addition, each repeated execution of the POP clause causes the value previously assigned to the single-valued variable to be overwritten with the new one.

SHIP AND RECEIVE KEYWORDS

In VP-Expert, a developer can send and receive text information through ASCII files. This requires use of the SHIP and RECEIVE keywords, which are discussed in the following sections.

SHIP Keyword

The SHIP keyword sends text to a separate file that it writes as an ASCII data file. SHIP is mainly used to transfer data to any external program that is able to read the ASCII file created.

The SHIP keyword is used as follows:

```
SHIP filename, variable
```

The first parameter, filename, is the name of a text file with no extension. If necessary, a path can be specified. The default path is the currently set path. The second parameter is a single-valued variable that contains the text being shipped out.

In Figure 6–6, HMOFLU2.KBS uses the SHIP keyword to place the patient's symptoms in an external file named AILMENTS. Each symptom is transferred to a separate line in the AILMENTS file. The DISPLAY clause is used here so that the user has visible evidence that transfer of the data has occurred, as shown in Figure 6–6.

RECEIVE Keyword

The RECEIVE keyword allows reading and retrieving data from a text or ASCII file. Each line in the file can have up to 80 characters. RECEIVE is often

Figure 6–6. Using the SHIP Keyword

Note: The name of this knowledge base file on the Sample Files disk is HMOFLU2.KBS.
The name of the ASCII data file used is AILMENTS.

```
ACTIONS
     WOPEN 1,1,1,20,77,3
     ACTIVE 1
     DISPLAY "

         ** WELCOME TO THE HMO SERVICE FLU SCREENING ASSISTANT **

         Please indicate the patient's symptom, press the HOME key,
         then enter a two-digit distress level factor.  Complete
         the entry by pressing the ENTER and ARROW keys.  Repeat the
         process until all of the patient's symptoms are accounted for.
         Press the END key when finished to continue the consultation.

              This example demonstrates use of the SHIP keyword.

                         PRESS ANY KEY TO CONTINUE~
"
   WCLOSE 1
   FIND symptom
   WHILEKNOWN symptom
      RESET symptom1
      SORT symptom
      POP symptom, symptom1
      SHIP ailments, symptom1            !SHIP sends found symptoms
      DISPLAY "{#symptom1}."             !to an external file called
   END                                   !AILMENTS
      DISPLAY "SHIP was executed successfully using the AILMENTS file.";

ASK symptom: "What are the patient's most distressing symptoms?";

CHOICES symptom: sore_throat, stomach_ache, headache, nausea,
                 severe_cough, G_I_discomfort;

PLURAL: symptom;
```

This KBS file produced this result after the opening screen.

```
What are the patient's most distressing symptoms?
 sore_throat 11 ◄          stomach_ache 22 ◄          headache 33 ◄
 nausea 66 ◄               severe_cough 55 ◄          G_I_discomfort ◄

nausea CNF 66.
severe cough CNF 55.
G I discomfort CNF 44.
headache CNF 33.
stomach ache CNF 22.
sore throat CNF 11.
SHIP was executed successfully using the AILMENTS file.
```

used to retrieve data from external programs. It is also useful to a KBS developer who wants to keep a rule base file less cluttered. This is possible by using RECEIVE to get text for DISPLAY messages from a separate file. It is also often paired with the SHIP keyword.

The RECEIVE keyword is used as follows:

```
RECEIVE filename, variable
```

The first parameter is the name of an ASCII text file, with specification of a path optional and no file extension. The second parameter must be a variable name into which one line of RECEIVEd text will be placed.

When the RECEIVE clause is executed, the current line is the first line of the file. Subsequent executions extract the next line, and so on. By placing RECEIVE and DISPLAY inside a WHILEKNOWN-END loop, the entire contents of a text file can be displayed during a consultation.

In Figure 6–7, the HMOFLU3.KBS example uses the text stored in the AILMENTS file created by HMOFLU2.KBS from Figure 6–6. The RECEIVE keyword is used to retrieve the symptoms stored in the AILMENTS file.

GRAPHICS CAPABILITIES AND FUNCTIONS

VP-Expert has a graphics mode, or GMODE, that permits the use of graphs. GMODE features require a compatible graphical interface adapter (Hercules, CGA, EGA, or VGA) and a mouse.

Figure 6–7. Using the RECEIVE Keyword

Note: The name of this knowledge base on the Sample Files disk is HMOFLU3.KBS.

```
ACTIONS
    WOPEN 1,1,1,20,77,3
    ACTIVE 1
    DISPLAY "

       ** WELCOME TO THE HMO SERVICE FLU SCREENING ASSISTANT **


         This example demonstrates use of the RECEIVE keyword.

                    PRESS ANY KEY TO CONTINUE~
"
  WCLOSE 1
  WHILEKNOWN symptom
    RESET symptom
    RECEIVE ailments, symptom          !RECEIVEs symptoms from AILMENTS file
    DISPLAY "The patient's most distressing symptoms are {#symptom}."
  END
    DISPLAY "RECEIVE was executed successfully using the AILMENTS file."
    DISPLAY "Note: The confidence factor (CNF) value does not get sent
     to the AILMENTS file.";
```

This KBS file produced this result after the opening screen.

```
The patient's most distressing symptoms are nausea CNF 100.
The patient's most distressing symptoms are severe cough CNF 100.
The patient's most distressing symptoms are G I discomfort CNF 100.
The patient's most distressing symptoms are headache CNF 100.
The patient's most distressing symptoms are stomach ache CNF 100.
The patient's most distressing symptoms are sore throat CNF 100.
The patient's most distressing symptoms are .
RECEIVE was executed successfully using the AILMENTS file.
Note: The confidence factor (CNF) value does not get sent
      to the AILMENTS file.
```

Graphic images, or *icons,* can communicate information immediately if they duplicate images that are already familiar to a user. Also, icons can eliminate the need for users to learn abbreviations or notation.

The GMODE keyword is used whenever the graphics mode is entered. When the GMODE keyword is executed, the normal consultation display is replaced by a graphics screen. To return to the default text-oriented consultation mode (TMODE) from GMODE, it is necessary to use the TMODE keyword. Figure 6–8 lists keywords used when working in the GMODE or graphics mode.

VP-Expert also offers a set of features called Dynamic Images. A **Dynamic Image** is a predefined graphic object, supplied with VP-Expert, that is dynamically linked to the value of a specified variable. When the value of the variable is modified, the graphic object associated with it is updated to reflect the new value. Dynamic Images include a gauge, button, formfield, meter, and time-series graph. They are used to communicate information to the user pictorially, as evident from the example in Figure 6–9. Figure 6–10 gives the KBS file coding for this example.

All Dynamic Images work only in GMODE, even though some are mainly text-based images (FORMFIELD and LBUTTON), while others are more traditional graphic images (METER and BUTTON). All require the specification of X and Y (column and row) coordinates. For text-based images, the X (column) coordinate can be from 0 to 79; the Y (row) coordinate from 0 to 24. For graphic images, the range depends on the present GMODE and screen resolution.

A Dynamic Image is not displayed on the screen until the variable to which it is linked is assigned a specific value other than UNKNOWN. Once it appears on screen, it can be removed by using the RESET keyword to reset the variable to UNKNOWN.

Using Prepared Images

Figures 6–9 and 6–10 (HMODEMO.KBS) give an example of using selected prepared Dynamic Images with a selection of graphic keywords. In the example, the patient's temperature is adjusted in four places—the two meters as well as the two formfield boxes above the meters—whenever a change is made in any *one* of the four places. Meter images are created with the METER keyword and are associated, in this example, with variables named FTEMP (Fahrenheit temperature) and CTEMP (Celsius/Centigrade temperature). All boxes in the figure are created with the FORMFIELD keyword.

SmartForms

Using advanced graphics features, it is possible to build knowledge-based systems with display screens that appear as regular paper forms—the type that one completes when visiting a doctor, preparing taxes, or applying for a loan. Such screens are referred to as **SmartForms** in VP-Expert. The top part of the form in Figure 6–9 is such an example, as is the form in Figure 6–11. A SmartForm has areas called formfields that appear on a simulated form to be filled out by a user.

Some SmartForms have several advantages:

- They avoid the confusion of regular paper forms, which require the user to determine which questions to complete and which to skip over.
- They permit a user to examine an entire group of questions at once and to respond to the formfield in any order.
- They allow the user to go back and modify a prior response.

Figure 6–8. Keywords Used in Graphics

Keyword	Brief Description (Consult the *VP-Expert Manual* for more detail.)
BUTTON	Displays a button image at the X (column) and Y (row) coordinates specified. Pressing a mouse button while pointing to a BUTTON image causes the value of the BUTTON variable to switch from "Yes" to "No" or vice versa.
DBFORM	Displays a vertical array of boxes corresponding to the fields of a .DBF database file
ELLIPSE	Draws an ellipse of given dimensions on the graphics screen
FILL	Fills an enclosed area with the current GCOLOR setting
FORMFIELD	Displays, at the X,Y (column, row) coordinates specified, a rectangular box containing text that is the value in the FORMFIELD variable
GBCOLOR	Sets the background color on the graphics screen
GCLS	Clears the graphics screen
GCOLOR	Sets the foreground color on the graphics screen
GDISPLAY	Displays text in GMODE at the current X (column) and Y (row) coordinates
GLOCATE	Sets the current X,Y (column, row) coordinates in GMODE. A subsequent GDISPLAY clause will begin text at the specified location.
GMODE	Causes a switch to graphics mode, allowing the use of VP-Expert graphics features
HGAUGE	Displays, at the specified X,Y (column, row) coordinates, a graphic horizontal "slide" gauge that has the value of the HGAUGE variable.
HOTREGION	Creates an invisible rectangular "hot region" on the screen. Pressing a mouse button while pointing to an area covered by a hot region causes the value of the HOTREGION variable to switch from "Yes" to "No" or vice versa.
HYPERTEXT	Displays a block of text, retrieved from an external file, that is linked by the current HYPERTEXT variable value. Any HYPERTEXT value is known as a "hyperword."
LBUTTON	Creates a rectangular "label button" image that contains "Yes" or "No" text or the name of the LBUTTON variable
LINETO	Draws a line on the graphics screen from the current X,Y (column, row) coordinates to the X,Y coordinates specified in the LINETO clause
METER	Displays a meter image with a value that is linked to the value in the METER variable
MOUSEOFF	Turns off display of the mouse pointer in GMODE
MOUSEON	Turns on display of the mouse pointer in GMODE
MOVETO	Sets the X,Y (column, row) coordinates before issuing a LINETO command to draw a line on the graphics screen
PSET	Draws a single pixel at the screen location specified by the X,Y (column, row) coordinates
RECTANGLE	Draws a rectangle on the graphics screen dimensioned by the X1,Y1 (upper left corner column and row) and X2,Y2 (lower right corner column and row) coordinates
TMODE	Resumes TMODE (text mode), the default VP-Expert screen mode
TRACK	Displays a time-series graph linked to the last 50 values of the TRACK variable
VGAUGE	Displays a graphic vertical slide gauge linked to the value of the VGAUGE variable

Figure 6–9. Example of Using Two Prepared (Dynamic) Graphic Images (FORMFIELD and METER)

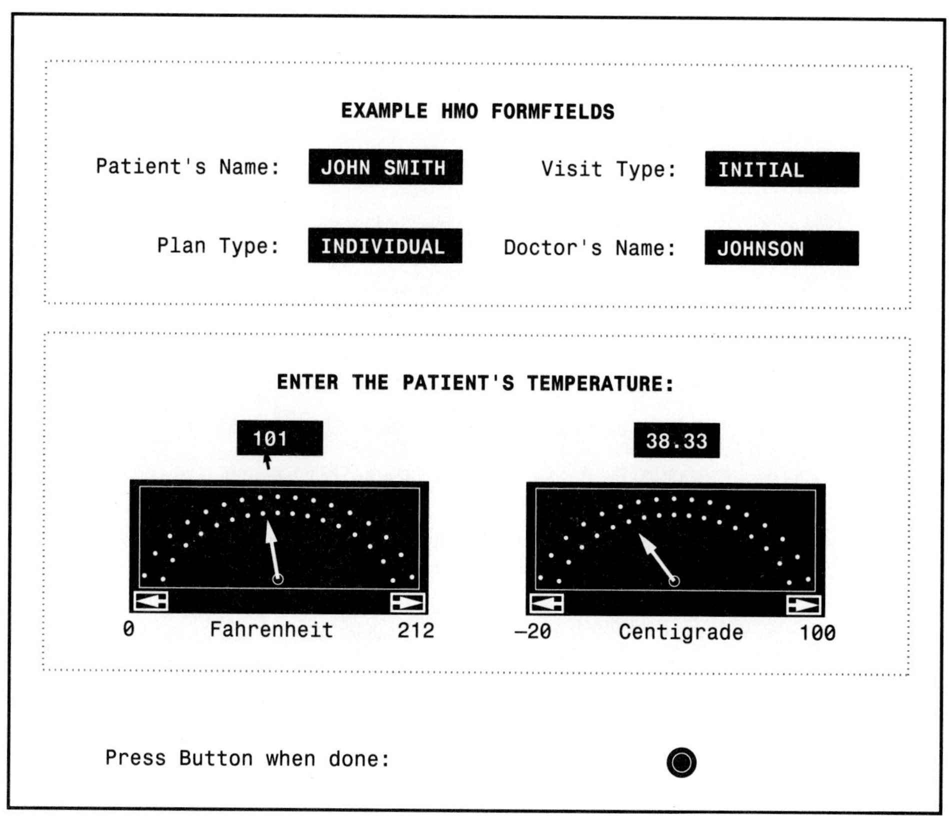

The following section explains the specific requirements to create a SmartForm.

Creation of a SmartForm. Creating a SmartForm, as apparent from the examples in Figures 6–10 and 6–12, requires a GMODE keyword to enter graphics mode, a WHILETRUE-END loop, and, if desired, a TMODE keyword to return to text mode after the user completes the form.

WHENEVER rules are conditions that are tested whenever a given variable is assigned a value. In a SmartForm application, WHENEVER rules may be used to offer advice to the user if certain information is entered into the form, remove irrelevant fields from the form, add new fields to the form, and/or maintain consistency between fields on the form.

A SmartForm application must also include at least two types of statements: a FORMFIELD statement to create the formfield rectangular box, and an LBUTTON statement to make a button labeled DONE or FINISHED, which the user can click on when the form is completed.

Consider the SMARTFM.KBS example given in Figure 6–12. It produces the SmartForm shown in Figure 6–11, which very simply demonstrates the capabilities of this feature. In the KBS file, the variable "temp" is initialized to "needed." It indicates to the user that this field cannot be left blank. When the mouse button is positioned and pressed on this formfield, the user is given the

Figure 6–10. Knowledge Base File to Create the Graphic Example in Figure 6–9

Note: The name of this knowledge base file on the Sample Files disk is HMODEMO.KBS. It requires a graphics-capable computer and a mouse.

```
RUNTIME;
ENDOFF;
BKCOLOR = 1;
ACTIONS
  COLOR = 15
  DISPLAY " HMODEMO.KBS

 This VP-Expert sample file demonstrates the use of
 FORMFIELDs combined with Dynamic Images.

 You must have an EGA or VGA display and a Microsoft-compatible mouse
 installed to use this demonstration rule base properly. You need to
 modify the rule base in order to have it support other display types."

 Find Continue

;  ! -- [ End of Actions ]

Ask Response: "
 Do you wish to procede?";
Choices Response: Yes, No;

Rule Show_Sample
If      Response = Yes
THEN    Continue = Yes
        CLS
        MOUSEON
        GMODE 16
        GCOLOR 15
        GBCOLOR 8
        Done = NO
        RECTANGLE 20, 5, 580, 130
        RECTANGLE 20, 150, 580, 300
        GLOCATE  27 , 2
        GDISPLAY "EXAMPLE HMO FORMFIELDS"
        GLOCATE  22 , 12
        GDISPLAY "ENTER THE PATIENT'S TEMPERATURE:"
        GLOCATE 15, 40
        GDISPLAY "Press Button when done:"
        GLOCATE 19, 21
        GDISPLAY "0  Fahrenheit  212      -20  Centigrade  100"
        FTEMP = 0
        CTEMP = 0
        Patient_Name = NEEDED
        Plan_Type = NEEDED
        Type_Visit = NEEDED
        Doctor_Name = NEEDED
        WHILETRUE Done = NO THEN END
ELSE    Continue = no;

!.......WHENEVER rules.........

WHENEVER FTEMP_Changes
IF    FTEMP <> ((CTEMP*1.8)+32)
THEN  CTEMP = ((FTEMP-32)*0.5555555555);

WHENEVER CTEMP_Changes
IF    CTEMP <> ((FTEMP-32)*0.5555555555)
THEN  FTEMP = ((CTEMP*1.8)+32);


!.......Dynamic Images.......

FORMFIELD Patient_Name: 22, 4, 12, 9;
ASK Patient_Name: "Patient's Name:";
FORMFIELD Plan_Type: 22, 7, 12, 9;
ASK Plan_Type: "Plan Type:";
CHOICES Plan_Type: INDIVIDUAL, FAMILY, GROUP, CO-PAYMENT, OTHER;
FORMFIELD Type_Visit: 55, 4, 10, 9;
ASK Type_Visit: "Visit Type:";
CHOICES Type_Visit: INITIAL, FOLLOW_UP, OTHER;
FORMFIELD Doctor_Name: 55, 7, 12, 9;
ASK Doctor_Name: "Doctor's Name:";


FORMFIELD FTEMP: 25, 15, 5, 8;
FORMFIELD CTEMP: 50, 15, 5, 8;
METER FTEMP: 145, 225, 0, 212;
METER CTEMP: 345, 225, 0, 100;
BUTTON Done: 400, 335, 1, 14;
```

Figure 6–11. Consultation Screen for the Knowledge-based System in Figure 6–12

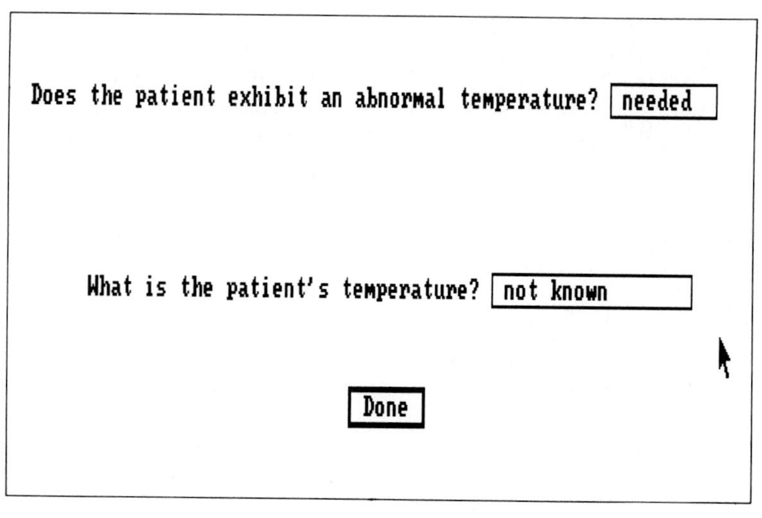

Figure 6–12. Using FORMFIELD and Related Keywords

Note: The name of this knowledge base file on the Sample Files disk is SMARTFM.KBS. It requires a graphics-capable computer and a mouse.

```
ACTIONS
     GMODE 14                           !Enters EGA graphics mode
     MouseAvailable = yes
     Done = no                          !These 4 lines initialize (assign
     temp = needed                      !values to) the variables Done,
     ftemp = not_known                  !Temp, and ftemp, causing
                                        !linked dynamic objects to appear
                                        !on screen.

     WHILETRUE Done = no THEN           !This loop keeps the form on
     END                                !screen until the user clicks on
                                        !the LBUTTON labeled 'Done.'

     TMODE;                             !Resumes text mode after loop
                                        !ends.

     LBUTTON Done: 37,20;               !Displays a button labeled 'Done.'
                                        !When the user clicks on this
                                        !button, variable Done is assigned
                                        !a 'yes' value and form disappears.
                                        !(Clicking on LBUTTONs toggle 'yes,'
                                        !'no' values.)

     FORMFIELD temp: 60, 7, 7;          !Displays a formfield showing the
                                        !value 'needed,' as assigned in the
                                        !ACTIONS Block.

     ASK temp: "Does the patient exhibit an abnormal temperature?";
     CHOICES temp: YES, NO;             !Labels the 'temp' formfield
                                        !and provides a menu of two choices.

     WHENEVER temp_status               !This WHENEVER rule is tested any
          IF temp = YES                 !time the variable temp is
          THEN ftemp = REQUIRED         !assigned a value. It passes if
          ELSE ftemp = NOT_REQUIRED     !temperature has a 'yes' value.

     FORMFIELD ftemp: 50, 15, 15;
     ASK ftemp: "What is the patient's temperature?";

     WHENEVER MouseAvailable
          IF MouseAvailable = yes
          THEN MOUSEON;

     WHENEVER temp1
          IF ftemp < 98.7
          THEN ftemp = normal;

     WHENEVER temp2
          IF ftemp > 98.6 and ftemp < 100.1
          THEN ftemp = abnormal;

     WHENEVER temp3
          IF ftemp > 100.0
          THEN ftemp = serious;
```

choice of either "YES" or "NO." If "YES" is selected, the next formfield, ftemp, will display the message "REQUIRED" and the user is alerted to enter a temperature. Depending on the entered number, the knowledge base returns the message "normal," "abnormal," or "serious." If "NO" is selected, the message "not required" appears in the second formfield.

In the HMODEMO.KBS example given in Figures 6–9 and 6–10, all formfields are initialized to "NEEDED." The fields "Patient's Name" and "Doctor's Name" require the user to type in the needed information. The "Plan Type" and "Visit Type" fields require the user to select from several choices, as indicated by the CHOICES statements in Figure 6–10.

The bottom half of the screen in Figure 6–9 demonstrates the use of the METER keyword. When the user indicates the patient's body temperature in either Fahrenheit or Centigrade, the corresponding meter and value adjusts to equal the value chosen.

Customized Objects

It is possible to create customized graphic objects by combining drawing keywords (such as ELLIPSE, FILL, GBCOLOR, GCOLOR, LINETO, MOVETO, PSET, and/or RECTANGLE) with the HOTREGION keyword. For instance, one could draw an image of a car with the front and rear tires and the windows designated as "hot regions," as shown in the CARPICT.KBS example given in Figures 6–13 and 6–14. If the user presses the mouse button while pointing to a hot region, or to a corresponding formfield button, the value of the linked variable changes from YES to NO, or vice versa. In this example, a hot region turns to blinking after being selected.

Hypertext

Hypertext is a VP-Expert feature that displays text information from an external file whenever a user encounters a hot word or button designated by the developer. This could be useful when a developer wants to alert the user of

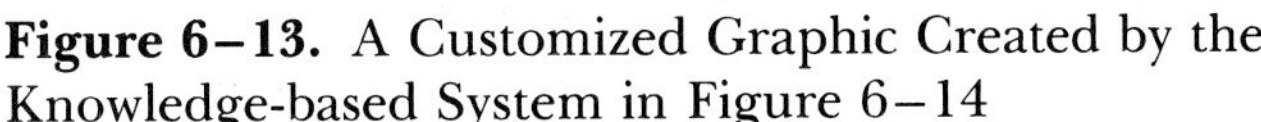

Figure 6–13. A Customized Graphic Created by the Knowledge-based System in Figure 6–14

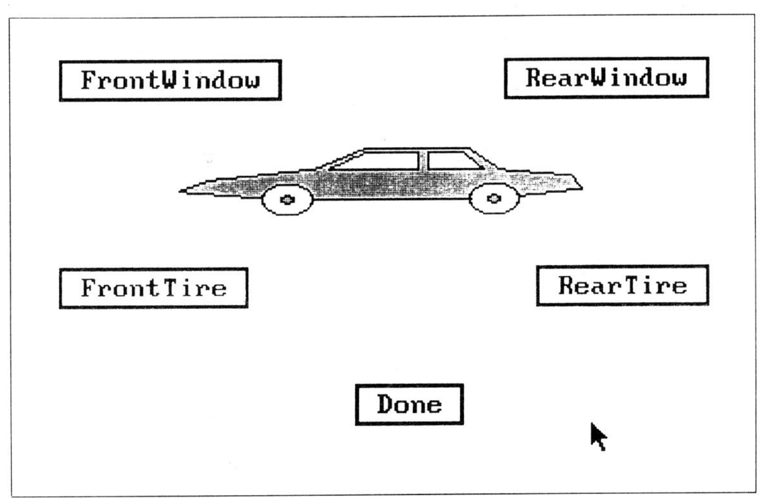

Figure 6–14. Knowledge Base File to Create the Custom Graphic Shown in Figure 6–13

Note: The name of this knowledge base file on the Sample Files disk is CARPICT.KBS
It requires a graphics-capable computer and a mouse.

```
RUNTIME;
ENDOFF;
BKCOLOR = 1;
ACTIONS
  MOUSEOFF
  COLOR = 15
  CLS
  DISPLAY " CARPICT.KBS

 This VP-Expert release 2 sample file demonstrates the ability of the
 graphic primitives combined with label buttons and WHENEVER rules.

 You must have an EGA or VGA display and a Microsoft-compatible mouse
 installed to use this demonstration rule base properly.  You need to
 modify the rule base in order to have it support other display types."

 Find Continue

;  ! -- [ End of Actions ]

Ask Response: "
 Do you wish to procede?";
Choices Response: Yes, No;

Rule Show_Sample
If     Response = Yes
THEN   Continue = Yes
       CLS
       MOUSEON
       GMODE 16
       FrontTire = no
       RearTire = no
       FrontWindow = no
       RearWindow = no
       Image = car
       Done = NO
       WHILETRUE Done = NO THEN END
ELSE   Continue = no;

WHENEVER pict_car
IF Image = CAR
THEN
! Draw the tires

GCOLOR 15
ELLIPSE 200,70,225,85
ELLIPSE 209,75,216,80
GCOLOR 11
FILL 213,78,15
GCOLOR 15
ELLIPSE 300,70,325,85
ELLIPSE 309,75,316,80
GCOLOR 11
FILL 313,78,15

! Draw the body outline of the car

GCOLOR 15
MOVETO 224,77
LINETO 301,77
MOVETO 200,76
LINETO 160,73
LINETO 175,68
LINETO 225,63
LINETO 250,53
LINETO 300,53
LINETO 315,63
LINETO 350,66
LINETO 355,73
LINETO 325,76

! Draw front window

MOVETO 232,63
LINETO 250,55
LINETO 275,55
LINETO 275,63
LINETO 232,63
```

```
! Draw rear window

MOVETO 280,63
LINETO 280,55
LINETO 297,55
LINETO 307,63
LINETO 280,63

! Paint the car

GCOLOR 14
FILL 260,70,15;

!.......WHENEVER rules to handle mouse-downs on HOTREGIONs........

WHENEVER Ftire
IF    FrontTire = yes
THEN  GLOCATE 19, 16
      GDISPLAY "You have selected the front tire.  "
      FOR Loop = 1 to 10
        GCOLOR 12
        FILL 205, 75, 15
        GCOLOR 0
        FILL 205, 75, 15
      END
      FrontTire = no;

WHENEVER Rtire
IF    RearTire = yes
THEN  GLOCATE 19, 16
      GDISPLAY "You have selected the rear tire.   "
      FOR Loop = 1 to 10
        GCOLOR 12
        FILL 305, 75, 15
        GCOLOR 0
        FILL 305, 75, 15
      END
      RearTire = no;

WHENEVER Fwindow
IF    FrontWindow = yes
THEN  GLOCATE 19, 16
      GDISPLAY "You have selected the front window."
      FOR Loop = 1 to 10
        GCOLOR 12
        FILL 250, 60, 15
        GCOLOR 0
        FILL 250, 60, 15
      END
      FrontWindow = no;

WHENEVER Rwindow
IF    RearWindow = yes
THEN  GLOCATE 19, 16
      GDISPLAY "You have selected the rear window. "
      FOR Loop = 1 to 10
        GCOLOR 12
        FILL 300, 60, 15
        GCOLOR 0
        FILL 300, 60, 15
      END
      RearWindow = no;


!........."Hidden" dynamic regions of the car graphic.........

HOTREGION FrontTire: 200, 70, 225, 85;
HOTREGION RearTire: 300, 70, 325, 85;
HOTREGION FrontWindow: 232, 55, 275, 63;
HOTREGION RearWindow: 280, 55, 307, 63;

!.........Label Buttons to allow easy access to a specific HOTREGION.......


LBUTTON FrontTire: 14, 9, 9, 10, FrontTire;
LBUTTON RearTire: 43, 9, 9, 10, RearTire;
LBUTTON FrontWindow: 14, 2, 9, 10, FrontWindow;
LBUTTON RearWindow: 41, 2, 9, 10, RearWindow;
LBUTTON Done: 32, 13, 0, 7, Done;
```

important information related to an action during a consultation. It can also be used effectively for displaying prompts and messages to users. When properly employed, hypertext can greatly increase system usability.

Hypertext is similar to RECEIVE text in that it is stored in an external file and read into a KBS file when required during a consultation. Hypertext, however, has a number of important differences:

- Hypertext can be used only in GMODE.
- Hypertext is displayed whenever a user clicks a mouse button over a hot word or button.
- Hypertext automatically appears inside a pop-up window.

An example of hypertext use is given in Figure 6–15.

Figure 6–16 shows the meaning of the parameters associated with the HYPERTEXT keyword. The first parameter is a variable name. For example, Topic is the name of the variable used with the HYPERTEXT keyword in Figure 6–15. Whenever this variable is assigned a value, it is considered by VP-Expert to be a *hyperword* whose text can be found in the associated .TXT file, which is named in the sixth parameter (in the example given in Figure 6–15, the

Figure 6–15. Example of Using HYPERTEXT Keyword

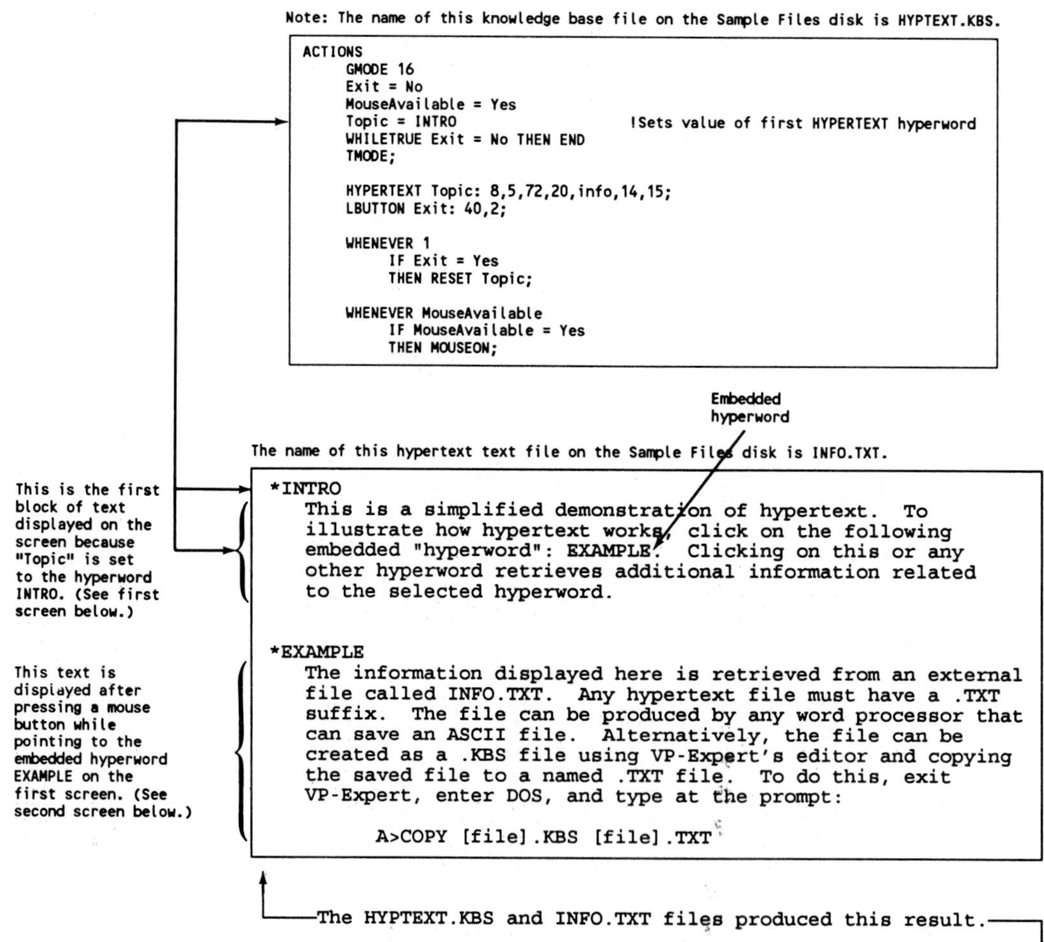

Figure 6–15 *continued*

Screen 1: Display for the INTRO hyperword.

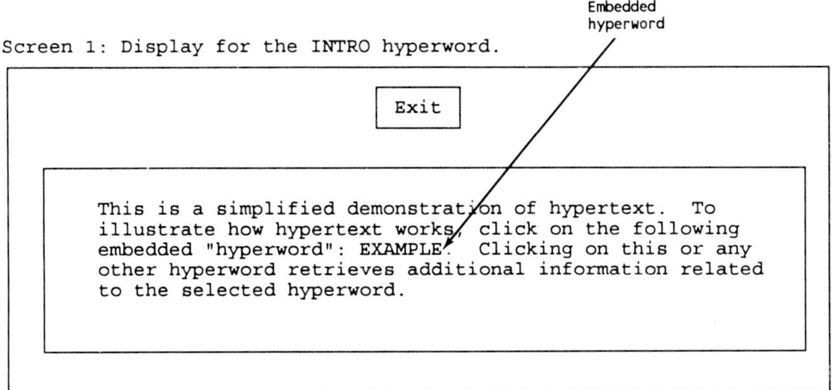

Screen 2: Display for the EXAMPLE hyperword.

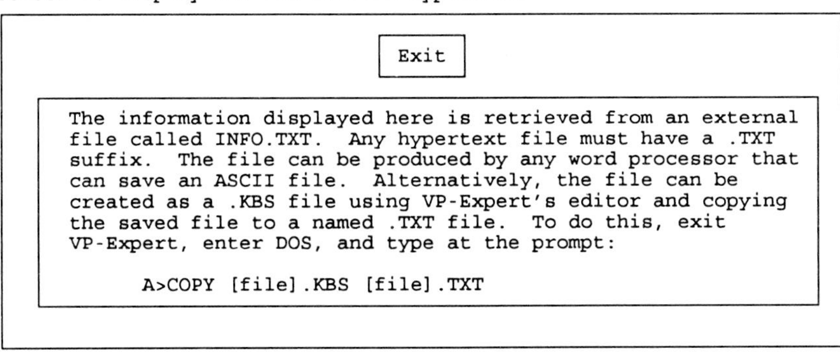

file is named info). Then the associated text contained in the file appears on the screen.

When displayed, hypertext can include embedded hot words, displayed in uppercase letters, called HYPERWORDS by VP-Expert. They cause the current text to be replaced with new text related to the chosen hyperword. For example, if this paragraph were HYPERTEXT text, a user could click on one of the two uppercase words, HYPERWORDS and HYPERTEXT. This would call a block of text to the display (in a window) on the subject of hyperwords or hypertext—whichever a user had chosen. In the sample file shown in Figure 6–15, the hyperwords are INTRO and EXAMPLE.

In a VP-Expert consultation, it is necessary to remove the hypertext window from the screen when it is no longer needed. One way to remove a hypertext window is to use the LBUTTON keyword to create an exit mechanism that users can click on when finished reading hypertext.

Although graphic capabilities and hypertext have been discussed here separately, they can be used together. The imaginative developer can create knowledge-based systems that use all these GMODE features. Imagine, for example, a SmartForm that uses hypertext to explain various sections of a questionnaire, or a KBS that combines graphics with hypertext to assist in PC repair. The latter system could display a custom-drawn graphic of the interior of a PC, with certain hardware designated as hot regions. When the user clicks on a specified hot region, hypertext or another graphic image corresponding to that region would appear.

Figure 6–16. The HYPERTEXT Keyword

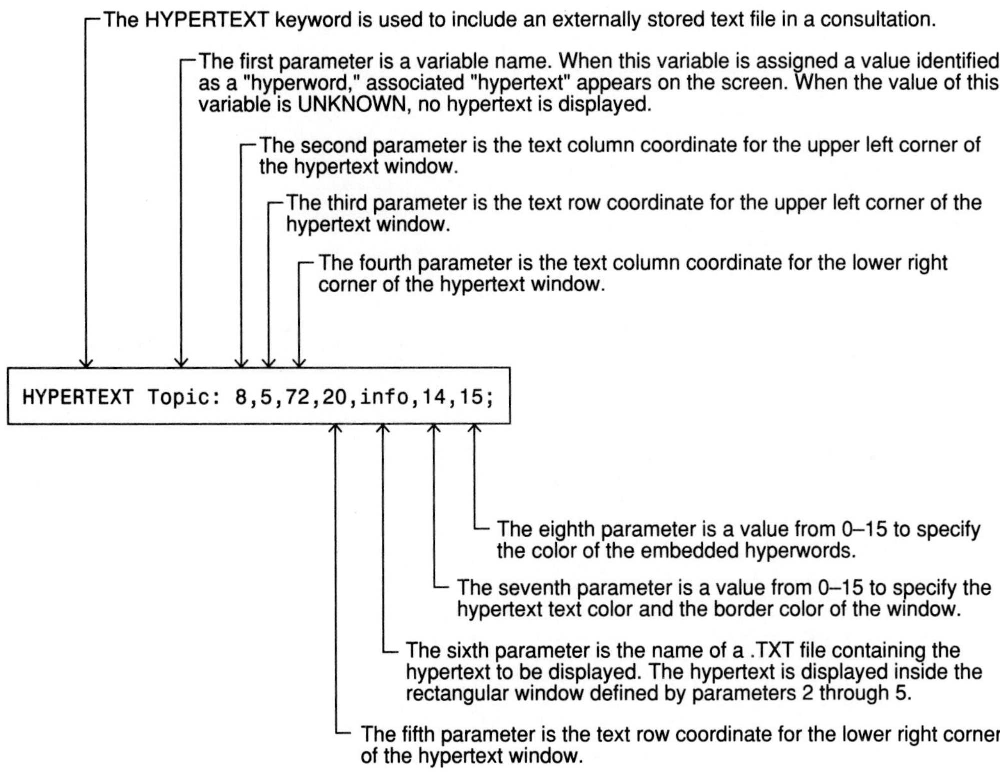

BCALL, CALL, AND CCALL KEYWORDS

One of VP-Expert's most useful features is its ability to call external program files. This capability allows a knowledge-based system to exit temporarily to perform the functions and operations of other software. A creative developer can build a KBS file that invokes sophisticated mathematical analysis programs or advanced telecommunications, a Pascal or BASIC routine, or spreadsheet operations, among others. A discussion of each type of VP-Expert call is given in the following sections.

BCALL Keyword

A developer can use BCALL (or batch program call) to run another program during a consultation.

A batch file is any so-called text or ASCII file. Most word processors can create ASCII text files. A word processing or DOS User's Guide should be consulted for more information about batch files.

An example of BCALL use is contained in the KBS in Figure 6–17. It helps schedule the number of doctors to assign in a hospital. After a user enters the day of the week planned for, as well as the anticipated weather on that day, the KBS uses BCALL to run a neural network program.

Figure 6–17. Using BCALL to Call a Batch .BAT File

Note: The name of this knowledge base file on the Sample Files disk is DOCTORS.KBS.

```
ACTIONS
     BCALL Reset                     !Invokes RESET.BAT file which deletes
                                     !       previous consultation files
     FIND Day                        !Makes system look for 1st variable
     FIND Weather                    !Makes system look for 2nd variable
     SHIP Patient, Day               !Puts day of week in Patient file
     SHIP Patient, Weather           !Puts expected weather in Patient file
     BCALL Nuroshll                  !Invokes NUROSHLL.BAT file which
                                     !       manages the flow of information
                                     !       with the neural network
     RECEIVE Patient, Patients       !Reads value in Patient text file back
                                     !       into VP-Expert
     FIND Doctors;                   !Fires rule set

Rule 1      IF  Patients <= 60
            AND Day < 6
            THEN Doctors = 8;

Rule 2      IF  Patients > 60
            AND Day < 6
            THEN Doctors = 12;

Rule 3      IF Patients <= 60
            AND Day > 5
            THEN Doctors = 14;

Rule 4      IF Patients > 60
            AND Day > 5
            THEN Doctors = 18;

ASK Day: "What day of the week is being planned for?
               1 = Sunday        5 = Thursday
               2 = Monday        6 = Friday
               3 = Tuesday       7 = Saturday
               4 = Wednesday";
CHOICES Day: 1, 2, 3, 4, 5, 6, 7;

ASK Weather: "Rate the weather expected using the following scale:
                     1 = Clear
                     2 = Cloudy
                     3 = Rainy
                     4 = Heavy rain, thunder";
CHOICES Weather: 1, 2, 3, 4;
```

This KBS file produced this result.

```
What day of the week is being planned for?
               1 = Sunday        5 = Thursday
               2 = Monday        6 = Friday
               3 = Tuesday       7 = Saturday
               4 = Wednesday
1                       2                       3
4                       5 ◄                     6
7

Rate the weather expected using the following scale:
                     1 = Clear
                     2 = Cloudy
                     3 = Rainy
                     4 = Heavy rain, thunder
1                       2 ◄                     3
4

[ RULES ]                          [ FACTS ]
Finding Doctors                    Patients = 54.8419 CNF 100
Testing 1                          Doctors = 8 CNF 100
RULE 1 IF
Patients <= 60 AND
Day < 6
THEN
Doctors = 8 CNF 100
```

In the example, the BCALL clause executes a DOS batch (.BAT) command file. Figure 6–18 gives an example of the batch files used (for reference only). At the conclusion of the batch file's execution, the VP-Expert consultation resumes where it left off.

The format of the BCALL clause is

```
BCALL filename
```

The SHIP keyword is used in the example to send data to an external ASCII file, which the neural network program uses to get data input. The neural net then uses its training on historical data to come up with the number of patients to expect. The number is received back into the KBS with the RECEIVE keyword. Then, based on the number of patients to expect and the day of the week planned for, the KBS recommends the number of doctors to schedule for duty.

A path can be optionally specified using the same format as that used by DOS. This informs VP-Expert where to locate the named file. The default is the currently set path. The filename supplied to the BCALL clause must be the name of an existing DOS file with a .BAT extension. The .BAT extension does not have to be provided.

Figure 6–18. Batch Files Used in DOCTORS.KBS File in Figure 6–17

A. NUROSHLL.BAT file manages the flow of information with the neural network.

(Note: The name of this ASCII text file on the Sample Files disk is NUROSHLL.BAT.)

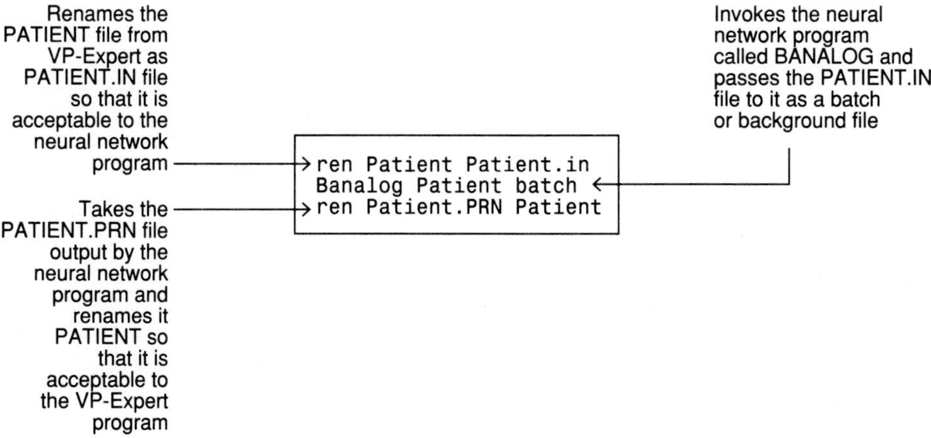

B. RESET.BAT file deletes previous consultation files (before starting a new consultation).

(Note: The name of this ASCII text file on the Sample Files disk is RESET.BAT.)

```
del Patient.in
del Patient
```

CALL Keyword

The CALL keyword suspends a VP-Expert consultation and loads an .EXE (or executable) program file. When execution of the program is completed, the KBS consultation resumes where it left off. More computer random access memory than is normally needed for running the .EXE program may be required.

The format to use CALL is as follows:

```
CALL filename
```

A path can optionally be specified using the same format as that used by DOS. This informs the KBS about where to find the named file. The default is the present path. The .EXE extension does not have to be provided.

CCALL Keyword

The CCALL keyword suspends a consultation and executes the named file. The filename supplied must be the name of a DOS command with a .COM (or command file) extension. The COM extension must not be explicitly provided, or a syntax error will result. When execution of the .COM program is finished, the consultation resumes where it left off. More computer random access memory than is normally necessary for the .COM program may be required.

The format for using the CCALL clause is

```
CCALL filename
```

As with CALL and BCALL, a path may be optionally specified using the identical format used by DOS.

FORMAT KEYWORD

The FORMAT keyword is used in conjunction with a DISPLAY or PDISPLAY clause to provide a format for displaying a floating-point number.

The keyword is used as follows:

```
FORMAT variable, integer1.integer2
```

The first parameter, variable, is the name of a variable that has a numeric value. The second parameter, integer1, specifies the total number of places, including decimal point, to format the variable. The last parameter, integer2, specifies the number of decimal places (to the right of the decimal point) to format the variable.

REVIEW QUESTIONS

1. What is the purpose of the MENU_SIZE keyword?
2. Name one way to prevent an "out-of-memory" condition caused by too many large menus being used in a KBS.
3. Why is it sometimes necessary to CLOSE a database file during a KBS consultation?

4. Discuss some uses for the RECORD_NUM keyword.
5. What are two methods of accessing spreadsheet data? What are the advantages and disadvantages of both?
6. What is a subscript?
7. How can a KBS arrange PLURAL variables by user preference order?
8. How is the POP keyword used to control separate values of a PLURAL variable?
9. How are data in an ASCII text file sent and received by a KBS?
10. How does the use of graphic images, or icons, enhance a KBS?
11. Identify three graphic capabilities of VP-Expert.
12. What keywords are used by a KBS to call external program files?
13. How is the FORMAT keyword used?

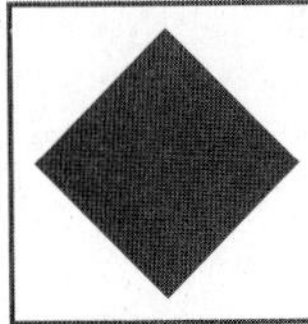

EXERCISES

1. This exercise explores how advanced database features appear in a consultation. It uses the HMODB1S.KBS file illustrated in Figure 6–1.
   a. Run a consultation with the knowledge base HMODB1S.KBS from the Sample Files disk. Use the "Procedure for Running a Consultation," given in Chapter 3, Figure 3–2, to run the consultation. Make any responses to the questions asked.
   b. Run another consultation entering different responses.
   c. Compare and record the results observed from the two consultations.
2. This exercise explores the mechanics of the SORT and POP keywords. It uses the HMOFLU1.KBS file illustrated in Figure 6–5.
   a. Run a consultation with the knowledge base HMOFLU1.KBS from the Sample Files disk. Make any responses desired to the questions asked and include a confidence factor value for each selection chosen.
   b. Run another consultation entering different confidence factors.
   c. Compare and record the results observed from the two consultations.
3. This exercise explores how the SHIP and RECEIVE keywords work. It uses the HMOFLU2.KBS and HMOFLU3.KBS files illustrated in Figures 6–6 and 6–7.
   a. Run a consultation with the knowledge base HMOFLU2.KBS from the Sample Files disk. Make any response desired to the question asked.
   b. At the conclusion of the consultation, exit VP-Expert and examine the contents of the external text file the SHIP keyword created. To do this, you must get to the DOS prompt. If your copy of VP-Expert is on a diskette drive, type

      ```
      A:>TYPE AILMENTS
      ```

      or alternatively, if you are working with a hard drive, type

      ```
      C:>cd\(directory_name)
      C:> TYPE AILMENTS
      ```

   c. Examine and record the contents of the AILMENTS file.
   d. Run a consultation with the knowledge base HMOFLU3.KBS from the Sample Files disk.
   e. Record the results observed from the consultation.

4. This exercise explores the features of a SmartForm. It uses the SMARTFM.KBS file illustrated in Figure 6–12. (Note: You will need a computer equipped with graphics and a mouse to complete this exercise.)
   - **a.** Run a consultation with the knowledge base SMARTFM.KBS from the Sample Files disk.
   - **b.** Make any response as indicated.
   - **c.** Record the results.
   - **d.** Run another consultation with the knowledge base SMARTFM.KBS from the Sample Files disk.
   - **e.** Choose different responses from the previous consultation.
   - **f.** Compare and record the results observed from the two consultations.
5. This exercise explores SmartForm features as well as other graphic features. It uses the HMODEMO.KBS file illustrated in Figure 6–10. (Note: You will need a computer equipped with graphics and a mouse to complete this exercise.)
   - **a.** Run a consultation with the knowledge base HMODEMO.KBS from the Sample Files disk.
   - **b.** Make any responses as indicated.
   - **c.** Observe and record the results obtained when a temperature is entered in either the Fahrenheit or Centigrade fields.
   - **d.** Run another consultation with the knowledge base HMODEMO.KBS.
   - **e.** Choose different responses from the previous consultation, including the figures in the Fahrenheit and/or Centigrade fields.
   - **f.** Compare and record the results of the two consultations.
6. The file FORMDEMO.KBS further demonstrates how to create entry systems based on SmartForms with Dynamic Images. (Note: You will need a computer equipped with graphics and a mouse to complete this exercise.)
   - **a.** Run a consultation with the knowledge base FORMDEMO.KBS from the Sample Files disk.
   - **b.** Make any response as indicated.
   - **c.** Record the results.
   - **d.** Run another consultation with the knowledge base FORMDEMO.KBS from the Sample Files disk.
   - **e.** Choose different responses from the previous consultation.
   - **f.** Compare and record the results observed from the two consultations.
7. This exercise explores the custom graphics features of VP-Expert. It uses the CARPICT.KBS file illustrated in Figure 6–14. (Note: You will need a computer equipped with graphics and a mouse to complete this exercise.)
   - **a.** Run a consultation with the knowledge base CARPICT.KBS from the Sample Files disk.
   - **b.** Click on the various "hot regions" on the car itself or the labels in the formfield boxes.
   - **c.** Observe and record the results.
   - **d.** Run several other consultations with CARPICT and study the printout of the code (Figure 6–14) during the consultations. Studying it in this manner can be very informative.
   - **e.** Consider using this custom graphics capability to enhance a knowledge-base system of your own design.
8. This exercise explores hypertext. It uses the HYPTEXT.KBS file illustrated in Figure 6–15. (Note: You will need a computer equipped with graphics and a mouse to complete this exercise.)
   - **a.** Run a consultation with the HYPTEXT.KBS knowledge base from the Sample Files disk.
   - **b.** Observe and record the results.

c. Exit VP-Expert and examine the contents of the external text file named INFO.TXT on the Sample Files disk. To do this, type

```
A:>TYPE INFO.TXT
```

or, if you are using a hard disk, type

```
C:>cd\(directory_name)
C:> TYPE INFO.TXT
```

d. Examine and make note of the results.

9. This exercise further explores hypertext. It uses the README.KBS file on the Sample Files disk. During a consultation, it uses the text file README.TXT. Repeat the instructions for Exercise 8. In part c, substitute README.TXT for INFO.TXT.

10. This exercise explores KBS integration with a neural network program through the use of a batch program. It uses the BCALL keyword contained in the DOCTORS.KBS file, illustrated in Figure 6–17, and a trained neural network called PATIENT.NET. The neural network is used to predict patient loads in a health care facility, based on the day of the week and the expected weather conditions. Patient load information is sent back to the DOCTORS.KBS, which then estimates the doctor staffing needed to meet patient load requirements. The integration between the KBS and the neural network occurs in the background and is largely invisible to a user.
    a. Run a consultation with the knowledge base DOCTORS.KBS from the Sample Files disk. Make any responses desired to the questions asked.
    b. Run another consultation entering different responses.
    c. Compare and record the results observed from the two consultations.

7

SUMMARY REFERENCE GUIDE

This chapter is designed to be a summary, as well as a reference guide, to the keywords and features covered in the tutorial in Part One of this book. It provides a single reference source to supplement information contained in Part One. In addition, this summary reference guide covers new material of interest to KBS developers, including

- Instructions to install VP-Expert
- Error messages

The *VP-Expert Manual* that comes with the full professional version of VP-Expert should be consulted if further detail is required.

SYSTEM REQUIREMENTS

VP-Expert runs on an IBM Personal Computer and compatible (clone) computers with

- 512K or more RAM
- DOS version 2.0 or higher

To use the graphics features, an IBM CGA, EGA, or VGA, a Hercules monochrome graphics adapter, or a compatible video adapter (graphics card) is required.

The software may not run with certain co-resident (terminate and stay ready—TSR) programs.

EDUCATIONAL VERSION LIMITATIONS

1. The size of the knowledge base is limited to 16 Kbytes.

2. The maximum number of knowledge base files that can be chained together is three.
3. The maximum number of database file records that can be read is 150.

INSTALLATION

It is strongly recommended that a duplicate backup copy of the disk accompanying this book be made. Save the original in a safe place and use the backup, or working copy, of the disk to install the programs onto diskettes or a hard drive. (Note: The distribution disk contains so-called zipped, or compressed, files. Files first must be unzipped to be usable. This is accomplished by running the Install program. Specific instructions follow.)

In this summary, the DOS prompt that is displayed on the screen is underlined. For instance, in A:\>install <Enter>, the A:\> is displayed by the computer on the screen. You would type only Install and then press Enter.

FOR A DISKETTE-DRIVE ONLY COMPUTER (NO HARD DRIVE)

If your computer has only diskette drives, place the distribution disk in drive A, change to an A> prompt, and type this command:

```
A:>install a: b:
```

At the first menu, choose option 1—Diskette Drive. This assumes that you have two high-density diskette drives and two formatted high-density diskettes ready to accept the unzipped files. Follow the instructions displayed.

When finished, label the first diskette created during the installation procedure "Sample Files." This diskette contains the VP-Expert shell program itself, as well as the systems referenced in Chapters 2 through 6. The second diskette should be labeled "Prototype Systems." These are the systems discussed in Part Two of this book, Chapters 8 through 10.

It is advisable to make a duplicate (backup) copy of the (unzipped) Sample Files diskette. The backup should be used as a working copy to do the exercises in Chapters 2 through 6. Before doing the exercises a second or third time, make a fresh working copy diskette to ensure that the correct sample files are used.

To start the program, insert the Sample Files diskette into the A: or B: disk drive and type VPX <Enter>.

FOR A HARD-DISK-DRIVE COMPUTER

The programs and files can be copied to a hard disk drive. There must be at least two megabytes of storage available on the hard disk. To check available hard disk storage space, log onto the hard disk (assumed to be the C: drive; if your hard disk is not the C: drive, substitute your hard disk identifier where you see C:) and enter the following command:

```
C:\>CHKDSK <Enter>
```

The amount of available disk space in bytes will be given.

It is helpful if the DOS prompt displays the path to the current subdirectory. This can be done by issuing this command:

```
C:\>prompt $p$g <Enter>
```

This installation is designed to begin at the root directory of the hard drive. If you are in the root directory, the prompt should display C:\>.

If you are in a subdirectory, for example, a subdirectory called WP, you can return to the root directory by entering the following command:

```
C:\WP>cd\
```

The prompt should now read C:\>.

Now place the distribution diskette in the A: drive. Change to the A: prompt by typing the following command:

```
C:\>A: <Enter>
```

Begin the install program by typing the following command:

```
A:>install a: c: <Enter>
```

At the opening menu of the install program, choose option 2—Hard Drive. Follow the instructions displayed to install the programs and files.

Once the installation is completed, change to the VP-Expert subdirectory by issuing the following command:

```
C:\>cd\VPEXPERT
```

The VP-Expert program is started by issuing the command vpx at the prompt. The screen should look like this:

```
C:\VPEXPERT>vpx <Enter>
```

PRINTING THE SAMPLE FILES

It is possible to get a printed copy of the knowledge bases provided on the disk. This is easily accomplished using the DOS print utility (PRINT.COM), the DOS COPY command, or a word processor. To use PRINT.COM, type the following command after DOS has been loaded into your computer's memory:

```
print filename.kbs
```

The computer will respond with the message

```
Name of list device (PRN):
```

If your printer is LPT1, press Enter to continue. If your printer is LPT2 or COM1, enter that information and then press Enter. If you do not know what to enter, experimentation usually produces good results.

To use the DOS COPY command, enter the following:

```
COPY filename.kbs lpt1
```

The sample knowledge base files are ASCII text files. To use your word processor to print the .KBS files, follow your system's instructions for retrieving and printing DOS or ASCII text files.

OBTAINING HELP

From anywhere in VP-Expert, you can press F1 to receive immediate help on the screen. Once in the Help sub-system, press the ESC escape key to bring up the

Topics Menu. Page through it for the keyword of interest. To get a printout of any material of interest from the Help sub-system

- Have the desired information displayed on the screen
- Check to see that your printer is on
- Press the Print Screen key on your computer, or the Shift and PrtSc key combination.

The Help sub-system is not available while a consultation session is in progress.

GENERAL KEYWORDS SUMMARY

Keyword	*Description*
ACTIONS	Must begin the Actions Block, which controls the action of a consultation
ACTIVE	Causes subsequent display text to appear in the specified window defined by a WOPEN keyword
ASK	Used to query the user for values to be assigned to a variable when the inference engine fails to find any values in the rules
AUTOQUERY	In the absence of an appropriate ASK statement, this statement automatically generates a generic question asking the user for a value to be assigned to the required variable.
BCALL	Executes a DOS batch (.BAT) command file
BKCOLOR	Used to set the background color of the consultation screen
CALL	Loads a DOS execution (.EXE) program file
CCALL	Executes a named DOS command (.COM) file
CHOICES	Used in conjunction with the ASK or AUTOQUERY statement to present a menu of allowable values that can be assigned to the requested variable. A CHOICES keyword may be followed by no more than 10 variables.
CLS	Used to clear the consultation window
COLOR	Used to set text color to be displayed
DISPLAY	Displays text and values in the consultation window
EJECT	Ejects the remainder of a page from the printer
END	The last word of a WHILEKNOWN-END loop
ENDOFF	Eliminates the need to hit the End key when finished choosing from a CHOICES menu
EXECUTE	Used to initiate a consultation automatically when Consult is chosen from the Main Menu. It eliminates the extra step of having to select Go from the Consult Menu before the consultation starts.
FIND	Used in a consultation to find goals
FORMAT	Used with a DISPLAY or PDISPLAY clause to provide a format for displaying a floating-point number
PDISPLAY	Prints text and values on the printer only. Text can contain a maximum of 1,000 characters, including spaces.

PLURAL	Used to declare a variable as one that may be assigned more than one value in a consultation. A PLURAL keyword may be followed by no more than 10 variables.
POP	Used to manipulate the separate values of a plural variable individually. When executed, the plural variable's top value is taken from the "stack" and assigned to the single-valued variable named in the clause.
PRINTOFF	Disables PRINTON
PRINTON	Prints text and values to both the screen and the printer
RECEIVE	Imports the current line of the named text file into a VP-Expert variable. Each line may be up to 80 characters in length.
RESET	Reinitializes a variable to the value UNKNOWN
RULE	Used to represent the expert knowledge in a knowledge base
RUNTIME	Eliminates the rules and facts windows from the consultation screen. Usually added after a system has been completely developed.
SHIP	Stores the contents of the named variable as the last item in the text file named in the SHIP clause
SORT	Sorts the values of a plural variable into descending order of confidence factor
TRUTHTHRESH	Sets the minimum confidence value required to fire a RULE
WHILEKNOWN	First word of a WHILEKNOWN-END loop. A WHILEKNOWN-END loop executes all clauses contained between the keywords WHILEKNOWN and END, provided that the variable used to control the loop has a value other than UNKNOWN whenever END is reached. Only one WHILEKNOWN-END loop can be active at one time.
WOPEN	Used with a corresponding ACTIVE keyword to generate windows around text displays during a consultation. A knowledge base can contain a maximum of nine WOPEN keywords.

DATABASE KEYWORDS SUMMARY

Keyword	*Description*
ALL	Used with GET and MENU keywords to indicate that no special condition needs to be met when selecting a record
CLOSE	Closes an open database file and resets the record pointer to the top (first record) of the database file

GET	Used to retrieve values from a database file
MENU	Used in conjunction with the ASK statement to generate a menu of allowable values that can be assigned to a variable based on the field values of a database file
MENU_SIZE	Specifies the number of options/values in a menu generated by the MENU command
MRESET	Releases the memory allocated to the last menu created with the MENU command
PUT	Used to update or change a record in a database file
RECORD_NUM	System variable that holds the number/value of the last database record accessed by the GET command

SPREADSHEET KEYWORDS SUMMARY

Keyword	*Description*
COLUMN	Used with the WKS or PWKS keywords to identify a column location in a spreadsheet
NAMED	Used with the WKS or PWKS keywords to identify a cell range in a spreadsheet
PWKS	Used to transfer values from a knowledge base variable into a spreadsheet
ROW	Used with the WKS or PWKS keywords to identify a row location in spreadsheet
WFORMAT	Defines the cell format for numeric values that will be transferred to a spreadsheet with the PWKS keyword
WKS	Used to transfer values from a spreadsheet into a knowledge base variable

GRAPHICS KEYWORDS SUMMARY

Keyword	*Description*
BUTTON	Displays a button image at the X (column) and Y (row) coordinates specified. Pressing a mouse button while pointing to a BUTTON image causes the value of the BUTTON variable to switch from "Yes" to "No" or vice versa.
DBFORM	Displays a vertical array of boxes corresponding to the fields of a .DBF database file
ELLIPSE	Draws an ellipse of given dimensions on the graphics screen
FILL	Fills an enclosed area with the current GCOLOR setting
FORMFIELD	Displays, at the X,Y (column, row) coordinates specified, a rectangular box containing text, which is the value in the FORMFIELD variable

GBCOLOR	Sets the background color on the graphics screen
GCLS	Clears the graphics screen
GCOLOR	Sets the foreground color on the graphics screen
GDISPLAY	Displays text in GMODE at the current X (column) and Y (row) coordinates
GLOCATE	Sets the current X,Y (column, row) coordinates in GMODE. A subsequent GDISPLAY clause will begin text at the specified location.
GMODE	Causes a switch to graphics mode, allowing the use of VP-Expert graphics features
HGAUGE	Displays, at the specified X,Y (column, row) coordinates, a graphic horizontal "slide" gauge, which has the value of the HGAUGE variable.
HOTREGION	Creates an invisible rectangular "hot region" on the screen. Pressing a mouse button while pointing to an area covered by a hot region causes the value of the HOTREGION variable to switch from "Yes" to "No" or vice versa.
HYPERTEXT	Displays a block of text, retrieved from an external file, that is linked by the current HYPERTEXT variable value. Any HYPERTEXT value is known as a hyperword.
LBUTTON	Creates a rectangular "label button" image that contains "Yes" or "No" text or the name of the LBUTTON variable
LINETO	Draws a line on the graphics screen from the current X,Y (column, row) coordinates to the X,Y coordinates specified in the LINETO clause
METER	Displays a meter image with a value that is linked to the value in the METER variable
MOUSEOFF	Turns off display of the mouse pointer in GMODE
MOUSEON	Turns on display of the mouse pointer in GMODE
MOVETO	Sets the X,Y (column, row) coordinates before issuing a LINETO command to draw a line on the graphics screen
PSET	Draws a single pixel at the screen location specified by the X,Y (column, row) coordinates
RECTANGLE	Draws a rectangle on the graphics screen dimensioned by the X1,Y1 (upper left corner column and row) and X2,Y2 (lower right corner column and row) coordinates
TMODE	Resumes TMODE (text mode), the default VP-Expert screen mode
TRACK	Displays a graphic time-series graph linked to the last 50 values of the TRACK variable
VGAUGE	Displays a graphic vertical slide gauge linked to the value of the VGAUGE variable

STRUCTURE OF A RULE

RULE label	*The keyword RULE followed by a label*
IF	Identifies the beginning of the RULE condition(s)
THEN	Identifies the beginning of the RULE conclusion
ELSE	Used optionally to identify the beginning of an alternative conclusion of a RULE
BECAUSE	Used optionally to offer an explanation of the premise, conclusion, and alternate conclusion of the RULE

A RULE must end with a semicolon. Conditions can be combined in rules using the logical operators:

AND	Both conditions must be met for the rule to be "true" and, therefore, "pass." Up to 20 conditions using AND can be combined in one rule.
OR	One or both conditions must be true. When both AND and OR are used in a rule, OR takes precedence over AND. It is as though parentheses surround the expressions connected by OR. Using OR with AND in a rule limits the number of conditions that can be combined to 10.

ARITHMETIC SYMBOLS (OPERATORS)

+	Used for addition of numbers
−	Used for subtraction of numbers
*	Used for multiplication of numbers
/	Used for division of numbers

RELATIONAL SYMBOLS (OPERATORS)

=	Used as the equal-to relation
>	Used as the greater-than relation
<	Used as the less-than relation
>=	Used as the greater-than-or-equal-to relation
<=	Used as the less-than-or-equal-to relation
<>	Used as the not-equal-to relation

ASSIGNMENT OPERATOR

=	Used to assign values to variables

SPECIAL SYMBOLS

! Exclamation	Used to identify comments
? Question mark	Used as a shorthand for the special value unknown

*** Wildcard character**	Used in an induction table column to indicate that a value is not required for the corresponding (asterisk) variable
~ Tilde	Used in text to initiate a pause until the user presses any key
# Pound sign	Used to display the confidence factor associated with the value of the variable that follows the pound sign
{ } Curly brackets	Used to display the value of a variable
( ) Parentheses	Used in (1) all math calculations and (2) assigning values to variables by indirect addressing
; Semicolon	Used at the end of Actions Block, each RULE, and each statement in the Questions Block
[ ] Square brackets	Used for indexing dimensioned variables
" Double quotes	Used to identify text in ASK, BECAUSE, DISPLAY, and PDISPLAY statements
UNKNOWN	The initial value of a variable
CNF	Used to assign confidence factors

TEXT COLOR

The keyword COLOR is used to change the color of the text when displayed on a color monitor and also to display blinking text. COLOR can be used to alter text color and text blinking as often as desired during a consultation. COLOR is followed by =, then a number from 0 to 31.

Number to Use for Normal Text	*Color*	*Number to Use for Blinking Text*
0	Black	16
1	Blue	17
2	Green	18
3	Cyan	19
4	Red	20
5	Magenta	21
6	Brown	22
7	White	23
8	Gray	24
9	Light blue	25
10	Light green	26
11	Light cyan	27
12	Light red	28
13	Light magenta	29
14	Yellow	30
15	Bright white	31

BACKGROUND COLOR

BKCOLOR sets the background color of the screen for a consultation. BKCOLOR is followed by =, then a number from 0 to 7. BKCOLOR may not be used to change the background color during a consultation. If more than one BKCOLOR statement is present in a program, only the last one will be used. (Note: On a monochrome monitor the numbers 0–6 display a black background.)

Number to Use	*Background Color*
0	Black
1	Blue
2	Green
3	Light blue
4	Red
5	Magenta
6	Brown
7	White

ERROR MESSAGES

This listing of some common error messages includes a short explanation of the message and some possible ways to correct the error situation.

Error in END clause	Each WHILEKNOWN clause in the knowledge base must contain an END clause.
Error in math	Illegal math expressions are usually due to unbalanced parentheses, illegal numeric formats or values, illegal functions, and so on.
Illegal color	Text Color values range from 0 to 15; blinking text colors range from 16 to 31. Background color values range from 0 to 7. Check assigned values.
Illegal confidence factor	Confidence factor values must range from 0 to 100 (use 0 for absolutely false and 100 for absolutely true). Check assigned values.
Illegal statement	Statement is not correct, usually due to a syntax or spelling error.
Illegal truth threshold	Truth threshold values must range from 0 to 100. Check assigned values.
Math expression too long	The limit is 256 characters.
Missing comma	Variable names must be separated by commas in ASK, CHOICES, and PLURAL statements.
Out of memory error	Memory limit has been exceeded. Try dividing the knowledge base into smaller units and CHAINing them together.
Premature end of the file	Usually occurs because of missing final semicolon in the knowledge base.

Recursion too deep	The limit is 10 sub-goal levels when using backward chaining.
Syntax error	Check spelling and usage.
Text string too long	The limit is 1,000 characters in ASK, BECAUSE, DISPLAY, and PDISPLAY text.
Too many columns	The limit is 11 columns in an induction table.
Too many examples	The limit is 120 rows in an induction table.
Trace file not present	The Tree Menu's Text and Graphics options require the existence of a .tbl file with the same file name as the current knowledge base. Use the Set Menu to create a trace file.
Trace file too big	The limit is 500 lines when using a tree.
Word too long	The limit is 40 characters for RULE labels and also for most variable names.

REVIEW QUESTIONS

1. How would you print a copy of a knowledge base provided on the Sample Files disk?
2. What is the structure of a rule?
3. How can conditions be combined in rules?
4. What are the arithmetic and relational symbols normally used in KBS development?
5. Identify what the assignment operator and some of the other special symbols are used for in the construction of a KBS file.
6. What are the keywords COLOR and BKCOLOR used for?
7. What are some common error messages that can occur during KBS development?

Part Two

SAMPLE PROTOTYPE SYSTEMS

8

BEGINNER-LEVEL SYSTEMS

8A Local-Area Network Client Screening Advisor

TECHNICAL PROFILE

Difficulty Level	Beginner
Special Feature	This system uses arithmetic operators to calculate a rough cost estimate of a proposed local-area network.
File Used	LANKBS.KBS
To Run	Load LANKBS.KBS from the disk accompanying this book.

OVERVIEW

The increasing popularity of local-area networks (LANs) has created a new career specialty: the network analyst. Firms that design and install LANs often are contacted by potential clients who telephone for service. The firm then dispatches a network analyst to meet with the potential client and evaluate the situation.

LAN consulting firms want to assign analysts to telephone "leads" as efficiently as possible. However, potential clients usually supply only basic information during the initial telephone conversation. Sometimes this makes it difficult to assess the business potential of each contact. The prototype expert system described here helps non-technicians make network analyst assignments based on information available through initial telephone contact with potential clients.

STUDYING THE SITUATION

There are many legitimate areas for expert system development in the local-area network field, as shown in Figure 8A–1. One is aiding network specialists to analyze and design a LAN system. Another is helping to assign network analysts to meet with potential clients. This latter area is the focus of the prototype expert system described here.

When potential customers contact a LAN consulting agency, they initially speak to a non-technician, usually an office support person. It is unrealistic to expect this person to obtain all of the technical details of the caller's networking needs. Instead, an appointment is made for a network analyst to visit the client.

The problem is in knowing which analyst to send to which client. Often, appointments are scheduled based on analyst availability rather than on matching the proficiency of the analyst with the complexity of the caller's needs. This

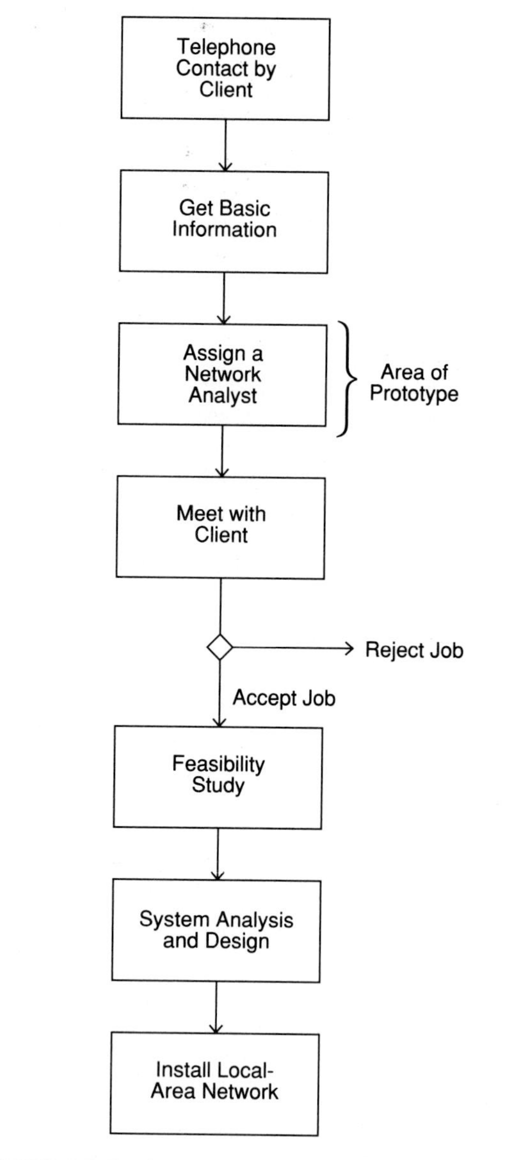

Figure 8A–1. Local-Area Network Client Screening Advisor: Block Diagram of Decision Situation

is expensive and, in the long run, inefficient. The system proposed here will help any non-technician to make better-informed analyst assignments.

To narrow the scope of the prototype system, it is limited to choosing a network analyst from one of three skill levels: trainee, experienced, and very experienced. Each skill level has different rates of pay and, based on experience, different probabilities of success in obtaining contracts.

The prototype system also estimates the raw cost of the client's proposed network. This estimate, which is very preliminary, is for internal use only to help decide the level of analyst required.

Critical Factors

Three critical factors are involved in the analyst assignment decision, as shown in Figure 8A–2.

1. *Organization size:* How large is the client organization? Does it have the resources to pay for the required system? Will this assignment lead to future jobs?
2. *Budget:* What is the amount of the estimated budget available for the LAN?
3. *Cost:* Does the estimated budget cover the estimated cost of the LAN? If not, how close is it to the estimated cost? A rough Cost Estimate is calculated from the number of nodes (computers connected to the LAN), buildings, and floors to be networked together by the projected LAN system.

   The final Cost factor is determined by dividing the Cost Estimate by the client's estimated Budget. This results in a Cost Index, which controls the value of Cost. These components of the Cost factor are shown in the detailed block diagram in Figure 8A–3.

Budget and size of the organization are important critical factors. At the lower extreme are small organizations with small budgets. Because such referrals are not very profitable, an analyst trainee will ordinarily suffice. At the other extreme are large organizations with generous budgets. Since these assignments are complex, sensitive, and profitable, they need a very experienced analyst. The in-between situation calls for experienced judgment to balance potential profitability against the level of expertise and expense required.

Figure 8A–2. Local-Area Network Client Screening Advisor: Overview Block Diagram of Decision to be Prototyped

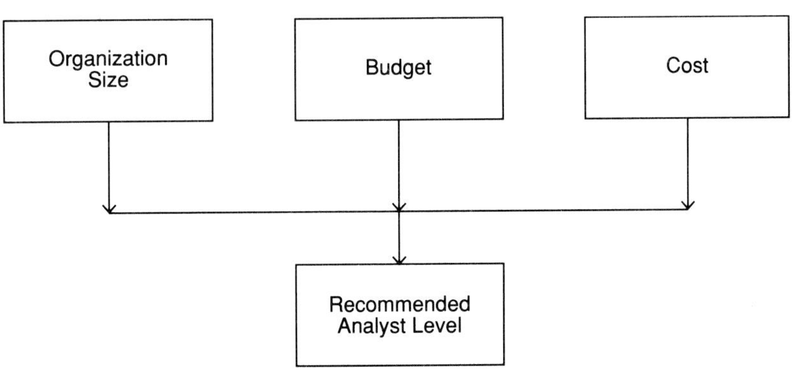

Figure 8A–3. Local-Area Network Client Screening Advisor: Detail Block Diagram of Decision to be Prototyped

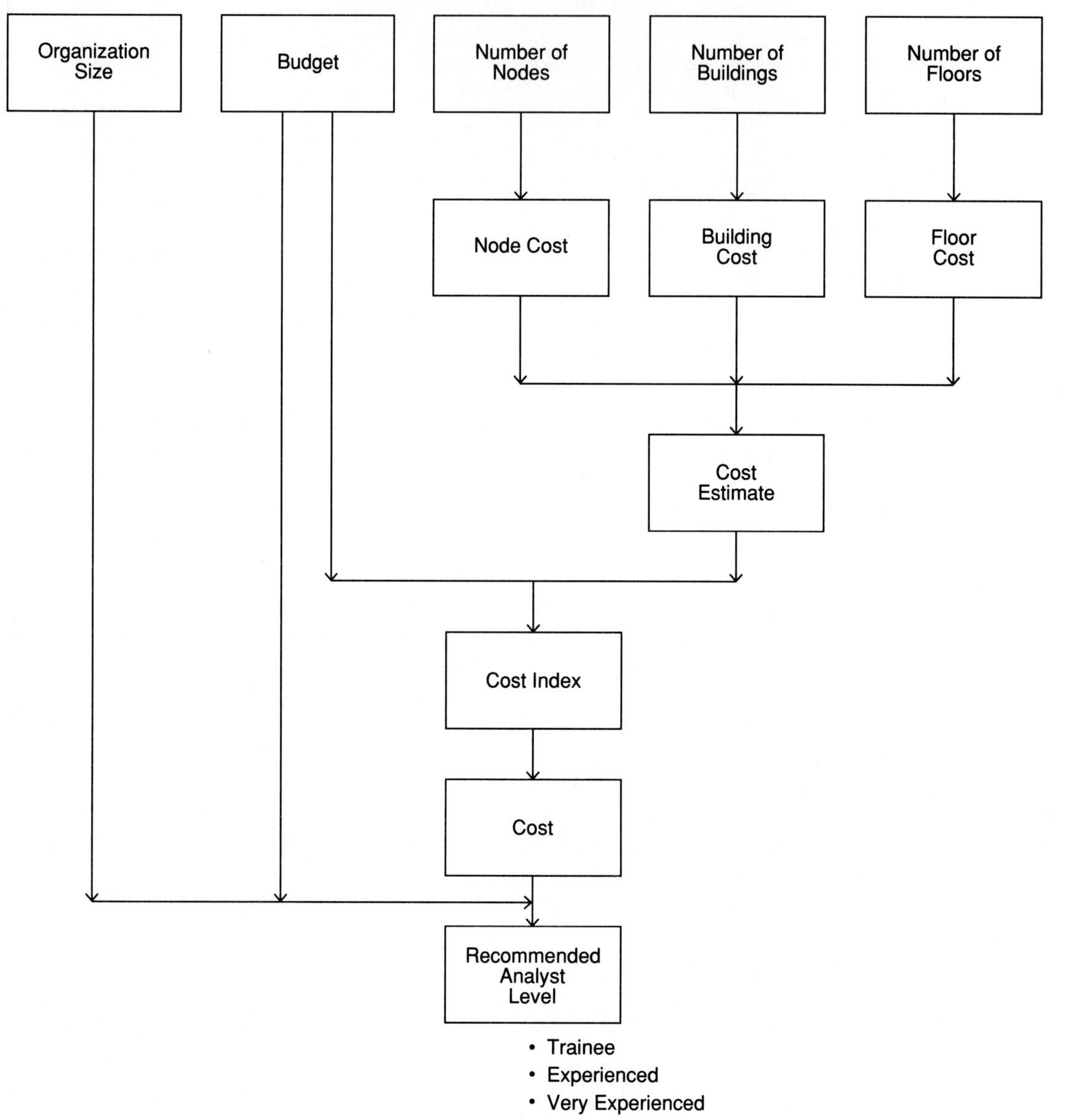

Questions Asked by the Expert System

Several questions are asked by the Local-Area Network Client Screening Advisor to determine values for the three critical factors:

1. *Organization size.* The system asks, "How many people work in your entire organization, not just in this office or division?" The answer choices are under 20, under 100, under 500, and over 500.
2. *Budget.* The system asks, "What is your estimated budget for this project?" The user enters a number and the system classifies the answer as less than 10,000, greater than or equal to 10,000 and less than 50,000, or greater than 50,000.

3. *Cost.* Four questions asked by the system combine to determine the estimated cost of the LAN:
   - "What is the number of microcomputers to be connected?"
   - "How many additional machines will be added to the network in the next two years?"
   - "How many total floors in all buildings will the network span?"
   - "How many different buildings will the network span?"

Cost Estimate is calculated as follows:

- Network interface cards: $600 × the number of nodes
- Cabling: $2,000 × number of floors, plus $8,000 × number of buildings
- Maintenance: 9 percent of cost
- Consultant's fee: $2,000 plus 6 percent of net cost (cost before maintenance and consultant fees)

If Cost Index (Cost Estimate divided by Budget) is less than 1, then Cost is considered to be OK. If Cost Index is greater than 1 but less than or equal to 1.5, Cost is "in range." Finally, if Cost Index is greater than 1.5, then Cost is Too High.

Typical Scenario

Kaye Bitz and Associates installs local-area networks. The company also does consulting and systems analysis and design for LANs. Its initial contact with customers is usually by telephone. Potential customers are often directors of small companies or computer managers of large organizations who want to investigate a LAN solution to their computing problems. After a brief conversation, the person who answers the telephone schedules a free on-site, preliminary consultation with an associate.

Ms. Bitz has six associates at three different skill and experience levels. Jane and Ann have more than 30 years of computer experience between them. Each has performed LAN installations for at least six years. Besides their obvious technical skills, they also possess keen interpersonal and managerial skills obtained from years of systems analysis experience. They are rated as *very experienced.*

Bob and Fred each have four years of computer experience. They started work at Kaye Bitz immediately after obtaining their MS degrees in computer information systems. Ms. Bitz has been giving them progressively increased responsibility over the years. Now each is capable of individually designing and installing fairly complex LANs. Bob and Fred are considered to be *experienced.*

Finally, Ted and Alice are presently *trainees.* They are finishing their MS degrees in computer information systems. Although they are both academically proficient, they lack real-world experience in a business environment. Ms. Bitz assigns them primarily maintenance tasks and smaller analysis jobs to give them incremental experience.

Jane and Ann, the very experienced analysts, earn $40 an hour plus a 4.5 percent commission on installations. They are very successful at obtaining clients, and Ms. Bitz prefers to send them only to accounts that are potentially lucrative. For middle-level customers, Fred or Bob, who earn $22.50 an hour plus 4.5 percent commission, is the better choice. Finally, Ted or Alice, who earn $12.50 an hour with no commission, are sent to small, simple accounts. Although these jobs are usually not very profitable, they are invaluable in giving Ted and Alice needed experience.

Ms. Bitz would like the office staff to be able to make the best analyst assignments possible, based on the limited information available from the caller. Making a wrong assignment, at best, results in overpaying more experienced analysts for smaller, less profitable jobs. At worst, it means losing profitable accounts because an inexperienced analyst is sent to jobs that he or she is not equipped to handle.

SYSTEM DOCUMENTATION

Figure 8A–4 is a dependency diagram of the local-area network analyst assignment decision. It shows all of the critical factors, rules, questions, and possible values associated with the decision.

Decision tables are given in Figures 8A–5 and 8A–6. Figure 8A–5 is an initial decision table that covers all of the possible combinations of factors that

Figure 8A–4. Local-Area Network Client Screening Advisor: Dependency Diagram

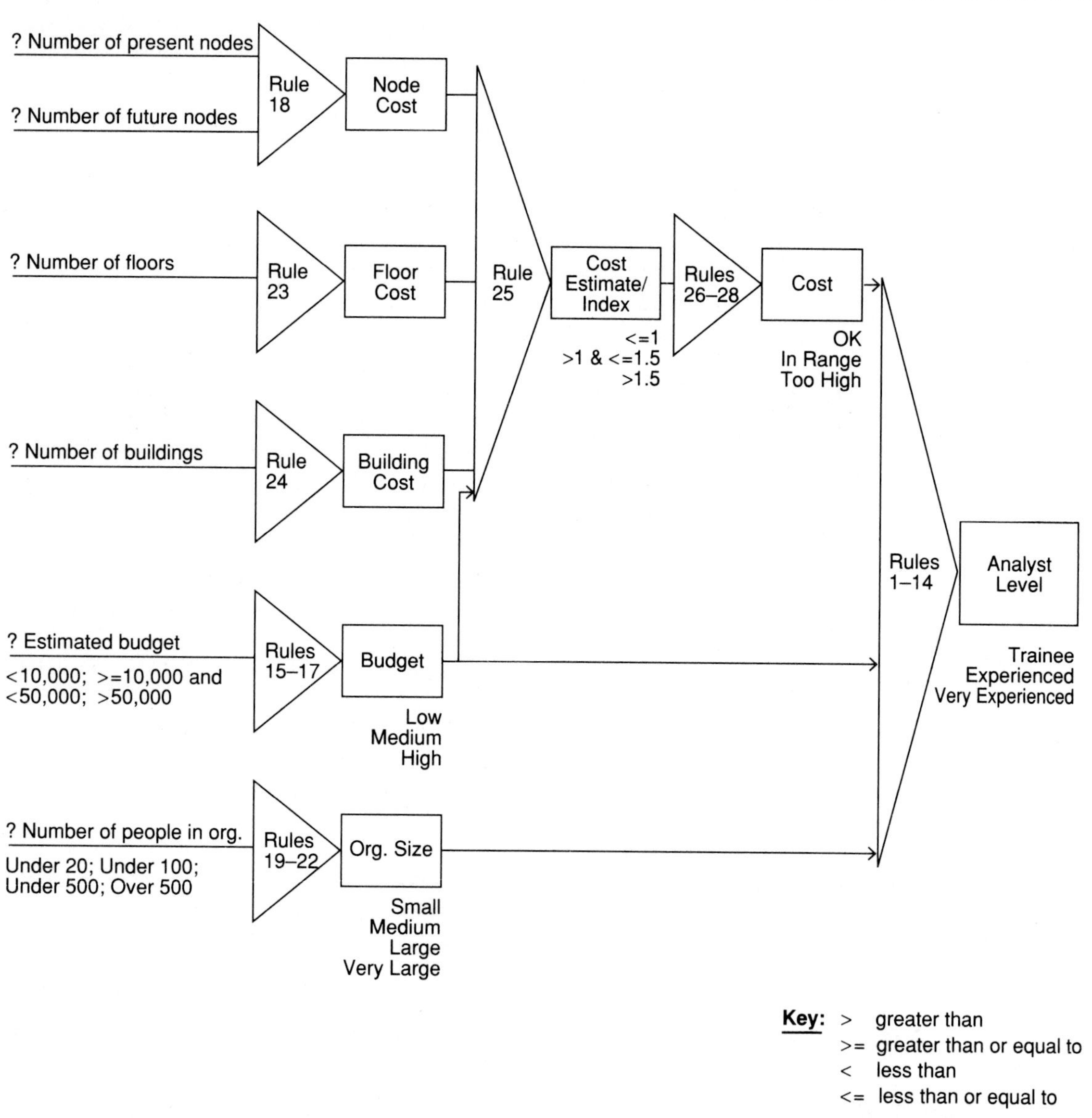

Figure 8A–5. Local-Area Network Client Screening Advisor: Final Rule Set—Decision Table

Budget	Organization Size	Cost	Recommended Analyst Level
Low	Small	OK	Trainee
Low	Small	In_Range	Trainee
Low	Small	Too_High	Trainee
Low	Middle	OK	Trainee
Low	Middle	In_Range	Trainee
Low	Middle	Too_High	Trainee
Low	Large	OK	Experienced
Low	Large	In_Range	Experienced
Low	Large	Too_High	Trainee
Low	Very_Large	OK	Experienced
Low	Very_Large	In_Range	Experienced
Low	Very_Large	Too_High	Experienced
Medium	Small	OK	Experienced
Medium	Small	In_Range	Experienced
Medium	Small	Too_High	Trainee
Medium	Middle	OK	Experienced
Medium	Middle	In_Range	Experienced
Medium	Middle	Too_High	Experienced
Medium	Large	OK	Experienced
Medium	Large	In_Range	Experienced
Medium	Large	Too_High	Experienced
Medium	Very_Large	OK	Very_Experienced
Medium	Very_Large	In_Range	Experienced
Medium	Very_Large	Too_High	Experienced
High	Small	OK	Very_Experienced
High	Small	In_Range	Experienced
High	Small	Too_High	Experienced
High	Middle	OK	Very_Experienced
High	Middle	In_Range	Very_Experienced
High	Middle	Too_High	Experienced
High	Large	OK	Very_Experienced
High	Large	In_Range	Very_Experienced
High	Large	Too_High	Very_Experienced
High	Very_Large	OK	Very_Experienced
High	Very_Large	In_Range	Very_Experienced
High	Very_Large	Too_High	Very_Experienced

can occur in the system's final recommendation. These combinations are then reduced to the decision table shown in Figure 8A–6.

The results of three sample consultations are given in Figure 8A–7. Figure 8A–8 is a printout of the entire knowledge base file.

Sample Consultations

In the first sample consultation of Figure 8A–7, the calling organization has an estimated budget of $49,000 and under 20 employees. Because the budget is *medium* and the firm size is *small,* the system must calculate a cost estimate. This organization wants to connect 20 microcomputers and plans to install 5

Figure 8A–6. Local-Area Network Client Screening Advisor: Final Rule Set—Reduced Decision Table

Budget	Organization Size	Cost	Recommended Analyst Level	Rule Number
Low	Small or Middle	—	Trainee	1
Low	Large	OK or In_Range	Experienced	2
Low	Large	Too_High	Trainee	3
Low	Very_Large	—	Experienced	4
Medium	Small	OK or In_Range	Experienced	5
Medium	Small	Too_High	Trainee	6
Medium	Middle or Large	—	Experienced	7
Medium	Very_Large	OK	Very_Experienced	8
Medium	Very_Large	In_Range or Too_High	Experienced	9
High	Small	OK	Very_Experienced	10
High	Small	In_Range or Too_High	Experienced	11
High	Middle	OK or In_Range	Very_Experienced	12
High	Middle	Too_High	Experienced	13
High	Large or Very_Large	—	Very_Experienced	14

Figure 8A–7. Local-Area Network Client Screening Advisor: Three Sample Consultations

<u>CONSULTATION 1</u>:

```
LOCAL-AREA NETWORK CLIENT SCREENING ADVISOR

Developed by Anthony Cantarella
under the direction and supervision of
Dr. D.G. Dologite
```

Text only

```
This program will choose the level of
analyst to assign to this project.

What is your estimated
budget for this project?
 49000

How many people work in your entire
organization, not just this office or division?
 Under 20 ◄              Under 100              Under 500
 Over 500

What is the number of microcomputers to be
connected?
 20

How many additional machines will be
added to the network in the next 2 years?
(Enter 0 for unknown)
  5

How many different buildings will the
network span?
(Enter number - 1 for unknown)
 1

How many total floors in all buildings
will the network span?
(Enter number [1 for each Bldg; 1 for unknown])
 1

Send someone whose level is: Experienced.
```

Consultation 2:

Text only

```
This program will choose the level of
analyst to assign to this project.

What is your estimated
budget for this project?
 9000

How many people work in your entire
organization, not just this office or division?.
 Under 20 ◄              Under 100                 Under 500
 Over 500

Send someone whose level is: Trainee.
```

Consultation 3:

Text only

```
This program will choose the level of
analyst to assign to this project.

What is your estimated
budget for this project?
 49000

How many people work in your entire
organization, not just this office or division?
 Under 20 ◄              Under 100                 Under 500
 Over 500

What is the number of microcomputers to be
connected?
 20

How many additional machines will be
added to the network in the next 2 years?
(Enter 0 for unknown)
 5

How many different buildings will the
network span?
(Enter number - 1 for unknown)
 10

How many total floors in all buildings
will the network span?
(Enter number [1 for each Bldg; 1 for unknown])
 10

Send someone whose level is: Trainee.
```

more within the next two years. The LAN will be confined to one floor in one building. The estimated cost is $30,750, well within the estimated budget. Because enough resources are committed for the project, the system assigns an *experienced* analyst to this client.

In the second consultation, a caller has an estimated budget of $9,000, which is considered to be *low* by the prototype system. The caller's firm has a total staff of under 20 people, which is evaluated to be *small.* In this example, the system reaches a conclusion after asking only two questions and assigns a *trainee* to the project. Because smaller projects tend to be less profitable, a trainee is usually adequate. Additionally, since the organization is small (less than 20 employees), there is a high likelihood that there will not be any significant future expansion. The organization's small size also suggests that it lacks substantial resources.

Figure 8A–8. Local-Area Network Client Screening Advisor: Printout of Knowledge Base File

```
! System name: Local-Area Network Client Screening Advisor
! Description: This expert system helps non-technicians make
!              local-area network analyst assignments based
!              on information from telephone calls with
!              potential clients.
! Microcomputer used: IBM PC compatible
! Saved file name: LANKBS.KBS

RUNTIME;
ENDOFF;
ACTIONS
WOPEN 1,1,1,20,77,3
ACTIVE 1
DISPLAY "
         LOCAL-AREA NETWORK CLIENT SCREENING ADVISOR

               Developed by Anthony Cantarella
           under the direction and supervision of
                      Dr. D.G. Dologite
              For further information, contact
                      Dr. D.G. Dologite
                  c/o Macmillan Publishing

          Press any key to begin the consultation~
WCLOSE 1
DISPLAY "This program will choose the level of
analyst to assign to this project.
  "
FIND Analyst_Level

DISPLAY "Send someone whose level is: {Analyst_Level}.~";

Rule 1
If Budget = Low
   and Org_Size = Small
    or Org_Size = Middle
Then Analyst_Level = Trainee;

Rule 2
If Budget = Low
   and Org_Size = Large
   and Cost = OK
    or Cost = In_range
Then Analyst_Level = Experienced;

Rule 3
If Budget = Low
   and Org_Size = Large
   and Cost = Too_high
Then Analyst_Level = Trainee;

Rule 4
If Budget = Low
   and Org_Size = Very_large
Then Analyst_Level = Experienced;

Rule 5
If Budget = Medium
   and Org_Size = Small
   and Cost = OK
    or Cost = In_range
Then Analyst_Level = Experienced;
```

```
Rule 6
If Budget = Medium
   and Org_Size = Small
   and Cost = Too_high
Then Analyst_Level = Trainee;

Rule 7
If Budget = Medium
   and Org_Size = Middle
    or Org_Size = Large
Then Analyst_Level = Experienced;

Rule 8
If Budget = Medium
   and Org_Size = Very_large
   and Cost = OK
Then Analyst_Level = Very_Experienced;

Rule 9
If Budget = Medium
   and Org_Size = Very_large
   and Cost = In_range
    or Cost = Too_high
Then Analyst_Level = Experienced;

Rule 10
If Budget = High
   and Org_Size = Small
   and Cost = OK
Then Analyst_Level = Very_Experienced;

Rule 11
If Budget = High
   and Org_Size = Small
   and Cost = In_range
    or Cost = Too_high
Then Analyst_Level = Experienced;

Rule 12
If Budget = High
   and Org_Size = Middle
   and Cost = OK
    or Cost = In_range
Then Analyst_Level = Very_Experienced;

Rule 13
If Budget = High
   and Org_Size = Middle
   and Cost = Too_high
Then Analyst_Level = Experienced;

Rule 14
If Budget = High
   and Org_Size = Large
    or Org_Size = Very_Large
Then Analyst_Level = Very_Experienced;

Rule 15
If  Est_Budget < 10000
Then Budget = Low;
```

Figure 8A–8. *continued*

```
Rule 16
If Est_Budget >=  10000
   and Est_Budget <= 50000
Then Budget = Medium;

Rule 17
If Est_Budget   > 50000
Then Budget = High;

Rule 18
If Node_Number > 0
   and Future_Number > -1
Then Node_Cost =
((Node_Number + Future_Number) *  600);

Rule 19
If Org_Size_Ques = Under_20
Then Org_Size = Small;

Rule 20
If Org_Size_Ques = Under_100
Then Org_Size = Middle;

Rule 21
If Org_Size_Ques = Under_500
Then Org_Size = Large;

Rule 22
If Org_Size_Ques = Over_500
Then Org_Size = Very_Large;

Rule 23
If Floors > 0
Then Floor_Cost = (2000*Floors);

Rule 24
If Buildings > 0
Then Building_Cost = (8000*Buildings):

Rule 25
If Node_Cost > 1
   and Building_Cost > 1
   and Floor_Cost > 1
```

In the third consultation, the budget is again $49,000, the organization is *small,* and there are 20 current and 5 future microcomputers to be connected to the LAN. But in this case, the project spans 10 buildings and 10 floors. The cost estimate for this project is $134,250, calculated as follows:

- Network interface cards: $600 × 25 = $15,000
- Cabling: $2,000 × 10 floors = $20,000
  $8,000 × 10 buildings = $80,000
- Maintenance: $115,000 × 9% = $10,350
- Consultant's fee: $115,000 × 6% + $2,000 = $8,900

Since the estimated budget is almost three times what the organization has budgeted, it is probable that this small firm does not have the resources to complete the project as outlined. Therefore, the system assigns a *trainee* to the account.

```
Then Cost_Est =
(((Building_Cost +
Floor_Cost +
Node_Cost) * 1.15)              !1.15 combines the 9% maintenance
+ 2000)                         !fee and 6% consultant's fee
Cost_Index =
(Cost_Est/Est_Budget);

Rule 26
If Cost_Index <= 1
Then Cost = OK;

Rule 27
If Cost_Index > 1
   and Cost_Index <= 1.5
Then Cost = In_range;

Rule 28
If Cost_Index > 1.5
Then Cost = Too_high;

ASK Est_Budget: "What is your estimated
budget for this project?";

ASK Org_Size_Ques: "How many people work in your entire
organization, not just this office or division?";
Choices Org_Size_Ques:Under_20,Under_100,Under_500,Over_500;

ASK Node_Number: "What is the number of microcomputers to be
connected?";

Ask Future_Number: "How many additional machines will be
added to the network in the next 2 years?
(Enter 0 for unknown)";

ASK Floors: "How many total floors in all buildings
will the network span?
(Enter number [1 for each Bldg; 1 for unknown])";

ASK Buildings: "How many different buildings will the
network span ?
(Enter number - 1 for unknown)";
```

Design Considerations

This prototype is designed for non-technicians, so ease of use is a primary consideration. Questions are straightforward and involve little technical jargon. They ask for information that callers should readily have at their disposal. Since the system makes only rough cost estimates, this information does not always have to be exact.

The heart of the calculation done to determine a rough cost estimate is given in Rule 25 of the knowledge base file shown in Figure 8A–8. The variables used in this rule, "node_cost," "floor_cost," and "building_cost," are calculated in Rules 18, 23, and 24. A fourth variable, "est-budget," is determined by the first user question, "What is your estimated budget for this project?" These and other rules in the knowledge base make use of arithmetic operators (+ and *), as well as relational operators (=, >, >=, <, and <=).

8B

College Major Advisor

TECHNICAL PROFILE

Difficulty Level	Beginner
Special Features	This is a small subset of a potentially larger expert system designed to help incoming college students select a major field of study. This prototype, which advises only computer majors, could easily be chained to additional modules to advise other majors.
File Used	MAJOR.KBS
To Run	Load MAJOR.KBS from the disk accompanying this book.

OVERVIEW

Students at one metropolitan area community college are required to choose a major area of study when they initially register at the school. Their choices are often based on incomplete or erroneous information. Once students begin classes, they often discover that they do not like their major or that they are not doing well in their major courses. A typical student changes majors four times during a college career.

To guide and advise students in the selection of a major, an expert system has been designed. The prototype of this system, the College Major Advisor, concentrates on students with pre-selected majors in the computer field. However, this system can be expanded to deal with all students and all majors.

STUDYING THE SITUATION

This prototype is designed for a two-year urban community college. The school year is divided into four 10-week quarters. The college is structured into four components, as shown in Figure 8B–1: Administration, Academic Affairs, Student Services, and Cooperative Education. The administration unit provides all support functions at the college, such as student admissions and financial aid. Faculty members are part of the Academic Affairs component. They are responsible for teaching courses and serving as faculty advisors to students. Student Services staff conduct an orientation course for incoming freshmen. They also provide individual counselling and academic advice. The final component, Cooperative Education, offers internship programs to full-time students in their major fields of study.

The college offers a wide selection of majors, ranging from liberal arts to animal health technology to computer science. Some of the programs, such as computer technology, are designed for students who plan to get a job after graduation. These are called career-oriented programs. Others, such as computer science, are transfer-oriented programs. They are designed for students who plan to continue their education at a four-year college after graduation.

Incoming freshmen declare a major before starting classes at the college. Their choice is based on personal preference as well as on discussions with counsellors and faculty. Counsellors and faculty agree on a best choice of major to recommend based on a student's interests, abilities, and financial need.

Figure 8B–1. College Major Advisor: Decision Area Under Study

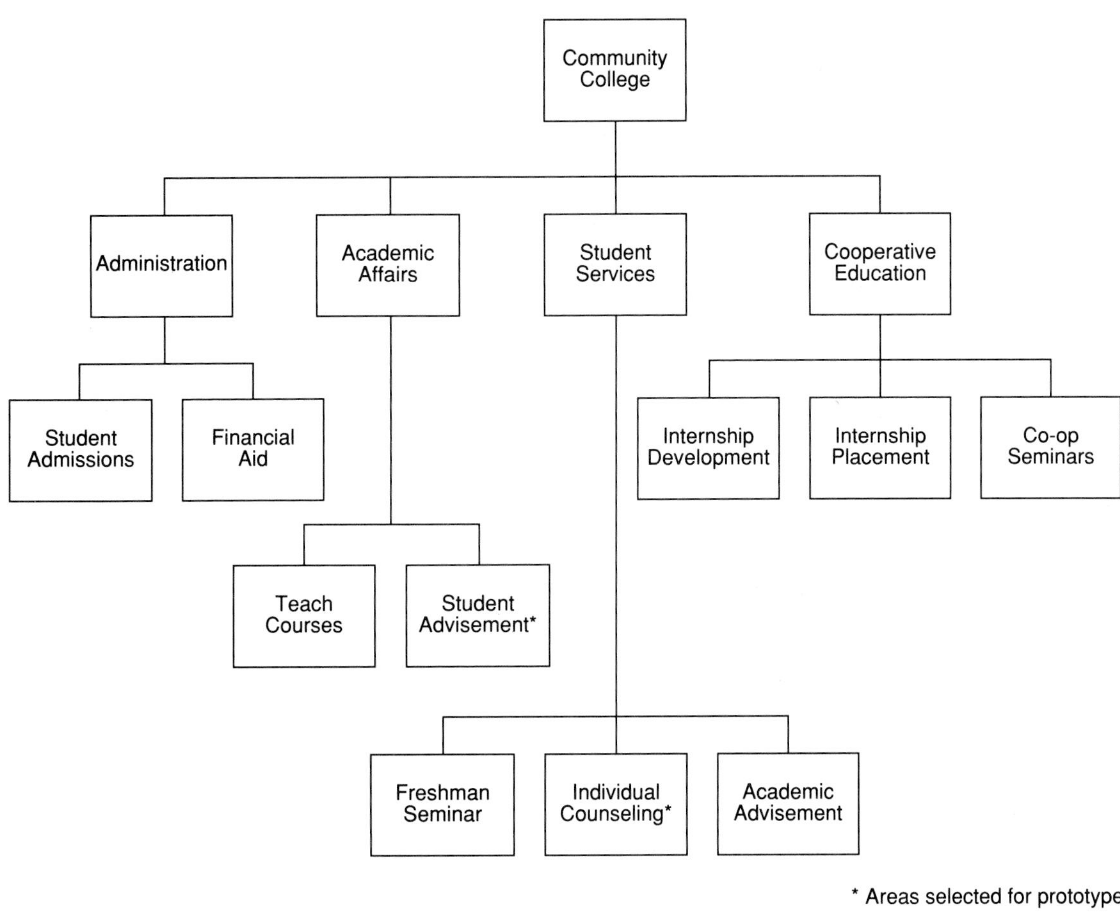

* Areas selected for prototype

Often students choose, however, without adequate information. Many discover that they never really understood the course of study or the skills required for the major selected. As a result, students change majors as many as four times during their two years at the college.

Unfortunately, opportunities to obtain advice are limited even after the student is enrolled. All students take a freshman seminar course in their first quarter. Taught by a counsellor, the course orients new students to the school. Counsellors may discuss choices of major, but they cannot address individual problems because of the large classes. Although students can make appointments to meet with a counsellor during office hours, there is not enough time to deal effectively with all problems. Alternatively, students can discuss concerns about a major with a faculty member. But the problem remains one of too many students and too little time.

If students can be better advised initially, they will not be groping for the correct major, they will not need to change majors, and they will save a great deal of time, energy, and money. An expert system designed to advise students on the selection of a major would make the knowledge of expert counsellors and faculty available to students at their convenience. Students could consult the system at any campus computer facility.

This particular problem lends itself to an expert system solution. The knowledge of experts is available and they agree on recommendations. For example, counsellors and faculty have many years of experience dealing with students. Faculty advisors are familiar with the skills required for particular majors, as well as with the profiles of students who do well in different majors. Counsellors are especially aware of skill requirements. Their psychological training helps them talk to students about interests, hobbies, and attitudes that may influence the choice of a major. Counsellors also are aware of results from various psychological tests, personality profiles, and interest inventories that help in student placement.

Narrowing the Focus

The prototype expert system developed here focuses on one particular major, computers. It advises students about whether a major in computers is appropriate for them. If it is, the system advises them to concentrate in one of three specialty areas: computer science, computer programming, or computer technology.

Critical Factors Affecting the Situation

The critical factors affecting a choice of major are a student's aptitude, interests, and financial need, as diagrammed in Figure 8B–2. Factors related to a student's *aptitude* for the computer field include mathematical skills, programming skills, and manual dexterity. Factors that determine *interests* are a student's enjoyment of computers, inclination toward problem solving and repairing things, and preference for working at a desk or in the field. A student's *financial need* is based on whether he or she needs to get a job after graduation. (The need to get a job eliminates the possibility of going directly to a four-year school after graduation.)

A detailed breakdown of the three critical factors is diagrammed in Figure 8B–3.

Possible Recommendations

After a student answers a series of questions, such as those shown in the sample consultation in Figure 8B–4, the system makes one of four final recommendations:

1. The student should major in computer science.
2. The student should major in computer programming.
3. The student should major in computer technology.
4. The student should major in some field other than computers.

Each of these recommendations is based on a combination of critical factor values. For example, students should major in computer science if their mathematical skills are good and if they demonstrate a strong aptitude for computer programming. They should like working with computers and enjoy problem-solving tasks. Computer science majors should not mind working at a desk for long periods of time. Finally, this major requires that students be willing and financially able to go on to a four-year school after graduation, since a computer science professional traditionally needs a four-year degree before employment.

A candidate for a computer programming major is someone who is a good logical thinker. A strong math orientation is not mandatory. The student should like working with computers and solving problems. This person must also be comfortable working at a desk. If financial need requires getting a job after

Figure 8B–2. College Major Advisor: Overview Block Diagram of Decision Situation for Prototype

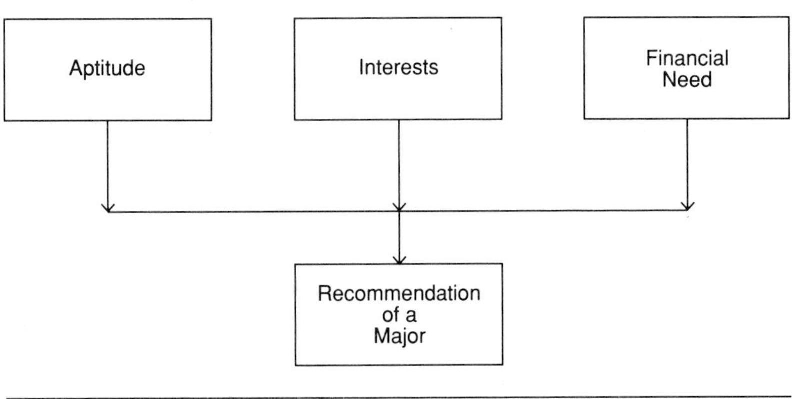

Figure 8B–3. College Major Advisor: Detailed Block Diagram of Critical Factors

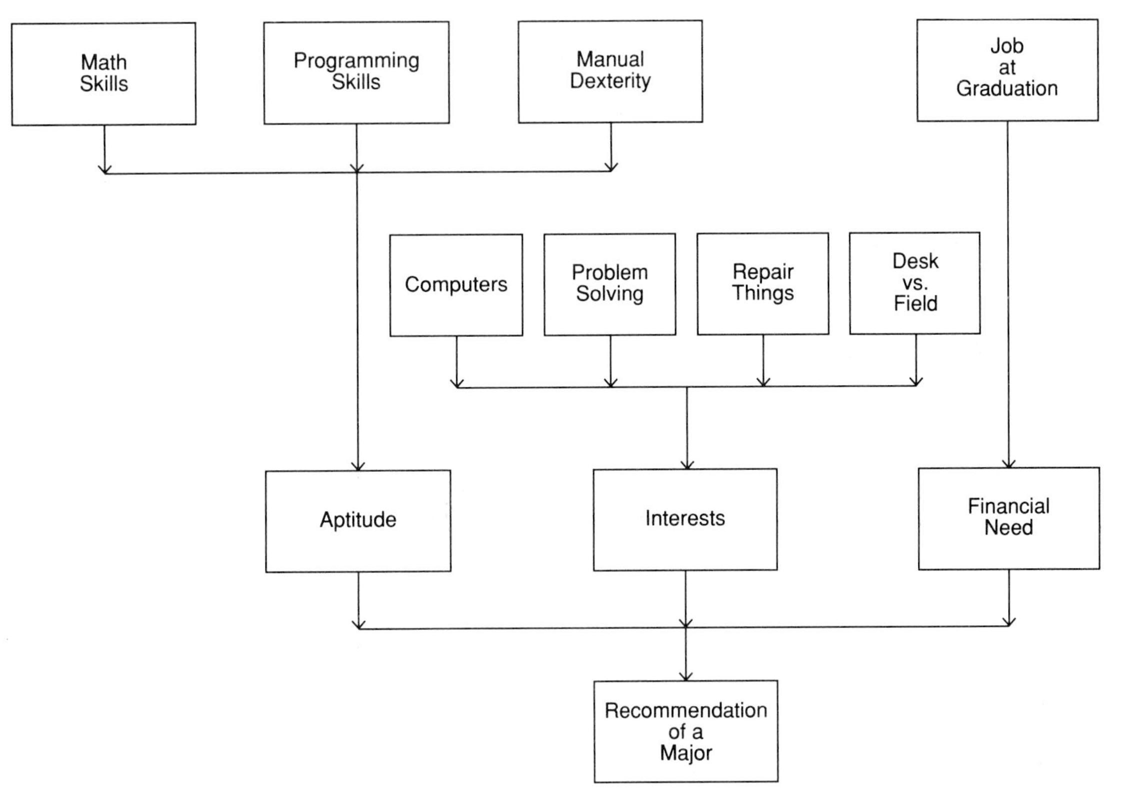

graduation, the student could do this and continue his or her education as appropriate in the future.

The third computer major is computer technology. This requires people who are good at working with their hands (have good manual dexterity) and enjoy fixing things. They need not have strong math skills, but they should like computers and be curious about how they work. This major requires someone

Figure 8B–4. College Major Advisor: Sample Consultation

```
*** COLLEGE MAJOR ADVISOR ***

Developed by Toby Shatzoff
under the direction and supervision of
Dr. D.G. Dologite
```

Actual screen

```
College Major Advisor

This system provides advice about choosing an
appropriate college major.  It asks you a series
of questions about your abilities, interests, and
financial needs.  The system then recommends an
appropriate major.


PLEASE PRESS ANY KEY TO BEGIN THE SESSION
```

Actual screen

```
INSTRUCTIONS
        When you are asked a question, use the arrow keys to move
        the light bar to a desired answer choice.
        Then press the ENTER key.
```

```
Are you good at math?
 yes ◂                    no

Are you good at programming?
 yes                      no ◂

Are you good at working with your hands?
 yes ◂                    no

Do you like working with computers?
 yes ◂                    no
```

Text only

```
Do you like solving problems?
 yes ◂                    no

Do you prefer working at a desk or in the field?
 desk                     field ◂

Do you like to repair things?
 yes ◂                    no



             Based on your answers, the College Major
             Advisor recommends that you major in:

                        computer technology.

          PLEASE PRESS ANY KEY TO CONCLUDE THIS SESSION
```

who likes to work in the field. It is especially appropriate for students who need to get a job immediately after graduation.

Finally, a student should major in some field other than computers if he or she has no interest in computers or problem solving.

A Typical Decision Situation

John Marcus is graduating from high school in June and applying to enter college in the fall. He plans to go to the community college near his home. On the admission application, John is asked to choose a major. He thinks he is interested in computers, so he looks on the application for the computer major choices. John sees Computer Science, Computer Technician: Computer Repair, and Computer Technician: Telecommunications. (Unfortunately, Programming and Operations are listed under Data Processing, a term that has no association to computers for John.) Not knowing the distinctions between the different computer majors, John checks the box labeled Computer Science.

His first quarter at the college, John is enrolled in the Freshman Seminar, Introduction to Computer Science, Pre-calculus, and two other courses. During the quarter, he sees that he is doing poorly in the pre-calculus course. He has mixed feelings about the computer science class, where a lot of time is devoted to programming in Pascal. John sets up a meeting with the counsellor who teaches his Freshman Seminar class. The counsellor and John start to discuss John's choice of a computer science major and whether it is the best choice.

The counsellor, Ms. Jones, asks John whether he likes computers. John says that he does like computers and that he especially likes to tinker with them. John also says that he likes to solve problems and to find out how things work. After further discussion, John reveals that he dislikes sitting at a desk for long periods of time.

Based on his responses, Ms. Jones concludes that John has the interest and personality traits for a computer major, but she is not certain which computer major is right for him. She questions him about his aptitude and skills. John explains that he is not doing very well in pre-calculus; he has a C average. He has a B average in the Introduction to Computer Science class, but he really is not very good at programming in Pascal. He is good, though, at learning about the different parts of the computer and how the hardware and software work together.

Ms. Jones now realizes that John is not strong in math or programming, which rules out a computer science or programming major. But his manual dexterity is strong and he is interested in computers. So she feels that he should switch his major to computer technology. To reach a final conclusion, she asks John about his financial situation and what he plans to do after graduation. John says that he wants to get a job instead of going on to a four-year school.

Ms. Jones concludes that John should switch his major to Computer Technology. This would allow him to learn all about computers and how to repair them. John has the interest in computers and repair, the necessary manual dexterity, and the need to get a job after graduation.

SYSTEM DOCUMENTATION

Figure 8B–5 shows the reduced decision tables developed to create the rules used in the College Major Advisor. A dependency diagram for the system is given in Figure 8B–6. A complete listing of the knowledge base file is shown in Figure 8B–7.

Figure 8B–5. College Major Advisor: Reduced Decision Tables

Decision Table for Final Rule Set (Set #1)

Rule	Aptitude	Interest	Financial Need	Recommendation for Major*
1_1	Level_0	—	—	Not_computers
1_2	—	Level_0	—	Not_computers
1_3	Level_1	Level_1	—	Computer_tech
1_4	Level_1	Level_2	Yes	Computer_program
1_5	Level_1	Level_2	No	Computer_science
1_6	Level_1	Level_3	Yes	Computer_program
1_7	Level_1	Level_3	No	Computer_science
1_8	Level_2	Level_1	Yes	Computer_program
1_9	Level_2	Level_1	No	Computer_science
1_10	Level_2	Level_2	Yes	Computer_program
1_11	Level_2	Level_2	No	Computer_science
1_12	Level_2	Level_3	Yes	Computer_program
1_13	Level_2	Level_3	No	Computer_science
1_14	Level_3	Level_1	—	Computer_tech
1_15	Level_3	Level_2	—	Computer_tech
1_16	Level_3	Level_3	—	Computer_tech
1_17	Level_4	Level_1	—	Computer_tech
1_18	Level_4	Level_2	—	Computer_program
1_19	Level_4	Level_3	—	Computer_program
1_20	Level_5	Level_1	—	Computer_program
1_21	Level_5	Level_2	—	Computer_program
1_22	Level_5	Level_3	—	Computer_program

***Explanation:**

Not_computers The student should major in some field other than computers.

Computer_science The student should major in computer science.

Computer_program The student should major in computer programming.

Computer_tech The student should major in computer technology.

Decision Table for Rule Set #2

Rule	Mathematical Aptitude	Programming Aptitude	Manual Dexterity	Aptitude Level†
2_1	Yes	Yes	Yes	Level_1
2_2	Yes	Yes	No	Level_2
2_3	Yes	No	Yes	Level_3
2_4	Yes	No	No	Level_0
2_5	No	Yes	Yes	Level_4
2_6	No	Yes	No	Level_5
2_7	No	No	Yes	Level_3
2_8	No	No	No	Level_0

†Explanation:

Level_0 No aptitude for the computer field

Level_1 Aptitude for math, programming, and manual dexterity

Level_2 Aptitude for math and programming

Level_3 Manual dexterity

Level_4 Aptitude for programming and manual dexterity

Level_5 Aptitude for programming

Figure 8B–5. *continued*

Decision Table for Rule Set #3

Rule	Computers‡	Problems	Place	Repair	Interest Level
3_1	Yes	Yes	Desk	Yes	Level_3
3_2	Yes	Yes	—	No	Level_2
3_3	Yes	Yes	Field	Yes	Level_1
3_4	Yes	No	—	—	Level_0
3_5	No	—	—	—	Level_0

‡Explanation:

Computers	An interest in computers
Problems	An interest in problem solving
Place	Desk/Field means an interest in a desk job or a field (non-desk) job
Repair	An interest in repairing things
Level_0	No interest in computers or problem solving
Level_1	An interest in computers and problem solving; an interest in a field job; an interest in repair
Level_2	An interest in computers and problem solving; an interest in a field or a desk job; no interest in repair
Level_3	An interest in computers and problem solving; an interest in a desk job; an interest in repair

Figure 8B–6. College Major Advisor: Dependency Diagram

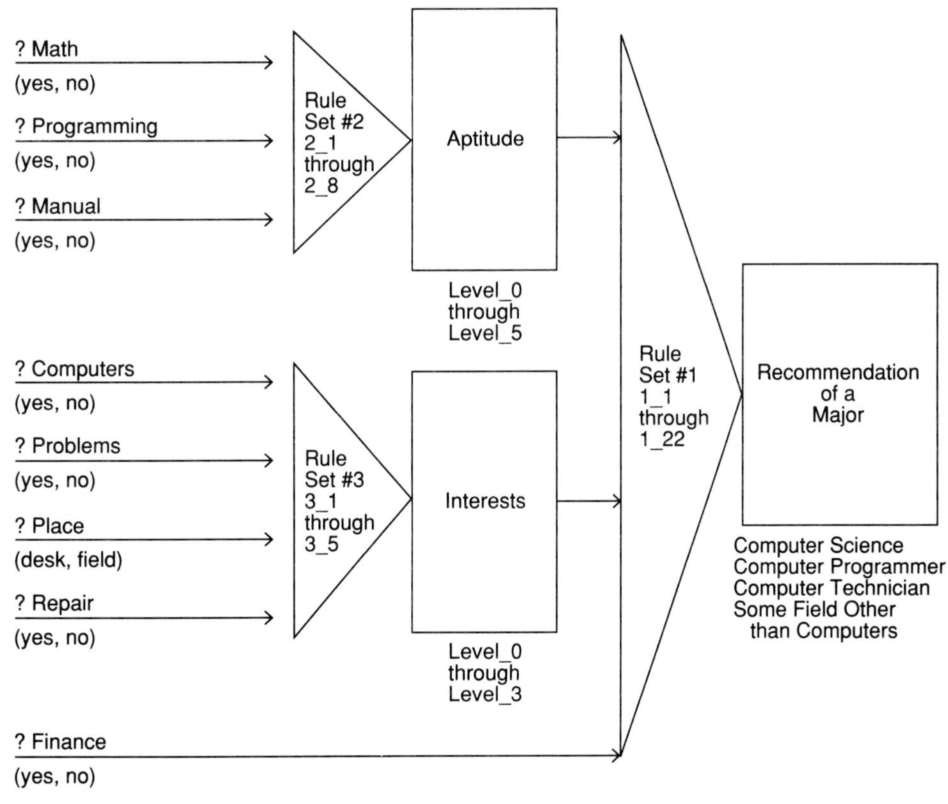

Figure 8B–7. College Major Advisor: Printout of Knowledge Base File

```
!College Major Advisor
!This prototype expert system assists students in choosing a major
!based on aptitude, interests, and financial need.
!The system is currently limited to CIS majors.
!Therefore, the recommended major is either computer science,
!computer programming, or computer technology.
!In addition, there is a recommendation to not major in computers,
!for students who show no aptitude or interest in computers.
!
!It was developed on an IBM-compatible ITT PC,
!using VP-Expert, Version 2.02.
!The KBS is saved under the filename MAJOR.KBS
!
!*****************************************************************
EXECUTE;     !Will start consultation without typing GO
RUNTIME;     !Will eliminate rules and facts window
ENDOFF;      !Will eliminate need for pressing END after ENTER
!
!
!
!Actions Block
!
ACTIONS
WOPEN 1,0,0,23,79,1
ACTIVE 1
DISPLAY "


                        *** COLLEGE MAJOR ADVISOR ***

                          Developed by Toby Shatzoff
                    under the direction and supervision of
                               Dr. D.G. Dologite
                       For further information, contact
                               Dr. D.G. Dologite
                           c/o Macmillan Publishing


                          Press any key to continue~"

WCLOSE 1
WOPEN 1,5,8,13,60,3          !Define opening window 1
ACTIVE 1
!Display opening message
!
DISPLAY  "
                College Major Advisor

     This system provides advice about choosing an
     appropriate college major.  It asks you a series
     of questions about your abilities, interests, and
     financial needs.  The system then recommends an
     appropriate major.

         PLEASE PRESS ANY KEY TO BEGIN THE SESSION~"
!
WCLOSE 1                     !Remove window 1
WOPEN 1,1,1,8,77,3           !Define instructions window 1
ACTIVE 1
!
!Display instructions for user
!
DISPLAY   "INSTRUCTIONS
        When you are asked a question, use the arrow keys to move
        the light bar to a desired answer choice.
        Then press the ENTER key."
!
WOPEN 2,7,1,14,77,2          !Define consultation screen, window 2
ACTIVE 2
FIND recommend               !recommend is the goal (a major)
WCLOSE 1
WCLOSE 2
```

```
CLS
WOPEN 1,5,13,9,48,3          !Define the recommendation window 1
ACTIVE 1

!
!Display the recommendation
DISPLAY     "  Based on your answers, the College Major
   Advisor recommends that you major in:

             {recommend}.


 PLEASE PRESS ANY KEY TO CONCLUDE THIS SESSION~"
;
!
!*********************************************************************
!Rules Block
!
!Rules for the final rule set, set #1
Rule 1_1
 IF aptitude = level_0
 THEN recommend = some_field_other_than_computers;
!
Rule 1_2
 IF interest = level_0
 THEN recommend = some_field_other_than_computers;
!
Rule 1_3
 IF aptitude = level_1 and
    interest = level_1
 THEN recommend = computer_technology;
!
Rule 1_4
IF aptitude = level_1 and
   interest = level_2 and
   finance = yes
 THEN recommend = computer_programming;
!
Rule 1_5
IF aptitude = level_1 and
   interest = level_2 and
   finance = no
THEN recommend = computer_science;
!
Rule 1_6
IF aptitude = level_1 and
   interest = level_3 and
   finance = yes
THEN recommend = computer_programming;
!
Rule 1_7
IF aptitude = level_1 and
   interest = level_3 and
   finance = no
THEN recommend = computer_science;
!
Rule 1_8
IF aptitude = level_2 and
   interest = level_1 and
   finance = yes
THEN recommend = computer_programming;
!
Rule 1_9
IF aptitude = level_2 and
   interest = level_1 and
   finance = no
THEN recommend = computer_science;
!
Rule 1_10
IF aptitude = level_2 and
   interest = level_2 and
   finance = yes
THEN recommend = computer_programming;
!
Rule 1_11
IF aptitude = level_2 and
   interest = level_2 and
   finance = no
THEN recommend = computer_science;
!
Rule 1_12
IF aptitude = level_2 and
   interest = level_3 and
   finance = yes
THEN recommend = computer_programming;
!
Rule 1_13
IF aptitude = level_2 and
   interest = level_3 and
   finance = no
THEN recommend = computer_science;
!
Rule 1_14
IF aptitude = level_3 and
   interest = level_1
THEN recommend = computer_technology;
!
Rule 1_15
IF aptitude = level_3 and
   interest = level_2
THEN recommend = computer_technology;
!
Rule 1_16
IF aptitude = level_3 and
   interest = level_3
THEN recommend = computer_technology;
!
Rule 1_17
IF aptitude = level_4 and
   interest = level_1
THEN recommend = computer_technology;
!
Rule 1_18
IF aptitude = level_4 and
   interest = level_2
THEN recommend = computer_programming;
!
Rule 1_19
IF aptitude = level_4 and
   interest = level_3
THEN recommend = computer_programming;
!
Rule 1_20
IF aptitude = level_5
   and interest = level_1
THEN recommend = computer_programming;
!
```

Figure 8B–7. *concluded*

```
Rule 1_21
IF aptitude = level_5 and
   interest = level_2
THEN recommend = computer_programming;
!
Rule 1_22
IF aptitude = level_5 and
   interest = level_3
THEN recommend = computer_programming;
!
!Rule set for rule set #2
!
Rule 2_1
IF math = yes and
   prog = yes and
   manual = yes
THEN aptitude = level_1;
!
Rule 2_2
IF math = yes and
   prog = yes and
   manual = no
THEN aptitude = level_2;
!
Rule 2_3
IF math = yes and
   prog = no and
   manual = yes
THEN aptitude = level_3;
!
Rule 2_4
IF math = yes and
   prog = no and
   manual = no
THEN aptitude = level_0;
!
Rule 2_5
IF math = no and
   prog = yes and
   manual = yes
THEN aptitude = level_4;
!
Rule 2_6
IF math = no and
   prog = yes and
   manual = no
THEN aptitude = level_5;
!
Rule 2_7
IF math = no and
   prog = no and
   manual = yes
THEN aptitude = level_3;
!
Rule 2_8
IF math = no and
   prog = no and
   manual = no
THEN aptitude = level_0;
!
!Rule set for rule set #3
!
Rule 3_1
IF computers = yes and
   problems = yes and
   place = desk and
   repair = yes
THEN interest = level_3;
!
Rule 3_2
IF computers = yes and
   problems = yes and
   repair = no
THEN interest = level_2;
!
Rule 3_3
IF computers = yes and
   problems = yes and
   place = field and
   repair = yes
THEN interest = level_1;
!
Rule 3_4
IF computers = yes and
   problems = no
THEN interest = level_0;
!
Rule 3_5
IF computers = no
THEN interest = level_0;
!

!
!Questions Block
!
ASK math: "Are you good at math?";
CHOICES math:yes,no;
!
ASK prog: "Are you good at programming?";
CHOICES prog:yes,no;
!
ASK manual: "Are you good at working with your hands?";
CHOICES manual:yes,no;
!
ASK computers: "Do you like working with computers?";
CHOICES computers:yes,no;
!
ASK problems: "Do you like solving problems?";
CHOICES problems:yes,no;
!
ASK place: "Do you prefer working at a desk or in the field?";
CHOICES place:desk,field;
!
ASK repair: "Do you like to repair things?";
CHOICES repair:yes,no;
!
ASK finance: "Do you need to get a job upon graduation?";
CHOICES finance:yes,no;
```

Testing and Validation

The College Major Advisor prototype system was initially tested by the system developer. Data was entered for "dummy" students with various responses to the input questions. The results were as expected. Then a more systematic test was done using all possible responses for all the questions. Again, the results were as expected.

The next step in the testing process will be to have a class of students test the system. First students will discuss their interests, aptitudes, and financial needs with a counsellor or a faculty advisor. The advisor will manually record the best major selection for the students. Then students will be asked to run the computerized College Major Advisor. They will report their results to the advisor, who will compare the computer results to the human expert's advice. This process will validate the results of the College Major Advisor.

8C Nonprofit Organization Loan Advisor

TECHNICAL PROFILE

Difficulty Level	Beginner
Special Features	The BECAUSE clause is used to provide explanations whenever a user asks "Why?" a question is being asked.
File Used	NFF.KBS
To Run	Load NFF.KBS from the disk accompanying this book.

OVERVIEW

Lending organizations want to ensure that borrowers pay back their loans. For this reason, a lending organization carefully scrutinizes all aspects of the borrower who is requesting the loan.

Loan evaluation processes are not the same from industry to industry. Each industry dictates a unique set of parameters that must be evaluated. For instance, nonprofit organizations in one metropolitan area can apply to the Nonprofit Facilities Fund for construction loans. These loan applications are evaluated in nonprofit terms, which consider factors such as the executive director's length of service and the organization's history.

The proposed expert system assists Nonprofit Facilities Fund personnel in the loan evaluation process. It helps a loan program associate to systematically evaluate the qualitative, or non-financial, aspects of loan applications from nonprofit organizations. Potential users of the system are lower- to middle-level loan program associates who work for the Nonprofit Facilities Fund or another nonprofit lending organization.

Justification for the Prototype

This prototype system will help to make loan evaluations less labor intensive, which is important because nonprofit lending organizations tend to be understaffed. The system also serves as a training tool. Personnel who perform credit analysis on a loan application are usually inexperienced junior associate staff members. The typical loan program associate is a recent college graduate and often a newcomer to the nonprofit sector.

Knowledge Sources

Several sources of knowledge were used to develop this prototype:

- Senior loan management personnel at nonprofit organizations
- Lending organizations, both private sector and nonprofit
- Financial consultants specializing in the nonprofit sector
- Government agencies involved in lending activities

STUDYING THE SITUATION

The Nonprofit Facilities Fund is divided into two main areas of service, as shown in Figure 8C–1. This prototype is concerned with only one of them, the Loan Program, the function of which is to process loans for qualified nonprofit organizations. The Loan Program sequence typically includes the following steps:

1. A completed loan application is received through the mail by a loan program associate.
2. The application is reviewed for completeness. The application package must include three years of financial statements (preferably certified audits); a description of the proposed project with projections for the benefits realized; financial projections for payback and general operations covering the term of the loan; and background information on the organization.
3. Information is entered on a credit analysis form. Scores, or credit ratings, are compiled to determine "suitability" in various categories.
4. On-site interviews with the borrower's senior management are conducted. Phone conversations provide additional information.
5. Based on the ratings determinations and the information gathered through conversations and interviews, a report is drafted either recommending or rejecting the application.

Figure 8C–1. Nonprofit Organization Loan Advisor: Block Diagram for Area Under Study

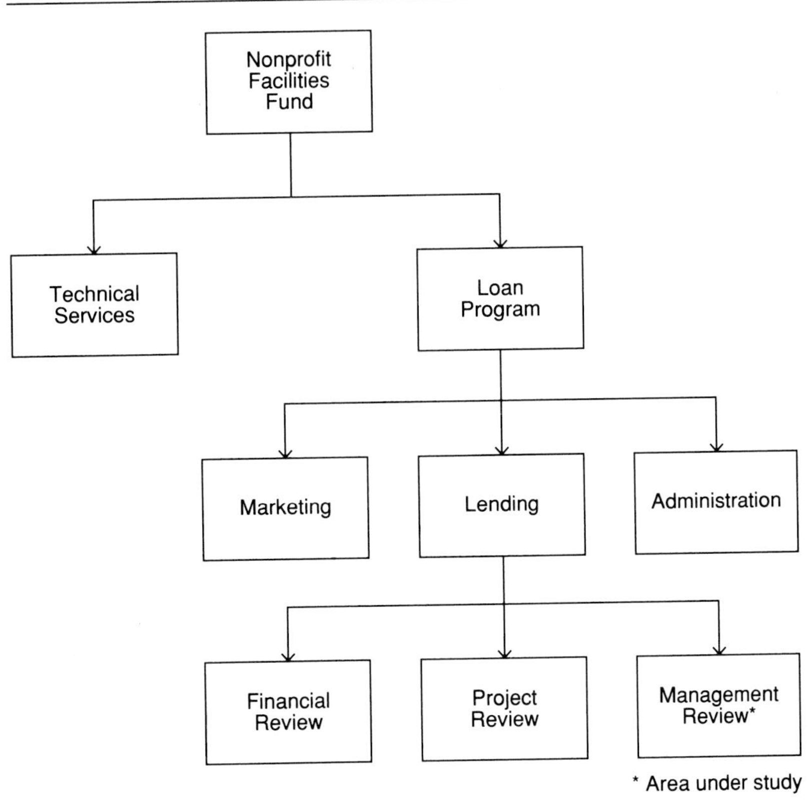

Many forms are filled out and used to perform a loan investigation. These documents, which serve as guidelines and information repositories for the loan staff, include

- A loan application
- Additional loan application checklist materials for follow-up meeting
- A loan summary
- A financial summary
- A credit score

Figure 8C–2. Nonprofit Organization Loan Advisor: Sample Forms (pp. 192–194)

LOAN APPLICATION

****

Background

Legal name of borrower:____________________________

Current address:____________________________

____

Address of project:____________________________

____

Name of executive director:____________________________

Telephone: ____________________ Fax: ____________

Contact name (if different):____________________________

Contact title:____________________________

Telephone:____________________ Fax:____________

Is your board of directors aware of this application?______
Has your board of directors formally approved the idea of borrowing for this project?______
Does your organization have 501(c)(3) tax-exempt status?______
Year organization was founded:______
Number of full-time equivalent employees:______
Number of people served annually:______

****

Project Information

Description of project:____________________________

____

Date funds will be needed:______________
Amount your organization will contribute to the cost: $ ____________

Total from other sources (explain as attachment 7): $ ____________

Amount of this loan request: $ ____________

Total $ ____________

How will you repay funds borrowed for this project?

____

____

****

Figure 8C–2 presents examples of two of these documents, a loan application and a loan summary. The application is filled out by the applicant and the loan summary is completed by the loan evaluator at the Nonprofit Facilities Fund.

Narrowing the Focus

Figure 8C–1 shows that the Loan Program is divided into three functions: marketing, lending, and administration. This prototype for the Nonprofit Organization Loan Advisor is concerned with the lending function. Lending in-

Property Information

Do you lease or own the facility to be financed?______
If you own, is your building mortgaged? [ ] Yes [ ] No
Mortgage lender:______________________________
Term: ______ yrs at ______ % interest   Monthly payments: $ ____________
Amount outstanding: $ ____________   Date of final payment: ____________
Does your mortgage contain any prohibitions/limitations on debt? ________
If you lease, when does your lease expire? ____________
Landlord: ______________________________   Annual rent: $ ____________

****

Financial Information

Name of bank:______________________________
Please attach:

1. Financial statements for your last three fiscal years
2. Year-to-date internal financial statement
3. Income/expense projections for the remainder of the current fiscal year (Use the same format as the Income Statement in your financial statement.)

If your borrowings have changed since your last audit, please note here:

____

____

____

****

ATTACHMENTS (These are a required part of the application; if any of these items are not available, please indicate so and note plans for obtaining them.)

In addition to financial information noted above, please attach:

4. Your most recent annual report, including a list of your board of directors and their affiliations
5. A brief statement describing your project and its importance to your organization (For example, you should indicate if the project will alleviate overcrowding, allow an increase in your client base, or generate additional revenue, and explain how the project will impact operating and maintenance costs.)
6. A project scope of work and budget, including a timetable
7. If this loan request represents partial funding for your project, a list of other funding received or committed and the total amount raised to date
8. A list of major program funders during most recent fiscal year

The information provided on this application and the accompanying documents are, to the best of my knowledge and belief, true, correct, and complete.

______________________   ______________________
Name (please print)   Signature

______________________   ______________________
Title   Date

Figure 8C–2 *concluded*

LOAN SUMMARY

Borrower: *Community One Stop,* Broadway at 116th Street
Business: Case work center for seniors, 70% funded by NYC Dept. F/T Aging 4,000 a year are served by 10 FTEs
Amount: $15,000
Purpose: Pay architectural and engineering fees in connection with COS's move to cheaper space (The landlord is paying for the renovations.)
Repayment: Operations

Credit

(FY=6/30)	87	88	89	90B	Loan as a % of:		Loan Scores	
Revenues	196	272	349	354	Revenues:	4%	Complexity:	I
Fd. Bal. Chg.	−3	−3	5	7	Fund Bal.:	200%	Overall:	138
End Fd. Bal.	4	9	15	22	Project:	15%E		

Other borrowings: None

Board

12 members, most with ties to other social service agencies involved with seniors. Chair = Fred Wilburn (Lenot Hse.) Ex. Dir. (for 4 yrs.) = May Lundorf (ACSW).

Technical Review

None, since landlord is paying for renovations and COS has retained their own architect (a well-regarded firm)

Proposed Loan

Amount:	$15,000	Rate:	11%
Amortztn:	8 equal qtly. payments	Fees:	waived
Maturity:	2 yrs. from signing	APR:	11%
Security:	None		

Discussion

This is a simple loan to a growing agency whose finances appear to be well under control. Its application reflected unusual maturity. The repayment burden will be very modest—well under the $18,000 per year in expected rent savings achieved by the move.

Dependence on one source of revenue is the greatest risk; however, the DFTA supervisor we spoke with spoke very favorably about the agency and its management. The contract is renewable annually (6/30) and has been in place since 1980, when the agency was established.

Recommendation

The staff recommends approval.

T.B.H. C.M.

volves reviewing all aspects of the loan application. It includes the loan applicant's financial statement and management profile, as well as a review of the project. The prototype is further narrowed to support only the review of the borrower's management profile.

Critical Factors Affecting the Situation

Recommendations given by this prototype expert system are based on three critical factors, the borrowing organization's management stability, board of directors' leadership and outside affiliations, and program history, as evident from Figure 8C–3.

Figure 8C–3. Nonprofit Organization Loan Advisor: Block Diagram for Loan Evaluation Decision

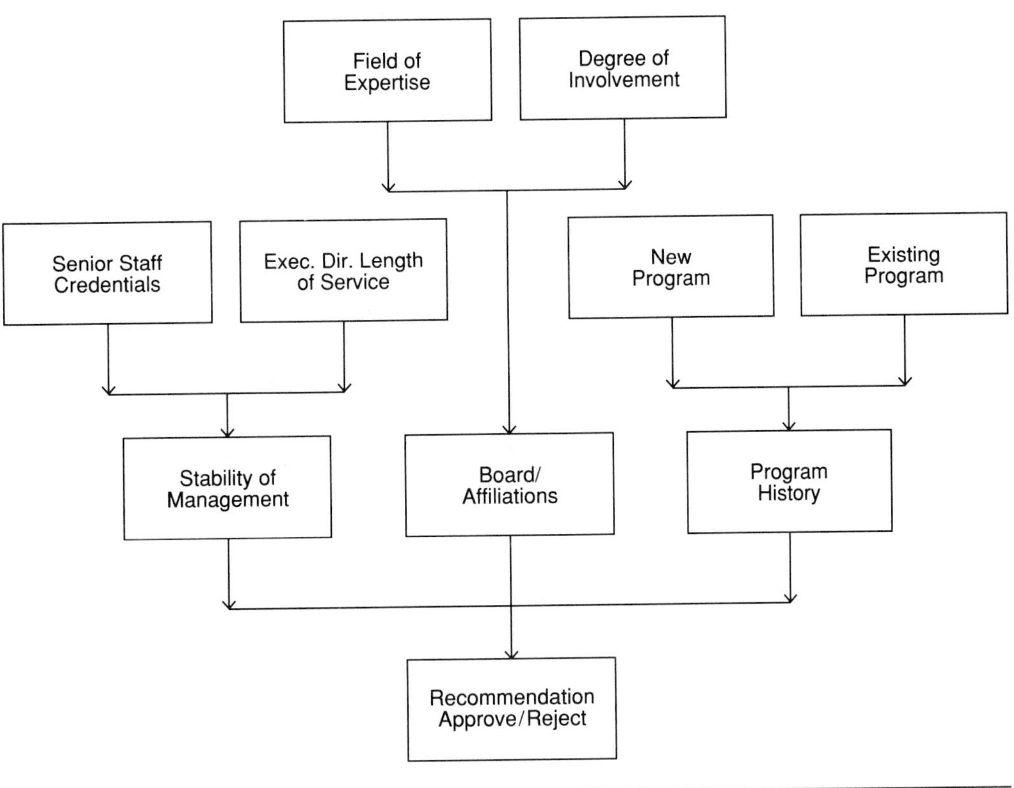

The stability of the applicant's management team is a leading indicator of its credit worthiness. Stability is measured in terms of how long the executive director and chief financial officer have worked for the nonprofit organization.

The next critical factor evaluates the leadership provided by the board of directors, as well as their outside affiliations. This examination provides valuable insight into the organizational culture and values as they relate to meeting financial obligations.

The third critical factor explores the organization's history in handling the type of program for which funding is being requested. Past performance is often one of the best indicators of future success.

Possible Recommendations Made by the System

After a user answers a series of questions, such as those shown in the sample consultations in Figure 8C–4, the Nonprofit Organization Loan Advisor prescribes one of four possible final recommendations:

1. Approve loan without collateral
2. Approve loan with collateral
3. Submit additional information
4. Reject loan application

Based on user responses to consultation questions, critical factors are determined to be strong, fair, or weak. There are multiple-factor combinations for

Figure 8C–4. Nonprofit Organization Loan Advisor: Sample Consultations

```
*** NONPROFIT ORGANIZATION LOAN ADVISOR ***
             Prototype Version

Developed by Denise Donovan and Maria Aguilar
     under the direction and supervision of
               Dr. D.G. Dologite
```

Consultation 1:

Text only

```
         Welcome to the Nonprofit Organization Loan Advisor

This system is designed to help a loan associate from the
Nonprofit Facilities Fund to evaluate loan applications.
Specifically, it helps the associate to evaluate the
qualitative, or non-financial, aspects of a loan application.

Several questions are asked during the consultation regarding
key decision factors.  The responses to these questions
determine the final recommendation.

           PLEASE PRESS ANY KEY TO BEGIN CONSULTATION
```

Actual screen

```
              Nonprofit Organization Loan Advisor

  Instructions:  Use the arrow keys to highlight the desired response,
                 then press the ENTER key.

How long has the Executive Director worked in this field?
 Less than 2 Years        2 to 5 Years             More than 5 Years ◄

How long has the Chief Financial Officer worked with the
organization?
 Less than 2 Years        2 to 5 Years             More than 5 Years ◄

Are the majority of Board members experienced with the type of
service the organization provides?
 Yes ◄                    No

What is the degree of the Board members' involvement with the
organization's operations?
 Low                      Moderate                 High ◄
```

Text only

```
Is the project meant to cover a new program area or to expand an
existing one?
 New ◄                    Existing

If this is a new program, does the applicant have any similar
experience?
 Yes ◄                    No
```

```
           The recommendation for the loan application is:

                 APPROVE LOAN WITHOUT COLLATERAL.

      This recommendation was determined by the combined evaluation
             of the critical factors.  They are as follows:

                 Management Stability - STRONG

         Board of Directors and their Affiliations - STRONG

                    Program History - STRONG

       Thank you for using the NONPROFIT ORGANIZATION LOAN ADVISOR.

            PLEASE PRESS ANY KEY TO CONCLUDE CONSULTATION
```

Consultation 2:

Text only

```
How long has the Executive Director worked in this field?
 Less than 2 Years        2 to 5 Years ◄           More than 5 Years

How long has the Chief Financial Officer worked with the
organization?
 Less than 2 Years ◄      2 to 5 Years             More than 5 Years

Are the majority of Board members experienced with the type of
service the organization provides?
 Yes ◄                    No

What is the degree of the Board members' involvement with the
organization's operations?
 Low                      Moderate ◄               High

Are any of the Board members willing to personally guarantee the
loan?
 Yes ◄                    No

Is the project meant to cover a new program area or to expand an
existing one?
 New                      Existing ◄

If it will expand an existing program, how long has the organization
been involved in this area or a similar one?
 Less than 2 Years        2 to 5 Years ◄           More than 5 Years


           The recommendation for the loan application is:

                 SUBMIT ADDITIONAL INFORMATION.

      This recommendation was determined by the combined evaluation
             of the critical factors.  They are as follows:

                 Management Stability - FAIR

         Board of Directors and their Affiliations - STRONG

                    Program History - FAIR

       Thank you for using the NONPROFIT ORGANIZATION LOAN ADVISOR.

            PLEASE PRESS ANY KEY TO CONCLUDE CONSULTATION
```

each recommendation. For example, there are three possible scenarios for a recommendation of "Approve loan without collateral." All three scenarios require that management stability, as well as at least one of the other two factors, be strong.

Figure 8C–5 shows the completed decision table for the final rule set, as well as the reduced decision table.

A Typical Decision Situation

Steven Lyman, loan program associate, Clara Johnson, executive director, and Tom Griffin, financial consultant, arrive at the 92nd St. Theatre Company for a 2 P.M. meeting with Rose Carlson, artistic director. By 3 P.M. the conversation has focused as follows:

CLARA JOHNSON. Well, Rose, what do you think? Are your board members committed enough to this construction to give us their personal guarantee to meet the quarterly payments if your funding should be delayed?

ROSE CARLSON. To be perfectly honest with you, Clara, about half the board is really excited about the new building. Of the other half, one or two hate it and the rest aren't saying very much during our meetings. I'll have to speak to them individually to see how committed they really are.

STEVE LYMAN. Forgive me, Rose, for not being up to date on this. How long has your chairperson been affiliated with the theatre?

ROSE CARLSON. Bob has been involved with the theatre and acting, in one way or another, since he was in college. I think if he could find a way to make it profitable, he wouldn't work in the private sector at all.

STEVE LYMAN. I'm glad he feels so strongly about it. How long did you say you have been artistic director?

ROSE CARLSON. I've been an artistic director for 10 years. Five of those were with another theatre, but I've been managing 92nd St. for the past five.

STEVE LYMAN. I was hoping to meet your chief financial officer. I'm sorry she couldn't make the meeting. How long has she been working for you?

ROSE CARLSON. She's been with the organization a little less than a year. She was a real find for us and has been doing a great job.

TOM GRIFFIN. Rose, is this a brand-new program for the theatre, or is it some kind of spin-off from last year?

ROSE CARLSON. Actually, Tom, the theatre has never attempted anything like this before. But three or four years ago, I was involved in a similar project in Chicago and it worked rather well. It took a lot of work, of course, and some very careful planning. It caught on gradually, and it was a big success in the end.

After the meeting ends, the Nonprofit Facilities Fund staff goes back to the office to discuss the results:

STEVE LYMAN. What do you think, Clara? Do you think the management is stable enough to see the payments through to term?

CLARA JOHNSON. Well, Rose has been in the business for 10 years. That's a big plus. On the other hand, the board doesn't seem to me to be really behind this project 100 percent.

TOM GRIFFIN. That's still to be seen after Rose speaks to her board members one-on-one. I do wish, though, that their financial person had been with the theatre longer. She hasn't even been there a year.

CLARA JOHNSON. Considering everything, it seems to me that we should get more information from the theatre staff before we make a final decision. What do you two think?

Figure 8C–5. Nonprofit Organization Loan Advisor: Decision Tables—Final Rule Set

A. Completed Decision Table

Rule	Stability of Management	Board of Directors	Program History	Concluding Recommendation
A1	Strong	Strong	Strong	Approve loan without collateral
A2	Strong	Strong	Fair	Approve loan without collateral
A3	Strong	Strong	Weak	Submit additional information
A4	Strong	Fair	Strong	Approve loan without collateral
A5	Strong	Fair	Fair	Approve loan with collateral
A6	Strong	Fair	Weak	Submit additional information
A7	Strong	Weak	Strong	Approve loan with collateral
A8	Strong	Weak	Fair	Approve loan with collateral
A9	Strong	Weak	Weak	Submit additional information
A10	Fair	Strong	Strong	Approve loan with collateral
A11	Fair	Strong	Fair	Submit additional information
A12	Fair	Strong	Weak	Reject loan application
A13	Fair	Fair	Strong	Submit additional information
A14	Fair	Fair	Fair	Submit additional information
A15	Fair	Fair	Weak	Reject loan application
A16	Fair	Weak	Strong	Submit additional information
A17	Fair	Weak	Fair	Reject loan application
A18	Fair	Weak	Weak	Reject loan application
A19	Weak	Strong	Strong	Submit additional information
A20	Weak	Strong	Fair	Reject loan application
A21	Weak	Strong	Weak	Reject loan application
A22	Weak	Fair	Strong	Reject loan application
A23	Weak	Fair	Fair	Reject loan application
A24	Weak	Fair	Weak	Reject loan application
A25	Weak	Weak	Strong	Reject loan application
A26	Weak	Weak	Fair	Reject loan application
A27	Weak	Weak	Weak	Reject loan application

B. Reduced Decision Table

Rule	Stability of Management	Board of Directors	Program History	Concluding Recommendation
B1	Strong	Strong	Strong/Fair	Approve loan without collateral
B2	Strong	Strong	Weak	Submit additional information
B3	Strong	Fair	Strong	Approve loan without collateral
B4	Strong	Fair	Fair	Approve loan with collateral
B5	Strong	Fair	Weak	Submit additional information
B6	Strong	Weak	Strong/Fair	Approve loan with collateral
B7	Strong	Weak	Weak	Submit additional information
B8	Fair	Strong	Strong	Approve loan with collateral
B9	Fair	Strong	Fair	Submit additional information
B10	Fair	Strong	Weak	Reject loan application
B11	Fair	Fair	Strong/Fair	Submit additional information
B12	Fair	Fair	Weak	Reject loan application
B13	Fair	Weak	Strong	Submit additional information
B14	Fair	Weak	Fair/Weak	Reject loan application
B15	Weak	Strong	Strong	Submit additional information
B16	Weak	Strong	Fair/Weak	Reject loan application
B17	Weak	Fair/Weak	—	Reject loan application

TOM GRIFFIN. I agree.

STEVE LYMAN. Me, too. I'll call Rose in the morning and ask her a few more questions.

SYSTEM DOCUMENTATION

A dependency diagram of the nonprofit organization loan evaluation decision is given in Figure 8C–6. The complete knowledge base can be examined in Figure 8C–7 and by printing out the file named NFF.KBS on the disk accompanying this book.

Design Considerations

An attempt was made to help make the system more user-friendly. This is evident in two ways:

1. The final values of the three decision factors of this system are displayed at the end of a consultation, along with a final recommendation. This helps a user to better understand why the system is making a specific recommendation.
2. The BECAUSE clause was used to provide explanations that are understandable whenever a user asks "Why?" a question is being asked.

Figure 8C–6. Nonprofit Organization Loan Advisor: Dependency Diagram

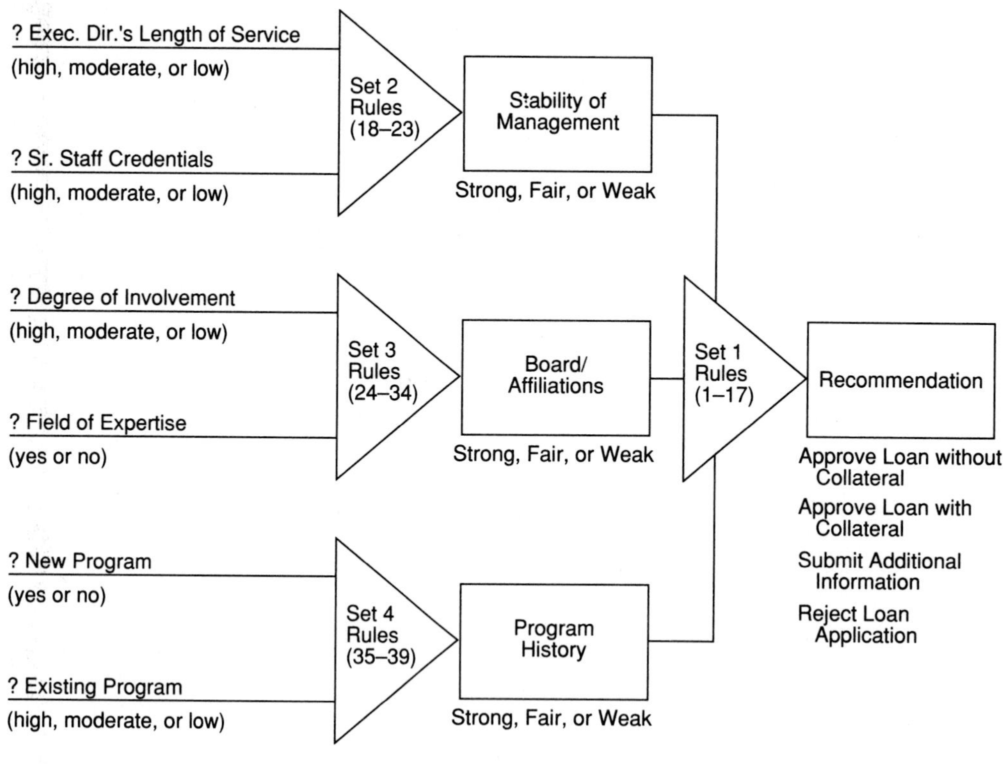

Figure 8C–7. Nonprofit Organization Loan Advisor: Printout of Knowledge Base File

```
!***************************************************************************
! KBS file name:       Nonprofit Organization Loan Advisor                  *
! Microcomputer Used:  IBM compatible                                       *
! Software Used:       VP-Expert, Educational Version 2.02                  *
! KBS Files Used:      NFF.KBS - There are no other files currently used.   *
!***************************************************************************
EXECUTE;
BKCOLOR = 1;
RUNTIME;
ENDOFF;


!*************** ACTION BLOCK *************************
ACTIONS
    WOPEN 1,0,0,23,79,1
    ACTIVE 1
    DISPLAY "

                    *** NONPROFIT ORGANIZATION LOAN ADVISOR ***
                                 Prototype Version

                   Developed by Denise Donovan and Maria Aguilar
                       under the direction and supervision of
                                 Dr. D.G. Dologite
                          For further information, contact
                                 Dr. D.G. Dologite
                              c/o Macmillan Publishing


                          PLEASE PRESS ANY KEY TO CONTINUE~"
    WCLOSE 1
    WOPEN 2,0,0,23,79,1
    ACTIVE 2
    DISPLAY "
             Welcome to the Nonprofit Organization Loan Advisor


      This system is designed to help a loan associate from the
      Nonprofit Facilities Fund to evaluate loan applications.
      Specifically, it helps the associate to evaluate the
      qualitative, or non-financial, aspects of a loan application.

      Several questions are asked during the consultation regarding
      key decision factors.  The responses to these questions
      determine the final recommendation.


                  PLEASE PRESS ANY KEY TO BEGIN CONSULTATION~"
    WCLOSE 2
    WOPEN 3,0,0,6,79,1
    ACTIVE 3
    DISPLAY
"                    Nonprofit Organization Loan Advisor

    Instructions:  Use the arrow keys to highlight the desired response,
                   then press the ENTER key."

    WOPEN 4,7,0,15,79,1
    ACTIVE 4
    FIND rec
    WCLOSE 4
    WCLOSE 3
    WOPEN 5,0,0,23,79,1
    ACTIVE 5
    DISPLAY
  "
                The recommendation for the loan application is:

                             {rec}.


          This recommendation was determined by the combined evaluation
                 of the critical factors.  They are as follows:

                         Management Stability - {STABILITY}
```

Figure 8C–7. *continued*

```
                Board of Directors and their Affiliations - {BOARD}

                            Program History - {PROGRAM}


          Thank you for using the NONPROFIT ORGANIZATION LOAN ADVISOR.

                 PLEASE PRESS ANY KEY TO CONCLUDE CONSULTATION~"
    WCLOSE 5

;

!*************** Rules Block for Final Recommendation***
!*************** STABILITY = STRONG *************************
RULE 1
IF STABILITY = STRONG AND
   BOARD     = STRONG AND
   PROGRAM   = STRONG OR
   PROGRAM   = FAIR
THEN REC = APPROVE_LOAN_WITHOUT_COLLATERAL;

RULE 2
IF STABILITY = STRONG AND
   BOARD     = STRONG AND
   PROGRAM   = WEAK
THEN REC = SUBMIT_ADDITIONAL_INFORMATION;

RULE 3
IF STABILITY = STRONG AND
   BOARD     = FAIR AND
   PROGRAM   = STRONG
THEN REC = APPROVE_LOAN_WITHOUT_COLLATERAL;

RULE 4
IF STABILITY = STRONG AND
   BOARD     = FAIR AND
   PROGRAM   = FAIR
THEN REC = APPROVE_LOAN_WITH_COLLATERAL;

RULE 5
IF STABILITY = STRONG AND
   BOARD     = FAIR AND
   PROGRAM   = WEAK
THEN REC = SUBMIT_ADDITIONAL_INFORMATION;

RULE 6
IF STABILITY = STRONG AND
   BOARD     = WEAK AND
   PROGRAM   = STRONG OR
   PROGRAM   = FAIR
THEN REC = APPROVE_LOAN_WITH_COLLATERAL;

RULE 7
IF STABILITY = STRONG AND
   BOARD     = WEAK AND
   PROGRAM   = WEAK
THEN REC = SUBMIT_ADDITIONAL_INFORMATION;

!*************** STABILITY = FAIR *************************
RULE 8
IF STABILITY = FAIR AND
   BOARD     = STRONG AND
   PROGRAM   = STRONG
THEN REC = APPROVE_LOAN_WITH_COLLATERAL;

RULE 9
IF STABILITY = FAIR AND
   BOARD     = STRONG AND
   PROGRAM   = FAIR
THEN REC = SUBMIT_ADDITIONAL_INFORMATION;

RULE 10
IF STABILITY = FAIR AND
   BOARD     = STRONG AND
   PROGRAM   = WEAK
THEN REC = REJECT_LOAN_APPLICATION;
```

```
RULE 11
IF STABILITY = FAIR AND
   BOARD     = FAIR AND
   PROGRAM   = STRONG OR
   PROGRAM   = FAIR
THEN REC = SUBMIT_ADDITIONAL_INFORMATION;

RULE 12
IF STABILITY = FAIR AND
   BOARD     = FAIR AND
   PROGRAM   = WEAK
THEN REC = REJECT_LOAN_APPLICATION;

RULE 13
IF STABILITY = FAIR AND
   BOARD     = WEAK AND
   PROGRAM   = STRONG
THEN REC = SUBMIT_ADDITIONAL_INFORMATION;

RULE 14
IF STABILITY = FAIR AND
   BOARD     = WEAK AND
   PROGRAM   = FAIR OR
   PROGRAM   = WEAK
THEN REC = REJECT_LOAN_APPLICATION;

!*************** STABILITY = WEAK ****************************
RULE 15
IF STABILITY = WEAK AND
   BOARD     = STRONG AND
   PROGRAM   = STRONG
THEN REC = SUBMIT_ADDITIONAL_INFORMATION;

RULE 16
IF STABILITY = WEAK AND
   BOARD     = STRONG AND
   PROGRAM   = FAIR OR
   PROGRAM   = WEAK
THEN REC = REJECT_LOAN_APPLICATION;

RULE 17
IF STABILITY = WEAK AND
   BOARD     = FAIR OR
   BOARD     = WEAK
THEN REC = REJECT_LOAN_APPLICATION;

!*************** FOR SECOND DECISION TABLE **************
!*************** ED.'S SERVICE = H **********************

RULE 18
IF EDSERV  = More_than_5_Years AND
   CFOSERV = 2_to_5_Years OR
   CFOSERV = More_than_5_Years
THEN STABILITY = STRONG
BECAUSE
"
Strong management stability is a leading indicator of credit worthiness.";


RULE 19
IF EDSERV  = More_than_5_Years AND
   CFOSERV = Less_than_2_Years
THEN STABILITY = FAIR
BECAUSE
"
Strong management stability is a leading indicator of credit worthiness.";

!*************** ED.'S SERVICE = M **********************

RULE 20
IF EDSERV  = 2_to_5_Years AND
   CFOSERV = More_than_5_Years
THEN STABILITY = STRONG
BECAUSE
"
Strong management stability is a leading indicator of credit worthiness.";
```

Figure 8C–7. *continued*

```
RULE 21
IF EDSERV  = 2_to_5_Years AND
   CFOSERV = Less_than_2_Years OR
   CFOSERV = 2_to_5_Years
THEN STABILITY = FAIR
BECAUSE
"
Strong management stability is a leading indicator of credit worthiness.";

!*************** ED.'S SERVICE = L **********************

RULE 22
IF EDSERV  = Less_than_2_Years AND
   CFOSERV = More_than_5_Years
THEN STABILITY = FAIR
BECAUSE
"
Strong management stability is a leading indicator of credit worthiness.";

RULE 23
IF EDSERV  = Less_than_2_Years AND
   CFOSERV = Less_than_2_Years OR
   CFOSERV = 2_to_5_Years
THEN STABILITY = WEAK
BECAUSE
"
Strong management stability is a leading indicator of credit worthiness.";


!*************** FOR THIRD DECISION TABLE ***************
!*************** BD.'S EXPER. = YES *********************

RULE 24
IF BDEXP = YES AND
   BDINV = HIGH
THEN BOARD = STRONG
BECAUSE
"
The organization's leadership is responsible for its financial obligations.";

RULE 25
IF BDEXP = YES AND
   BDINV = MODERATE AND
   BDGRN = YES
THEN BOARD = STRONG
BECAUSE
"
The organization's leadership is responsible for its financial obligations.";

RULE 26
IF BDEXP = YES AND
   BDINV = MODERATE AND
   BDGRN = NO
THEN BOARD = FAIR
BECAUSE
"
The organization's leadership is responsible for its financial obligations.";

RULE 27
IF BDEXP = YES AND
   BDINV = LOW AND
   BDGRN = YES
THEN BOARD = STRONG
BECAUSE
"
The organization's leadership is responsible for its financial obligations.";

RULE 28
IF BDEXP = YES AND
   BDINV = LOW AND
   BDGRN = NO
THEN BOARD = FAIR
BECAUSE
"
The organization's leadership is responsible for its financial obligations.";
```

```
!*************** BD.'S EXPER. = NO **********************

RULE 29
IF BDEXP = NO AND
   BDINV = HIGH AND
   BDGRN = YES
THEN BOARD = FAIR
BECAUSE
"
The organization's leadership is responsible for its financial obligations.";

RULE 30
IF BDEXP = NO AND
   BDINV = HIGH AND
   BDGRN = NO
THEN BOARD = WEAK
BECAUSE
"
The organization's leadership is responsible for its financial obligations.";

RULE 31
IF BDEXP = NO AND
   BDINV = MODERATE AND
   BDGRN = YES
THEN BOARD = FAIR
BECAUSE
"
The organization's leadership is responsible for its financial obligations.";

RULE 32
IF BDEXP = NO AND
   BDINV = MODERATE AND
   BDGRN = NO
THEN BOARD = WEAK
BECAUSE
"
The organization's leadership is responsible for its financial obligations.";

RULE 33
IF BDEXP = NO AND
   BDINV = LOW AND
   BDGRN = YES
THEN BOARD = FAIR
BECAUSE
"
The organization's leadership is responsible for its financial obligations.";

RULE 34
IF BDEXP = NO AND
   BDINV = LOW AND
   BDGRN = NO
THEN BOARD = WEAK
BECAUSE
"
The organization's leadership is responsible for its financial obligations.";

!*************** FOR FOURTH DECISION TABLE **************
!*************** NEW PROGRAM ****************************

RULE 35
IF PGM = NEW AND
   SIMEXP  = YES
THEN PROGRAM = STRONG
BECAUSE
"
Past experience is a key indicator of future success.";
```

Figure 8C–7. *concluded*

```
RULE 36
IF PGM = NEW AND
   SIMEXP  = NO
THEN PROGRAM = FAIR
BECAUSE
"
Past experience is a key indicator of future success.";
!*************** EXIST PROGRAM **************************

RULE 37
IF PGM    = EXISTING AND
   LEXP   = More_than_5_Years
THEN PROGRAM = STRONG
BECAUSE
"
Past experience is a key indicator of future success.";

RULE 38
IF PGM    = EXISTING AND
   LEXP   = 2_to_5_Years
THEN PROGRAM = FAIR
BECAUSE
"
Past experience is a key indicator of future success.";

RULE 39
IF PGM    = EXISTING AND
   LEXP   = Less_than_2_Years
THEN PROGRAM = WEAK
BECAUSE
"
Past experience is a key indicator of future success.";


!*************** QUESTIONS *********************************
ASK EDSERV:"How long has the Executive Director worked in this field?";
CHOICES EDSERV: Less_than_2_Years, 2_to_5_Years, More_than_5_Years ;

ASK CFOSERV:"How long has the Chief Financial Officer worked with the
organization?";
CHOICES CFOSERV: Less_than_2_Years, 2_to_5_Years, More_than_5_Years ;

ASK BDEXP:"Are the majority of Board members experienced with the type of
service the organization provides?";
CHOICES BDEXP: Yes, No;

ASK BDINV:"What is the degree of the Board members' involvement with the
organization's operations?";
CHOICES BDINV: Low, Moderate, High;

ASK BDGRN:"Are any of the Board members willing to personally guarantee the
loan?";
CHOICES BDGRN: Yes, No;

ASK PGM:"Is the project meant to cover a new program area or to expand an
existing one?";
CHOICES PGM: New, Existing;

ASK SIMEXP:"If this is a new program, does the applicant have any similar
experience?"; CHOICES SIMEXP: Yes, No;

ASK LEXP:"If it will expand an existing program, how long has the organization
been involved in this area or a similar one?";
CHOICES LEXP: Less_than_2_Years, 2_to_5_Years, More_than_5_Years ;
```

Testing and Validation

To test performance, completed loan applications that were submitted to several nonprofit loan organizations were entered into the Nonprofit Organization Loan Advisor prototype system. Results from the system were then compared to decisions made by staff loan program associates.

Careful attention was paid to the selection of test cases. Since the requirements for nonprofit organizations vary according to the sector they serve—for example, education, health, or social service—it was important that each sector be properly represented in testing. It was also significant that cases chosen for validation span at least two to five years. This smoothed out whatever effects the general economic conditions played in the final disposition of the applications.

One more consideration was the complexity of the loan application. Test cases included loans that involved only one lender and a simple project, as well as those involving multiple lending institutions and multi-site, complex projects. This approach guaranteed that a representative range of possible scenarios and outcomes could be accommodated by the expert system.

A decision match of 70 percent between the human decision maker and the expert system is considered within an acceptable range. The initial set of test cases used here achieved a 78 percent match ratio.

REFERENCES

Various documentation and interviews with staff, New York City Department of Cultural Affairs, Capital Revolving Loan Fund Program.

Various documentation and interviews with staff, New York State Council on the Arts, Revolving Construction Loan Fund for Arts Organizations Program.

Various documentation and interviews with staff, United Parcel Service, Loan Fund for Arts Organizations Program.

Various documentation and interviews with staff, Nonprofit Facilities Fund, Loan Fund Program.

8D

Job Applicant Screening Assistant

TECHNICAL PROFILE

Difficulty Level	Beginner
Special Features	This system uses the PLURAL keyword. It also uses a numeric rating scheme that helps to determine a final recommendation.
File Used	PROJECT1.KBS
To Run	Load PROJECT1.KBS from the disk accompanying this book

OVERVIEW

Often, considerable human resources are devoted to hiring the "right" person for a job. One organization where this is especially true is at the headquarters of the United Nations (UN) Organization. Applicants for UN jobs are plentiful and the screening process is exhaustive. Some UN employees must, for example, be able to adapt to living in foreign countries, have exceptional interpersonal skills, and speak more than one language.

The Job Applicant Screening Assistant prototype expert system is designed for screening job applicants at one branch of the UN, the United Nations Development Programme (UNDP). As shown in Figure 8D–1, the UNDP is just one of many branches that make up the UN. The goal of the UNDP is to provide assistance for 4 billion people in countries of the developing world. The UNDP is the central funding, planning, and coordinating organization for technical assistance in the UN system. It provides grant assistance to build skills and develop resources in areas such as agriculture, industry, health, education, economic planning, transportation, and communications. The UNDP's country program funds are apportioned to go to the poorest countries in the world.

Consider these examples of UNDP programs that have had an impact on developing countries:

- Organizing construction of a bridge to truck food into famine-stricken Chad
- Providing skills training for women who are income providers in Bangladesh
- Supporting audiovisual training programs for Peruvian farmers to learn farm production and storage skills
- Supporting groundwater drilling in drought-stricken Mali
- Providing training for more than 1 million teachers throughout the world's developing countries

The UNDP was chosen as a prototype development area for several reasons:

- The high demand for UNDP employees, especially those required on a temporary basis
- The large volume of job applicants who must be screened on a continuing basis
- The recognized field and personnel experts who are readily available for interviews and who can articulate the methods used to reach a hiring decision
- The chief developer's firsthand knowledge of the UNDP personnel area

Figure 8D–1. Job Applicant Screening Assistant: Organization Chart of the United Nations

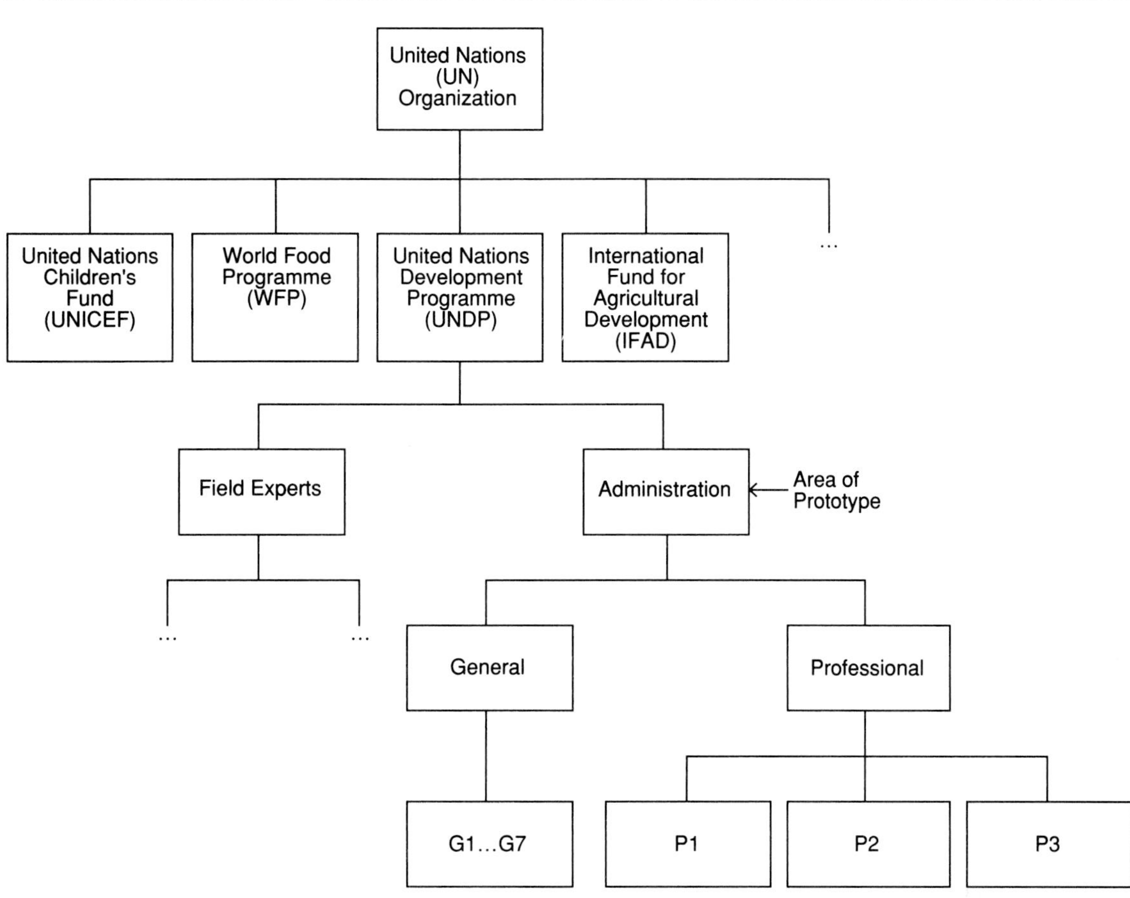

The intended users of the system are data entry operators in the UNDP personnel department. They enter an applicant's information directly into a computer from the application form. The expert system then recommends the applicant's suitability for available job positions.

The system's main benefit is that it reduces the time top management must devote to screening job applicants. By using an expert system for preliminary screening, high-level management avoids spending valuable time going through volumes of application forms. In addition, the ethnic diversity of the UN staff makes integrity a sensitive issue. Because the Job Applicant Screening Assistant evaluates applicants objectively, it adds integrity to the screening and hiring process.

STUDYING THE SITUATION

Four thousand people staff the UNDP's worldwide network. As Figure 8D–1 shows, staff is divided into field experts and administrative personnel. The administrative division has general (G) and professional (P) staff members. Both types are assigned position grades, such as G2 or P3. Employees can move up in grade over time, for example, from a P3 to a P4 position.

General staff consists of office support personnel, such as secretaries and clerical help, as well as lower-level managers. Professional staff includes upper- and middle-level management. They are professionals in any number of fields, such as administration, economics, finance, engineering, and project management. Their job responsibilities depend on their area of expertise and on the department in which they are employed, such as Africa, Asia, or Latin America. For example, a grade P2 project manager in the African department may be responsible for budgeting and evaluating ongoing UNDP projects in that country.

The initial concept-testing phase for this expert system is limited to screening job applicants for professional positions in the administrative division of the UNDP. It is further limited to only grade P2 positions. For prototyping purposes, the system considers job openings in four UNDP departments: Africa, Asia, Arab countries, and Latin America.

Critical Factors Affecting the Situation

The diagrams in Figures 8D–2 and 8D–3 identify the critical factors in the UNDP professional job applicant screening process. An applicant's *education level* must match the requirements of a particular job level. In some cases, relevant *work experience* in the UNDP or related areas can compensate for not meeting the education requirement. Applicants with an education lower than the level required for a particular job, and who cannot compensate for it with work experience, would not be considered.

The official *languages* required for UNDP employees are English, French, Spanish, Chinese, Arabic, and Russian. Knowledge of these official languages, with English as a requirement, is a key factor in departmental (such as Asia, Africa, or Latin America) recruiting. Within a department, the right candidate would be fluent in at least one of the official languages of the region. The ability to speak several languages increases the level of flexibility and mobility of an employee within the organization.

A *personal background* check determines if an applicant fits the job profile. It also determines if there are any conflicts with organizational hiring policies. For example, when there is a vacancy for an entry-level position, the organization is inclined to hire someone who is not approaching retirement. On the other hand, high-level positions demand people with more expertise and maturity. Also, it is common practice in the organization to favor applicants who are already UN employees, since they already know the organization's policies and procedures.

Another factor considered in personal background screening is the applicant's willingness to relocate and/or travel on overseas missions. Professional staff personnel are stationed both in the United States and foreign countries; foreign tours typically last two years. Even those with stateside assignments typically go on overseas missions frequently.

Any familiarity with world regions assisted by UNDP, especially a region with a job opening, is a positive indicator of the applicant's fit for the job.

A final personal background factor considers whether the applicant will be a financial burden to the organization. The organization has a policy of providing benefits, such as child care and other family expense coverage, for employees who go on missions abroad. Management is, nevertheless, concerned with the costs involved. So if there are a number of equally qualified applicants, the one who is the least eligible for family (dependent) benefits would be the most attractive to the organization.

Each of the three critical factors is determined by a series of questions asked by the expert system, as evident from the printout of a sample consultation in Figure 8D–4.

Figure 8D–2. Job Applicant Screening Assistant: Block Diagram of Decision Situation

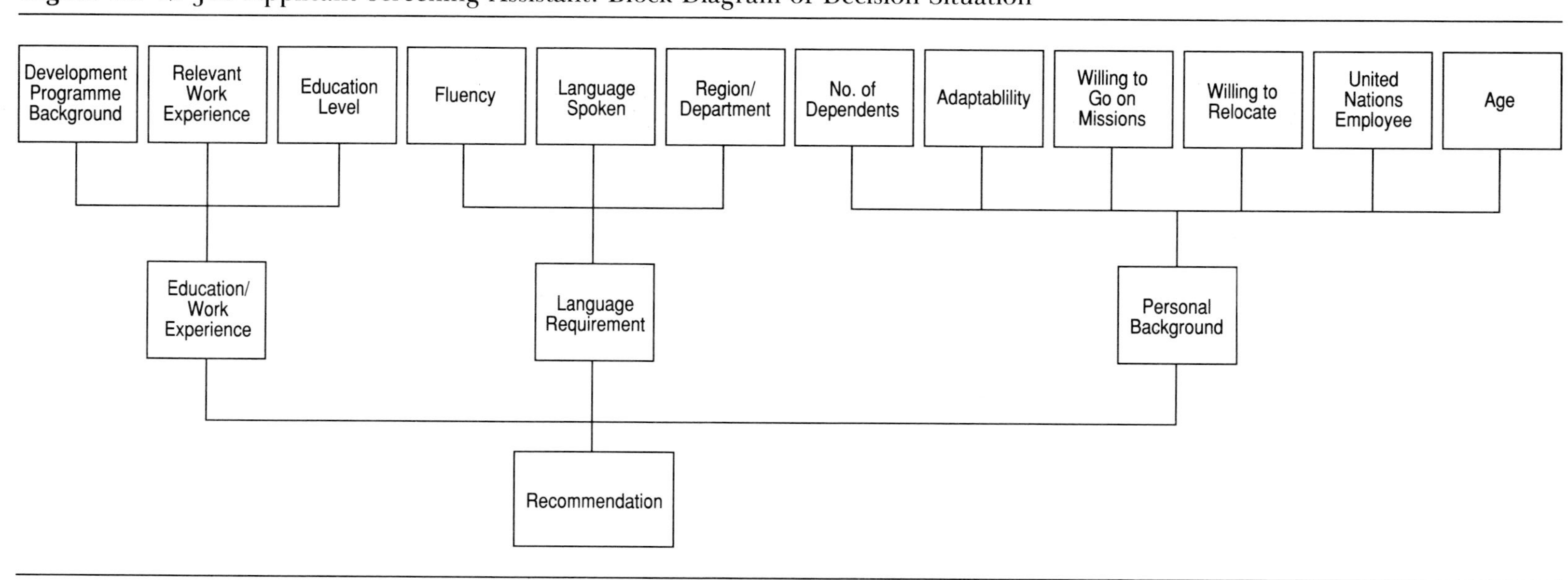

Figure 8D–3. Job Applicant Screening Assistant: Dependency Diagram

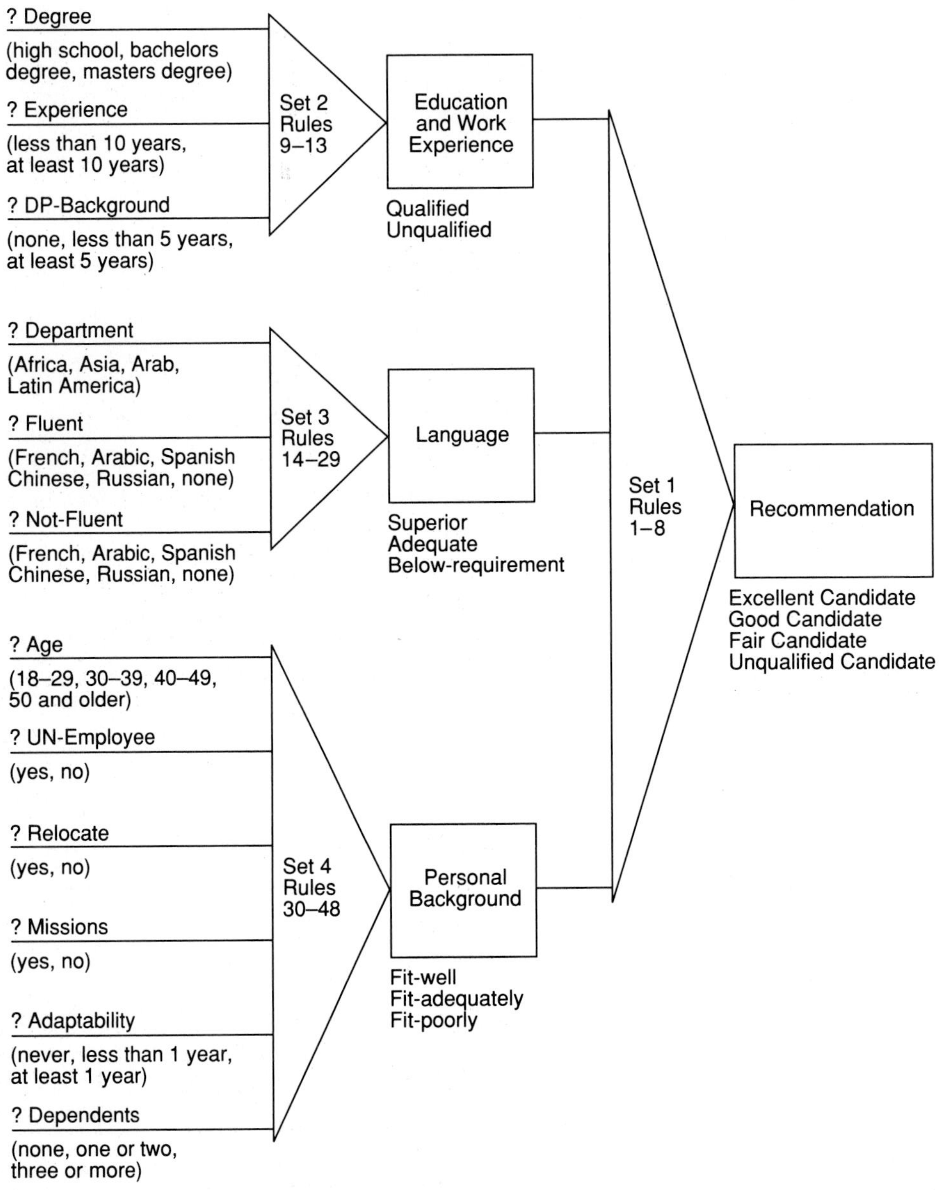

Possible Recommendations

The Job Applicant Screening Assistant gives one of four final recommendations:

1. *Excellent candidate:* The applicant's skills and personal background exceed the job position requirements. The applicant should be selected for an interview.
2. *Good candidate:* The applicant fits the profile of the job well. Select the applicant for an interview if there are not enough "excellent" candidates.

Figure 8D–4. Job Applicant Screening Assistant: Sample Consultation

```
                    Welcome To The
         Job Applicant Screening Assistant

            Developed by T.M. Wan Bok Nale
       under the direction and supervision of
                   Dr. D.G. Dologite
```

Text only

```
                   Job Applicant Screening Assistant

        This system is designed to help you screen an applicant
        applying for a job with the UNDP.  Please answer the
        questions using answers from the application form.
        The applicant will be categorized as being a(n):

                        Excellent candidate
                        Good candidate
                        Fair candidate
                        Unqualified candidate

                     Press any key to continue...




What is the applicant's highest level of education achieved?
High school             Bachelors Degree ◂      Masters Degree

What experience does the applicant have in the development programme?
None                    Less than 5 years ◂     At least 5 years

In which department is the position available?
Africa ◂                Asia                    Arab
Latin America

Which of these official languages does the applicant speak fluently?
(Press the END key after making your selection(s).)
French ◂                Arabic ◂                Spanish
Chinese                 Russian                 None

What is the age range of the applicant?
18-29 ◂                 30-39                   40-49
50 and older

Is the applicant already a UN employee?
Yes                     No ◂

Is the applicant willing to relocate?
Yes ◂                   No

Is the applicant willing to go on missions abroad?
Yes ◂                   No

How long has the applicant lived in the region represented
by the department?
Never ◂                 Less than 1 year        At least 1 year

How many dependent(s) does the applicant claim?
None ◂                  One or two              Three or more


Based on the information given, the applicant may be a(n)

Good candidate.

         (Press any key to conclude this consultation.)
```

3. *Fair candidate:* The applicant marginally meets the requirements of the job. Select the applicant for an interview only if there are not enough "excellent" and "good" candidates.
4. *Unqualified candidate:* The applicant is not qualified for the job. Reject the application.

In determining a final recommendation, a numbering scheme assigns points that represent how well an applicant's personal background fits a job profile. For example, points are assigned for the age factor as follows:

Age Range	*Points*
18–29	2
30–39	3
40–49	2
50 and over	1

As another example, an applicant receives five points for being a UN employee and two points for being willing to go on foreign missions. Details of the points used in this numbering scheme are given in Figure 8D–5.

At the end of the personal background section of a consultation, the total points accumulated determine how good is the fit of an applicant to a job.

Total Points	*Value*
greater than 13	fits well
greater than 9 and less than or equal to 13	fits adequately
less than or equal to 9	fits poorly

Figure 8D–5. Job Applicant Screening Assistant: Point Scheme for Rule Set 4

Factor	Rule No.	Total Points*	Value
Age	30	2	18–29
	31	3	30–39
	32	2	40–49
	33	1	50 and older
United Nations employee	34	5	Yes
	35	0	No
Relocate	36	2	Yes
	37	0	No
Missions	38	2	Yes
	39	0	No
Adaptability	40	1	Never
	41	2	Less than 1 year
	42	3	At least 1 year
Dependents	43	3	None
	44	2	One or two
	45	1	Three or more
Personal background	46	> 13	Fit well
	47	>9 and <=13	Fit adequately
	48	<= 9	Fit poorly

*> greater than; <= less than or equal to.

The final value is used with the other two critical factors to determine a final recommendation, as shown in the top of Figure 8D–6.

A Typical Scenario Situation

The African department has advertised vacancies for a P2, a P1, and three G3 level positions. The day after the deadline, it is estimated that about 2,500 people applied for the jobs. Mr. Yves La-Hale, the vice director of the department, is, among other things, responsible for interviewing and selecting job applicants. Recommendations about whom to hire are subsequently submitted to a superior. The prospect of going through 2,500 application forms does not appeal to the vice director at all, especially when there are so many other things to do.

The vice director starts to screen the first applicant, Ms. Sheila Rajani, for the P2 position. She holds a master's degree. She is originally from Lebanon and she speaks French as well as Arabic. Mr. La-Hale finds that she qualifies for the job's *education* and *language* requirements.

Next he looks at her application to determine if Ms. Rajani has any background in the UNDP. The application indicates three years of previous experience, which qualifies her in terms of *working experience.*

Finally, Mr. La-Hale evaluates Ms. Rajani's *personal background.* She is 30 years old, which is in the ideal range for this particular position, and she is currently employed in another branch of the UN. She lived in North Africa for 15 years and she is willing to relocate and go on missions. This indicates that she can easily adapt, reasons Mr. La-Hale, to the conditions of the African countries where she might be sent. Because Ms. Rajani does not have any dependents, the department will not have to provide additional family benefits.

Given her qualifications and personal background, Mr. La-Hale evaluates Ms. Rajani as an excellent candidate for the position. He will have her scheduled for a face-to-face interview.

SYSTEM DOCUMENTATION

Figure 8D–3 shows a dependency diagram for the Job Applicant Screening Assistant prototype system. The final decision tables appear in Figures 8D–5 and 8D–6.

In the sample consultation shown in Figure 8D–4, the applicant is recommended to be a "good" candidate for the job. By comparing the answers given in the consultation to the complete listing of the knowledge base file given in Figure 8D–7, it is possible to trace how the final recommendation was reached.

Rule 9 determines that an applicant with a bachelor's degree and some UNDP background (DP-Background <> [not equal to] None) is *qualified* in the education and work experience area. Because the job opening is in the department of Africa and the applicant is fluent in French, Rule 14 judges the language factor as *superior.*

To determine the final value for the personal background section, the points received for all items are considered:

	Points	*Rule #*
Age is 18–29	2	30
Not a UN employee	0	35
Is willing to relocate	2	36
Is willing to go on missions	2	38
Never lived in Africa	1	40
No dependents	3	43
Total points	10	

Figure 8D–6. Job Applicant Screening Assistant: Sample Decision Tables

Reduced decision table for Rule Set 1—Final Recommendation*

Rule	Education/ Work experience	Language	Personal background	Recommendation
1	Qualified	Superior	Fit-well	Excellent-candidate
2	Qualified	Superior	Fit-adequately	Good-candidate
3	Qualified	Superior	Fit-poorly	Fair-candidate
4	Qualified	Adequate	Fit-well	Good-candidate
5	Qualified	Adequate	Fit-adequately	Fair-candidate
6	Qualified	Adequate	Fit-poorly	Fair-candidate
7	Qualified	Below-requirement	—	Unqualified-candidate
8	Unqualified	—	—	Unqualified-candidate

Reduced decision table for Rule Set 2—Education Level

Rule	Degree	Development Programme background	Experience	Recommendation
9	Masters or Bachelors	<> None	—	Qualified
10	Masters or Bachelors	None	—	Unqualified
11	High-school	At-least-5-years	At-least-10-years	Qualified
12	High-school	<> At-least-5-years	—	Unqualified
13	High-school	—	<> At-least-10-years	Unqualified

Reduced decision table for Rule Set 3—Language Proficiency

Rule	Department	Fluent	Not Fluent	Recommendation
14	Africa	French	—	Superior
15	Africa	Arabic	French	Superior
16	Africa	Arabic	<> French	Adequate
17	Africa	<> French <> Arabic	—	Below-requirement
18	Asia	Chinese	—	Superior
19	Asia	Russian	<> None	Superior
20	Asia	Russian	None	Adequate
21	Asia	<> Chinese <> Russian	—	Below-requirement
22	Arab	Arabic	—	Superior
23	Arab	French	Arabic	Superior
24	Arab	French	<> Arabic	Adequate
25	Arab	<> Arabic	<> French	Below-requirement
26	Latin-America	Spanish	—	Superior
27	Latin-America	<> Spanish <> None	Spanish	Adequate
28	Latin-America	None	Spanish	Below-requirement
29	Latin-America	<> Spanish	<> Spanish	Below-requirement

*<> not equal to; — any value.

Figure 8D–7. Job Applicant Screening Assistant: Printout of the Knowledge Base File

```
! * * * * * * * * * * * * * * * * * * * * * * * * * * * * * * * * * *
! * * * * * * * * * * * * * * * * * * * * * * * * * * * * * * * * * *
! * * *                                                           * * *
! * * *          JOB APPLICANT SCREENING ASSISTANT                * * *
! * * *                                                           * * *
! * * * * * * * * * * * * * * * * * * * * * * * * * * * * * * * * * *
! * * * * * * * * * * * * * * * * * * * * * * * * * * * * * * * * * *
!
! Saved as PROJECT1.KBS
! Description:  An expert system to help United Nations Development
!               Programme (UNDP) personnel screen job applicants.

RUNTIME;
ENDOFF;
ACTIONS
     WOPEN 1,3,17,18,45,7                 !Window for opening message.
     ACTIVE 1                             !Activate the window.
     DISPLAY "


              Welcome To The
     Job Applicant Screening Assistant

       Developed by T.M. Wan Bok Nale
   under the direction and supervision of
             Dr. D.G. Dologite
     For further information, contact
             Dr. D.G. Dologite
         c/o Macmillan Publishing


         Press any key to continue.
     ~
     "
     WCLOSE 1                             !Remove window 1.

     WOPEN 1,3,4,16,72,7                  !Open explanation window.
     ACTIVE 1                             !Activate it.
     DISPLAY"
               Job Applicant Screening Assistant

      This system is designed to help you screen an applicant
      applying for a job with the UNDP.  Please answer the
      questions using answers from the application form.
      The applicant will be categorized as being a(n):

                    Excellent candidate
                    Good candidate
                    Fair candidate
                    Unqualified candidate

                Press any key to continue...
      ~"

     WCLOSE 1

     WOPEN 2,1,1,5,77,2                   !Instructions window defined.
     ACTIVE 2                             !Activate it.
     DISPLAY"
                             INSTRUCTIONS
             To select a choice(s), move the lightbar to the
             desired answer choice(s), then press the enter key."

     WOPEN 3,7,1,14,77,3                  !Consultation window defined.
     ACTIVE 3                             !Activate it.
     Ppoints = 0                          !Initialize accumulator.
     FIND Recommendation
     WCLOSE 2                             !Close instructions window.
     WCLOSE 3                             !Close consultation window.
     WOPEN 4,5,13,12,48,7                 !Concluding window defined.
     WOPEN 5,6,5,10,70,7                  !Nest in window 4.
     ACTIVE 5                             !Activate concluding window.
     LOCATE 1,9                           !Location for next display.
     DISPLAY"
      Based on the information given, the applicant may be a(n)

      {Recommendation}.

             (Press any key to conclude this consultation.)~"
```

Figure 8D–7. *continued*

```
! * * * * * * * * * * * * * * * * * * * * * * * * * * * * * * * * * * *
! *       Set 1 ( Rules to determine the recommendation. )            *
! * * * * * * * * * * * * * * * * * * * * * * * * * * * * * * * * * * *

!Begin set 1.

Rule 1
     IF     Education-workexperience = Qualified  AND
            Language = Superior   AND
            Go-thru-personal-background = Yes AND
            Check-point-personal-background = Yes AND
            Personal-background = Fit-well
     THEN   Recommendation = Excellent_candidate;

Rule 2
     IF     Education-workexperience = Qualified  AND
            Language = superior   AND
            Go-thru-personal-background = Yes AND
            Check-point-personal-background = Yes AND
            Personal-background = Fit-adequately
     THEN   Recommendation = Good_candidate;

Rule 3
     IF     Education-workexperience = Qualified  AND
            Language = Superior   AND
            Go-thru-personal-background = Yes AND
            Check-point-personal-background = Yes AND
            Personal-background = Fit-poorly
     THEN   Recommendation = Fair_candidate;

Rule 4
     IF     Education-workexperience = Qualified  AND
            Language = Adequate   AND
            Go-thru-personal-background = Yes AND
            Check-point-personal-background = Yes AND
            Personal-background = Fit-well
     THEN   Recommendation = Good_candidate;

Rule 5
     IF     Education-workexperience = Qualified  AND
            Language = Adequate   AND
            Go-thru-personal-background = Yes AND
            Check-point-personal-background = Yes AND
            Personal-background = Fit-adequately
     THEN   Recommendation = Fair_candidate;

Rule 6
     IF     Education-workexperience = Qualified  AND
            Language = Adequate   AND
            Go-thru-personal-background = Yes AND
            Check-point-personal-background = Yes AND
            Personal-background = Fit-poorly
     THEN   Recommendation = Fair_candidate;

Rule 7
     IF     Education-workexperience = Qualified  AND
            Language = Below-requirement
     THEN   Recommendation = Unqualified_candidate;

Rule 8
     IF     Education-workexperience = Unqualified
     THEN   Recommendation = unqualified_candidate;

!End of set 1.
```

```
! * * * * * * * * * * * * * * * * * * * * * * * * * * * * * * * * * * *
! *       Set 2 ( Rules to determine the education level. )           *
! * * * * * * * * * * * * * * * * * * * * * * * * * * * * * * * * * * *

!Begin set 2.

Rule 9
     IF     Degree = Masters_Degree OR Degree = Bachelors_Degree AND
            DP-background <> None
     THEN   Education-workexperience = Qualified;

Rule 10
     IF     Degree = Masters_Degree OR Degree = Bachelors_Degree AND
            Dp-background = None
     THEN   Education-workexperience = Unqualified;

Rule 11
     IF     Degree = High_school AND
            Dp-background = At_least_5_years AND
            Experience = At_least_10_years
     THEN   Education-workexperience = Qualified;

Rule 12
     IF     Degree = High_school AND
            Dp-background <> At_least_5_years
     THEN   Education-workexperience = Unqualified;

Rule 13
     IF     Degree = High_school AND
            Dp-background <> At_least_10_years
     THEN   Education-workexperience = Unqualified;

ASK Degree: " What is the applicant's highest level of education achieved?";
CHOICES Degree: High_school, Bachelors_Degree, Masters_Degree;

ASK Experience:" How many years of relevant working experience does the applicant
have?";
CHOICES Experience: Less_than_10_years, At_least_10_years;

ASK Dp-background:" What experience does the applicant have in the development
programme?";
CHOICES Dp-background: None, Less_than_5_years, At_least_5_years;

!End of set 2.

! * * * * * * * * * * * * * * * * * * * * * * * * * * * * * * * * * * *
! *      Set 3 ( Rules to determine the language proficiency. )       *
! * * * * * * * * * * * * * * * * * * * * * * * * * * * * * * * * * * *

!Begin set 3.

Rule 14
     IF     Department = Africa AND
            Fluent = French
     THEN   Language = Superior;

Rule 15
     IF     Department = Africa AND
            Fluent = Arabic AND
            Not-fluent = French
     THEN   Language = Superior;

Rule 16
     IF     Department = Africa AND
            Fluent = Arabic AND
            Not-fluent <> French
     THEN   Language = Adequate;

Rule 17
     IF     Department = Africa AND
            Fluent <> French AND
            Fluent <> Arabic
     THEN   Language = Below-requirement;

Rule 18
     IF     Department = Asia AND
            Fluent = Chinese
     THEN   Language = Superior;
```

Figure 8D–7. *continued*

```
Rule 19
     IF     Department = Asia AND
            Fluent = Russian AND
            Not-fluent <> None
     THEN   Language = Superior;

Rule 20
     IF     Department = Asia AND
            Fluent = Russian AND
            Not-fluent = None
     THEN   Language = Adequate;

Rule 21
     IF     Department = Asia AND
            Fluent <> Chinese AND
            Fluent <> Russian
     THEN   Language = Below-requirement;

Rule 22
     IF     Department = Arab AND
            Fluent = Arabic
     THEN   Language = Superior;

Rule 23
     IF     Department = Arab AND
            Fluent = French AND
            Not-fluent = Arabic
     THEN   Language = Superior;

Rule 24
     IF     Department = Arab AND
            Fluent = French AND
            Not-fluent <> Arabic
     THEN   Language = Adequate;

Rule 25
     IF     Department = Arab AND
            Fluent <> Arabic AND
            Fluent <> French
     THEN   Language = Below-requirement;

Rule 26
     IF     Department = Latin_America AND
            Fluent = Spanish
     THEN   Language = Superior;

Rule 27
     IF     Department = Latin_America AND
            Fluent <> Spanish AND
            Fluent <> None AND
            Not-fluent = Spanish
     THEN   Language = Adequate;

Rule 28
     IF     Department = Latin_America AND
            Fluent = None AND
            Not-fluent = Spanish
     THEN   Language = Below-requirement;

Rule 29
     IF     Department = Latin_America AND
            Fluent <> Spanish AND
            Not-fluent <> Spanish
     THEN   Language = Below-requirement;

ASK Department:" In which department is the position available?";
CHOICES Department: Africa, Asia, Arab, Latin_America;

ASK Fluent:" Which of these official languages does the applicant speak fluently?
(Press the END key after making your selection(s).)";
CHOICES Fluent: French, Arabic, Spanish, Chinese, Russian, None;

ASK Not-fluent:" Which of the following languages does the applicant speak,
but without fluency?
```

```
(Press the END key after making your selection(s).)";
CHOICES Not-fluent: French, Arabic, Spanish, Chinese, Russian, None;

PLURAL: Fluent, Not-fluent;

!End of set 3.

! * * * * * * * * * * * * * * * * * * * * * * * * * * * * * * * * * * *
! *   Set 4 ( Rules to determine how well the personal background     *
! *           of the applicant fits the profile of the job. )         *
! * * * * * * * * * * * * * * * * * * * * * * * * * * * * * * * * * * *

!Begin set 4.

Rule 30
     IF     Age = 18-29
     THEN   Dummy-Age = Yes
            Ppoints = ( Ppoints + 2 );
Rule 31
     IF     Age = 30-39
     THEN   Dummy-Age = Yes
            Ppoints = (Ppoints + 3);

Rule 32
     IF     Age = 40-49
     THEN   Dummy-Age = Yes
            Ppoints = (Ppoints + 2);

Rule 33
     IF     Age = 50_and_older
     THEN   Dummy-age = Yes
            Ppoints = (Ppoints + 1);

Rule 34
     IF     Un-employee = Yes
     THEN   Dummy-Un-employee = Yes
            Ppoints = ( Ppoints + 5 );

Rule 35
     IF     Un-employee = No
     THEN   Dummy-Un-employee = Yes
            Ppoints = ( Ppoints + 0 );

Rule 36
     IF     Relocate = Yes
     THEN   Dummy-Relocate = Yes
            Ppoints = ( Ppoints + 2 );

Rule 37
     IF     Relocate = No
     THEN   Dummy-Relocate = Yes
            Ppoints = ( Ppoints + 0 );

Rule 38
     IF     Missions = Yes
     THEN   Dummy-Missions = Yes
            Ppoints = ( Ppoints + 2 );

Rule 39
     IF     Missions = No
     THEN   Dummy-Missions = Yes
            Ppoints = ( Ppoints + 0 );

Rule 40
     IF     Adaptability = Never
     THEN   Dummy-Adaptability = Yes
            Ppoints = ( Ppoints + 1 );
```

Figure 8D–7. *concluded*

```
Rule 41
     IF     Adaptability = Less_than_1_year
     THEN   Dummy-Adaptability = Yes
            Ppoints = ( Ppoints + 2 );

Rule 42
     IF     Adaptability = At_least_1_year
     THEN   Dummy-Adaptability = Yes
            Ppoints = ( Ppoints + 3 );

Rule 43
     IF     Dependents = None
     THEN   Dummy-Dependents = Yes
            Ppoints = ( Ppoints + 3 );

Rule 44
     IF     Dependents = One_or_two
     THEN   Dummy-Dependents = Yes
            Ppoints = ( Ppoints + 2 );

Rule 45
     IF     Dependents = Three_or_more
     THEN   Dummy-Dependents = Yes
            Ppoints = ( Ppoints + 1 );

Rule 46
     IF     Ppoints > 13
     THEN   Check-point-personal-background = Yes
            Personal-background = Fit-well;

Rule 47
     IF     Ppoints > 9 AND Ppoints <= 13
     THEN   Check-point-personal-background = Yes
            Personal-background = Fit-adequately;

Rule 48
     IF    Ppoints <= 9
     THEN Check-point-personal-background = Yes
          Personal-background = Fit-poorly;

ASK Age:" What is the age range of the applicant?";
CHOICES Age: 18-29, 30-39, 40-49, 50_and_older;

ASK Un-employee:" Is the applicant already a UN employee?";
CHOICES Un-employee: Yes, No;

ASK Relocate:" Is the applicant willing to relocate?";
CHOICES Relocate: Yes, No;

ASK Missions:" Is the applicant willing to go on missions abroad?";
CHOICES Missions: Yes, No;

ASK Adaptability:" How long has the applicant lived in the region represented
 by the department?";
CHOICES Adaptability: Never, Less_than_1_year, At_least_1_year;

ASK Dependents:" How many dependent(s) does the applicant claim?";
CHOICES Dependents: None, One_or_two, Three_or_more;

!End of set 4.

! Rule to force all the user questions about personal background.

Rule Dummy-for-personal-background
     IF     Dummy-Age = Yes AND
            Dummy-Un-employee = Yes AND
            Dummy-Relocate = Yes AND
            Dummy-Missions = Yes AND
            Dummy-Adaptability = Yes AND
            Dummy-Dependents = Yes
     THEN   Go-thru-personal-background = Yes;
```

According to Rule 47, if the applicant's total points are greater than 9 and less than or equal to 13, the personal background factor is *fit-adequately*. Rule 2 states that if education-work experience is *qualified*, language is *superior*, and personal background is *fit-adequately*, the applicant is a *good* candidate for the job.

Future Development

This prototype system is designed to test the concept and structure of a larger job applicant screening system within the UNDP, and even possibly within the UN as a whole. The Job Applicant Screening Assistant can be examined as one of a series of expert systems to encompass all the existing job position levels of the administrative side of the UNDP. Eventually, a more complex expert system could be developed to help the UNDP personnel department select personnel to oversee projects financed by the UN throughout the world. This larger system could link into UN personnel databases to help identify qualified personnel for a variety of positions.

8E

Motorcycle Troubleshooting Advisor

TECHNICAL PROFILE

Difficulty Level	Beginner
Special Features	This is an example of a common class of expert systems called diagnostic systems.
File Used	BIKE.KBS
To Run	Load BIKE.KBS from the disk accompanying this book.

OVERVIEW

Note: This prototype does not provide conclusions for all possible combinations of values found in the decision tables. So certain combinations of answers do not give a recommendation during a consultation. To ensure getting a final recommendation, use the decision tables shown in Figure 8E–4 as a guide to enter responses when running the system.

This is a small prototype example of a potentially larger expert system designed to diagnose, or "troubleshoot," problems encountered when operating a motorcycle. It is an example of the type of expert system that manufacturers can supply on disk to customers to encourage and facilitate customer self-repair of malfunctioning goods. By providing such a disk, manufacturers can eliminate a substantial overhead cost for their service network.

STUDYING THE SITUATION

The various problems that can be encountered when operating a motorcycle can be divided into the following categories:

- Difficult to start: This is the most common problem and often the toughest to solve. The usual causes are a failure in the fuel, ignition, or compression systems.
- Erratic performance: This problem is evident from the bike's running "rough" or missing gears. Common causes include malfunctioning fuel, ignition, compression, or lubrication systems.
- Insufficient power and/or overheating: In addition to the causes just mentioned, this problem can be induced by mechanical problems, such as piston seizure or engine wear.
- Excessive smoke: This is often due to problems in engine lubrication or a malfunctioning compression system, and it can cause spark plug fouling as well as poor performance.
- Excessive noise: This can include too much engine vibration as well as extreme abnormal clutch, transmission, or drive train noise.
- Frame and running gear problems: They often show up as inadequate braking, uneven tire wear, and generally poor handling of the motorcycle. Some common causes are worn brake linings, incorrect adjustments, and defective shock absorbers.

- Clutch problems: They can result from incorrect free-play adjustment. Too much free play prevents the clutch from disengaging completely. Too little free play causes the clutch to slip and eventually be destroyed.
- Transmission problems: When transmission parts wear, it becomes difficult to shift properly. Transmission malfunctions usually require that the engine be disassembled to locate the cause.
- Electrical problems: Electrical problems can entail malfunctioning of many parts on a motorcycle, including ignition, battery, lights, horn, and so forth. Tracing the root of an electrical problem is often a time-consuming process.

Technical manuals that explain the troubleshooting process in detail are widely available. But most motorcycle owners have neither the time nor the patience to go through a manual. Moreover, reading a manual provides theoretical detail necessary to understand the bike. It does not teach the thought process that an expert mechanic goes through to fix a problem bike. The Motorcycle Troubleshooting Advisor prototype expert system has the potential to provide help normally associated with consulting an expert mechanic.

By supplying bike customers with a disk containing the Motorcycle Troubleshooting Advisor, the bike manufacturer can realize benefits such as

- Securing a competitive marketing edge over the competition
- Providing a quick and efficient way for customers to self-diagnose bike problems
- Reducing the cost overhead associated with servicing sold merchandise
- Facilitating signing up new dealers to sell the bikes, because they can devote fewer resources to servicing them
- Promoting a "hi-tech," state-of-the-art image, especially in relation to customer support

Such benefits can be generalized beyond motorcycles. Manufacturers of house and garden appliances, transportation and leisure equipment, and so on can adopt a similar approach to supply diagnostic expert systems on disk to their customers. As personal computer use continues to increase in the home, this approach can be expected to escalate.

Narrowing the Focus

"Difficulty in starting" is the most common and usually the toughest problem to solve in the motorcycle troubleshooting process. This is the problem isolated for the initial concept-testing and prototyping phase. The problem can occur for three reasons: (1) fault in the fuel system, (2) fault in the ignition system, and (3) fault in the compression system. The Motorcycle Troubleshooting Advisor identifies the causes of each of these problems and suggests corrective action.

Critical Factors Affecting the Situation

The three critical factors in the motorcycle troubleshooting decision are fuel, ignition, and compression, as shown in Figure 8E–1. Figure 8E–2 provides more detail about the decision-making process followed during troubleshooting.

Problems in the *fuel* system can be caused by either not enough or too much fuel. It is also important to have the right fuel-air mixture. This is accomplished by adjusting the carburetor. If the fuel reaches the carburetor and the engine head, and if the carburetor adjustment is correct, then the fuel system is functioning properly.

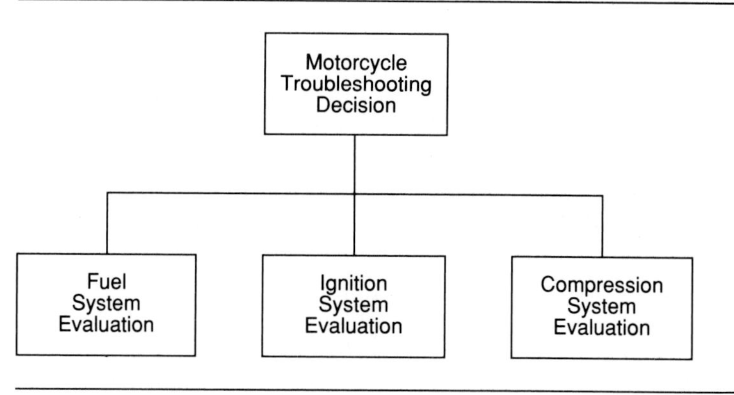

Figure 8E–1. Motorcycle Troubleshooting Advisor: Block Diagram of Diagnostic Situation

Figure 8E–2. Motorcycle Troubleshooting Advisor: Detail Block Diagram of Diagnostic Situation for Prototyping

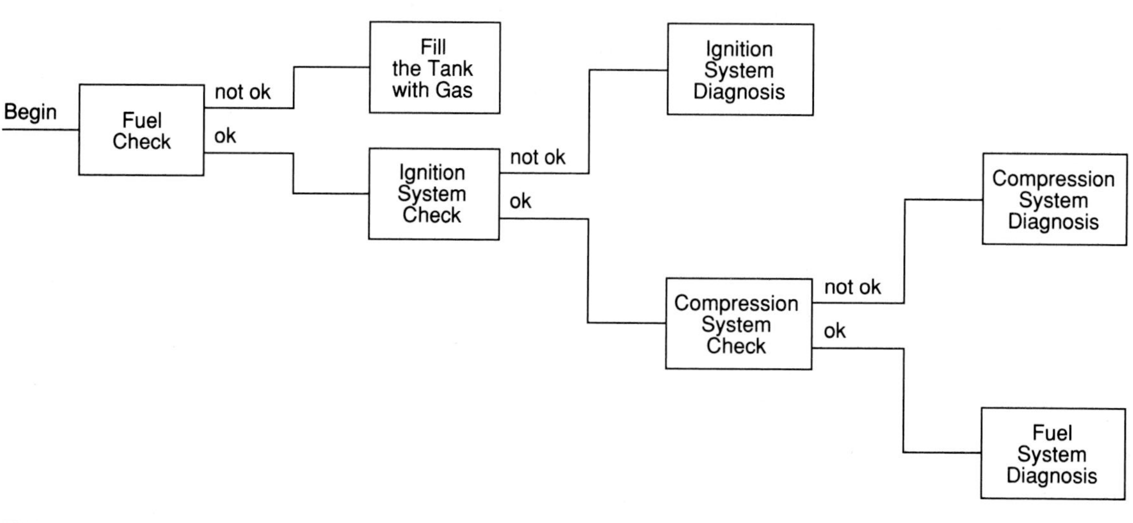

If the spark plug is wet, fuel is getting into the cylinder and the trouble is probably in the *ignition* system, which consists of primary (or low-tension) and secondary (or high-tension) circuits. Some basic tests must be performed to isolate ignition problems. The first step is to be certain the trouble is not being caused by the spark plug itself. The plug insulator could be cracked, the gap in the spark plug may be too wide, the gap may be bridged, or the spark plug may be fouled because it lacks a high-tension spark. The problem may also be due to a faulty condenser or ignition coil.

Compression is the third critical factor. An engine requires a compression of between 90 and 120 pounds per square inch (psi) to start. Faulty seals or gaskets may cause a loss of compression.

The dependency diagram in Figure 8E–3 shows the breakdown of the critical factors, as well as the questions asked and recommendations made by the prototype, which are examined in the next sections.

Figure 8E–3. Motorcycle Troubleshooting Advisor: Dependency Diagram

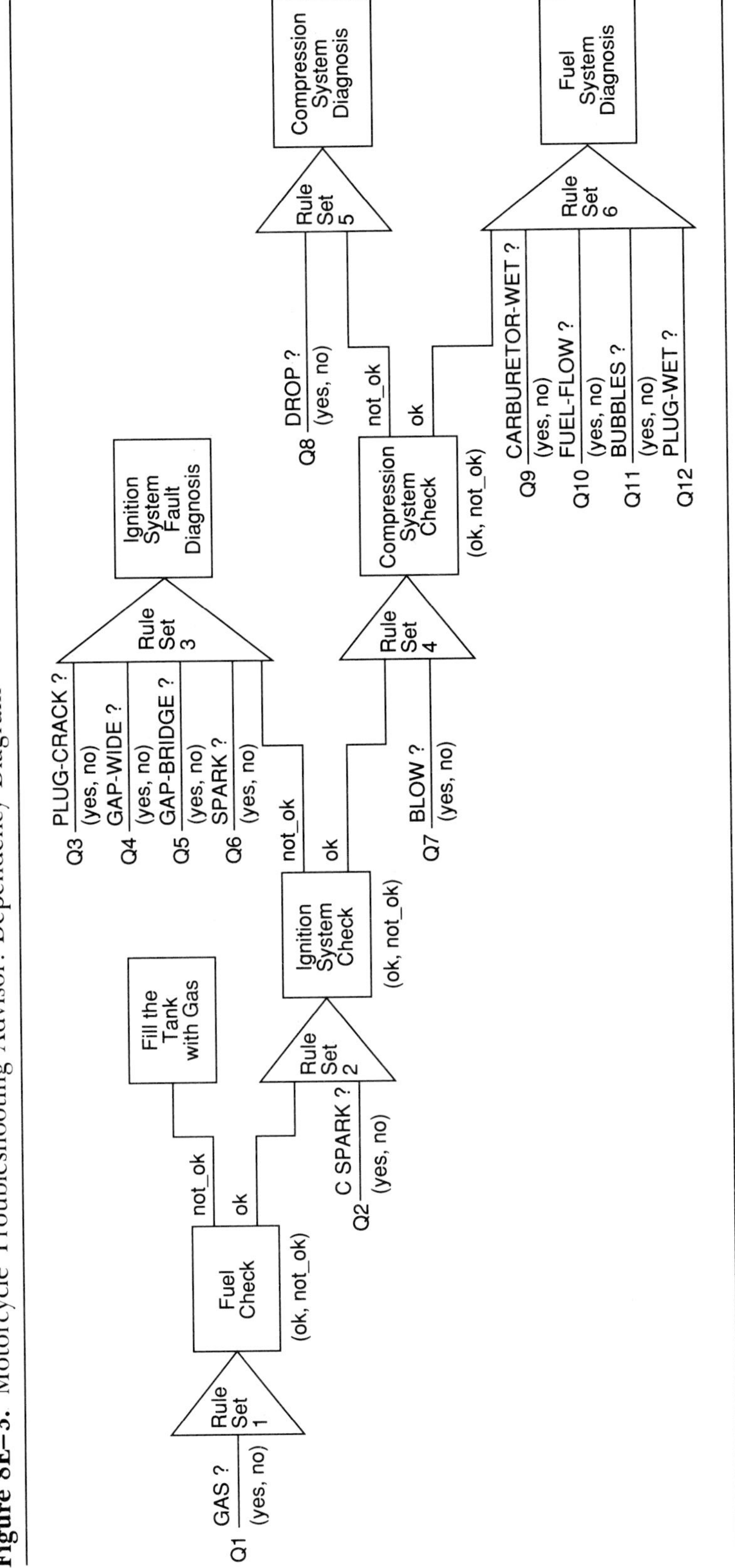

Questions Asked by the Prototype System

The Motorcycle Troubleshooting Advisor asks the following questions during a user consultation (also given are explanations of why the question is being asked):

- Is there gas in the tank? (yes, no)
  Reason: The engine cannot start without fuel.
- Remove the spark plug from the engine head and hold it near the head. Then operate the kick starter. Is there a spark? (yes, no)
  Reason: If there is a spark, the ignition system is OK.
- Is the spark plug insulator cracked? (yes, no)
  Reason: If it is cracked, the spark plug is fouled.
- Is the spark plug gap excessively wide? (yes, no)
  Reason: If the gap is too wide, there will be no spark.
- Is the spark plug gap bridged? (yes, no)
  Reason: If it is, there will be no spark.
- Remove the spark plug from the ignition wire. Insert a screwdriver into the cap. Hold the screwdriver approximately ¼-inch from the cylinder head and operate the kick starter. Is there a spark? (yes, no)
  Reason: If there is a spark, the spark plug is defective. If there is no spark, either the battery is defective or the condenser has a short or the ignition coil is defective.
- Remove the spark plug and crank the engine while holding your thumb over the hole. Does your thumb get blown off the hole? (yes, no)
  Reason: If it does not get blown off, there is not enough compression.
- Set the piston at the bottom dead center of its cycle and then remove the carburetor. Hold your hand over the intake port and blow on the exhaust port. Does the pressure drop? (yes, no)
  Reason: If it does drop, the seals or the gaskets are faulty.
- Is the inside of the carburetor throat wet? (yes, no)
  Reason: If it is wet, the fuel is reaching the carburetor.
- Does the fuel flow out when the fuel line is removed? (yes, no)
  Reason: If the fuel does not flow out, the fuel line is pinched, preventing the fuel from reaching the carburetor.
- Remove the fuel tank cap and blow back through the line. Do you hear bubbles? (yes, no)
  Reason: If you do not hear bubbles, there is a plugged vent in the fuel tank cap or something in the tank floating over the petcock is shutting off the flow.
- Is the spark plug wet? (yes, no)
  Reason: If the spark plug is wet, the fuel is getting into the cylinder.

Recommendations Made by the System

This prototype diagnostic system makes the following final recommendations:

- Fill the tank with gasoline.
- Clean the surface of the spark plug. If the motorcycle still does not start, either the condenser has a short or the ignition coil is defective.
- Change the spark plug.
- Adjust the contact point gap.
- Have the piston rings changed.
- Take the motorcycle to a mechanic.
- Adjust the carburetor.
- Clean the vent and the petcock.

A Typical Decision Scenario

John owns a Suzuki motorcycle, which he uses to commute to school every day. One morning the bike will not start. John checks the battery by turning on the lights. The lights are working, so he concludes that the battery is OK. He then looks into the fuel tank, which is half full. John does not know what else to check, so he takes the motorcycle to his neighborhood garage.

Peter Brown is the mechanic at the garage who specializes in motorcycle tune-ups and repairs. John tells Peter that the battery is OK and that he has already checked for fuel in the tank. So Peter begins the troubleshooting process by checking the *ignition system.* He removes the spark plug from the engine head and holds it near the engine head. Then he operates the kick starter. There is a distinct spark, which tells Peter that the ignition system is OK.

Next he checks the *compression system.* He puts his thumb on the spark plug hole and slowly cranks the engine. He feels pressure building up inside the cylinder, indicating that the problem is not with the compression. So Peter cleans the spark plug and puts it back into the cylinder head. He kicks the kick starter and removes the spark plug again. It is dry, which indicates the fuel is not reaching the engine. This means that there is a problem with the fuel system.

To pinpoint the *fuel system* problem, Peter must check the fuel line. He opens the carburetor and touches the inside of the carburetor throat. It is also dry, indicating that fuel is not reaching the carburetor. When Peter disconnects the fuel line, there is no fuel flowing out. He removes the fuel tank cap and blows back into the line. He can feel pressure building up in the fuel line, meaning that the vent is clogged. By examining the vent, Peter discovers that it is clogged with very fine iron particles. He takes a thin wire and unclogs the vent. Then he reassembles the carburetor. A few kicks and the engine starts.

SYSTEM DOCUMENTATION

Figure 8E–4 shows the decision tables developed for the Motorcycle Troubleshooting Advisor prototype system. Sample consultations are shown in Figure 8E–5. The three consultations test each of the major sub-systems considered in this prototype: the fuel system, the ignition system, and the compression system.

The first consultation requires seven questions to reach a conclusion. Since there is a spark when the kick starter is operated, this implies that the ignition system is OK. The third question checks the compression in the cylinder. The pressure inside the cylinder is great enough to blow the thumb off, indicating that the compression system is also OK. This means that the problem is probably with the fuel system. From the responses to the last four questions, the Motorcycle Troubleshooting Advisor concludes that the problem is in the fuel tank and the vent, and the petcock should be cleaned.

The second consultation shown in Figure 8E–5 asks six questions before reaching a final conclusion. Because there is no spark, the ignition is implicated as the problem source. Questions 3 through 5 check the physical condition of the spark plug. Question 6 checks the ignition coil. Since all these components are OK, the expert system concludes that the problem is with the spark plug surface.

The third consultation detects a fault in the compression system. The fuel system and the ignition system are checked first. The last two questions determine that there is a drop in pressure in the cylinder. This can only be due to defective piston rings. The user is advised to have the piston rings replaced.

A complete listing of the knowledge base file is given in Figure 8E–6.

Figure 8E–4. Motorcycle Troubleshooting Advisor: Decision Tables

Rule Set 1

		1	2
IF	gas	y	n
THEN			R1
	fuel-check	ok	

Rule Set 2

		1	2
IF	fuel-check	ok	ok
	cspark	y	n
THEN	ignition-check	ok	nok

Rule Set 3

	1	2	3	4	5	6	7
IF ignition-check	nok	nok	nok	nok	nok	nok	nok
plug-crack	n	n	n	n	y	y	y
gap-wide	n	n	y	y	n	n	y
gap-bridge	n	y	n	n	n	y	n
spark	n	n	n	y	n	n	n
THEN	R2	R3	R4	R4	R3	R3	R3

Rule Set 4

	1	2
IF ignition-check	ok	ok
blow	y	n
THEN compression-check	ok	nok

Rule Set 5

	1	2
IF compression-check	nok	nok
drop	y	n
THEN	R5	R6

Rule Set 6

	1	2	3	4	5	6	7	8	9	10	11	12	13
IF carburetor-wet	y	n	y	y	n	y	y	n	n	y	y	n	n
fuel-flow	y	y	n	n	n	y	y	y	y	n	n	n	n
bubbles	y	y	y	y	y	n	n	n	n	n	n	n	n
plug-wet	n	n	y	n	n	y	n	y	n	y	n	y	n
compression-check	ok	ok	ok	ok	ok	ok	ok	ok	ok	ok	ok	ok	ok
THEN	R7	R7	R8	R8	R8	R8	R8	R8	R8	R8	R8	R8	R8

Key:

y = yes.
n = no.
nok = not ok.
R1 = fill the tank with gasoline.
R2 = clean the surface of the spark plug. If the motorcycle still does not start, either the condenser has a short or the ignition coil is defective.
R3 = change the spark plug.
R4 = adjust the contact point gap.
R5 = have the piston rings changed.
R6 = take the motorcycle to a mechanic.
R7 = adjust the carburetor.
R8 = clean the vent and the petcock.

Figure 8E–5. Motorcycle Troubleshooting Advisor: Sample Consultations

```
MOTORCYCLE TROUBLESHOOTING ADVISOR

Developed by Rajive B. Jain
under the direction and supervision of
Dr. D.G. Dologite
```

Consultation 1:
Text only

```
Welcome to the Motorcycle Troubleshooting Advisor

Is there gas in the tank?
YES ◄                   NO

Remove the spark plug from the engine head and hold it
near the head. Then operate the kick starter. Is there a spark?
YES ◄                   NO

Remove the spark plug and crank the engine while holding
your thumb over the hole.  Does your thumb get blown off the hole?
YES ◄                   NO

Is the inside of the carburetor throat wet?
YES ◄                   NO

Does the fuel flow out when the fuel line is removed?
YES ◄                   NO

Remove the fuel tank cap and blow back through the line.
Do you hear bubbles?
YES                     NO ◄

Is the spark plug wet?
YES ◄                   NO

Based on the answers you have given,
  I recommend that you:  Clean the vent and the petcock
```

Figure 8E–5. *concluded*

Consultation 2:

Text only

```
Is there gas in the tank?
YES ◄                   NO

Remove the spark plug from the engine head and hold it
near the head. Then operate the kick starter. Is there a spark?
YES                     NO ◄

Is the spark plug insulator cracked?
YES                     NO ◄

Is the spark plug gap excessively wide?
YES                     NO ◄

Is the spark plug gap bridged?
YES                     NO ◄

Remove the spark plug from the ignition wire.  Insert a
screwdriver into the cap.  Hold the screwdriver approximately 1/4-inch
from the cylinder head and operate the kick starter. Is there a spark?
YES                     NO ◄

Based on the answers you have given,
  I recommend that you:  Clean the surface of the spark plug
```

Consultation 3:

Text only

```
Is there gas in the tank?
YES ◄                   NO

Remove the spark plug from the engine head and hold it
near the head. Then operate the kick starter. Is there a spark?
YES ◄                   NO

Remove the spark plug and crank the engine while holding
your thumb over the hole.  Does your thumb get blown off the hole?
YES                     NO ◄

Set the piston at the bottom dead center of its cycle and
then remove the carburetor.  Hold your hand over the intake port and blow
on the exhaust port.  Does the pressure drop?
YES ◄                   NO

Based on the answers you have given,
  I recommend that you:  Have the piston rings changed
```

Figure 8E–6. Motorcycle Troubleshooting Advisor: Knowledge Base

```
! Name of the expert system: MOTORCYCLE TROUBLESHOOTING ADVISOR
! Description: This system assists a user in diagnosing motorcycle
!              problems and in finding out how to solve them.
! Microcomputer used: IBM PC compatible
! Saved file name: BIKE.KBS

ENDOFF;
RUNTIME;

! ACTIONS BLOCK
ACTIONS
WOPEN 1,0,0,23,79,2
ACTIVE 1
DISPLAY "


                    MOTORCYCLE TROUBLESHOOTING ADVISOR

                       Developed by Rajive B. Jain
                   under the direction and supervision of
                             Dr. D.G. Dologite
                      For further information, contact
                             Dr. D.G. Dologite
                          c/o Macmillan Publishing


                          Press any key to continue~"
WCLOSE 1

   DISPLAY " Welcome to the Motorcycle Troubleshooting Advisor"
   FIND RECO
   DISPLAY " Based on the answers you have given,
   I recommend that you: {RECO}";


RULE 1-1
IF        GAS = YES
THEN      FUEL-CHECK = OK
BECAUSE   " Engine cannot run without fuel.";

RULE 1-2
IF        GAS = NO
THEN      RECO = Fill_the_tank_with_gasoline;

RULE 2-1
IF        FUEL-CHECK = OK
          AND CSPARK = YES
THEN      IGNITION-CHECK = OK
BECAUSE   "If there is a spark, the ignition system is ok.";

RULE 2-2
IF        FUEL-CHECK = OK
          AND CSPARK = NO
THEN      IGNITION-CHECK = NOK;

RULE 3-1
IF        IGNITION-CHECK = NOK
          AND PLUG-CRACK = NO
          AND GAP-WIDE = NO
          AND GAP-BRIDGE = NO
          AND SPARK = NO
THEN      RECO = Clean_the_surface_of_the_spark_plug;

RULE 3-2
IF        IGNITION-CHECK = NOK
          AND PLUG-CRACK = NO
          AND GAP-WIDE = NO
          AND GAP-BRIDGE = YES
          AND SPARK = NO
THEN      RECO = Change_the_spark_plug;
```

Figure 8E–6. *continued*

```
RULE 3-3
IF       IGNITION-CHECK = NOK
         AND PLUG-CRACK = NO
         AND GAP-WIDE = YES
         AND GAP-BRIDGE = NO
         AND SPARK = NO
THEN     RECO = Adjust_the_contact_point_gap;

RULE 3-4
IF       IGNITION-CHECK = NOK
         AND PLUG-CRACK = NO
         AND GAP-WIDE = YES
         AND GAP-BRIDGE = NO
         AND SPARK = YES
THEN     RECO = Adjust_the_contact_point_gap;

RULE 3-5
IF       IGNITION-CHECK = NOK
         AND PLUG-CRACK = YES
         AND GAP-WIDE = NO
         AND GAP-BRIDGE = NO
         AND SPARK = NO
THEN     RECO = Change_the_spark_plug;

RULE 3-6
IF       IGNITION-CHECK = NOK
         AND PLUG-CRACK = YES
         AND GAP-WIDE = NO
         AND GAP-BRIDGE = YES
         AND SPARK = NO
THEN     RECO = Change_the_spark_plug;

RULE 3-7
IF       IGNITION-CHECK = NOK
         AND PLUG-CRACK = YES
         AND GAP-WIDE = YES
         AND GAP-BRIDGE = NO
         AND SPARK = NO
THEN     RECO = Change_the_spark_plug;

RULE 4-1
IF       IGNITION-CHECK = OK
         AND BLOW = YES
THEN     COMPRESSION-CHECK = OK;

RULE 4-2
IF       IGNITION-CHECK = OK
         AND BLOW = NO
THEN     COMPRESSION-CHECK =NOK;

RULE 5-1
IF       COMPRESSION-CHECK =NOK
         AND DROP = YES
THEN     RECO = Have_the_piston_rings_changed;

RULE 5-2
IF       COMPRESSION-CHECK =NOK
         AND DROP = NO
THEN     RECO = Take_the_motorcycle_to_a_mechanic;

RULE 6-1
IF       CARBURETOR-WET = YES
         AND FUEL-FLOW = YES
         AND BUBBLES = YES
         AND PLUG-WET = NO
         AND COMPRESSION-CHECK = OK
THEN     RECO = Adjust_the_carburetor;

RULE 6-2
IF       CARBURETOR-WET = NO
         AND FUEL-FLOW = YES
         AND BUBBLES = YES
         AND PLUG-WET = NO
         AND COMPRESSION-CHECK = OK
THEN     RECO = Adjust_the_carburetor;
```

```
RULE 6-3
IF       CARBURETOR-WET = YES
         AND FUEL-FLOW = NO
         AND BUBBLES = YES
         AND PLUG-WET = YES
         AND COMPRESSION-CHECK = OK
THEN     RECO = Clean_the_vent_and_the_petcock;

RULE 6-4
IF       CARBURETOR-WET = YES
         AND FUEL-FLOW = NO
         AND BUBBLES = YES
         AND PLUG-WET = NO
         AND COMPRESSION-CHECK = OK
THEN     RECO = Clean_the_vent_and_the_petcock;

RULE 6-5
IF       CARBURETOR-WET = NO
         AND FUEL-FLOW = NO
         AND BUBBLES = YES
         AND PLUG-WET = NO
         AND COMPRESSION-CHECK = OK
THEN     RECO = Clean_the_vent_and_the_petcock;

RULE 6-6
IF       CARBURETOR-WET = YES
         AND FUEL-FLOW = YES
         AND BUBBLES = NO
         AND PLUG-WET = YES
         AND COMPRESSION-CHECK = OK
THEN     RECO = Clean_the_vent_and_the_petcock;

RULE 6-7
IF       CARBURETOR-WET = YES
         AND FUEL-FLOW = YES
         AND BUBBLES = NO
         AND PLUG-WET = NO
         AND COMPRESSION-CHECK = OK
THEN     RECO = Clean_the_vent_and_the_petcock;

RULE 6-8
IF       CARBURETOR-WET = NO
         AND FUEL-FLOW = YES
         AND BUBBLES = NO
         AND PLUG-WET = YES
         AND COMPRESSION-CHECK = OK
THEN     RECO = Clean_the_vent_and_the_petcock;

RULE 6-9
IF       CARBURETOR-WET = NO
         AND FUEL-FLOW = YES
         AND BUBBLES = NO
         AND PLUG-WET = NO
         AND COMPRESSION-CHECK = OK
THEN     RECO = Clean_the_vent_and_the_petcock;

RULE 6-10
IF       CARBURETOR-WET = YES
         AND FUEL-FLOW = NO
         AND BUBBLES = NO
         AND PLUG-WET = YES
         AND COMPRESSION-CHECK = OK
THEN     RECO = Clean_the_vent_and_the_petcock;
```

Figure 8E–6. *concluded*

```
RULE 6-11
IF        CARBURETOR-WET = YES
          AND FUEL-FLOW = NO
          AND BUBBLES = NO
          AND PLUG-WET = NO
          AND COMPRESSION-CHECK = OK
THEN      RECO = Clean_the_vent_and_the_petcock;

RULE 6-12
IF        CARBURETOR-WET = NO
          AND FUEL-FLOW = NO
          AND BUBBLES = NO
          AND PLUG-WET = YES
          AND COMPRESSION-CHECK = OK
THEN      RECO = Clean_the_vent_and_the_petcock;

RULE 6-13
IF        CARBURETOR-WET = NO
          AND FUEL-FLOW = NO
          AND BUBBLES = NO
          AND PLUG-WET = NO
          AND COMPRESSION-CHECK = OK
THEN      RECO = Clean_the_vent_and_the_petcock;

!STATEMENTS BLOCK

ASK GAS: " Is there gas in the tank?";
CHOICES GAS: YES,NO;

ASK CSPARK: " Remove the spark plug from the engine head and hold it
 near the head. Then operate the kick starter. Is there a spark?";
CHOICES CSPARK: YES,NO;

ASK PLUG-CRACK: " Is the spark plug insulator cracked?";
CHOICES PLUG-CRACK : YES,NO;

ASK GAP-WIDE: " Is the spark plug gap excessively wide?";
CHOICES GAP-WIDE : YES,NO;

ASK GAP-BRIDGE: " Is the spark plug gap bridged?";
CHOICES GAP-BRIDGE : YES,NO;

ASK SPARK : " Remove the spark plug from the ignition wire.  Insert a
 screwdriver into the cap.  Hold the screwdriver approximately 1/4-inch
 from the cylinder head and operate the kick starter. Is there a spark?";
CHOICES SPARK : YES,NO;

ASK BLOW : " Remove the spark plug and crank the engine while holding
 your thumb over the hole.  Does your thumb get blown off the hole?";
CHOICES BLOW : YES,NO;

ASK DROP : " Set the piston at the bottom dead center of its cycle and
 then remove the carburetor.  Hold your hand over the intake port and blow
 on the exhaust port.  Does the pressure drop?";
CHOICES DROP : YES,NO;

ASK CARBURETOR-WET :" Is the inside of the carburetor throat wet?";
CHOICES CARBURETOR-WET : YES, NO;

ASK FUEL-FLOW : " Does the fuel flow out when the fuel line is removed?";
CHOICES FUEL-FLOW : YES, NO;

ASK BUBBLES : " Remove the fuel tank cap and blow back through the line.
 Do you hear bubbles?";
CHOICES BUBBLES : YES, NO;

ASK PLUG-WET : " Is the spark plug wet?";
CHOICES PLUG-WET : YES, NO;
```

REFERENCES

Crawford, Charles W. *Glenn's Suzuki One Cylinder Repair and Tuneup Guide.* New York, NY: Crown Publishers, 1972.

Lockwood, Tim. *Suzuki Service-Repair Handbook.* Los Angeles, Calif.: Clymer Publications, 1973.

9

INTERMEDIATE-LEVEL SYSTEMS

9A Personal Computer Diagnosis and Repair Assistant

TECHNICAL PROFILE

Difficulty Level	Intermediate
Special Features	This diagnostic system uses the VP-Expert APPEND clause to add records to the end of a dBASE database file. The records store data gathered during a consultation. In this system the main KBS file chains to a smaller second KBS file that functions only to print the contents of the dBASE file. The printout is useful for management decision-making purposes.
Files Used	PCARE.KBS (main file), PCARE2.KBS (chained file), ERR1.DBF (dBASE file), and TEMPDATA (temporary file used only to transfer data from the main file to the chained file)
To Run	Load PCARE.KBS from the disk accompanying this book.

OVERVIEW

Today's computer users have varying degrees of personal computer (PC) knowledge. The majority know little about how a computer actually operates; they know only the software packages they are trained to use. If a problem occurs, especially one that is hardware related, most users are not able to diagnose and correct it.

In many large organizations, the computer department has a "help desk," usually a division of the information center, to assist users with computer-related problems. Smaller companies often buy contracts from outside service companies to provide telephone and on-site support. Whether support comes from an in-house or outside source, it is both time consuming and costly to have to rely on others for all PC troubleshooting. User departments in large organizations, as well as service companies, are overburdened and often unable to give immediate attention to many help requests.

This situation calls for an automated system to assist non-technical users in tackling some of the problems that arise during PC operation. The diagnostic prototype expert system described here is designed to accomplish this task. It can be distributed to PC user departments on a diskette and used by anyone who encounters problems operating a PC. End-user dependence on computer support personnel is thereby reduced and troubleshooting experts are freed from handling routine problems.

Given the range of problems that can occur during PC operation, it is not difficult to imagine the scope of such a diagnostic system. For this initial concept-testing phase, the focus of the prototype is narrowed to one problem symptom: the user does not get a "C:\" prompt on the screen when the computer is turned on, or booted. Personal Computer Diagnosis and Repair Assistant (PC/CARE) diagnoses the problem and directs the user on how to remedy the situation.

An automatic by-product of the PC/CARE system is its ability to provide management with information about the problems users are having. The system saves information about the types and quantity of PC problems encountered in a database file created during PC/CARE user consultations. This management control feature is described at the end of this discussion of the PC/CARE system.

Justification for the Prototype System

The primary justification for PC/CARE is cost savings. When non-technical users encounter PC problems, they will not always have to resort to costly service technician calls. Users also will not lose valuable time waiting for technicians to arrive and correct the difficulty. Instead, this prototype enables users to troubleshoot and fix many PC problems on their own.

A second reason for this prototype system is user convenience. Because most computer users are not experienced technicians, they find it difficult to pore over manuals looking for answers to their problems. It is a time-consuming and often confusing process. Even users with the necessary patience frequently do not have the time to troubleshoot PC problems using a manual.

PC/CARE also helps to make less experienced users more at ease with computers by decreasing their "technophobia."

STUDYING THE SITUATION

Various problem symptoms may occur when operating a personal computer. Often they originate from one of the following sources:

- *Power supply:* The system does not respond when it is turned on (for example, the fan does not turn or the display screen, or monitor, is blank) or the power supply fan starts, then abruptly stops.
- *Monitor:* The system's fan is running, but the display screen remains blank.
- *Keyboard:* The keyboard does not work.
- *RAM* (Random Access Memory): The system does not respond when the power is turned on, or the fan runs but the display screen remains blank.
- *Parallel port or device:* The printer or other parallel device does not respond to incoming data from the system unit.

- *Serial port or device:* The serial printer or other serial device (such as a mouse or a modem) does not respond to incoming data.
- *Disk drive* (hard and diskette drives): The system reports a problem with a diskette and/or hard drive.
- *DOS:* Error messages include "Bad command or filename," "Disk error reading drive X—Abort, Retry, Ignore?", "File not found," "Invalid date," and "Write protect error writing drive X—Abort, Retry, Ignore?".

Narrowing the Focus

One problem is especially difficult to diagnose and repair unless a user is experienced with PC troubleshooting: the system is booted but does not respond with the "C:\>" prompt message. This problem is the area selected for initial testing and prototyping. It can be caused by one or more of four source factors: power supply, monitor, RAM, or hard disk. The PC/CARE prototype system identifies which factor is the source of the problem and makes recommendations for repair.

Critical Factors Affecting the System

The four critical factors considered by the PC/CARE prototype system are power supply, monitor, RAM, and hard disk. Their possible values, as determined by a consultation session, are

Critical Factor	*Values*
Power supply	(ok, not_ok)
Monitor	(ok, not_ok)
RAM	(ok, not_ok)
Hard disk	(ok, not_ok)

Problems with the *power supply* may be caused by the following conditions:

- The power switch is not turned on or the power supply cable is not properly installed in the rear of the system unit.
- The computer's power cord is not securely plugged into an electrical outlet.
- The volt selector switch (110/220) on the back of the unit is not properly set.
- The controller boards in the system unit are not properly seated in their slots on the system board.
- The cable running from the power supply to the system board is not seated properly.
- The cables from the power supply to the disk drives are not seated properly.

Problems with the *monitor* may be due to the following:

- The monitor is not turned on.
- The monitor is not plugged into an outlet.
- The brightness and/or contrast controls are not adjusted properly.
- The monitor data cable is not properly connected to the port at the rear of the system unit.
- The video adapter board is not properly seated in its slot on the system board.
- SW1 jumper pins are not set correctly for the type of monitor being used. For example, monochrome monitors need only one pin set on the SW1 jumper. Otherwise, the jumper should be set with both pins.

Problems that occur with *RAM* are usually due to faulty Bank 0 RAM chips or RAM chips that are not properly seated on the system board. Once a system boots, a short RAM test is performed on the system board. If the system does not respond when the power is turned on or the fan runs but the display remains blank, it may be because the RAM chips in Bank 0 are not fully seated in their sockets. If the system beeps continuously, it is either because a key on the keyboard is stuck or Bank 0 RAM chips are not properly seated in their sockets.

Finally, problems with the *hard disk* may be caused by two conditions, as considered by this prototype:

1. The hard disk is not formatted.
2. The hard disk is not configured correctly.

These four critical factors are identified in the decision diagram in Figure 9A–1. Because this is a prototype of a PC diagnosis and repair system, it considers only a limited number of the possible problem conditions. The conditions included in this system are described in the next section and identified in Figure 9A–2.

Typical User Questions Grouped by Critical Factors

Each consultation begins with a user entering his or her full name and position (staff or managerial). This information begins a record that is stored in a database file that keeps track of people and problems encountered.

All the other questions in this consultation require a simple "yes" or "no" response. The first two questions are asked to determine if the computer is displaying a C:> prompt and if the computer's motor is running:

- Is the C:\> displayed on the screen of the computer?
- Do you hear the motor running on the PC?

To determine the first critical factor, power supply, the following questions are asked:

- Is the computer's power cord plugged into an outlet?
- Is the computer's power switch turned on?
- Is the connection to the power supply secure?

The next questions determine the second critical factor, monitor:

- Is the brightness turned all the way up on the monitor?
- Is the cable connection between the computer and the monitor secure?
- Is the monitor turned on?
- Does the monitor display anything on the screen?

To determine the third critical factor, hard disk, the following questions are asked:

- Does the hard disk light flicker on and off?
- Does the screen display the following message: "Hard Disk failure—Run SETUP"?

The last set of questions determines the fourth critical factor, RAM:

- Does the computer beep continuously?
- Is the keyboard stuck?

Figure 9A–1. Personal Computer Diagnosis and Repair Assistant: Block Diagram of Diagnostic Decision Situation

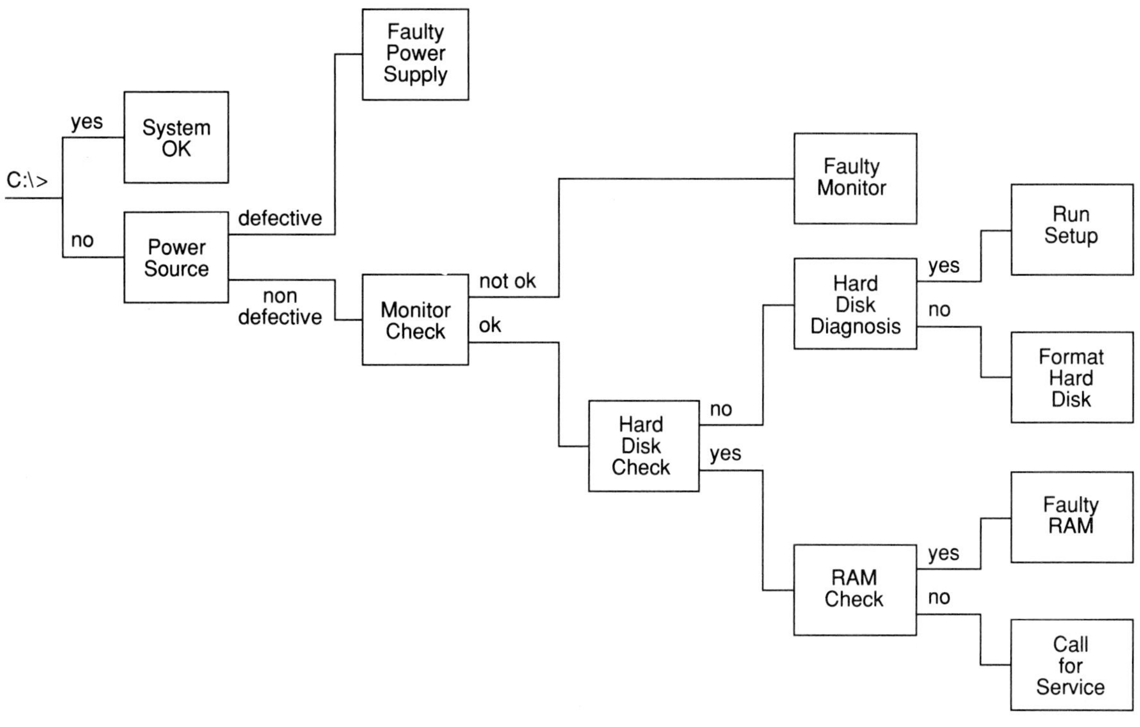

Figure 9A–2. Personal Computer Diagnosis and Repair Assistant: Detail of Diagnostic System for Prototyping

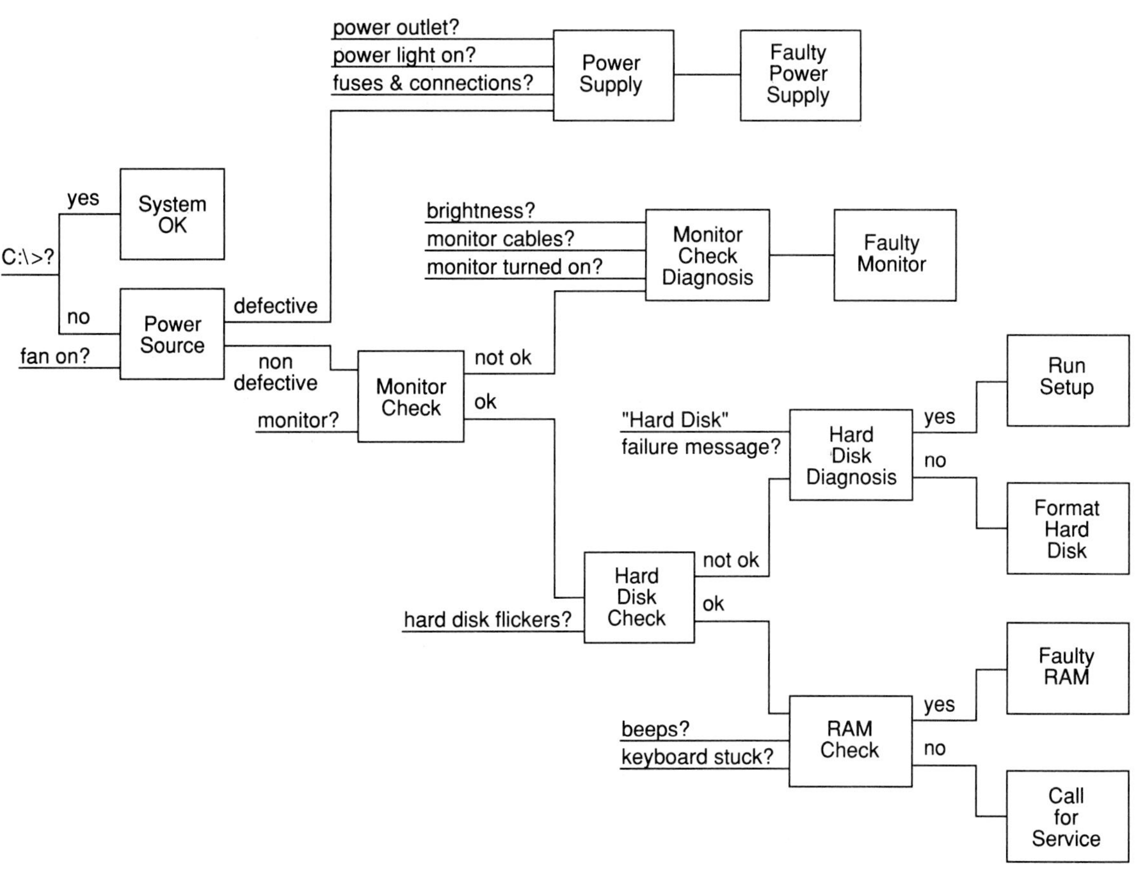

Recommendations Made by the System

The following 14 recommendations made by this prototype system depend on the problem(s) experienced by the user:

1. You do not need PC/CARE. The computer is OK.
   Reason: The user got the C:\> prompt message.
2. Have the power supply checked.
   Reason: The power supply is defective.
3. Secure the power cord.
   Reason: The computer must be plugged in securely for it to work.
4. Plug the PC securely into an outlet.
   Reason: The computer will not run if it is not plugged securely into an electrical outlet.
5. Turn on the PC to display the C prompt.
   Reason: The computer's power must be on in order for the system to boot.
6. Try a different outlet.
   Reason: The problem may be that the electrical outlet is defective.
7. Replace the monitor.
   Reason: The monitor is damaged.
8. Secure the monitor cable connection.
   Reason: The cable connection is loose or damaged.
9. Check the plug and turn the monitor on.
   Reason: If the monitor is not plugged in or turned on, it will not be able to display anything.
10. Adjust the brightness level.
    Reason: If the monitor is on but the intensity or contrast controls are too low, the screen display will not be seen.
11. Run the Setup program.
    Reason: There was a "Hard Disk failure" message on the screen.
12. Reformat the hard disk.
    Reason: There was no message on the screen, but the hard disk flickered.
13. Call CompuTec to check Bank 0 of RAM.
    Reason: If RAM chips are not properly seated or defective, the system may beep continuously and will not display anything on the monitor.
14. Call CompuTec 1-800-SYS-HELP.
    Reason: The system's problem could not be determined. Call for service.

A Typical Scenario

Maria, an accountant for a Big Six accounting firm, uses an IBM PC to perform various office duties. One morning when she turned on the computer and the monitor, the system did not display the C:\> prompt message; it was blank. Maria checked the plugs for the system and the monitor to be certain they were firmly plugged into the wall outlet. Then she adjusted the brightness and the contrast controls on the monitor. She still did not see a C:\> prompt.

Since Maria is not a technical computer person, she did not know what else to try. She reported the problem to her supervisor, who called CompuTec Service Company to service the PC.

The help desk representative at CompuTec sent Michael Sullivan, a technician, to service the call. Maria told Mike that the system and the monitor were plugged in and that she had adjusted the brightness and contrast controls. Mike asked Maria if she heard the fan running. Maria said yes. Mike then proceeded to check the fuses and cables. He tested the fuse with a voltmeter and saw that it was OK. Then he checked the cables to make sure they were not loose. They were properly secured, so he concluded that the power supply was OK.

Next Mike checked the monitor. He checked the connection from the monitor to the rear of the system unit and realized that the connection was loose. That was the reason Maria was not getting a C:\> prompt message on the PC. Once the monitor cable was secured, the monitor and the computer worked perfectly.

SYSTEM DOCUMENTATION

Figure 9A–3 gives three sample decision tables for rules in this prototype system. Similar decision tables are prepared for all the rule sets in the system. Figure 9A–4 is a completed dependency diagram of the PC/CARE prototype system.

Figure 9A–3. Personal Computer Diagnosis and Repair Assistant: Sample Decision Tables

Rule Set 1:

Determines whether user has a problem or not (This prototype assumes the PC is OK if the user gets a C:\> prompt message.)

IF	C_prompt	yes	no	no
	fan	—	yes	no
THEN		R13	PS nondef	PS def

R13 = the system is OK.
PS def = power source is defective.
PS nondef = power source is non-defective.

Rule Set 2:

IF	PS	def	def	def	def
	power_outlet	yes	no	yes	yes
	power_light	yes	—	no	no
	connections	yes	—	yes	no
THEN	recommend	R4	R11	R1	R12

PS = power source
def = defective
R1 = turn computer on.
R4 = the power supply should be checked.
R11 = plug the computer into an outlet.
R12 = replace the power supply cable.

Rule Set 3:

IF	PS	nondef	nondef
	CRT_monitor	no	yes
THEN	CRT_check	not_ok	ok

def = defective
nondef = non_defective

Figure 9A–4. Personal Computer Diagnosis and Repair Assistant: Dependency Diagram

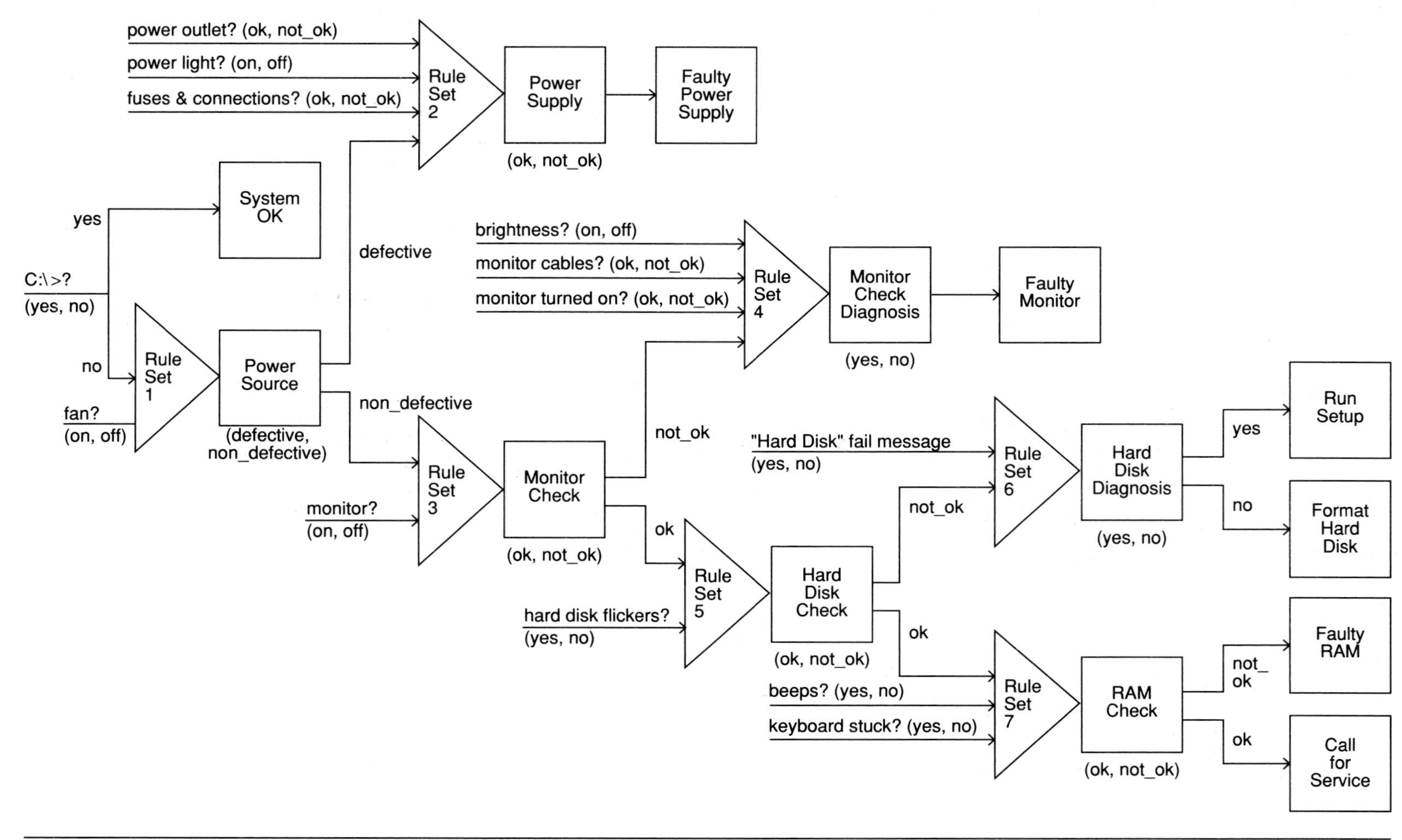

Figure 9A–5 gives the record structure and some sample records for the dBASE database file used by this system.

Two sample consultations are shown in Figure 9A–6. As the consultations demonstrate, as soon as the source of the problem is determined, the system does not explore other areas. Instead, it proceeds directly to a recommendation screen.

For example, in the first consultation, the user answers "no" to the question, "Is the computer's power cord plugged into an outlet?" At this point, there is no need to continue the consultation with questions about the monitor, the hard drive, and RAM. None of those components will function properly unless the power unit is plugged in. So PC/CARE immediately concludes the session with a recommendation to plug the PC securely into an outlet.

The second consultation determines the source of the problem while evaluating the second critical factor, the monitor.

A third sample consultation, given in Figure 9A–7, shows a manager requesting a printout of the names of staff members who received the system recommendation to replace their monitors. The concluding screen shows that two users received this recommendation.

A printout of the two knowledge bases in the PC/CARE system is given in Figure 9A–8.

Testing and Validation

For the testing phase of this expert system project, the knowledge engineer must test at least 15 different cases. It is necessary to trace each path of the dependency diagram to ensure that all logical bugs have been eliminated. Once this is done and the user interface is developed, the prototype can be turned over to the staff of a specific end-user department for further testing.

Figure 9A–5. Personal Computer Diagnosis and Repair Assistant: Database File

Database Structure

Field Name	Field Type	Width	Description
E_NAME	Character	16	Name of the user
ERROR_TYPE	Character	40	Error message/recommendation

Sample Database Records

E_NAME	ERROR_TYPE
Kayla Connelli	plug_the_PC_securely_into_an_outlet
Charles Duncan	replace_the_monitor
Phyllis Grimson	replace_the_monitor
Laura Lucchesi	do_not_need_PC_CARE_The_computer_is_OK
Mark Donaghan	have_the_power_supply_checked
Maria Angrisani	call_CompuTec_1-800-SYS-HELP
Sandra Mullin	reformat_the_hard_disk
David Wildner	run_the_Setup_Program
Paula Johnson	adjust_the_brightness_level
Pamela Brady	secure_the_monitor_cable_connection

Figure 9A–6. Personal Computer Diagnosis and Repair Assistant: Sample Consultations—Normal User Segment (Part 1)

CONSULTATION 1:

```
PERSONAL COMPUTER DIAGNOSIS AND REPAIR ASSISTANT (PC/CARE)

              Developed by Laura Lucchesi
        under the direction and supervision of
                   Dr. D.G. Dologite
```

Text only

```
Welcome to the PC/CARE  Personal Computer Diagnosis
                           and Repair Assistant

Press any key to continue ...




              *** I N T R O D U C T I O N ***

  This consultation assists a non-technical user in
  troubleshooting problems encountered while using a
  personal computer.  It asks a series of questions
  about the problem then recommends a way to correct it.

  Please press any key to begin the consultation.
```

Actual screen

```
                  I N S T R U C T I O N S
     Use the arrow keys to move the lightbar to a desired answer
     choice then press the ENTER key.

What is your name (full name, please)?
 Kayla Connelli

Which of the following best describes your position?
 staff worker ◄           manager

Is the C:\> displayed on the screen of the computer?
 yes                      no ◄

Do you hear the motor running on the PC?
 yes                      no ◄
```

Users in the accounting department, for example, run the system for a trial period of approximately one month. During this time, they provide input and suggest modifications. The knowledge engineer incorporates enhancements from the users' suggestions and returns the revised system to them. Therefore, by the end of the trial period, the final system is user-friendly and operates correctly.

Text only

```
Is the computer's power cord plugged into an outlet?
  yes                    no ◄



                *** R E C O M M E N D A T I O N ***

         Kayla Connelli, based on the answers given, I recommend
         that you plug the PC securely into an outlet.

         (Press any key to conclude the consultation.)
```

CONSULTATION 2:

Text only

```
What is your name (full name, please)?
 Phyllis Grimson

Which of the following best describes your position?
 staff worker ◄        manager

Is the C:\> displayed on the screen of the computer?
 yes                   no ◄

Do you hear the motor running on the PC?
 yes ◄                 no

Does the monitor display anything on the screen?
 yes                   no ◄

Is the brightness turned all the way up on the monitor?
 yes ◄                 no

Is the cable connection between the computer and the monitor
secure?
 yes ◄                 no

Is the monitor turned on?
 yes ◄                 no



              *** R E C O M M E N D A T I O N ***

       Phyllis Grimson, based on the answers given, I recommend
       that you replace the monitor.

       (Press any key to conclude the consultation.)
```

Design Issues

The initial difficulty in the development phase of this prototype was narrowing the focus, or scope, of the project. Once the initial prototype was focused, the next challenge was to make user questions easy and friendly enough to be understood by a computer novice or non-technical person. After many rewordings, acceptable questions were developed and implemented.

Figure 9A–7. Personal Computer Diagnosis and Repair Assistant: Sample Consultation—Management Segment (Part 2)

Text only

```
What is your name (full name, please)?
 Gary Greene

Which of the following best describes your position?
 staff worker         manager ◄



                       PC/CARE ERROR LOG KEEPER

           This produces a printout of the recommendations
           given for the PC problems staff members have been
           experiencing.

           (Press any key to continue ... )



             CAUTION !!!!!
Please check to make sure the printer is ON.
Press any key to continue.
Gary Greene, what type of error are you interested in
searching for?
 plug the PC securely     replace the monitor ◄    call CompuTec 1-800-
 do not need PC CARE      have the power suppl     reformat the hard di
 run the Setup Progra     check the plug and t     adjust the brightnes
 turn on the PC to di     secure the monitor c



The following database records meet your criteria:

Recommendation: replace the monitor

                   NAME
                 --------
              Charles Duncan
              Phyllis Grimson

*    E N D   O F   E R R O R   L O G   F I L E    *

Press any key when done.
```

The design of this system is relatively simple. During a consultation, the main program, PCARE.KBS, appends each user's name and consultation outcome to the ERR1.DBF dBASE database file. The structure of this database file and representative records are given in Figure 9A–5.

When a user indicates that he or she is a manager, PCARE.KBS chains to a second file called PCARE2.KBS. The manager's name is passed to the second KBS file using a temporary file called TEMPDATA. PCARE2.KBS accesses the database file to print out the names of all users who receive a specific error type, for example, users who have been advised to replace the monitor.

A limited number of the questions asked by the system include the VP-Expert BECAUSE keyword to provide explanatory text in response to the Why? or How? command given by a user during a consultation. An expanded version of this diagnostic system would include explanations for all of the questions asked.

MANAGEMENT CONTROL

An important by-product of the PC/CARE expert system is the information it provides to management. A database file of PC user problems is a helpful tool to

Figure 9A–8. Personal Computer Diagnosis and Repair Assistant: Printout of Knowledge Base File

```
!____________________________________________________________________!
!                                                                    !
! Personal Computer Diagnosis and Repair Assistant (PC/Care) - Part 1 !
!                                                                    !
! This system will help a user find and correct personal computer errors. !
! This file links to pcare2.kbs, which prints out a management report.  !
!____________________________________________________________________!
!                                                                    !
! Saved filename      : pcare.kbs                                    !
! Shell used          : VP-Expert, Educational Version 2.02          !
! Microcomputer used: IBM AT compatible                              !
! Chained file        : pcare2.kbs (to print out the manager's report) !
! Temporary file      : tempdata (saves user's name for chaining to  !
!                       pcare2.kbs)                                  !
!____________________________________________________________________!

bkcolor = 3;                    !set screen background color to blue
runtime;                        !eliminates rules and facts window
endoff;                         !eliminates need to press END after a choice
!============================== Actions Block ==========================
actions
  wopen 1,1,1,20,77,3           !define opening credit window
  active 1
  display "


         PERSONAL COMPUTER DIAGNOSIS AND REPAIR ASSISTANT (PC/CARE)

                        Developed by Laura Lucchesi
                   under the direction and supervision of
                            Dr. D.G. Dologite
                     For further information, contact
                            Dr. D.G. Dologite
                        c/o Macmillan Publishing


                        Press any key to continue~
     "
  wclose 1
  cls
  display "


            Welcome to the PC/CARE  Personal Computer Diagnosis
                                       and Repair Assistant



       Press any key to continue ... ~"
  cls
  wopen 2,2,9,15,62,6          !define outer frame
  active 2                     !activate window 2
  display "
            *** I N T R O D U C T I O N ***

  This consultation assists a non-technical user in
  troubleshooting problems encountered while using a
  personal computer.  It asks a series of questions
  about the problem then recommends a way to correct it.

  Please press any key to begin the consultation.~

     "
  wclose 2                     !remove window 2
  wopen 3,1,1,5,77,6           !define instructions window 3
  active 3                     !activate window 3
  display "                          I N S T R U C T I O N S
        Use the arrow keys to move the lightbar to a desired answer
        choice then press the ENTER key."
  wopen 4,7,1,14,77,7          !define consultation window 2
  active 4                     !activate window 4
  display "    "
```

Figure 9A–8. *continued*

```
  whileknown end_switch
      reset emp_name
      find  emp_name
      e_name = (emp_name)
      reset recommend
      find recommend
      wclose 3                    !remove window 3
      wopen 5,5,7,10,65,7         !define recommendations window
      active 5                    !activate window 5
      display "                ***     R E C O M M E N D A T I O N  ***

      {emp_name}, based on the answers given, I recommend
      that you {recommend}.

      (Press any key to conclude the consultation.)~"
      wclose 5
      error_type = (recommend)
      append errl                 !adds to existing DB file
      close  errl                 !closes DB file
end;
!============================== Rules Block ==============================
rule D-1                          !rule that links to another
     if title = manager           !KBS file called pcare2
     then recommend = dummy
          savefacts tempdata
          chain pcare2;

rule 1-1
     if   c_prompt  = yes
     then recommend = do_not_need_PC_CARE_The_computer_is_OK;

rule 1-2
     if   c_prompt  = no  and
          fan =  no
     then ps = defective
     because "The motor is not running, so problem is with power supply";

rule 1-3
     if   c_prompt  = no  and
          fan = yes
     then ps = non_defective
     because "The motor is running, so power supply is OK";

rule 2-1
     if   ps = defective  and
          power_outlet = yes and
          power_lite   = yes and
          connections  = yes
     then recommend = have_the_power_supply_checked;

rule 2-2
     if   ps = defective  and
          power_outlet = yes and
          power_lite   = yes and
          connections  = no
     then recommend = secure_the_power_cord;

rule 2-3
     if   ps = defective  and
          power_outlet = no
     then recommend = plug_the_PC_securely_into_an_outlet;

rule 2-4
     if   ps = defective  and
          power_outlet = yes and
          power_lite   = no  and
          connections  = yes
     then recommend = turn_on_the_PC_to_display_c_prompt;

rule 2-5
     if   ps = defective and
          power_outlet = yes and
          power_lite   = no  and
          connections  = no
     then recommend =  try_a_different_outlet;
```

```
rule 3-1
     if   ps = non_defective and
          CRT_monitor = no
     then CRT_check = not_ok
     because "The monitor must be on to display anything";

rule 3-2
     if   ps = non_defective and
          CRT_monitor = yes
     then CRT_check = ok;

rule 4-1
     if   CRT_check  = not_ok and
          briteness  = yes and
          cables     = yes and
          plugged_in = yes
          then recommend = replace_the_monitor;

rule 4-2
     if   CRT_check = not_ok and
          briteness = yes and
          cables    = no
     then recommend = secure_the_monitor_cable_connection;

rule 4-3
     if   CRT_check  = not_ok and
          briteness  = yes and
          cables     = yes and
          plugged_in = no
     then recommend  = check_the_plug_and_turn_the_monitor_on;

rule 4-4
     if   CRT_check = not_ok and
          briteness = no
     then recommend = adjust_the_brightness_level;

rule 5-1
     if   CRT_check = ok and
          HD_flicks = yes
     then HD_check  = ok
     because "If hard disk flickers & monitor is OK, then RAM is the
     problem";

rule 5-2
     if   CRT_check = ok and
          HD_flicks = no
     then HD_check  = not_ok
     because "If hard disk does not flicker & monitor is OK, then hard
     disk is the problem";

rule 6-1
     if   HD_check = not_ok and
          HD_fail_msg = yes
     then recommend = run_the_Setup_Program;

rule 6-2
     if   HD_check = not_ok and
          HD_fail_msg = no
     then recommend = reformat_the_hard_disk;

rule 7-1
     if   HD_check = ok and
          beeps = yes and
          keyboard_stuck = yes
     then recommend = call_CompuTec_to_check_bank_0_of_RAM
     because "Bank 0 of RAM is either loose or defective";
```

Figure 9A–8. *continued*

```
rule 7-2
     if   HD_check = ok and
          beeps = no and
          keyboard_stuck = no
     then recommend = call_CompuTec_1-800-SYS-HELP;

rule 7-3
     if   HD_check = ok and
          beeps = no and
          keyboard_stuck = yes
     then recommend = call_CompuTec_1-800-SYS-HELP;

rule 7-4
     if   HD_check = ok and
          beeps = yes and
          keyboard_stuck = no
     then recommend = call_CompuTec_1-800-SYS-HELP;

!========================== Questions Block ============================

ask c_prompt: "Is the C:\> displayed on the screen of the computer?";
choices c_prompt: yes, no;

ask power_lite: "Is the computer's power switch turned on?";
choices power_lite: yes, no;

ask fan: "Do you hear the motor running on the PC?";
choices fan: yes, no;

ask power_outlet: "Is the computer's power cord plugged into an outlet?";
choices power_outlet: yes, no;

ask connections: "Is the connection to the power supply secure?";
choices connections: yes, no;

ask plugged_in: "Is the monitor turned on?";
choices plugged_in: yes, no;

ask briteness:  "Is the brightness turned all the way up on the monitor?";
choices briteness: yes, no;

ask cables: "Is the cable connection between the computer and the monitor
secure?";
choices cables: yes, no;

ask HD_flicks: "Does the hard disk light flicker on and off?";
choices HD_flicks: yes, no;

ask HD_fail_msg:  "Does the screen display the following message:
    'Hard disk failure - Run SETUP'?";
choices HD_fail_msg: yes, no;

ask beeps:  "Does the computer beep continuously?";
choices beeps: yes, no;

ask keyboard_stuck:  "Is the keyboard stuck?";
choices keyboard_stuck: yes, no;

ask CRT_monitor:  "Does the monitor display anything on the screen?";
choices CRT_monitor: yes, no;

ask emp_name: "What is your name (full name, please)?";

ask title: "Which of the following best describes your position?";
choices title: staff_worker, manager;
```

```
= = = = = = = = = = = = = = = = = = = = = = = = = = = = = = = = = = = = = = = = =
!_______________________________________________________________________________!
!                                                                               !
! PC/CARE - Personal Computer Diagnosis and Repair Assistant - Part 2          !
!                                                                               !
! This part of the system prints out the error log for management control      !
! purposes.                                                                     !
!_______________________________________________________________________________!
!                                                                               !
! Saved filename    : pcare2.kbs                                                !
! Purpose           : This KBS file is accessed by a CHAIN command in           !
!                     pcare.kbs.  It retrieves records from the database        !
!                     file err1.dbf for printout.  The printout is for a        !
!                     manager's use to see what type of errors staff            !
!                     members are experiencing.                                 !
! Technical note    : This KBS does not save any variables.                     !
! Micro used        : IBM AT compatible PC                                      !
! Shell used        : VP-Expert, Educational Version, 2.02                      !
!_______________________________________________________________________________!
!                                                                               !

execute;                          !start consultation immediately
bkcolor = 3;                      !set screen background color to light blue
runtime;                          !eliminate rules and facts windows
endoff;                           !eliminate need to press end


!============================== Actions Block ============================
actions
     loadfacts tempdata           !load into memory all variable names and values
                                  !stored in the temporary file called TEMPDATA
     wopen 1,5,12,8,57,7          !defines opening window
     active 1                     !activates window 1
     display "
               PC/CARE ERROR LOG KEEPER

     This produces a printout of the recommendations
     given for the PC problems staff members have been
     experiencing.

     (Press any key to continue ... )~"
     wclose 1                     !removes window 1
     color = 20                   !set caution message to blinking red
     display "              C A U T I O N !!!!!"
     color = 4
     display "Please check to make sure the printer is ON"
     display "Press any key to continue.~"
     color = 0                    !reset text back to black lettering
     menu err_type,all,err1,error_type
     find err_type
     cls
     display " "
     display " The following database records meet your criteria:"
     display " "
     display " Recommendation: {err_type}"
     display " "
     display "                        NAME    "
     display "                        --------  "
     whileknown error_type
               get err_type = error_type,err1,all
               reset message
               printon            !send display text to screen and printer
               find message
     end
;
!============================== Rules Block ==============================
rule 1
     if error_type <> unknown
     then message = displayed
          display "               {e_name} "
      else message = displayed
          display " "

          display " *    E N D   O F   E R R O R   L O G   F I L E    * "
          display " "
          display "Press any key when done.~";

!============================== Questions Block ==========================
ask err_type: "{emp_name}, what type of error are you interested in
searching for?";
```

monitor the volume of calls that come to the help-desk support function. Too high a volume could indicate the need to have more PC training for selected individuals or workgroups.

In addition, the tracking file allows an organization to monitor the condition of the company's computer hardware. For example, the hardware may be reaching a point of obsolescence if a large number of users are experiencing recommendations to replace their monitors or repeatedly reformat their hard drives.

The database file created during PC/CARE consultations can also be manipulated through the dBASE program itself. Managers can design customized dBASE reports using the data in the file to help control PC operations.

REFERENCES

Alperson, B., A. Fluegelman, and L. Magid. *The Fully Powered PC.* New York, NY: Brady Books, 1985.

MS/DOS User's Reference Manual. Redmond, Wash.: Microsoft Corp., 1990.

9B Foreign Tourism Authority Travel Assistant—For Thailand

TECHNICAL PROFILE

Difficulty Level	Intermediate
Special Features	This system uses eight dBASE database files of information about the different vacation sites recommended by the prototype.
Files Used	TAT.KBS and the dBASE database files WATER.DBF, MOUNTAIN.DBF, CITY.DBF, M_CITY.DBF, M_HOTEL.DBF, AR_CITY.DBF, AR_HOTEL.DBF, and TATDATA.DBF.
To Run	Load TAT.KBS from the disk accompanying this book.

OVERVIEW

Note: This is an exploratory customer service system. It is designed to test the feasibility of using expert system technology to help answer traveller inquiries at a tourism bureau. For this prototype, The Tourism Authority of Thailand in New York City was chosen as the test case because of the developer's familiarity with this environment and the availability of tourism information for Thailand.

The Tourism Authority of Thailand in New York City TAT (NYC) acts on behalf of Thailand's government to promote and develop the nation's tourism industry. In 1987, Thailand's government declared that year as "Visit Thailand Year" and made the event part of the celebration honoring the king's 60th birthday. Since then, Thailand has become increasingly popular for travellers. Tourism is now a major source of income. As a result, Thailand's government has supported the staging of various activities to increase tourism.

TAT (NYC) plays an active role in helping to meet the goal of increased travel to Thailand. TAT (NYC) has four major responsibilities:

1. To provide necessary information to travellers who wish to go to Thailand by supplying them with travel brochures or by assisting them with helpful recommendations.
2. To promote Thailand's tourism industry by hosting or participating in travel exhibitions throughout the United States in cooperation with other major travel agencies.
3. To respond reasonably, actively, and effectively to complaints from travellers; to bring issues to Thailand's government's attention for further consideration; and to act as an arbitrator to settle issues.
4. To provide needed assistance to people in tourism or the travel industry who may, in turn, help promote Thailand tourism, such as newspaper reporters, magazine writers, travel photographers, travel book writers, and the like.

Although it is a major center on America's East Coast, TAT(NYC) is understaffed. Often the public relations officer is unable to help visitors who come in for travel advice because she is busy on the telephone.

An automated travel information system would provide immediate and accurate assistance to customers when office personnel are not available. The system could offer information on Thailand such as travel requirements, sightseeing and other available activities, and climate and currency.

The benefits of a computerized travel information system outweigh the costs. For example, while the system is in service, a public relations officer is freed from helping waiting visitors and can handle other business efficiently and promptly. The computerized system would provide consistent and complete travel information at all times. In addition, Thailand's image would be enhanced by showcasing its technological know-how and innovative approach to tourism.

Once developed, the system could be copied and installed in any TAT location in the world. A copy could even be placed on a computer located outside TAT offices to provide travel information when offices are closed, for example, during holidays. The system could also be helpful during periods of personnel shortages and during peak tourist seasons.

The expertise needed to develop a complete tourism advisory system can be acquired from in-house travel experts, travel brochures, travel magazines, and inquiries originating from the travellers themselves.

STUDYING THE SITUATION

TAT (NYC) is located in the World Trade Center in Manhattan. It has four employees: the director, an assistant to the director, a public relations officer, and a mail clerk. The public relations officer is responsible for answering all telephone calls, handling all calls for travel information, and assisting visitors who are potential travellers. Office hours are from 9:30 A.M. to 5:30 P.M., and peak hours are from about 10:00 A.M. to 2:30 P.M.

The office has three telephone lines. On the average, two lines ring simultaneously every seven minutes. Under all circumstances, telephone calls are given first priority. Since TAT(NYC) is involved in a wide range of activities, a call may be either local or long distance from

- A Thailand government consulate
- Another Tourism of Thailand office
- A travel agency asking for specific information, such as train or ferry schedules
- A potential traveller interested in visiting Thailand
- An organization that arranges ongoing promotion trips to Thailand and needs current status information

The length of the calls varies, depending on the nature of the call.

The situation that initiated this prototype system occurred when a potential traveller came into the office while the public relations officer was busy on the telephone, handling one call after another. The traveller waited patiently for a while. Finally, he grabbed some brochures and left. The public relations officer regretted not being able to assist the traveller. The situation, however, could not be avoided. She brought the matter to the attention of the director and explained how an expert system could be used to give potential travellers information while she is on the telephone.

The system could be installed near the brochures table to generate curiosity. Visitors would be invited to sit down and answer a few simple questions on the computer. In turn, the automated travel system would recommend travel sites based on the user's preferences.

Critical Factors Affecting the Decision Area

The four critical factors affecting the travel information decision area are shown in Figure 9B–1. They are activity preference, interest preference, transportation preference, and lifestyle/comfort level.

Figure 9B–1. Foreign Tourism Authority Travel Assistant—For Thailand: Block Diagram of Decision Situation

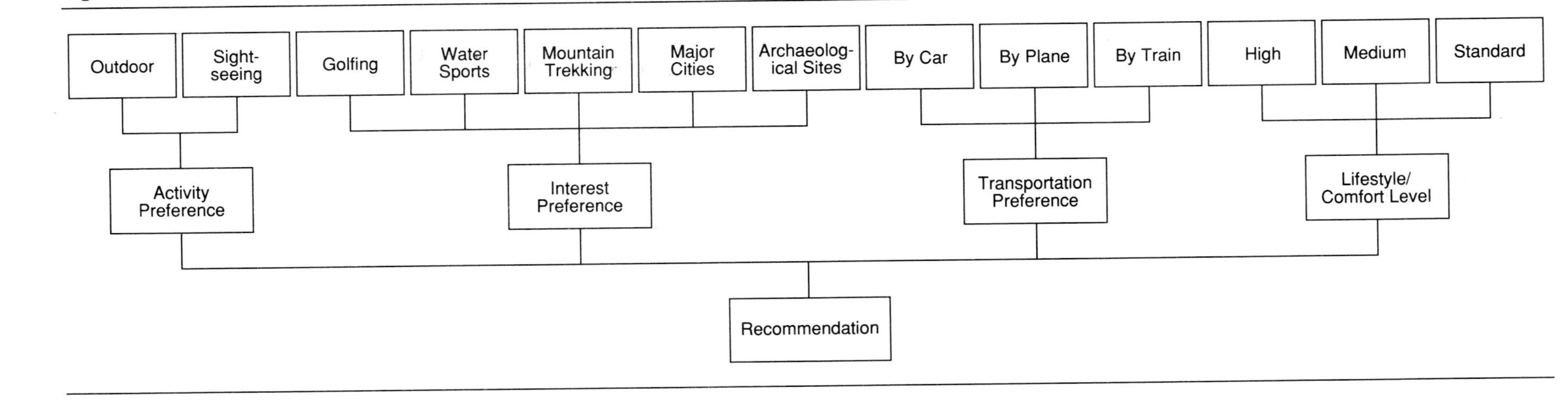

Activity Preference. People enjoy a vacation the most when they can do what they want. The system recommends vacation areas based on two categories of popular activities—outdoor activities and sightseeing.

Interest Preference. Depending on the type of activity chosen (outdoor or sightseeing), the system offers a number of options to fit varying interests. For example, for those who prefer outdoor activities, Thailand is famous for its golf courses. It is also a paradise of water sports and offers exciting mountain trekking.

No trip to Thailand is complete without seeing some of the country. While some people prefer to tour the major cities, others enjoy a classical tour, such as visiting archaeological sites. Because Thailand is more than 2,000 years old, it has plenty of heritage and history to be uncovered by adventurous travellers.

Transportation Preference. Although Thailand is comparable in size to France, it does not have the same transportation conveniences. So the expert system provides users with an estimate of the time required to travel to a destination by each type of available transportation (car, plane, or train), where appropriate. This helps tourists with time restrictions to choose vacation areas and transportation methods best suited to their schedules.

Lifestyle/Comfort Level. Vacationers are most satisfied when treated with the level of service and comfort to which they are accustomed. Lifestyle, or level of comfort and services, is classified by this system in terms of high, medium, and standard. As expected, the higher the level of comfort, the more luxurious (and the more expensive) the accommodations recommended.

Questions Asked by the System

The Foreign Tourism Authority Travel Assistant prototype system asks the following questions during a consultation:

- What do you prefer to do on your vacation? (Outdoor activities, Sightseeing)
- (If the user prefers outdoor activities) Which activity interests you the most? (Golfing, Mountain trekking, Water sports)
- (If the user prefers sightseeing) What kind of sights do you prefer to see? (Major cities, Archaeological sites)
- (If the user prefers outdoor activities or sightseeing in major cities) How do you plan to travel to your vacation destination? (By car, By plane, By train)
- (If the user prefers sightseeing at archaeological sites) How do you like to travel? (By car, By train)
- What level of comfort do you require on a vacation? (High, Medium, Standard)

Recommendations Made by the Prototype System

The 34 final recommendations made by the Foreign Tourism Authority Travel Assistant depend on the user's choice of transportation, activities, and lifestyle preference. A complete list of all of the recommendations and their corresponding critical factor values is given in the decision table in Figure 9B–2. There are two situations where this prototype does not have a suitable site recommendation for the choices made (for example, for a combination of golfing, travelling by train, and a high lifestyle preference). In these cases, the system displays a message that a "mismatch" has occurred.

Figure 9B–2. Foreign Tourism Authority Travel Assistant—For Thailand: Decision Table for Final Rule Set

Activity	Interest	Transportation	Preference	Recommendation
Outdoor	Golfing	By car	High	Bangkok (Rose Garden)
Outdoor	Golfing	By plane	High	Phuket (Phuket)
Outdoor	Golfing	By train	High	Mismatch
Outdoor	Golfing	By car	Medium	Bangkok (Navatanee)
Outdoor	Golfing	By plane	Medium	Chieng Mai (Lanna)
Outdoor	Golfing	By train	Medium	Pattaya (Bangpla)
Outdoor	Golfing	By car	Standard	Bangkok (Krungthep)
Outdoor	Golfing	By plane	Standard	Mismatch
Outdoor	Golfing	By train	Standard	HuaHin (Royal HuaHin)
Outdoor	Mountain trekking	—	High	Chieng Mai (Orchid Hotel)
Outdoor	Mountain trekking	—	Medium	Chieng Mai (Mae Ping Hotel)
Outdoor	Mountain trekking	—	Standard	Chieng Mai (Cheing Mai Hills Hotel)
Outdoor	Water sports	By car	High	Pattaya (Royal Cliffs)
Outdoor	Water sports	By plane	High	Phuket (Phuket Resort)
Outdoor	Water sports	By train	High	HuaHin (Sofitel Cntrl)
Outdoor	Water sports	By car	Medium	Pattaya (Montien Patt)
Outdoor	Water sports	By plane	Medium	Phuket (Karon Noi)
Outdoor	Water sports	By train	Medium	HuaHin (Royal Gardens)
Outdoor	Water sports	By car	Standard	Pattaya (Ocean View)
Outdoor	Water sports	By plane	Standard	Phuket (Patong Resort)
Outdoor	Water sports	By train	Standard	HuaHin (Sailom Hotel)
Sightseeing	Major cities	By car	High	Bangkok (The Oriental)
Sightseeing	Major cities	By plane	High	Chieng Mai (Dusit Inn)
Sightseeing	Major cities	By train	High	Mismatch
Sightseeing	Major cities	By car	Medium	Bangkok (Royal Orchid)
Sightseeing	Major cities	By plane	Medium	Chieng Mai (Ch. Orchid)
Sightseeing	Major cities	By train	Medium	Ayutthaya (U-Thong)
Sightseeing	Major cities	By car	Standard	Bangkok (Nari Hotel)
Sightseeing	Major cities	By plane	Standard	Chieng Mai (Chieng Inn)
Sightseeing	Major cities	By train	Standard	Ayutthaya (Thai Sena)
Sightseeing	Arch. sites	By car	High	Sukhothai (Rajthanee)
Sightseeing	Arch. sites	By train	High	Kanchanaburi (Rama of River Kwai)
Sightseeing	Arch. sites	By car	Medium	Sukhothai (Wiang)
Sightseeing	Arch. sites	By train	Medium	Kanchanaburi (River Kwai Village Hotel)
Sightseeing	Arch. sites	By car	Standard	Sukhothai (Nanchao)
Sightseeing	Arch. sites	By train	Standard	Kanchanaburi (Kanchanaburi Inn)

Lifestyle and comfort are categorized as follows:

1. *High:* First-class travellers prefer and can presumably afford superior and luxurious accommodations. For example, they do not mind spending $300 a night or more for a hotel room.
2. *Medium:* This type of traveller has some budget constraints but still desires comfort and services. An appropriate recommendation might be a hotel priced from $100 to $200 a night.
3. *Standard:* Money is a major consideration for these travellers. The system assumes that they would not spend more than $100 a night for a hotel room. Appropriate accommodations range from $60 to $100 a night.

Here is an example of a typical recommendation. If a user chooses golf as a vacation interest, likes to travel by car, and prefers a high level of comfort, the system makes the following recommendation:

Our recommendation is: BANGKOK-ROSE GARDEN GOLF COURSE

> Restaurants: Thai, Japanese, Chinese, Western
> VIP & function rooms
> Pro shop, lockers, and shower & changing rooms
> Tel: 66-034-311-171
>
> Cultural: Daily performances on aspects of Thai
> Center &: village life.
> Gardens :

All of the final recommendation site information is saved in database files accessed by the main TAT.KBS file during a consultation.

After the system makes a final recommendation, users are asked if they would like to know more about Thailand. If the answer is "yes," the system provides the following information: climate, entry requirements, health regulations, Thailand currency conversion, and the airline reservation telephone number. This option is available for every consultation session.

Typical Scenario

The following scenario takes place at TAT(NYC). A visitor comes in while the public relations officer (PR) is busy on the phone. He waits patiently until the PR officer is free to help him.

PR. Sorry to keep you waiting. How can I help you, sir?

VISITOR. I am going to make a trip to Thailand. It will be my first trip, so I want to know as much as possible about the country.

The PR officer points at the information table across the reception desk where the travel brochures are kept. The brochures depict various activities that might interest visitors to Thailand, such as golfing, water sports, and sightseeing.

PR. There are some travel brochures and a travel guide. Please skim through them and tell me what interests you the most. Then I can make some suggestions.

VISITOR. It looks like there are many beautiful beaches in Thailand. I think that's what I want to do when I go there.

PR. Very well, sir. Do you also like water sports?

VISITOR. Yes, I do indeed. I like to scuba dive and snorkel. Is there a place I can do these things in Thailand?

PR. Certainly. How would you prefer to travel while in Thailand? Would you prefer car, plane, or train?

VISITOR. I think I would prefer to travel by car so I can see more of the country.

PR. What is your preference in terms of comfort and services: high, medium, or standard level of comfort?

VISITOR. Since this is a special vacation for my wife and myself, I would like to have the best accommodations available.

PR. Then my recommendation for you would be to go to Pattaya. You prefer to travel by car and Pattaya is only a two-hour drive from Bangkok. It's located on the east coast of the Gulf of Thailand and is known as the "Queen of Asia's Resorts" because so many colorful and lively activities go on there night and day. I can assure you that there will never be a dull moment at Pattaya. The first-class hotel there is the Royal Cliff Beach Hotel. You will enjoy your own private beach with full-facility water sports. You can contact your travel agent for hotel and airline reservations. Here is the hotel's address and fax number.

VISITOR. You've been very helpful. Thanks a lot for your help. Bye.
PR. You're welcome. Enjoy your stay in Thailand.

SYSTEM DOCUMENTATION

Figure 9B–3 is a dependency diagram of the Foreign Tourism Authority Travel Assistant prototype system. Since there are 34 possible recommendations, only a few are listed on the dependency diagram.

Figure 9B–4 shows a sample of the records in each of the eight dBASE database files used in this prototype system. The first one, TATDATA.DBF, is a database file of golfing vacation sites in Thailand. The second is MOUNTAIN-.DBF and has recommended sites for mountain trekking vacations. The next file, WATER.DBF, contains the hotel name and other related information about water sports. Another file, CITY.DBF, holds descriptions of the three recommended water sports cities, as well as some of the activities available there.

The other four databases hold information for sightseeing vacations. M_CITY.DBF and M_HOTEL.DBF contain records that store the names of major cities to visit, as well as recommended hotels in these cities. The records in

Figure 9B–3. Foreign Tourism Authority Travel Assistant—For Thailand: Dependency Diagram

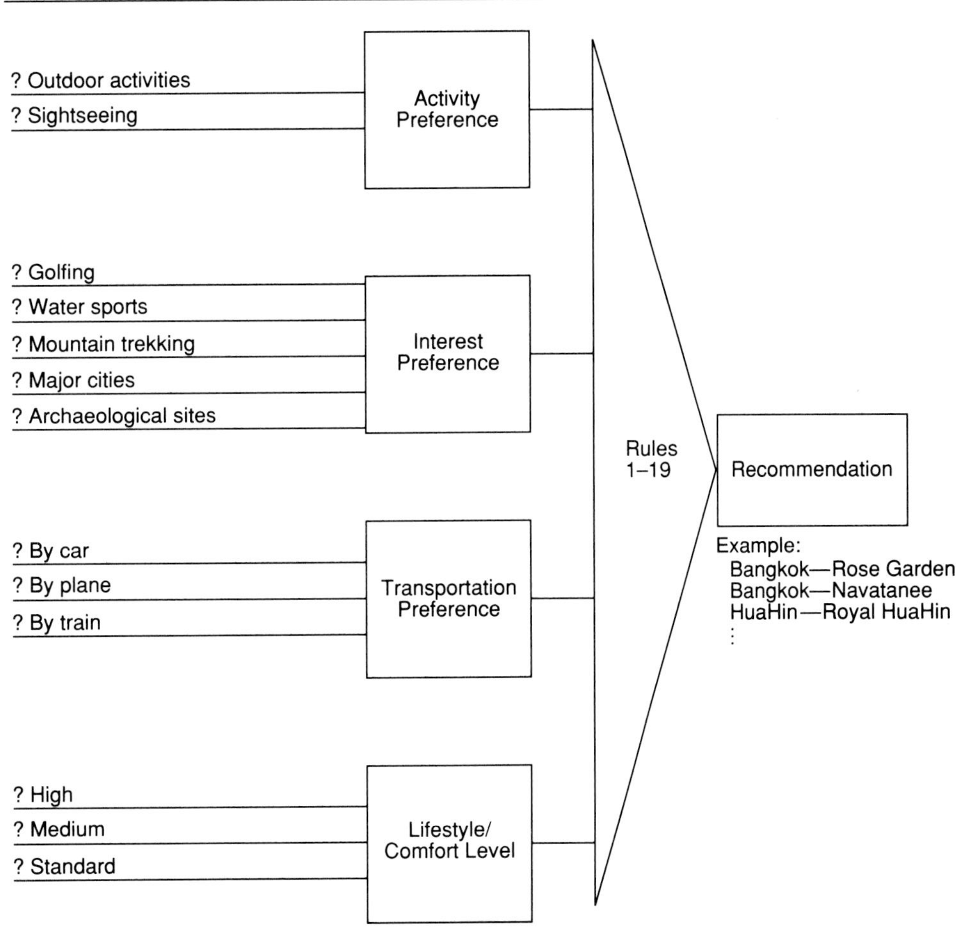

Figure 9B–4. Foreign Tourism Authority Travel Assistant—For Thailand: Samples of Records in Eight Database Files

Database filename: TATDATA.DBF

PLACE_ ID	DBPLACE	DESC1	DESC2	DESC3	HOTEL	CULTURAL	TEL
01	BANGKOK—ROSE GARDEN GOLF COURSE	Restaurants: Thai, Japanese, Chinese, Western	VIP & function rooms	Pro-shop, lockers, shower & changing rooms	80 first-class rooms and suites, swimming pool, and tennis court	Daily performances on aspects of Thai village life	66-034-311-171
02	PHUKET—PHUKET GOLF & COUNTRY CLUB	Driving range	Various restaurants	Pro-shop, lockers, shower & changing rooms, sauna		Tennis courts, swimming pool, jogging, hiking, horseback riding	66-076 231-388
03	BANGKOK—NAVATANEE GOLF COURSE	Driving range, restaurant	Pro-shop, lockers, shower & changing rooms	Meeting rooms, banquet rooms		Swimming, tennis	66-2 374-6127
04	CHIENG MAI—LANNA GOLF COURSE	Driving range	Restaurant	Pro-shop, lockers, shower & changing rooms			66-053 211-911

Database filename: MOUNTAIN.DBF

DB_PREFER	HOTEL	ADDRESS1	LOCAL_TEL	BKK_OFFICE	BKK_TEL
HIGH	Chieng Mai Orchid Hotel	100-102 Huai Kaeo Road, Chieng Mai	053-221-625	5th Floor Yada Bldg., 56 Silom Road	02-233-8261-3
MEDIUM	Mae Ping Hotel	Sridonchai Road, Chieng Mai	053-251-060		02-391-4096
STANDARD	Chieng Mai Hills Hotel	18 Huai Kaeo Road, Chieng Mai	053-221-255	8th Floor, Silom Road, Bangkok	02-235-0240-5

Database filename: WATER.DBF

DBTRANS	DBPREFER	HOTEL	DBPLACE	LOCAL__TEL	BKK__OFFICE	BKK__TEL
By__car	Medium	Montien Pattaya Hotel	Pattaya Beach Resort, Chonburi	038-428-155-6	c/o Montien Hotel 54 Surawongse Road	02-234-8060-9
By__car	Standard	Ocean View Hotel	Pattaya Beach Resort, Pattaya City, Chonburi	038-428-084		02-859-1373
By__car	High	Royal Cliff Beach Hotel		038-428-511		02-282-0999
By__plane	Medium	Karon Noi Beach, Phuket	Meridian Phuket	076-321-480-5		02-252-8545
By__plane	Standard	Patong Resort Hotel	Patong Beach, Phuket	076-321-333-5		02-235-9040

Database filename: CITY.DBF

DBCITY	TRVL__INFO	LOC__DESC1	LOC__DESC2	LOC__DESC3	SPRT__DESC1	SPRT__DESC2
PATTAYA	Travel by car is approximately 1 hour and 45 minutes.	Located on the east coast of the gulf of Thailand.	A two hour drive from Bangkok.		Sailing, water skiing, parasailing, windsurfing,	scuba diving, deep-sea fishing, and more.
PHUKET	Travel by plane is 1 hour.	Located on the southeast coast, just an hour's flight from	Bangkok. Phuket is Thailand's largest island and a	province in its own right.	Windsurfing, sailing, fishing, parasailing, and	much more.
HUA__HIN	Travel by train is 4 hours.	A sleepy coastal town on the sunrise side of Thai gulf.	Hua Hin was Thailand's first beachside resort and has been	the Thai royal family's summer residence since 1925.	Windsurfing, sailing, parasailing, water skiing,	deep-sea fishing, and a lot more.

Figure 9B–4. *continued*

Database filename: M_CITY.DBF

DBMAJOR	CITY_DESC1	CITY_DESC2	CITY_DESC3	SIGHT1—SIGHT6
CHIENG_MAI	Thailand's second largest city and capital of the northern	provinces.		Wat Prathat Doi Suthep Doi Inthanont National Park Mae Klang Falls Borichinda Cave Chieng Mai National Museum Phu Phing Palace
AYUTTHAYA	Thai capital for 417 years. Ayutthaya is one of Thailand's	major attractions. Many ancient ruins and art work can be	seen in this city founded in 1350.	Vihara Phra Mongkok Bopitr Bang Pa-In Summer Palace open every day from 8:30 AM—noon and from 1:00 PM—3:00 PM The Chao Sam Phraya National Museum Chandra Kasem Palace

Database filename: M_HOTEL.DBF

DBPREFER	DBTRANS	HOTEL	DBPLACE	BKK_TEL
HIGH	BY_CAR	The Oriental	48 Oriental Avenue, Bangkok 10500	662-236-1936
STANDARD	BY_CAR	Nari Hotel	222 Silom Road, Bangkok 10500	662-233-3350
MEDIUM	BY_CAR	Royal Orchid Sheraton	@ Captain Rush Lane Siphaya Road, Bangkok 10500	662-236-8320
MEDIUM	BY_TRAIN	U-Thong Hotel	80 U-Thong Road, Ayuthaya	251-136
STANDARD	BY_TRAIN	Thai Sena	268 Sena—Navin Soi 2, Sena District, Ayuthaya	201-032

Database filename: AR_CITY.DBF

DB_ARCH	CITY_DESC1	CITY_DESC2	ATTR1—ATTR6
KANCHANABURI	Known among war historians as the site of the notorious	"Death Railway" and the "Bridge over the River Kwai"	Kanchanaburi War Cemetery Death War Museum Ban Kao Neolithic Museum Prasat Muang Singh Historical Park Kanchanaburi Cultural Center River Kwai Railway Camp
SUKHOTHAI	It is believed that the Thai people originated some 4,500	years ago and Sukhothai was their first kingdom in 1238.	The Sukhothai Historical Park The Ramkhamhaeng Historical Park The Wall of the old city San-Ta-Pha deang or city shrine King Ramkhamhaeng National Monument Ruin of old celadon factory

Database filename: AR_HOTEL.DBF

DBCITY	DBPREFER	HOTEL	ADDRESS	TEL
KANCHANABURI	HIGH	Rama of River Kwai Hotel	284-3 Saeng Chut Road, Kanchanaburi	034-511-184
KANCHANABURI	MEDIUM	River Kwai Village Hotel	74 Ban Phutakhian Tamban, Amphor Saiyok, Kanchanaburi	034-517-552
KANCHANABURI	STANDARD	Kanchanaburi Inn	55 Rajavithi Road, Kanchanaburi	034-517-828
SUKHOTHAI	HIGH	Rajthanee Hotel	229 Charodai Road, Amphor Muang, Sukhothai 61103	055-511-910
SUKHOTHAI	MEDIUM	Wiang Sukhothai Hotel	25/3 Mahatthai Bumrung Road, Sukhothai	055-511-910
SUKHOTHAI	STANDARD	Nanchao Hotel	242 Raromtriloknat Road, Sukhothai	055-259-511

the final two database files, AR_CITY.DBF and AR_HOTEL.DBF, contain cities and hotels for recommended archaeological sightseeing vacations.

Other system documentation, which includes sample consultations and a printout of the knowledge-based system, is given in Figures 9B–5 and 9B–6. The first consultation shows a recommendation for a traveller who likes water sports, wants to travel by car, and desires a medium level of comfort. It also shows the two display screens of further information about Thailand.

The second consultation is for a traveller who desires to go sightseeing to archaeological sites by train, with a standard level of comfort.

Figure 9B–5. Foreign Tourism Authority Travel Assistant—For Thailand: Sample Consultations

CONSULTATION 1:

```
                    Welcome to
             FOREIGN TOURISM AUTHORITY
          TRAVEL ASSISTANT - for Thailand

          Developed by Vantanee Hoontrakul
       under the direction and supervision of
                  Dr. D.G. Dologite
```

Actual screen

```
Use the arrow keys to move the lightbar to a desired selection.
Press the Enter key to make a selection.
Press the End key to move to the next question.
```

```
What do you prefer to do on your vacation?
 Outdoor Activities ◄      Sightseeing

Which activity interests you the most?
 Golfing                   Mountain trekking
 Water sports ◄

How do you plan to travel to your vacation destination?
 By car ◄                   By plane
 By train

What level of comfort do you require on a vacation?
 High                      Medium ◄
 Standard
```

Actual screen

```
Our recommendation is: Pattaya.

PATTAYA: Located on the east coast of the gulf of Thailand.
         A two hour drive from Bangkok.

Sport:   Sailing, water skiing, parasailing, windsurfing,
         scuba diving, deep-sea fishing, and more.


 Hotel:  Montien Pattaya Hotel
 Place:  Pattaya Beach Resort, Chonburi
 Tel:    038-428-155-6

 Bangkok Office: c/o Montien Hotel, 54 Surawongse Road
 Tel:  02-234-8060-9

                     Press any key to continue
```

Text only

```
Would you like to know more about Thailand?
 Yes ◂                        No


CLIMATE
             Hot Season   : March - May
             Rainy Season: June - September
             Cool Season : October - February
             Average Temperature: 28C (82.4F)

ENTRY REQUIREMENTS
  Passports: All visitors entering Thailand must
             possess valid passports.
  Visas:     American citizens visiting Thailand
             for the purpose of vacation or pleasure are
             exempt from applying for entry visas if they
             plan to stay in Thailand for less than 15 days.

             Other nationalities please consult the
             Thai consulate at 53 Park Place, 5th Floor,
             New York City,  Tel: 212-732-8166.

                          Press any key to continue



HEALTH REGULATIONS
  No inoculations or vaccinations are required unless
  you are coming from or passing through contaminated
  areas.

THAI CURRENCY
  1 US. Dollar = 25 Baht (Approximately)

AIRLINE
  Thai Airways reservation toll-free telephone number is
  1-800-426-5204.

                    Press any key to continue


      Thank you for using the Foreign Tourism Authority
      Travel Assistant - for Thailand.  Please ask our travel
      consultants any specific questions you may have.

                Press any key to end this consultation
```

CONSULTATION 2:

Text only

```
What do you prefer to do on your vacation?
 Outdoor Activities        Sightseeing ◂

What kind of sights do you prefer to see?
 Major Cities              Archaeological sites ◂

How do you like to travel?
 By car                    By train ◂

What level of comfort do you require on a vacation?
 High                      Medium
 Standard ◂

Our recommendation is: Kanchanaburi.
KANCHANABURI: Known among war historians as the site of the notorious
              "Death Railway" and the "Bridge over the River Kwai"

Attraction:   Kanachanaburi War Cemetary
              Death War Museum
              Ban Kao Neolithic Museum
              Prasat Muang Singh Historical Park
              Kanachanburi Cultural Center
              River Kwai Railway Camp
Hotel         Kanachanburi Inn
Address:      55 Rajavithi Road, Kanchanaburi
Tel:          034-517-828
```

Figure 9B–6. Foreign Tourism Authority Travel Assistant—For Thailand: Printout of Knowledge Base File

```
! Foreign Tourism Authority Travel Assistant (TAT) - for Thailand
! Saved as tat.kbs
! This program links to the following dBASE III+ files:

!          dBASE Filename        Description
!          tatdata.dbf           Golf vacation sites
!          mountain.dbf          Mountain trekking sites
!          water.dbf             Hotel information for water activities
!          city.dbf              Cities for water activities
!          m_city.dbf            Major cities for sightseeing
!          m_hotel.dbf           Hotels in major cities
!          ar_city.dbf           Archaeological cities for sightseeing
!          ar_hotel.dbf          Hotels in archaeological cities

        runtime;                          ! Eliminate rules and facts windows

! ====================== Action Blocks ==============================

actions
        outdoor = Outdoor_Activities
        sight = Sightseeing
        major = Major_Cities
        arch  = Archaeological_sites
        wopen  1,1,1,20,77,3              ! Define opening window 1
        active 1                          ! Activate window 1
        display "


                                Welcome to
                            FOREIGN TOURISM AUTHORITY
                         TRAVEL ASSISTANT - for Thailand

                         Developed by Vantanee Hoontrakul
                      under the direction and supervision of
                                Dr. D.G. Dologite
                         For further information, contact
                                Dr. D.G. Dologite
                            c/o Macmillan Publishing

              Please press any key to begin the consultation ~ "
        wclose 1                          ! Remove window 1

        wopen 1,1,6,5,68,5                ! Define instructions window 1
        active 1                          ! Activate window 1

        display"Use the arrow keys to move the lightbar to a desired selection."
        display"Press the Enter key to make a selection."
        display"Press the End key to move to the next question."
        wopen 2,7,5,17,70,3               ! Define consultation window 2
        active 2                          ! Activate window 2

        find place

        wopen 1,5,5,10,70,4
        active 1
        display "
       Thank you for using the Foreign Tourism Authority
       Travel Assistant - for Thailand.  Please ask our travel
       consultants any specific questions you may have.



                 Press any key to end this consultation~"
        wclose 1;

!******************* OUTDOOR RULES START HERE ************************

RULE 1
if      area=(outdoor) and
        interest=Golfing and
        trans=By_car and
        prefer=High
```

```
then    place= 01    ! Assign a value to a variable for tatdata.dbf
        find golfing_desc
        find more_detail
        find detail_desc;

RULE 2
if      area=(outdoor) and
        interest=Golfing and
        trans=By_plane and
        prefer=High
then    place=02     ! Assign a value to a variable for tatdata.dbf
        find golfing_desc
        find more_detail
        find detail_desc;

RULE 3
if      area=(outdoor) and
        interest=Golfing and
        trans=By_train and
        prefer=High
then    wclose 2                    ! Close window 2
        wopen 2,7,5,6,70,4          ! Open new window 2
        active 2
        display "                  Selection is a mismatch."

        display"          Press any key to go back to consultation screen.~"
        wclose 2                    ! Close window 2
        place = mismatch;           ! Place = dummy value

RULE 4
if      area=(outdoor) and
        interest=Golfing and
        trans=By_car and
        prefer=Medium
then    place=03   ! Assign a value to a variable for tatdata.dbf
        find golfing_desc
        find more_detail
        find detail_desc;

RULE 5
if      area=(outdoor) and
        interest=Golfing and
        trans=By_plane and
        prefer=Medium
then    place=04   ! Assign a value to a variable for tatdata.dbf
        find golfing_desc
        find more_detail
        find detail_desc;

RULE 6
if      area=(outdoor) and
        interest=Golfing and
        trans=By_train and
        prefer=Medium
then    place=05
        find golfing_desc
        find more_detail
        find detail_desc;

RULE 7
if      area=(outdoor) and
        interest=Golfing and
        trans=By_car and
        prefer=Standard
then    place=06
        find golfing_desc
        find more_detail
        find detail_desc;

RULE 8
if      area=(outdoor) and
        interest=Golfing and
        trans=By_plane and
        prefer=Standard
```

Figure 9B–6. *continued*

```
then    wclose 2
        wopen 2,7,5,6,70,4
        active 2
        display "                      Selection is a mismatch."
        display"         Press any key to go back to consultation screen.~"
        wclose 2
        place = mismatch;

RULE 9
if      area=(outdoor) and
        interest=Golfing and
        trans=By_train and
        prefer=Standard
then    place=07
        find golfing_desc
        find more_detail
        find detail_desc;

RULE 10
if      area=(outdoor) and
        interest=Mountain_trekking then
        find trans
        find prefer
        place=Chieng_Mai
        find mountain_desc
        find more_detail
        find detail_desc;

RULE 11
if      area=(outdoor) and
        interest=Water_sports and
        trans=By_car
then    place=Pattaya
        find prefer
        find water_desc
        find more_detail
        find detail_desc;

RULE 12
if      area=(outdoor) and
        interest=Water_sports and
        trans=By_plane
then    place=Phuket
        find prefer
        find water_desc
        find more_detail
        find detail_desc;


RULE 13
if      area=(outdoor) and
        interest=Water_sports and
        trans=By_train
then    place=Hua_HIN
        find prefer
        find water_desc
        find more_detail
        find detail_desc;

! ************** MAJOR CITY RULE STARTS HERE ********************

RULE 14
IF      area=(sight) and
        sight_prefer = (major) and
        trans=By_plane
then    place=Chieng_Mai
        find prefer
        find major_desc
        find more_detail
        find detail_desc;
RULE 15
if      area=(sight) and
        sight_prefer = (major) and
        trans=By_car
THEN    place=Bangkok
        find prefer
```

```
        find major_desc
        find more_detail
        find detail_desc;
RULE 16
if      area=(sight) and
        sight_prefer = (major) and
        trans=By_train and
        prefer <> High
then    place=Ayutthaya
        find major_desc
        find more_detail
        find detail_desc;
RULE 17
if      area=(sight) and
        sight_prefer = (major) AND
        trans=By_train and
        prefer = High
then    wclose 2
        wopen 2,7,5,6,70,4
        active 2
        display "                        Selection is a mismatch."
        display"            Press any key to go back to consultation screen.~"
        wclose 2
        place = mismatch;

!   ***************  Archaeological_sites Rule Starts Here ******************

RULE 18
if      area=(sight) and
        sight_prefer = (arch) and
        arch_trans = By_train
then    place=Kanchanaburi
        find prefer
        find arch_desc
        find more_detail
        find detail_desc;
RULE 19
if      area=(sight) and
        sight_prefer = (arch) and
        arch_trans  = By_car
then    place=Sukhothai
        find prefer
        find arch_desc
        find more_detail
        find detail_desc;

RULE MOUNTAIN_RULE
if      interest = Mountain_trekking
then
        wclose 1
        wclose 2
        wopen 1,0,3,23,72,5
        active 1
        display "Our recommendation is: {PLACE}.
                                                          "
        get prefer = db_prefer, mountain,all
        display "  Hotel: {HOTEL}"
        display "         {ADDRESS1}"
        display "  Tel:   {LOCAL_TEL}"
        display "  Bangkok Office: {BKK_OFFICE}"
        display "  Tel:   {BKK_TEL}                   "
        display "                                     "
        wopen 2,9,3,15,72,3
        active 2
        display "       Hill tribe trekking in Chieng Mai to see four major"
        display "       hilltribes: Karen, Meo Lahu, Yao, and Akha."
        display "                                                 "
        display "  Average cost:  2 days and 1 night      1,000  Baht."
        display "  -----------    3 days and 2 nights     1,800  Baht."
        display "                 4 days and 3 nights     2,200  Baht."
        display "                                                  "
        display "  Please contact TAT Chieng Mai office for authorization at"
        display "              105/1 Chieng Mai-Lamphun Road            "
```

Figure 9B–6. *continued*

```
        display "              Amphur Muang, Chieng Mai 50000          "
        display "              Tel. (053) 248-604, 248-607             "
        display "              Fax. (053) 248-605                      "
        display "                                                      "

        display "                         Press any key to continue ~"

        wclose 1
        wclose 2
        mountain_desc=(hotel);          ! mountain_desc = any dummy value.

RULE PLACE_DESC
if      interest = Golfing
then
        wclose 1
        wclose 2
        wopen 1,1,3,5,73,4
        active 1
        get place = place_id,tatdata,all
        display " Our recommendation is: {DBPLACE}               "
        display "                                                "
        wopen 2,6,1,18,78,3
        active 2
        display "      {DESC1}"
        display "      {DESC2}"
        display "      {DESC3}"
        display "      {HOTEL}"
        display "Tel:  {TEL}"
        display "              "
        display "Cultural:  {CULTURAL}"
        display "Center &"
        display "Gardens"
        display""
        display""
        display""
        display""
        display""
        display""
        display"                          Press any key to continue ~"
        close tatdata
        wclose 1
        wclose 2
        golfing_desc=dbplace;

RULE WATER_DET
        if interest = Water_sports
then
        wclose 1
        wclose 2
        wopen 1,3,3,21,72,5
        active 1
        display "Our recommendation is: {PLACE}."
        display "                              "
        get place = dbcity,city,all
        display "{DBCITY}: {LOC_DESC1}"
        display "          {LOC_DESC2}"
        display "          {LOC_DESC3}"
        display "                     "
        display "Sport:    {SPRT_DESC1}"
        display "          {SPRT_DESC2}"
        display "          {SPRT_DESC3}"
        display "                      "
        get prefer = dbprefer and trans = dbtrans,water,all
        display " Hotel:   {HOTEL}"
        display " Place:   {DBPLACE}"
        display " Tel:     {LOCAL_TEL}"
        display "                     "
        display " Bangkok Office: {BKK_OFFICE}"
        display " Tel:  {BKK_TEL}                 "
        display "                                 "
        display "                                 "
        display "                        Press any key to continue ~"
        wclose 1
        water_desc=(hotel);
```

```
RULE MAJOR_DET
        if sight_prefer = (major)
then
        wclose 1
        wclose 2
        wopen 1,3,3,21,72,5
        active 1
        display "Our recommendation is: {PLACE}."
        display "                                  "
        get place = dbmajor,m_city,all
        display "{DBMAJOR}: {CITY_DESC1}"
        display "           {CITY_DESC2}"
        display "           {CITY_DESC3}"
        display "           {CITY_DESC4}"
        display "                      "
        display "Sightseeing: {SIGHT1}"
        display "             {SIGHT2}"
        display "             {SIGHT3}"
        display "             {SIGHT4}"
        display "             {SIGHT5}"
        display "             {SIGHT6}"
        display "                      "
        get prefer = dbprefer and trans = dbtrans,m_hotel,all
        display "  Hotel:     {HOTEL}"
        display "  Address:   {DBPLACE}"
        display "                    "
        display "  Tel:       {BKK_TEL}              "
        display "                      "
        display "                         Press any key to continue ~"
        wclose 1
        major_desc=(hotel);

RULE ARCH_DET
        IF sight_prefer = (arch)
THEN
        wclose 1
        wclose 2
        wopen 1,3,3,21,72,5
        active 1
        display "Our recommendation is: {PLACE}."
        display "                                  "
        get place = DB_ARCH,AR_CITY,ALL
        display "{DB_ARCH}: {CITY_DESC1}"
        display "           {CITY_DESC2}"
        display "           {CITY_DESC3}"
        display "           {CITY_DESC4}"
        display "                      "
        display "Attraction:  {ATTR1}"
        display "             {ATTR2}"
        display "             {ATTR3}"
        display "             {ATTR4}"
        display "             {ATTR5}"
        display "             {ATTR6}"
        get prefer = dbprefer and place = dbcity,ar_hotel,all
        display "  Hotel:     {HOTEL}"
        display "  Address:   {ADDRESS}"
        display "                    "
        display "  Tel:       {TEL}              "
        display "                          "
        display "                          Press any key to continue ~"
        wclose 1
        arch_desc=(hotel);

RULE MORE_DET
if      more_detail = Yes
then    cls
        wopen 1,1,3,23,74,3
        active 1
        display "  CLIMATE                            "
        display "
               Hot Season   : March - May
               Rainy Season: June - September
               Cool Season  : October - February
               Average Temperature: 28C (82.4F)
```

Figure 9B–6. *concluded*

```
ENTRY REQUIREMENTS"
  display "                                                        "
  display "     Passports: All visitors entering Thailand must"
  display "                possess valid passports."
  display "                                                              "
  display "     Visas:     American citizens visiting Thailand "
  display "                for the purpose of vacation or pleasure are"
  display "                exempt from applying for entry visas if they"
  display "                plan to stay in Thailand for less than 15 days."
  display "                                                           "
  display "                Other nationalities please consult the"
  display "                Thai consulate at 53 Park Place, 5th Floor,"
  display "                New York City,  Tel: 212-732-8166.      "
  display ""
  display "                        Press any key to continue~"
       wclose 1
       wopen 1,1,3,23,74,3
       active 1
       display"  HEALTH REGULATIONS"
       display"                                      "
       display"    No inoculations or vaccinations are required unless"
       display"    you are coming from or passing through contaminated"
       display"    areas."
       display"                                                  "
       display"  THAI CURRENCY

  1 US. Dollar = 25 Baht (Approximately)

 AIRLINE

  Thai Airways reservation toll-free telephone number is
  1-800-426-5204.



                    Press any key to continue~"
       wclose 1
       detail_desc = Yes;

ask area: "What do you prefer to do on your vacation?";
choices area: Outdoor_Activities,Sightseeing;

ask interest: "Which activity interests you the most?";
choices interest: Golfing,Mountain_trekking,Water_sports;

ask sight_prefer: "What kind of sights do you prefer to see?";
choices sight_prefer: Major_Cities,Archaeological_sites;

ask trans: "How do you plan to travel to your vacation destination?";
choices trans: By_car,By_plane,By_train;

ask arch_trans: "How do you like to travel?";
choices arch_trans: By_car,By_train;

ask prefer: "What level of comfort do you require on a vacation?";
choices prefer: High,Medium,Standard;

ask more_detail: "Would you like to know more about Thailand?";
choices more_detail: Yes,No;
```

REFERENCES

Tourism Authority of Thailand, Tourist Service Division Information Development Section. *A Traveller's Guide to Thailand 1989–1990.* Bangkok, Thailand: O.S. Printing House, 1989.

Thailand Travel Manual 1989–1990 and other assorted 1990 travel brochures from the Tourism Authority of Thailand.

Golf Thailand: A Player's Guide to Golf in Asia's Most Exotic Thailand. Bangkok, Thailand: Asia Images Co., Ltd., 1989.

9C Student Financial Aid Advisor

TECHNICAL PROFILE

Difficulty Level	Intermediate
Special Features	This prototype uses the VP-Expert RANGE statement to limit the range of values that can be assigned to specified variables, such as a student's grade point average (GPA). A dBASE database file stores detail for the recommended financial aid programs listed at the end of a consultation. FOR/END and COUNT keywords are used to execute a loop that prints all recommended financial aid programs. The final recommendation can be displayed on the screen or output to a printer. Some user questions have explanatory BECAUSE statements.
Files Used	FAA.KBS (KBS file) and FAA.DBF (dBASE database file)
To Run	Load FAA.KBS from the disk accompanying this book

OVERVIEW

Students often find it difficult to locate financial aid programs for which they are eligible. Doing research for the information using financial aid source books in a library is a tedious job. In addition, every college has its own private financial aid programs as well as processing procedures. To compound the problem, financial aid experts are a scarce resource and not all students have an opportunity to meet with such an expert at their institution.

This lack of readily accessible information creates a need to effectively collect, organize, and distribute knowledge about financial aid programs. Meeting this need could improve the educational services offered to incoming students.

The Financial Aid Advisor is an expert system developed for this purpose. It helps students to select the appropriate financial aid programs for which to apply. Although the expert system concentrates on the major financial sources available at one major metropolitan college, it could easily be adapted by other institutions that provide financial aid services.

The system evaluates the financial aid eligibility of each student user by asking direct questions. At the end of a consultation, the system displays and/or prints a list of applicable financial aid sources. Each recommendation includes the name of the financial aid offering, a contact source, telephone number, and the dollar or other value of the financial aid available.

Narrowing the Focus

The Financial Aid Advisor prototype expert system narrows its development scope to financial aid programs managed or directly related to the college and available only to graduate MBA students. All outside resources are excluded. This area was selected for prototyping because the expertise of the college's financial aid personnel was readily available. Also, the chief developer of this system had a working familiarity with the programs and procedures of the financial aid office.

Justification for the Prototype System

From an economic viewpoint, the implementation of the Financial Aid Advisor is feasible because financial aid advisors are expensive to hire and retain. In some cases, it is not easy to recruit personnel who have consulting experience. More importantly, budget constraints often prevent a college from hiring adequate and competent staff.

The hardware investment for this project is minimal. The only real cost is software design and implementation, which could be amortized over several years.

The Financial Aid Advisor expert system may be installed in student activity halls, government offices, libraries, or other locations around the college where students assemble. It can provide expert advice on financial aid programs to a larger number of students than human advisors are able to handle. In addition, human advisors will have more time to concentrate on problematic individual cases.

STUDYING THE SITUATION

More than 16,000 students attend the urban-centered college considered for this prototype expert system. A high percentage of the students receive some kind of financial aid. The financial aid office is, understandably, constantly flooded with students. They ask about the financial aid programs available and the necessary application procedures. Because of the large number of programs and complex individualized criteria set by each program, it is difficult for a student to pinpoint appropriate programs without the aid of an advisor.

Financial aid advisors must know basic information about a student before they can suggest appropriate financial aid programs to pursue. For example, only full-time students who have lived in the state for more than two years are eligible for the Tuition Assistance Program.

The major financial aid sources may be categorized as follows:

1. Federal Programs
   - Pell Grant
   - Supplemental Educational Opportunity Grant
   - College Work-Study Program
   - Federal Aid to Native Americans
2. State/City Programs
   - Tuition Assistance Program
   - Student Tuition Assistance
   - Regent Scholarship
   - Child of Veteran Award
   - Empire State Mathematics and Science Teacher Scholarship
   - Aid for Part-time Study
   - Mayor's Scholarship Program
3. Loan Programs
   - Carl Perkins' National Direct Student Loan
   - Guaranteed Student Loan Program
   - Auxiliary Loans to Assist Students
   - Parent Loan for Undergraduate Student
4. College Financial Aid Programs
   - There are a number of scholarships sponsored by alumni, corporate, and personal donations.
5. Outside resources
   - Fellowships, scholarships, and grants offered by companies, professional organizations, and government agencies

Critical Factors Considered by the System

As evident in Figures 9C–1 and 9C–2, there are four critical factors used to determine an MBA graduate student's eligibility for financial aid programs: financial need, academic progress, loan credibility, and other factors.

Financial Need factors solicit information about a student's financial situation. Estimated education cost is calculated based on citizenship and state residency status and the number of credit hours for which a student is enrolled. The graduate tuition structure at the selected college is as follows:

Graduate	*Full-Time (6 or more credit hours)*	*Part-Time (under 6 credit hours)*
State residents	\$950/semester	\$82 per credit
Out-of-state residents	\$2,350/semester	\$198.50 per credit

The difference between estimated education cost (calculated tuition plus a fixed amount of \$7,000 for living expenses) and self-support amount (money a student and his or her family can contribute toward education costs) is used to determine the need for financial aid.

Academic Progress factors evaluate the student's performance and category. Successful academic progress for an MBA student, as indicated by a GPA score of 3.0 or better, is an eligibility consideration for some types of financial aid. If an individual is a new, incoming MBA student, he or she is automatically considered to be making satisfactory academic progress.

Loan Credibility determines if a student has defaulted on a student loan. In such cases, financial aid will not be granted until repayment arrangement is made.

Other Factors provide supplementary information to determine eligibility for specific financial aid programs. If employed off campus, for example, a student may not be awarded a Graduate Assistantship. If a student is a full-time city employee, he or she is eligible to apply for the Mayor's Graduate Scholarship. Additional considerations are the number of years at the college and the student's GMAT score and undergraduate GPA.

Each critical factor has specific questions asked during a consultation to determine a correct value. The questions, along with their possible values, are apparent from the dependency diagram in Figure 9C–3, as well as from the sample consultations in Figure 9C–4.

Recommendations Made by the System

For prototyping purposes, the Financial Aid Advisor expert system is limited to making six financial aid recommendations for graduate students. They

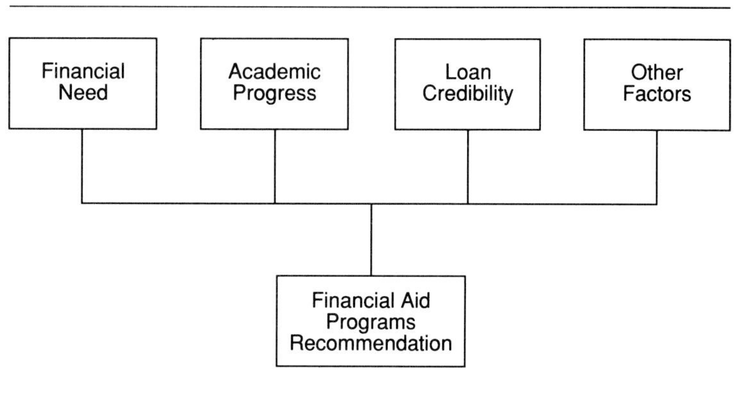

Figure 9C–1. Student Financial Aid Advisor: Overview Block Diagram of Decision Situation

Figure 9C–2. Student Financial Aid Advisor: Detailed Block Diagram of Decision Situation

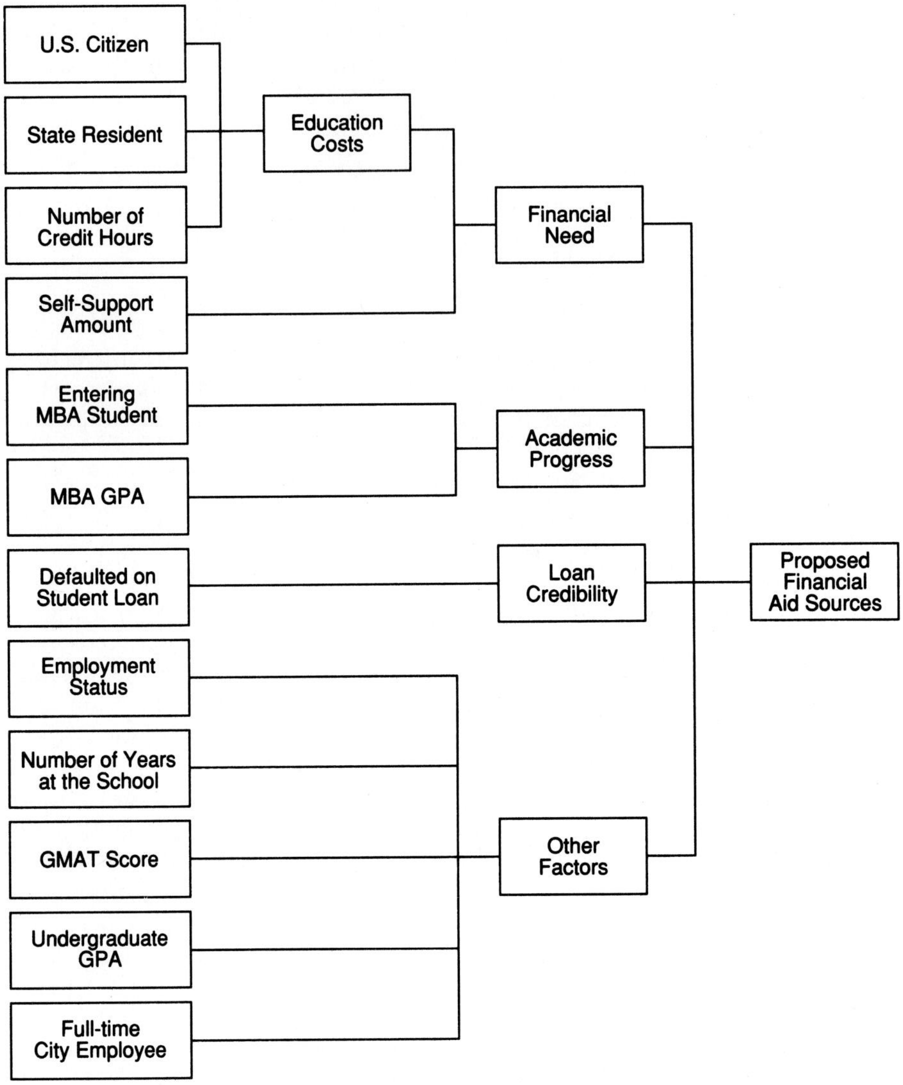

are contained in a dBASE database file and are identified in Figure 9C–5. All programs, except Graduate Fellowships, are need-based financial aid. To be eligible, a student must have financial need, good credibility on student loans, and be making satisfactory progress toward a degree. Brief descriptions of the recommendations follow.

- *Graduate Research Assistantship (GRA):* Graduate research assistants are expected to devote full time (12 credits of course work or equivalent) to graduate study during the period of the award. No outside employment is permitted. Fifteen hours of service a week must be rendered to the department to which the student is assigned. The annual award can range up to $5,000.

Figure 9C–3. Student Financial Aid Advisor: Dependency Diagram

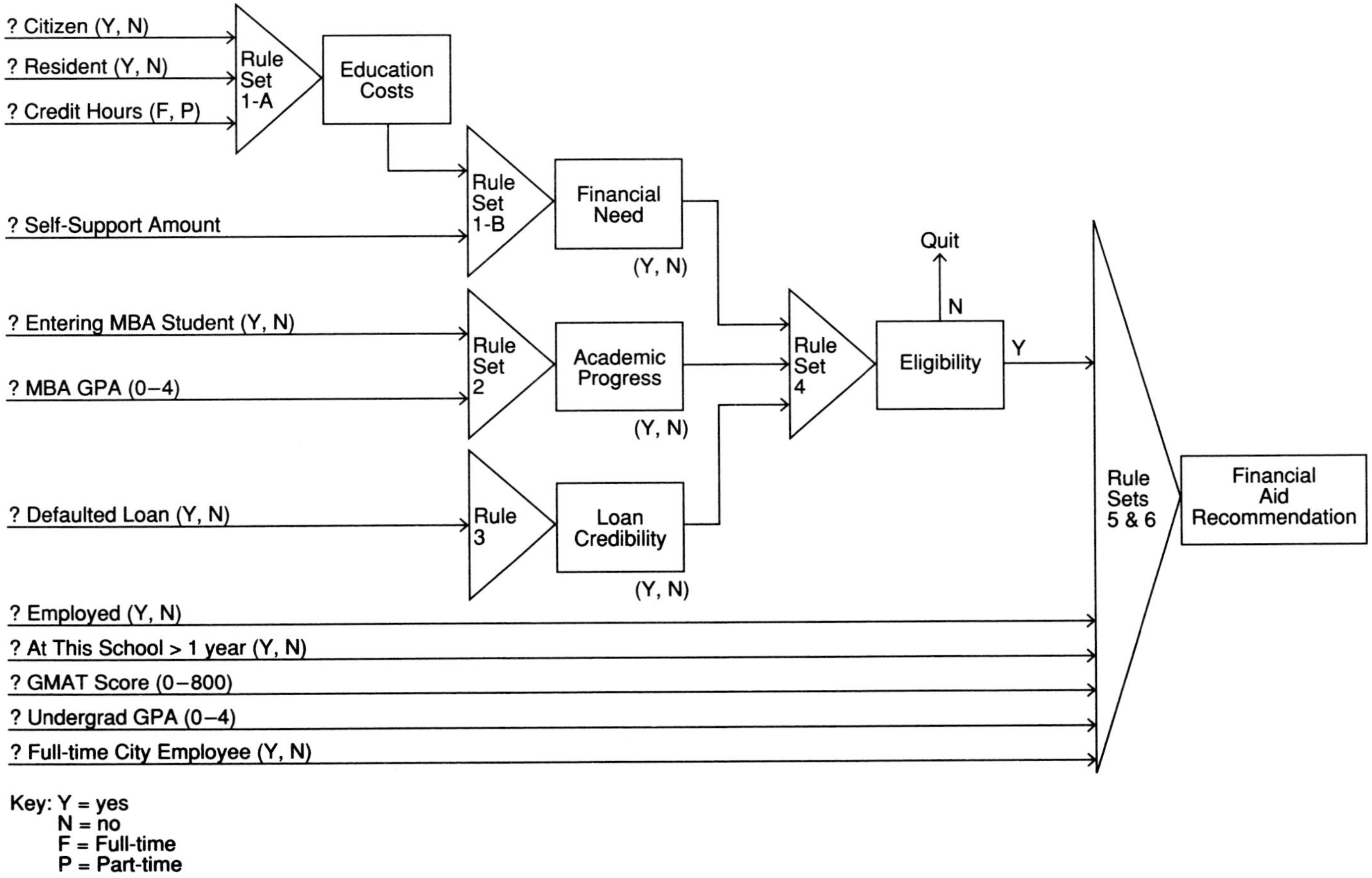

Figure 9C–4. Student Financial Aid Advisor: Sample Consultations

```
*** STUDENT FINANCIAL AID ADVISOR ***

Developed by Sheng Guo
under the direction and supervision of
Dr. D.G. Dologite
```

Consultation 1:

Text only

```
Welcome to the Student Financial Aid Advisor

Do you have a printer attached to your computer?
 Yes ◂                    No

Please turn on your printer. Press any key to continue ...

How much can you and your family afford for tuition and expenses
per year?
 5000

Are you a US citizen or Permanent Resident?
 Yes ◂                    No

Have you lived in this state for more than one year?
 Yes                      No ◂

Are you an entering MBA student?
 Yes ◂                    No

Have you ever defaulted on a student loan?
 Yes                      No ◂

How many credit hours do you plan to take per semester?
 9

Are you employed?
 Yes                      No ◂

THE FOLLOWING IS A LIST OF FINANCIAL AID SOURCES FOR WHICH
YOU MAY APPLY
Guaranteed Student Loan
CONTACT: A bank of your choice
TEL:
THE MAXIMUM AWARD AMOUNT IS: $7500

Tuition Waiver Program
CONTACT: Financial Aid Office, Room 206, 155 E. 24th St.
TEL: 212-555-3069
THE MAXIMUM AWARD AMOUNT IS: Tuition Waiver
```

- *Guaranteed Student Loan:* U.S. citizens or permanent residents enrolled for a minimum of six credits per semester may apply for a Guaranteed Student Loan through most banks. This is a long-term, low-interest loan granted to assist students in meeting their education expenses. Graduate students may apply for a maximum of $7,500 yearly.
- *Tuition Waiver Program:* This program provides partial tuition waivers to students who demonstrate financial need. Foreign students must have studied at the college for one year before they can apply.
- *Tuition Assistance Program:* This program is available to all full-time, matriculated U.S. citizens or permanent residents who have resided in the state at least two years.
- *Graduate Fellowship:* Full-tuition awards are available to full-time entering MBA students with outstanding academic credentials. Recipients are se-

Consultation 2:

Text only

```
Welcome to the Student Financial Aid Advisor

Do you have a printer attached to your computer?
 Yes ◂                   No

Please turn on your printer.  Press any key to continue ...

How much can you and your family afford for tuition and expenses
per year?
 0

Are you a US citizen or Permanent Resident?
 Yes                     No ◂

How many credit hours do you plan to take per semester?
 12

Are you an entering MBA student?
 Yes ◂                   No

Have you ever defaulted on a student loan?
 Yes                     No ◂

Are you employed?
 Yes ◂                   No

Have you been at this school for more than one year?
 Yes                     No ◂

Please enter your GMAT score.
 680

Please enter your undergraduate GPA.
 3.7

Are you a full-time city employee?
 Yes                     No ◂


FOLLOWING IS A LIST OF FINANCIAL AID SOURCES FOR WHICH
YOU MAY APPLY
Graduate Fellowship
CONTACT: Admissions Office, Room 527, 155 E. 24th St.
TEL: 212-555-3078
THE MAXIMUM AWARD AMOUNT IS: Tuition Waiver
```

lected primarily on the basis of a high GMAT score (630 or above) and a high undergraduate GPA (3.2 or above).

- *Mayor's Graduate Scholarship:* This scholarship provides a tuition waiver of up to six credits per semester for full-time city employees.

In addition to these final recommendations, the system can also determine if a student has *no* financial need. In this instance, the system displays the message "It is determined that you are not eligible for financial aid because no financial difficulty seems evident." Other messages displayed in place of a final recommendation include:

- "It is determined that you are not eligible for financial aid now because of a GPA that is lower than required."
- "It is determined that you are not eligible for financial aid at this time. Please make arrangements to pay the current loan before submitting a new application."

Figure 9C–5. Student Financial Aid Advisor: Database File (FAA.DBF) of Possible Recommendations

Database File Record Data Structure

Field	Field Name	Type	Width
1	AID_ID	Character	3
2	NAME	Character	35
3	CONTACT	Character	60
4	TEL	Character	12
5	MAX_AMT	Character	25
Total			136

Database File Content

AID_ID	NAME	CONTACT	TEL	MAX_AMT
GRA	Graduate Research Assistantship	Office of Graduate Studies, Room 910, 46 E. 26th St.	212-555-3250	$5000
GSL	Guaranteed Student Loan	A bank of your choice		$7500
TWP	Tuition Waiver Program	Financial Aid Office, Room 206, 155 E. 24th St.	212-555-3069	Tuition Waiver
TAP	Tuition Assistance Program	Financial Aid Office, Room 206, 155 E. 24th St.	212-555-3069	Tuition Waiver
BGF	Graduate Fellowship	Admissions Office, Room 527, 155 E. 24th St.	212-555-3078	Tuition Waiver
MGS	Mayor's Graduate Scholarship	Your agency's Personnel Office		Tuit.waiver for 6 credits

The final consultation recommendations, as well as the not eligible messages, are either displayed on the screen and output to a printer, or just displayed on the screen if a user indicates that no printer is available.

Sample decision tables, for Rule Sets 1 to 3, are shown in Figure 9C–6. A printout of the complete knowledge base file is given in Figure 9C–7.

A Typical Scenario

Mark Stevens is a first-year, full-time MBA student majoring in Computer Information Systems. He works 15 hours a week in a small consulting firm as an assistant systems analyst. In the past, the part-time job has provided just enough money for tuition fees and living expenses. With increasing rent, transportation, and other expenses, Mark is now unable to meet his financial obligations. He visits the financial aid office at the college to see if he is eligible for financial aid.

A financial aid advisor interviews Mark in the office. Mark briefly describes his financial situation. Then the advisor compiles the following personal information about Mark:

Figure 9C–6. Student Financial Aid Advisor: Sample Decision Tables

Rule Set 1-A: Calculates estimated education costs

	1	2	3	4	5	6
IF is a US citizen permanent resident Possible values: Y (yes) or N (no)	Y	Y	Y	Y	N	N
IF Resident in state for more than 1 year Possible values: Y (yes) or N (no)	Y	Y	N	N	*	*
IF Credit hours taken Possible values: P (part-time) for <12, F (full-time) for >=12	F	P	F	P	F	P
THEN:						
Resident rate, full-time $950	X					
Out-of-state rate, full-time $2350			X		X	
Resident rate, part-time $82/credit		X				
Out-of-state rate, part-time $198.50/credit				X		X

Rule Set 1-B: Determines financial necessity

	1	2
IF Education costs greater than self-support amount	Y	N
THEN Financial need	Y	N

Rule Set 2: Checks academic progress

	1	2	3
IF Entering MBA Student	N	N	Y
IF GPA > 3.0	Y	N	—
THEN Satisfactory academic progress	Y	N	Y

Rule Set 3: Determines loan credibility

	1	2
IF Had defaulted student loan	Y	N
THEN Good loan credibility	N	Y

- The difference between tuition cost and the amount Mark can afford to contribute is about $3,000 a year.
- Mark is a U.S. citizen who has lived in the city for three years.
- He is a first-year, full-time MBA student majoring in computer information systems.
- His accumulated undergraduate GPA is 3.5.
- He has not defaulted on any student loans.

Figure 9C–7. Student Financial Aid Advisor: Knowledge Base File

```
! System name:     FINANCIAL AID ADVISOR
! Description:     An expert system to help students select appropriate
!                  financial aid programs to apply for.
! KBS file name:   FAA.KBS
! DB file name:    FAA.DBF

RUNTIME;
ENDOFF;

! Action Block
ACTIONS
      WOPEN 1,0,0,23,79,1
      ACTIVE 1
      DISPLAY "


                   *** STUDENT FINANCIAL AID ADVISOR ***

                           Developed by Sheng Guo
                   under the direction and supervision of
                            Dr. D.G. Dologite
                      For further information, contact
                            Dr. D.G. Dologite
                         c/o Macmillan Publishing


                          Press any key to continue~"

      WCLOSE 1
      PRINTOFF
      DISPLAY "Welcome to the Student Financial Aid Advisor"
      DISPLAY " "
      ! Decide if printer is available or not
      FIND PRTCTRL
      ! living expense is assigned as a constant here
      Living = 7000
      FIND Support
      ! Decide the eligibility of a student before searching for
      ! suitable programs.
      FIND Continue;


! Rules Block

! Rule set 1-printer is used to control output through printer or screen.
RULE 1-printer
IF Printer = Yes
THEN PRTCTRL = ON

     DISPLAY "Please turn on your printer. Press any key to continue ...~"
     DISPLAY " "
     PRINTON
     EJECT;

! Rule set 1-A calculates the education costs

RULE 1-A-1
IF Citizen= Yes
   AND Resident = Yes
   AND Hour >= 12
THEN Edu_Cost = (living + 2*950)
BECAUSE "In-State full-time tuition is $950";

RULE 1-A-2
IF Citizen= Yes
   AND Resident = Yes
   AND Hour <12
THEN Edu_Cost = (living + 2*Hour*82)
BECAUSE "In-State part-time tuition is $82 per credit hour";

RULE 1-A-3
IF Citizen= Yes
   AND Resident = No
   AND Hour >= 12
THEN Edu_Cost = (living + 2*2350)
BECAUSE "Out-of-State full-time tuition is $2350";
```

```
RULE 1-A-4
IF Citizen= Yes
   AND Resident = No
   AND Hour <12
THEN Edu_Cost = (living + 2*Hour*198.5)
BECAUSE "Out-of-State part-time tuition is $198.50 per credit hour";

RULE 1-A-5
IF Citizen= No
   AND Hour >=12
THEN Edu_Cost = (living + 2*2350)
BECAUSE "Out-of-State full-time tuition is $2350";

RULE 1-A-6
IF Citizen= No
   AND Hour <12
THEN Edu_Cost = (living + 2*Hour*198.5)
BECAUSE "Out-of-State part-time tuition is $198.50 per credit hour";

! Rule set 1-B decides financial necessity.
RULE 1-B
IF Edu_Cost <= (Support)
THEN Need = No
     DISPLAY "It is determined that you are not eligible for financial"
     DISPLAY "aid because no financial difficulty seems evident."
ELSE Need = Yes;

! Rule set 2 checks the academic progress of a student.
RULE 2-A
IF ENTERING = NO
   AND GPA >= 3.0
THEN PROGRESS = OK;

RULE 2-B
IF ENTERING = NO
   AND GPA < 3.0
THEN PROGRESS = NOT_OK
     DISPLAY "It is determined that you are not eligible for financial"
     DISPLAY "aid now because of a GPA that is lower than required";

RULE 2-C
IF ENTERING = YES
THEN PROGRESS = OK;

! Rule 3 decides the credibility of a student.

RULE 3
IF Defaulted = Yes
THEN Credibility = Bad
       DISPLAY "It is determined that you are not eligible for financial"
       DISPLAY "aid at this time.  Please make arrangements to pay off"
       DISPLAY "the current loan before submitting a new application."
ELSE Credibility = Good;

! Rule set 4 decides the eligibility of a student.
RULE 4-A
IF Need = No
THEN Eligible = No;

RULE 4-B
IF Progress = NOT_OK
THEN Eligible = No;

RULE 4-C
IF Credibility = Bad
THEN Eligible = No;

RULE 4-D
IF Credibility = Good
   AND Progress = Ok
   AND Need = Yes
THEN Eligible = Yes;

! Rule 5 searches for matched programs if a student is eligible for financial
! aid and retrieves information stored in a database.
RULE 5
IF Eligible = Yes
```

Figure 9C–7. *continued*

```
THEN  Continue = Yes
      FIND Program
      COUNT Program, Pnumber
      DISPLAY "THE FOLLOWING IS A LIST OF FINANCIAL AID SOURCES FOR WHICH"
      DISPLAY "YOU MAY APPLY"
      FOR Pcount= 1 to @Pnumber
         GET Program=Aid_ID, FAA, ALL
         DISPLAY "{NAME}"
         DISPLAY "CONTACT: {CONTACT}"
         DISPLAY "TEL: {TEL}"
         DISPLAY "THE MAXIMUM AWARD AMOUNT IS: {MAX_AMT}"
         DISPLAY "  "
      END
      PRINTOFF;

! Rule set 6 defines the criteria for each financial aid program.

RULE 6-1
IF Hour >= 12
   AND Employed = No
THEN Program = GRA;

RULE 6-2
IF Hour >= 6
   AND Citizen = Yes
THEN Program = GSL;

RULE 6-3-A
IF Citizen = Yes
THEN Program = TWP;

RULE 6-3-B
IF Citizen = No
   AND Years_at_School = Yes
THEN Program = TWP;

RULE 6-4
IF Citizen = Yes
   AND Resident = Yes
THEN Program = TAP;

RULE 6-5
IF Entering = Yes
   AND Hour >= 12
   AND GMAT >= 630
   AND Under_GPA >= 3.2
THEN Program = BGF;
```

Based on this information, the advisor recognizes that Mark has a need for financial aid. Having lived in the city for more than one year and never having defaulted on a student loan, Mark is eligible for financial aid from federal, state, and city sources. The high GPA indicates Mark's satisfactory progress toward an MBA degree.

The advisor then analyzes the possible financial resources with Mark:

- *Graduate Research Assistantship (GRA):* Fifteen hours of weekly service must be rendered to the student's assigned department. The assistantship pays $5,000 a year. It is college policy that it can only be awarded to full-time students who are not employed off campus. Mark doesn't want to quit his part-time job because it provides good experience in his major field. Therefore, he is not eligible for a GRA.
- *Tuition Waiver Program:* Mark may apply for a tuition waiver from the school and the state.
- *Guaranteed Student Loan:* Graduate students may apply for a long-term, low-interest loan of up to $7,500 a year through the bank of their choice. Mark could consider applying for a $3,000 loan to make up the difference between expenses and income.

```
RULE 6-6
IF Employed = Yes
   AND FT_CITY_EMP = Yes
THEN Program = MGS;

! Questions Block

PLURAL: Program;

ASK Citizen: "Are you a US citizen or Permanent Resident?";
CHOICES Citizen: Yes, No;

ASK Resident: "Have you lived in this state for more than one year?";
CHOICES Resident: Yes, No;

ASK Hour: "How many credit hours do you plan to take per semester?";
RANGE Hour: 1, 21;

ASK Support: "How much can you and your family afford for tuition and expenses
per year?";
RANGE Support: 0, 100000;

ASK Entering: "Are you an entering MBA student?";
CHOICES Entering: Yes, No;

ASK GPA: "Please input your GPA in the MBA Program (on a 4.0 scale).";
RANGE GPA: 0,4;

ASK Defaulted: "Have you ever defaulted on a student loan?";
CHOICES Defaulted: Yes, No;

ASK Employed: "Are you employed?";
CHOICES Employed: Yes, No;

ASK Years_at_School: "Have you been at this school for more than one year?";
CHOICES Years_at_School: Yes, No;

ASK GMAT: "Please enter your GMAT score.";
RANGE GMAT: 0,800;

ASK Under_GPA: "Please enter your undergraduate GPA.";
RANGE Under_GPA: 0,4;

ASK FT_CITY_EMP: "Are you a full-time city employee?";
CHOICES FT_CITY_EMP: Yes, No;

ASK Printer: "Do you have a printer attached to your computer?";
CHOICES Printer: Yes, No;
```

After considering the advantages and disadvantages of several kinds of financial aid, the advisor suggests that Mark

- Fill out the Student Aid Form (SAF) to make an application for the Tuition Waiver Program
- Select a bank and apply for a Guaranteed Student Loan

Design Issues

While designing and implementing the Student Financial Aid Advisor prototype expert system, several issues had to be addressed.

Error Control. It is common for a user to make mistakes while answering questions during a consultation. The Student Financial Aid Advisor system is designed to reduce possible input errors by using the RANGE statement to constrain upper and lower values. For example,

```
ASK GMAT: "Please enter your GMAT score";
RANGE GMAT: 0,800;

ASK Under_GPA: "Please enter your undergraduate GPA";
RANGE Under_GPA: 0,4;
```

In the first question, input values from 0 to 800 are valid, while values from 0 to 4 are valid in the second question.

Redundancy Control. The system tries to ask only questions relevant to the decision-making task. If a combination of conditions is used, VP-Expert evaluates all conditions using the logical operator OR. For example,

```
IF Need = No
   OR Progress = Not_OK
   OR Credibility = Bad
THEN Eligible = No;
```

When VP-Expert executes this rule, it searches for the Progress and Credibility variables, even if Need = No. Ideally, when a student has no financial need, the system should not ask questions related to academic progress or loan credibility. The following method, which uses several rules to replace the single rule, is used to eliminate question redundancy.

```
RULE 4-A
  IF Need = No
  THEN Eligible = No;
RULE 4-B
  IF Progress = Not_OK
  THEN Eligible = No;
RULE 4-C
  IF Credibility = Bad
  THEN Eligible = No;
RULE 4-D
  IF Credibility = Good
     AND Progress = OK
     AND Need = Yes
  THEN Eligible = Yes;
```

Plural Variable. Because a student is often eligible for more than one financial aid program, a plural variable is required and is defined as

```
PLURAL: Program;
```

This causes the expert system to search for all financial sources for which a student may apply.

Database File. A database file stores detailed information on each financial aid program that could appear in a recommendation. Using database information means that anyone familiar with dBASE can update the information stored there. Expert system programming knowledge is not required.

The structure of the database and its contents is shown in Figure 9C–5. It is apparent there that the maximum amount of an award sometimes cannot be expressed in numeric format. For example, it is possible to get a partial tuition waiver. Also, the maximum amount may vary for full-time and part-time students, as well as state and other residents.

Loop Structure. A FOR loop is implemented to print information about each eligible financial aid source. The following code from Rule 5 of the program counts the number of programs the student is eligible for and stores it in a variable, Pnumber. The loop is executed Pnumber times to print all the relevant program information.

```
FIND Program
COUNT Program, Pnumber
DISPLAY "THE FOLLOWING IS A LIST OF FINANCIAL AID
SOURCES FOR WHICH"
DISPLAY "YOU MAY APPLY"
FOR Pcount= 1 to @Pnumber
   GET Program=Aid_ID, FAA, ALL
   DISPLAY  "{NAME}"
   DISPLAY  "CONTENT: {CONTACT}"
   DISPLAY  "TEL: {TEL}"
   DISPLAY  "THE MAXIMUM AWARD AMOUNT IS: {MAX_AMT}"
   DISPLAY  "  "
END
```

User Interface. In future versions of the prototype, some improvements in the user interface will be needed to enhance its usefulness. For example, at times a student is eligible for more programs than fit on one screen. A control facility to allow a user to scroll up and down the screen may be necessary, especially in the case where no printer is attached to the computer.

9D Small Business Acquisition Advisor

TECHNICAL PROFILE

Difficulty Level	Intermediate
Special Features	This prototype system uses the CALL keyword to call external programs written in the Pascal program language. The called programs are used to display introduction and recommendation screens.
Files Used	SBPA.KBS (KBS file) and EXPERT.EXE, GOOD.EXE, CAUTION.EXE, POOR.EXE (Pascal files)
To Run	Load SBPA.KBS from the disk accompanying this book

OVERVIEW

The general objective of this prototype expert system is to help an individual make a decision about acquiring a small business. The prototype assumes that the business will be a kiosk, or newspaper shop, or similar small retail outlet.

Many buyers of small businesses are first-time entrepreneurs who do not have the experience necessary to know what to look for when evaluating the investment. Overlooking even one key factor can lead to catastrophic financial loss. This prototype system, called the Small Business Acquisition Advisor, can help an investor make a thorough and systematic evaluation before purchasing a small retail business.

Sources of Knowledge

The experts consulted in developing this prototype system included merchants and retailers with 10 to 30 years of experience. In addition, the books listed in the reference section were helpful.

STUDYING THE SITUATION

The small business acquisition decision is based on three critical factors, as shown in Figure 9D–1.

1. *Money*—concerns financing and income. Financing establishes how much the store is worth, given its sales and expenses for three years compared to the asking price and the terms of the lease. Income, on the other hand, uses sales and expense figures for determining whether the business can generate a 15 percent profit.
2. *Location*—concerns the condition of the neighborhood where the business is located and other characteristics about the business. If either is unacceptable, the system recommends, at best, that the purchaser proceed with caution.
3. *Lease/Ownership*—evaluates the business' chance for future growth. This is determined, for example, by restrictions found in the business' lease and tax situation.

Figure 9D–1. Small Business Acquisition Advisor: Block Diagram of Decision Situation

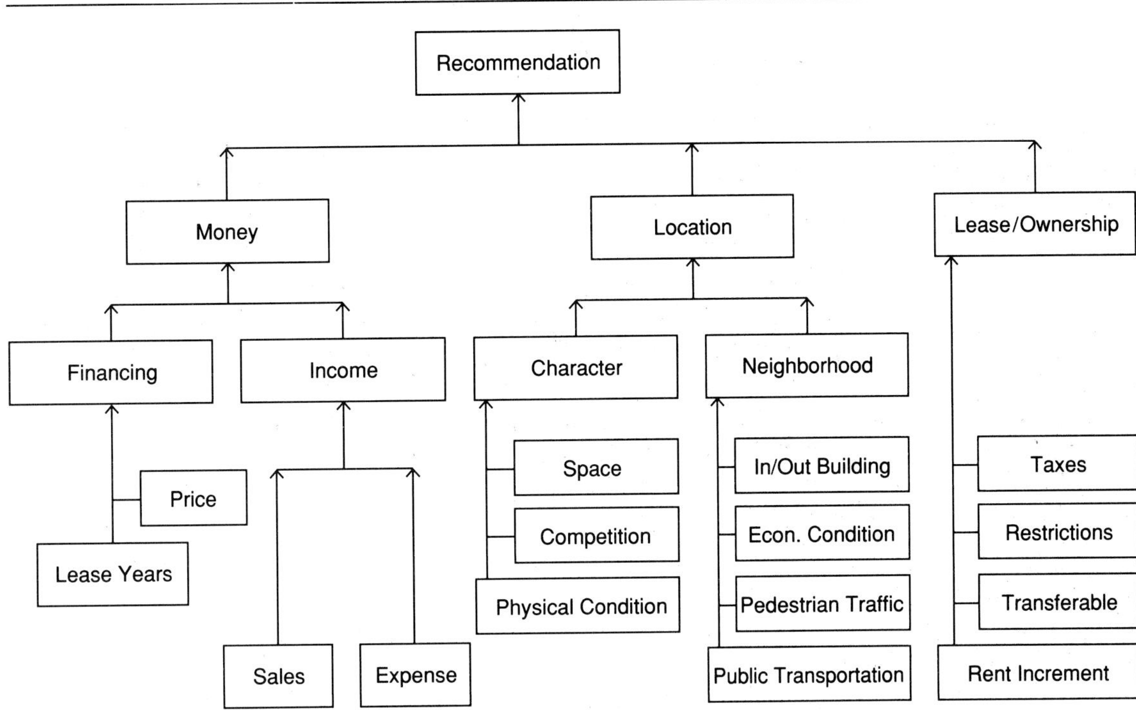

Questions Asked by the Prototype System

The system asks the user questions about the three critical factors to arrive at a recommendation. To keep the prototype system to a manageable size, it is not as comprehensive as a true "expert" would be in an evaluation. It does strive, however, to touch on all the major factors in the decision area by asking the following questions:

1. The questions asked to determine the *money* critical factor are
- How much does the owner want to sell the business for?
- How much does the store collect in revenue per year?
- What are the yearly expenses? Include rent, utilities, taxes, salaries, and other expenses.
- How many years is the lease for?

2. The questions asked to determine the *location* critical factor are
- What is the economic condition of the neighborhood? (Good, Fair, Bad)
- What is the volume of pedestrian traffic? (Heavy, Moderate, Light)
- How heavy is the traffic generated by public transportation? (Heavy, Moderate, Light)
- Is the store inside the building or outside the building? (Outside, Inside)
- What is the physical condition of the store? (Good, Fair, Poor)
- How heavy is the competition near the business that you are considering? (Heavy, Moderate, Light)

- What is the size of the store in square feet? (Under or equal to 400, Over 400)

3. The questions asked to determine the *lease/ownership* critical factor are
   - Is the lease transferable when the current owner sells it to you, and can you transfer it? (Yes, No, Do Not Know)
   - Are there any restrictions to selling any item which you may want to sell in the future? (Yes, No, Do Not Know)
   - Who pays the Real Estate taxes? (Us, Them, Do Not Know)
   - Is there a yearly rent increase? (Yes, No)

Recommendations Made by the System

Based on a user's answers to the above questions, the system provides one of the following recommendations:

- Good: Purchase ONLY after ALL evaluations are completed.
- Caution: Negotiate and bargain as much as possible before investing. The location factor or the lease factor is fair.
- Poor: Do not purchase. The business does not seem to be profitable or the lease or location is bad.

Typical Scenario

One day Jatin received a call from a friend who alerted him about a store for sale on Church Street in downtown New York City. Jatin immediately went to the store owner and asked for further information about the sale. He had been coached by his parents, who own three other stores, about what information is needed to evaluate a purchase.

That night after dinner, Jatin's parents discussed the matter with him.

FATHER. How much is the owner asking?
JATIN. Somewhere around $125,000.
FATHER. How much is the rent and how long is the lease for?
JATIN. He said the rent is about $2,500 a month and the lease is for 5 years, but extendable.
FATHER. I wish the lease was longer.
MOTHER. How much does he collect in revenues?
JATIN. About $25,000 per month.
FATHER. How about lottery sales?
JATIN. Commissions average about $3,000 per month.
MOTHER. Well, so far it sounds good. But I think the asking price is too high. Why don't we try to negotiate it down? What is the required down payment?
JATIN. About $55,000.
FATHER. I hope that's negotiable.
JATIN. I have a feeling he will come down on that. How do you feel about the location, Dad?
FATHER. The location seems great. A lot of pedestrians walk by there and it's near a bus stop and a subway station. Approximately how big is the store?
JATIN. Around 600 square feet.
FATHER. What about the total monthly expenses?
JATIN. Expenses are in the $7,000 to $10,000 range.
FATHER. Going by the information you have given us so far, it sounds promising.
MOTHER. I agree. But is the lease transferable and are there any restrictions?

JATIN. The lease is transferable. As far as the restrictions go, we cannot sell liquor and sandwiches. That shouldn't matter, because we don't intend to sell those items anyway.
MOTHER. Is there competition?
FATHER. No, not on that block, anyway.

After discussing the matter for about half an hour, Jatin and his family decided that they would need to negotiate and bargain as much as possible before purchasing the store. They felt they could not buy the store unless the owner reduced his selling price and down payment. Jatin's father warned that they must proceed with caution to get the best possible price.

SYSTEM DOCUMENTATION

Figure 9D–2 shows a dependency diagram for the Small Business Acquisition Advisor. The decision table for the final recommendation rule set is given in Figure 9D–3. A sample consultation is shown in Figure 9D–4 (pp. 296–298).

Figure 9D–2. Small Business Acquisition Advisor: Dependency Diagram

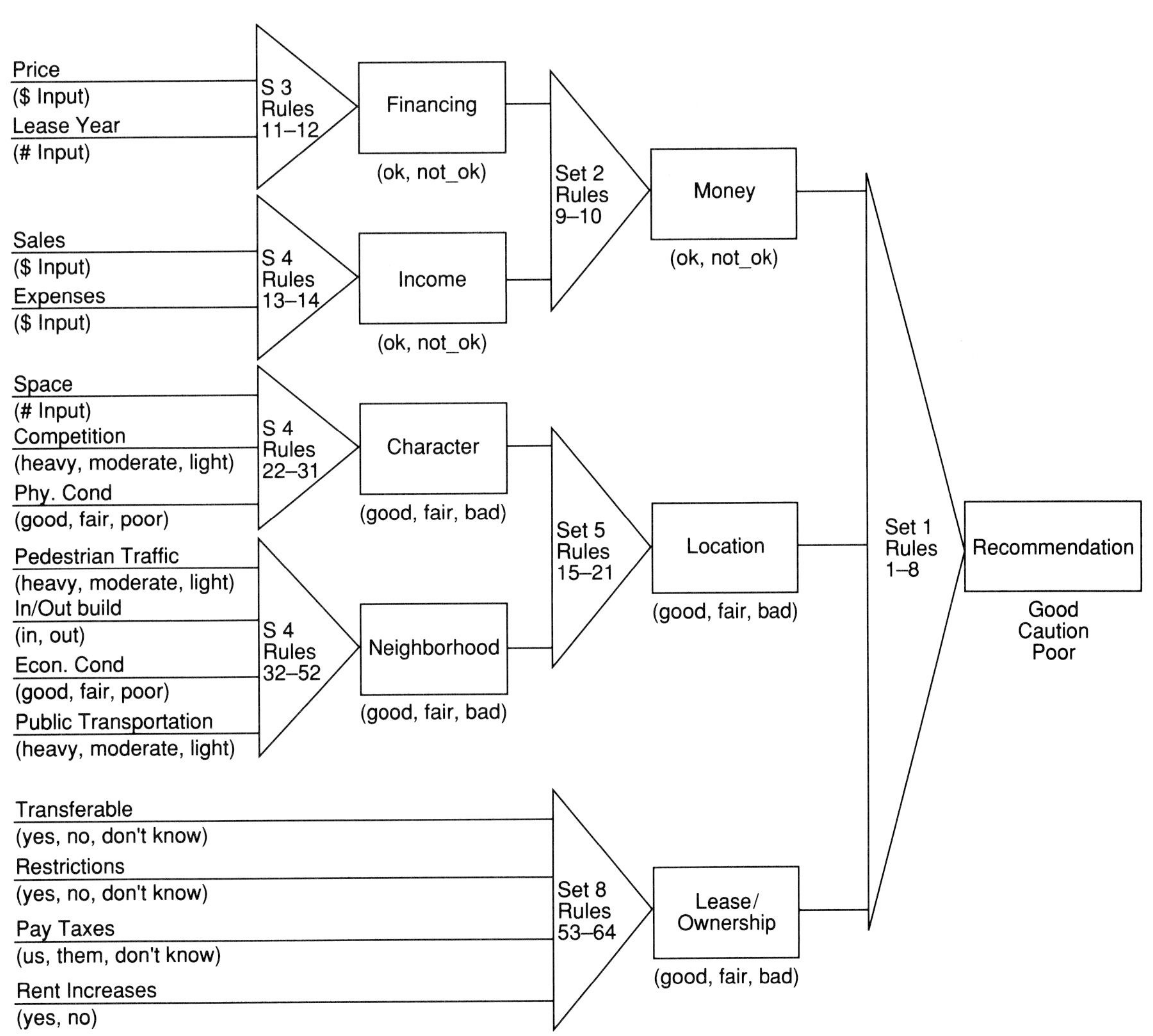

Figure 9D–3. Small Business Acquisition Advisor: Decision Table for Final Rule Set

Rule	Money	Location	Lease	Recommendation
1	Not Ok	—	—	Poor
2	—	Bad	—	Poor
3	Ok	Fair	Bad	Poor
4	Ok	Good	Bad	Poor
5	Ok	Fair	Good	Caution
6	Ok	Fair	Fair	Caution
7	Ok	Good	Good	Good
8	Ok	Good	Fair	Good

Figure 9D–4. Small Business Acquisition Advisor: Sample Consultation

```
S M A L L   B U S I N E S S
A C Q U I S I T I O N   A D V I S O R

Developed by Hiren B. Patel
under the direction and supervision of
Dr. D.G. Dologite
```

The

Small Business
Acquisition Advisor

will assist you

in making a decision regarding the purchase
of a small business. It will arrive at
a proper conclusion based on the answers
you provide. The Small Business Acquisition
Advisor will base its decision on
the following critical factors:
Financing * Income * Location * Ownership

press any key to start

Figure 9D–4. *continued*

Text only

```
How much does the owner want to sell the business for?
 90000

How much does the store collect in revenue per year?
 280000

What are the yearly expenses?
Do NOT forget to include:     Rent
                              Utilities
                              Taxes
                              Salaries
                              Other
 190000

How many years is the lease for?
 5

What is the economic condition of the neighborhood?
 Good                      Fair ◄                  Bad

What is the volume of pedestrian traffic?
 Heavy ◄                   Moderate                Light

How heavy is the traffic generated by public
transportation?
 Heavy                     Moderate ◄              Light

Is the store inside the building or outside the
building?
 Outside                   Inside ◄

What is the physical condition of the store?
 Good                      Fair ◄                  Bad

How heavy is the competition near the business
that you are considering?
 Heavy                     Moderate ◄              Light

What is the size of the store in square feet?
 Under \ Equal to 400      Over 400 ◄

Is the lease transferable when the current
owner sells it to you, and can you transfer it?
 Yes ◄                     No                      Do Not Know

Are there any restrictions to sell any item
which you may want to sell in the future?
 No ◄                      Yes                     Do Not Know

Who pays the Real Estate taxes?
Us                         Them                   Do Not Know ◄

        Try to find out who is going to pay the real
     estate taxes.  They are important for your income.

                  Press any key to continue.
```

The complete knowledge base can be examined by printing out the SBPA. KBS file from the disk accompanying this book. An excerpt from it is included in Figure 9D–5 to show the code that calls Pascal programs. The CALL keyword temporarily suspends the VP-Expert consultation to run an .EXE program.

Figure 9D–6 shows the program code for one of the four Pascal programs used in this consultation. It is the GOOD.EXE program, which generates the recommendation screen that concludes "purchase the business only after all evaluations are completed." A "good" conclusion, as shown in the decision table in Figure 9D–3, is reached if the money factor is OK, the location is good, and the lease is either fair or good. The other two Pascal programs used for recom-

Figure 9D–4. *concluded*

Small Business
Acquisition Advisor

Recommends

that you take

Caution

Negotiate and bargain as much as possible before investing.
The location is fair and/or the lease is fair.

press any key to continue

mendation screens, CAUTION.EXE and POOR.EXE, look very similar to the GOOD.EXE program code. They can be examined by printing out the files named CAUTION.PAS and POOR.PAS on the disk accompanying this book.

The fourth Pascal program, EXPERT.EXE, displays the introductory screen shown in Figure 9D–4. The code for the screen display is in a file named EXPERT.PAS on the disk accompanying this book.

The files GOOD.PAS, CAUTION.PAS, POOR.PAS, and EXPERT.PAS are ASCII text files. They are the "uncompiled" versions, called "source" files, of the Pascal programs used to display the screens in this expert system. Once these source files are entered into the computer and saved, they are translated into machine language by a compiler. The Pascal compiler processes the source file and, if there are no syntax errors, creates an "object" file which is executable by a computer. These executable .EXE files are the ones called by the VP-Expert program to create the screens: GOOD.EXE, CAUTION.EXE, POOR.EXE, and EXPERT.EXE. An .EXE file is normally incomprehensible to humans.

The program code for the display screens were created using the Turbo Pascal version 5.5 program. The idea for designing the Pascal screens for this expert system prototype came from observing examples in the user's manual for the Pascal program.

Figure 9D–5. Small Business Acquisition Advisor: Partial Printout of Knowledge Base File

```
! KBS name:      Small Business Acquisition Advisor                      !
! Description:   This prototype expert system helps a user to make a      !
!                decision about buying a small retail business.           !
! File names:    The KBS file is named SBPA.KBS.  Four external Pascal   !
!                language programs are called to display the introduction :
!                and recommendations screens.  They are:                  !
!                   GOOD.EXE (for a "good" recommendation screen)         !
!                CAUTION.EXE (for a "caution" recommendation screen)      !
!                   POOR.EXE (for a "poor" recommendation screen)         :
!                 EXPERT.EXE (for an introductory screen)                 !
! Hardware:      IBM-PC compatible                                        !

Execute;
Runtime;
Endoff;
BkColor=1;

                              !Action Block Starts
ACTIONS
         Color = 12           !Light Red
         Display "


                          S M A L L   B U S I N E S S
                     A C Q U I S I T I O N   A D V I S O R"
         Color = 13           !Light Magenta
         Display "


                         Developed by Hiren B. Patel"
         Color = 12           !Light Red
         Display "
                    under the direction and supervision of
                              Dr. D.G. Dologite
                      For further information, contact
                              Dr. D.G. Dologite
                          c/o Macmillan Publishing



                         Press any key to continue.~"

         Call Expert, ""       ! Calls Pascal program for opening screen
         Color = 12
         Find Price
         Find Sales
         Find Expenses
         Find LeaseYears
         Find Recommendation
;

                        !Rule Block Starts

        !**********RECOMMENDATION BLOCK STARTS**********

Rule Recommendation.1.1
IF          Money = Not_OK
THEN        Recommendation = Poor
            Call Poor, ""        ! Calls Pascal program for POOR screen
;
Rule Recommendation.2.2
IF          Location = Bad
THEN        Recommendation = Poor
            Call Poor, ""        ! Calls Pascal program for POOR screen
;
Rule Recommendation.3.3
IF          Money = OK
     and    Location = Fair
     and    LeaseOwnership = Bad
THEN        Recommendation = Poor
            Call Poor, ""        ! Calls Pascal program for POOR screen
;
Rule Recommendation.4.4
IF          Money = OK
     and    Location = Good
     and    LeaseOwnership = Bad
```

Figure 9D–5. *concluded*

```
THEN       Recommendation = Poor
           Call Poor, ""           ! Calls Pascal program for POOR screen
;
Rule Recommendation.5.5
IF         Money = OK
     and   Location = Fair
     and   LeaseOwnership = Good
THEN       Recommendation = Caution
           Call Caution, ""        ! Calls Pascal program for CAUTION screen
;
Rule Recommendation.6.6
IF         Money = OK
     and   Location = Fair
     and   LeaseOwnership = Fair
THEN       Recommendation = Caution
           Call Caution, ""        ! Calls Pascal program for CAUTION screen
;
Rule Recommendation.7.7
IF         Money = OK
     and   Location = Good
     and   LeaseOwnership = Good
THEN       Recommendation = Good
           Call Good, ""           ! Calls Pascal program for GOOD screen
;
Rule Recommendation.8.8
IF         Money = OK
     and   Location = Good
     and   LeaseOwnership = Fair
THEN       Recommendation = Good
           Call Good, ""           ! Calls Pascal program for GOOD screen
;

             !**********MONEY BLOCK STARTS**********

Rule Money.1.9
IF         Financing = OK
     and   Income = OK
THEN       Money = OK
;
Rule Money.2.10
IF         Financing <> OK
     or    Income <> OK
THEN       Money = Not_OK
;

           !**********FINANCING BLOCK STARTS**********
        ! Store price should not be more than 3 year profit

Rule Financing.1.11
IF         Price < ((Sales-Expenses)*3)
     and   LeaseYears >= 3
THEN       Financing = OK
;
Rule Financing.2.12
IF         Price >= ((Sales-Expenses)*3)
     and   LeaseYears < 3
THEN       Financing = Not_Ok
           Display "

             You need to negotiate the store price.
           It is high when comparing three year profits.
             Also, the lease is less than three years.


                   Press any key to continue.~
 "
 ;
```

Note: The rest of the knowledge base file not included here can be examined by printing out the file named SBPA.KBS on the disk accompanying this book.

Figure 9D–6. Small Business Acquisition Advisor: Printout of Pascal Program (GOOD.EXE) for "Purchase" Recommendation Screen

Note: This printout of GOOD.EXE shows one of four Pascal programs written to display screens in this consultation. The four programs, which are very similar to each other, are: GOOD.EXE (for a "good" recommendation screen); CAUTION.EXE (for a "caution" recommendation screen); POOR.EXE (for a "poor" recommendation screen); and EXPERT.EXE (for an introductory screen).

```
Program GoodScreen;   { THIS PROGRAM WILL DISPLAY THE 'PURCHASE' SCREEN
                        FOR THE SMALL BUSINESS ACQUISITION ADVISOR  }

uses Crt,
     Graph,     { library of graphics routines }
     Drivers,   { all the BGI drivers }
     Fonts;     { all the BGI fonts }

var CheckBreak,
    FuncKey:     Boolean;
    Ch:          char;

Procedure CheckForDriversandfonts;

  Procedure Abort(Msg : string);
    begin
      Writeln(Msg, ': ', GraphErrorMsg(GraphResult));
      Halt(1);
    end;

begin {CheckForDriversandfonts}
  { Register all the drivers }
  if RegisterBGIdriver(@CGADriverProc) < 0 then
    Abort('CGA');
  if RegisterBGIdriver(@EGAVGADriverProc) < 0 then
    Abort('EGA/VGA');
  if RegisterBGIdriver(@HercDriverProc) < 0 then
    Abort('Herc');
  if RegisterBGIdriver(@ATTDriverProc) < 0 then
    Abort('AT&T');
  if RegisterBGIdriver(@PC3270DriverProc) < 0 then
    Abort('PC 3270');

  { Register all the fonts }
  if RegisterBGIfont(@GothicFontProc) < 0 then
    Abort('Gothic');
  if RegisterBGIfont(@SansSerifFontProc) < 0 then
    Abort('SansSerif');
  if RegisterBGIfont(@SmallFontProc) < 0 then
    Abort('Small');
  if RegisterBGIfont(@TriplexFontProc) < 0 then
    Abort('Triplex');

end; {CheckForDriversandfonts}

Procedure SelectDriver;

var
     C,
     GraphDriver,
     GraphMode,
     ErrorCode : integer;

begin  {SelectDriver}

  GraphDriver := Detect;                          { It autodetects the hardware }
  InitGraph(GraphDriver, GraphMode, '');          { and activates the graphics }
  if GraphResult <> grOk then                     { Checks for any errors }

  begin
    Writeln('Graphics init error: ', GraphErrorMsg(GraphDriver));
    Writeln('Sorry No Graphics Driver was found.  Therefore, Program
       aborted...');
    Halt(1);
  end;
```

Figure 9D–6. *concluded*

```
end;    {SelectDriver}


{ This Procedure occurs only when the program is started.  It draws the
  3 borders that changes color and in it displays company name with
  software developer's name. }

Procedure WaitToGo; { Wait for the user to continue }

var
  Ch : char;

 begin { WaitToGo }
    repeat until KeyPressed;
    Ch := ReadKey;
    if ch = #0 then ch := readkey;       { trap function keys }
    ClearDevice;                         { clear screen,   }
 end; { WaitToGo }

Procedure Good;

    Begin
       SetBKcolor(BLUE);
       Setcolor(LightCyan);
       Rectangle(0,0, GetMaxX, GetMaxY);         {draws full screen box}
       Setcolor(LightMagenta);
       Rectangle(5,5, GetMaxX-5, GetMaxY-5);             {   3   }
       Setcolor(LightCyan);
       Rectangle(10,10, GetMaxX-10, GetMaxY-10);         { Times }

       SetTextJustify(CenterText, CenterTExt);        { Centers text}

       SetTextStyle(Triplexfont, HorizDir, 6);
       SetColor(LightRed);
       SetUserCharSize(2, 1, 4, 2);          { REMINDER-this line will make next
                                                  line bigger }
       OutTextXY(GetMaxX div 2, GetMaxY-400, 'Small Business');
       SetTextStyle(Triplexfont, HorizDir, 6);
       OutTextXY(GetMaxX div 2, GetMaxY-325, 'Acquisition Advisor');
       SetTextStyle(Triplexfont, HorizDir, 4);
       OutTextXY(GetMaxX div 2, GetMaxY-250, 'Recommends');
       OutTextXY(GetMaxX div 2, GetMaxY-200, 'that you');
       SetTextStyle(Triplexfont, HorizDir, 5);
       OutTextXY(GetMaxX div 2, GetMaxY-150, 'Purchase');
       SetTextStyle(Triplexfont, HorizDir, 1);
       OutTextXY(GetMaxX div 2, GetMaxY-100,
      'this business ONLY after ALL evaluations are completed');

       SetColor(LightRed);
       SetTextStyle(SansSeriffont, HorizDir, 3);
       OutTextXY(GetMaxX div 2, GetMaxY-70 div 2, 'press any key to continue');
       WaitToGo;        { Waits for user to press any key }
       RestoreCrtMode; {Lets system goback to regular mode}
       CloseGraph;
    End;


Begin {GoodScreen}
     CheckBreak := False;        {Because of this line program will ignore
                                    CONTROL-BREAK}
     CheckForDriversandfonts;  {Checks to see if it has fonts that will be used
                                    by the program}
     SelectDriver;               {Selects appropriate Graphics Driver for the
                                    system}
     Good;                       {Main Graphic Good Screen}
End.  {GoodScreen}
```

REFERENCES

Meigs, R. F., and W. B. Meigs. *Financial Accounting.* New York, NY: McGraw-Hill, 1987.

Horngren, C. T., and G. L. Sundem. *Introduction to Management Accounting.* Englewood Cliffs, NJ: Prentice-Hall, 1989.

Francis, Jack Clark. *Management of Investments.* New York, NY: McGraw-Hill, 1988.

10

ADVANCED-LEVEL SYSTEMS

10A Juvenile Delinquent Disposition Advisory System

TECHNICAL PROFILE

Difficulty Level	Advanced
Special Features	This system is divided into four modules chained together into a single seamless consultation.
Files Used	PRESOFF.KBS (main file), PROINV.KBS, DIAGASMT.KBS, and DISP.KBS (chained files), and TEMP1, TEMP2, and TEMP3 (temporary files)
To Run	Load PRESOFF.KBS from the disk accompanying this book.

OVERVIEW

Note: This is an exploratory system. It is designed to test the feasibility of using expert system technology to help reduce the backlog of legal cases that often occur in major city courts. For this prototype, New York City (NYC) was chosen as the test case because of the system developer's familiarity with the situation, as well as the availability of public and other sources of information.

This prototype expert system has two main purposes:

1. To determine whether a person is a juvenile delinquent in accordance with established procedures and due process of law
2. To determine an appropriate order and level of disposition of those who are formally judged to be juvenile delinquents

The system also considers the needs and best interests of the juvenile (called a "respondent") as well as the community's need for protection.

The Juvenile Delinquent Disposition Advisory System supports the work of prosecuting and defense attorneys as well as judges or magistrates assigned to juvenile cases. By using this system, an attorney can establish a probable court outcome. This helps in designing an appropriate strategy to defend a client or prosecute a respondent.

In addition, judges or court magistrates hear and determine an appropriate order of disposition for numerous cases everyday. This expert system can assist them to reach fair, appropriate, consistent, and unbiased decisions without regard to race, sex, age, or religious preference.

Appropriateness of Expert System Technology

Expert system technology is appropriate for the juvenile delinquent disposition situation because intermediate evaluations and final recommendations

1. Are done by experts/professionals (judges, magistrates)
2. Require reasoning and informed judgments, as opposed to common sense
3. Are done more than a few times a year by these experts
4. Do not have a quantitative or procedural structure

Since the situation to be prototyped is highly judgmental and qualitative in nature, it is better handled by expert system technology than conventional computer tools, such as spreadsheets or databases.

Four sources were used to obtain the knowledge for developing this expert system:

1. *Juvenile Justice Information Services* (NYC Mayor's Office)
2. *Family Law of the State of New York* (Family Court Act; Family Court Rules)
3. *Penal Law of the State of New York*
4. *Juvenile Justice Case Processing: Volume I (Draft)* (NY State Division of Criminal Justice Services, 1990 Albany, New York)

STUDYING THE SITUATION

As with any litigation proceeding, a typical juvenile delinquent case can take months from time of arrest to court order of disposition. It is true that a proceeding may be delayed for various circumstances beyond the court's control. For example, it may be held for additional evidence or issuance of warrants and subpoenas. In many instances, however, delays are due simply to the enormous caseloads of attorneys and judges.

Decisions on all NYC Family Court cases are made in the family courts of the county in which the incident occurred. There are five family courts in NYC: Manhattan, Brooklyn, Queens, Bronx, and Staten Island.

After considering and weighing all the evidence, the presiding judge determines the extent and severity of the offense and renders an appropriate order of disposition against the respondent. The prosecuting and defense attorneys determine what strategies are most appropriate in prosecuting or defending the respondent.

Identification of Knowledge Domain to Be Prototyped

Figure 10A–1 is a flowchart of the decision-making process in a typical juvenile proceeding within the Family Court system in NYC. The knowledge

Figure 10A–1. Juvenile Delinquent Disposition Proceedings: Overall Decision-Making Process

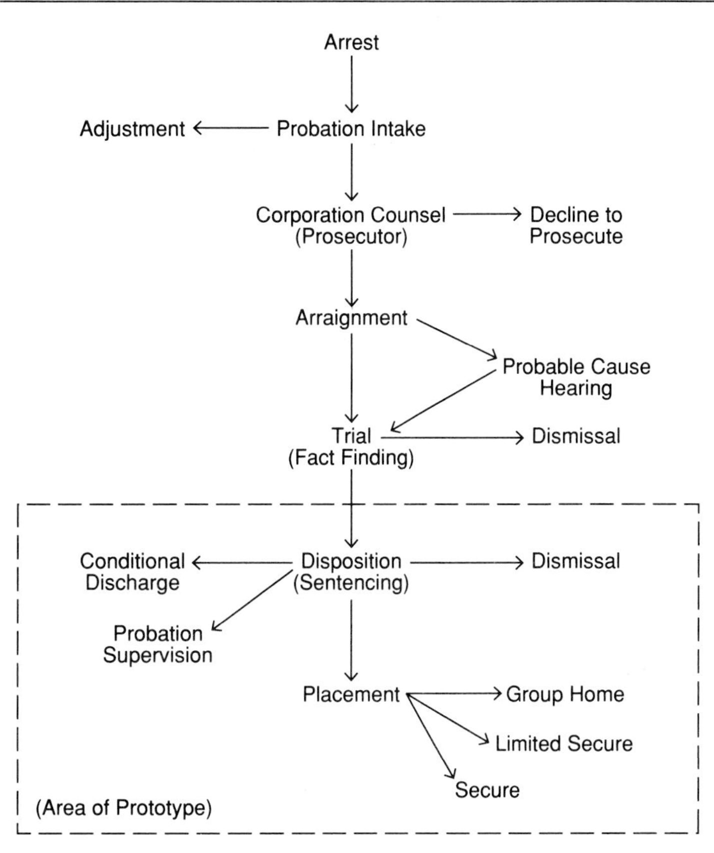

domain to be prototyped in this expert system is the bottom one-third of the flowchart: Disposition (Sentencing) and Placement.

Critical Factors Considered

As shown in the overview block diagram of the decision to be prototyped, in Figure 10A–2, three critical factors are examined in the Juvenile Delinquent Disposition Advisory System.

A "weighing" scheme is used when considering the values of these factors. For the first critical factor, Present Offense Weight Evaluation, the scale for the three weighable values—high, medium, and low—is more weighted at the high end. This type of scale corresponds with real-life legal decisions. For example, if a juvenile has committed a serious crime or caused serious injury or damage to others (meaning a high value for this factor), the courts place additional emphasis on this fact. The other two critical factors in the disposition decision, Probation Investigation Evaluation and Diagnostic Assessment Evaluation, are weighted into three equal parts, poor, fair, and good.

The meanings of the critical factors are described next and identified in the detailed block diagram shown in Figure 10A–3.

Present Offense Weight Evaluation. This critical factor considers several elements: the age of the respondent; the classification of the offense (Designated Class A Felony, Designated Felony, Other); and prior convictions and dispositions, if legally available. A felony is defined as a major crime for which the law provides greater punishment than for a misdemeanor offense. When it is rele-

Figure 10A–2. Juvenile Delinquent Disposition Advisory System: Overview Block Diagram of Decision to Be Prototyped

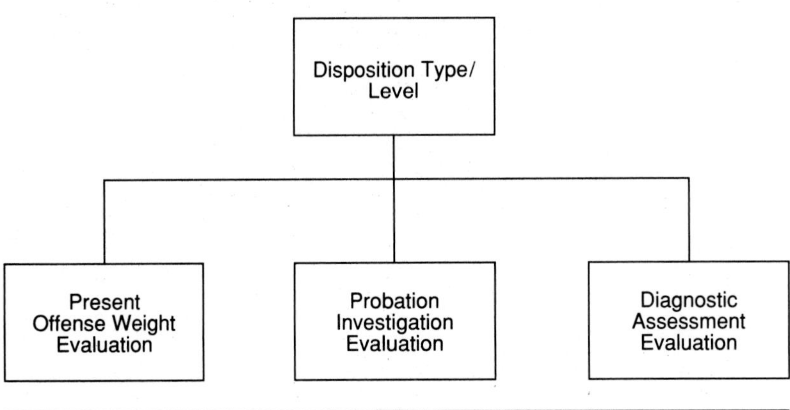

Figure 10A–3. Juvenile Delinquent Disposition Advisory System: Detailed Block Diagrams of Critical Factors

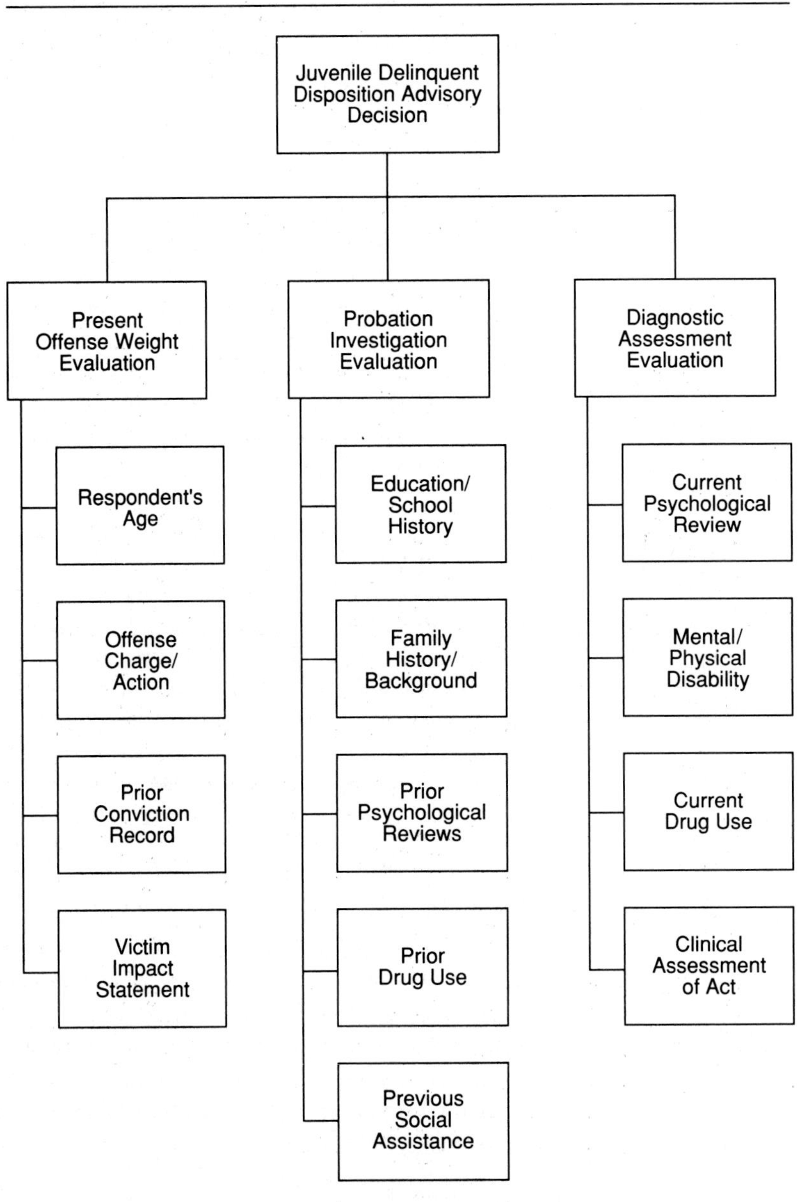

vant to the order of disposition, a victim impact statement is also considered. Such a statement includes an analysis of the victim's version of the offense, the extent of injury or economic loss or damage to the victim, and the views of the victim relating to disposition, including the amount of restitution sought, if any.

Possible values for the Present Offense Weight Evaluation and their weight scale are

- High (2.67–5.00)
- Medium (1.33–2.66)
- Low (0.00–1.32)
- Other (no weight scale applicable)
- Designated Felony (DF) Class A (no weight scale applicable)

Probation Investigation Evaluation. Probation Investigation includes, but is not limited to, the history of the juvenile. This includes school adjustment, the family situation, previous psychological and psychiatric reports, drug or alcohol use, and previous social assistance provided by voluntary or public agencies and the response of the juvenile to such assistance. Possible weighted values for Probation Investigation are

- Poor (2.67–4.00)
- Fair (1.33–2.66)
- Good (0.00–1.32)

Diagnostic Assessment Evaluation. Diagnostic Assessment includes, but is not limited to, the factors shown in Figure 10A–3. These involve psychological tests and psychiatric interviews to determine mental capacity and achievement, emotional stability, and mental disabilities. It also considers current drug use and a clinical assessment of situational factors that may have contributed to the criminal act or acts. When feasible, expert opinion is rendered about the risk presented by the juvenile to others or himself or herself, with a recommendation about the need for restrictive placement.

Possible weighted values for Diagnostic Assessment are

- Poor (2.67–4.00)
- Fair (1.33–2.66)
- Good (0.00–1.32)

These explanations are taken in part from the New York State Family Court Act and the Family Law of the State of New York.

Specific Questions Asked

The expert system asks four questions to guide the Present Offense Weight Evaluation:

1. What is the age of the respondent? (Between 7 and 11, Between 12 and 16, Other)
2. What is the classification of the top adjudicated charge? (Des Felony Class A, Designated Felony, Other Felony)
3. Does the respondent have two or more total convictions where at least one was a felony finding? (yes, no)
4. What is the extent of the injury, economic loss, or damage to the victim? (severe, not severe)

Next, the system asks five specific questions to conduct the Probation Investigation:

1. What is the history of the respondent's general overall school attendance record and behavior? (good, poor)
2. Does the respondent come from a broken family which has not been supportive or is unable to meet his/her physical or social needs? (yes, no)
3. After reviewing any previous psychiatric and/or general personal history reports, what is the evaluation of the respondent's prior psychological condition? (good, poor)
4. Has the respondent previously been involved with drugs/alcohol? (yes, no)
5. If social assistance was ever administered to the respondent or his/her family concerning the above matters, what were the results? (if never administered, assume it could be "helpful" to the respondent) (helpful, not helpful)

Finally, four specific questions are asked to conduct a Diagnostic Assessment:

1. Based on current psychiatric reports, what is the evaluation of the respondent's psychological condition? (good, poor)
2. Does the respondent exhibit any noticeable mental disability(s) or signs of physical abuse? (yes, no)
3. Is the respondent currently involved with drugs/alcohol? (yes, no)
4. To what extent, based on the clinical assessment, have external factors contributed to or caused the offense(s) the respondent has committed? (great extent, little extent)

Recommendations Determined by the Expert System

There are nine possible recommendations to be made by this prototype system:

1. *Dismissal:* A dismissal may be granted when the existence of some compelling further consideration or circumstance clearly demonstrates that the continuing proceeding would constitute or result in an injustice to the respondent. These considerations and circumstances include
   - a. The seriousness and circumstances of the crime
   - b. The extent of harm caused by the crime
   - c. Any exceptionally serious misconduct of law enforcement personnel in the investigation and arrest of the respondent or in the presentment of the petition
   - d. The history, character, and condition of the respondent
   - e. The needs and best interest of the respondent
   - f. The need for protection of the community
   - g. Any other relevant fact indicating that an alternative disposition would serve no useful purpose.

   From the Final Recommendation decision table shown in Figure 10A–4, the only combination of values that yields a disposition of dismissal are

   Present Offense Weight Evaluation = low
   Diagnostic Assessment Evaluation = good
   Probation Investigation Evaluation = good

2. *Conditional Discharge:* The court may conditionally discharge the respondent if the court, having regard for the nature and circum-

Figure 10A–4. Juvenile Delinquent Disposition Advisory System: Decision Tables

Final Recommendation—Reduced Decision Table

Rule	Present Offense	Diagnostic Assessment	Probation Investigation	Conclusion
1D	Designated Felony Class A	—	—	Placement level 3
2D	Other	—	—	Other jurisdiction
3D	High	Good	Good	Probation level 1
4D	High	Good	Fair	Probation level 2
5D	High	Good	Poor	Probation level 3
6D	High	Fair	Good	Probation level 2
7D	High	Fair	Fair	Probation level 3
8D	High	Fair	Poor	Placement level 1
9D	High	Poor	Good	Probation level 3
10D	High	Poor	Fair	Placement level 1
11D	High	Poor	Poor	Placement level 2
12D	Medium	Good	Good	Conditional discharge
13D	Medium	Good	Fair	Probation level 1
14D	Medium	Good	Poor	Probation level 2
15D	Medium	Fair	Good	Probation level 1
16D	Medium	Fair	Fair	Probation level 2
17D	Medium	Fair	Poor	Probation level 3
18D	Medium	Poor	Good	Probation level 2
19D	Medium	Poor	Fair	Probation level 3
20D	Medium	Poor	Poor	Placement level 1
21D	Low	Good	Good	Dismissed
22D	Low	Good	Fair	Conditional discharge
23D	Low	Good	Poor	Probation level 1
24D	Low	Fair	Good	Conditional discharge
25D	Low	Fair	Fair	Probation level 1
26D	Low	Fair	Poor	Probation level 2
27D	Low	Poor	Good	Probation level 1
28D	Low	Poor	Fair	Probation level 2
29D	Low	Poor	Poor	Probation level 3

Relative Weights of Values

Present Offense	Diagnostic Assessment	Probation Investigation	Conclusion
High = 3 Medium = 2 Low = 1 Designated Felony Class A = not applicable (n/a) Other = n/a	Good = 0 Fair = 1 Poor = 2	Good = 0 Fair = 1 Poor = 2	Dismissed = 1 Conditional discharge = 2 Probation level 1 = 3 Probation level 2 = 4 Probation level 3 = 5 Placement level 1 = 6 Placement level 2 = 7 Placement level 3 = Des Felony Class A only Other jurisdiction = n/a

Figure 10A–4. *continued*

Present Offense Weight Evaluation—Reduced Decision Table

Rule	Respondent's Age	Top Adjudicated Charge	Two Total Felony Convictions	Victim Impact Statement	Conclusion
1A	Other	—	—	—	Other Jurisdiction
2A	7–11 or 12–16	Designated Felony Class A	—	—	Designated Felony Class A
3A	Between 7 and 11	Designated Felony	Yes	Severe	High
4A	Between 7 and 11	Designated Felony	Yes	Not severe	High
5A	Between 7 and 11	Designated Felony	No	Severe	High
6A	Between 7 and 11	Designated Felony	No	Not severe	Medium
7A	Between 7 and 11	Other Felony	Yes	Severe	High
8A	Between 7 and 11	Other Felony	Yes	Not severe	Medium
9A	Between 7 and 11	Other Felony	No	Severe	Medium
10A	Between 7 and 11	Other Felony	No	Not severe	Low
11A	Between 12 and 16	Designated Felony	Yes	Severe	High
12A	Between 12 and 16	Designated Felony	Yes	Not severe	High
13A	Between 12 and 16	Designated Felony	No	Severe	High
14A	Between 12 and 16	Designated Felony	No	Not severe	Medium
15A	Between 12 and 16	Other Felony	Yes	Severe	High
16A	Between 12 and 16	Other Felony	Yes	Not severe	High
17A	Between 12 and 16	Other Felony	No	Severe	High
18A	Between 12 and 16	Other Felony	No	Not severe	Medium

Relative Weights of Values

Respondent's Age	Top Adjudicated Charge	Two Total Felony Convictions	Victim Impact Statement	Conclusion
Between 7 and 11 = 0	Designated Felony Class A = n/a	Yes = 1	Severe = 1	Low = 0.00–1.32
Between 12 and 16 = 1	Designated Felony = 2	No = 0	Not severe = 0	Medium = 1.33–2.66
	Other Felony = 1			High = 2.67–5.00

Probation Investigation Evaluation—Reduced Decision Table

Rule	Education/ School	Family Status	Psychological Evaluation	Drug Use	Social Assistance	Conclusion	
1C	Good	Yes	Good	Yes	Helpful	Fair	(2)
2C	Good	Yes	Good	Yes	Not helpful	Fair	(3)
3C	Good	Yes	Good	No	Helpful	Good	(1)
4C	Good	Yes	Good	No	Not helpful	Fair	(2)
5C	Good	Yes	Poor	Yes	Helpful	Fair	(3)
6C	Good	Yes	Poor	Yes	Not helpful	Poor	(4)
7C	Good	Yes	Poor	No	Helpful	Fair	(2)
8C	Good	Yes	Poor	No	Not helpful	Fair	(3)
9C	Good	No	Good	Yes	Helpful	Good	(1)
10C	Good	No	Good	Yes	Not helpful	Fair	(2)
11C	Good	No	Good	No	Helpful	Good	(0)
12C	Good	No	Good	No	Not helpful	Good	(1)
13C	Good	No	Poor	Yes	Helpful	Fair	(2)
14C	Good	No	Poor	Yes	Not helpful	Fair	(3)
15C	Good	No	Poor	No	Helpful	Good	(1)
16C	Good	No	Poor	No	Not helpful	Fair	(2)
17C	Poor	Yes	Good	Yes	Helpful	Fair	(3)
18C	Poor	Yes	Good	Yes	Not helpful	Poor	(4)
19C	Poor	Yes	Good	No	Helpful	Fair	(2)
20C	Poor	Yes	Good	No	Not helpful	Fair	(3)
21C	Poor	Yes	Poor	Yes	Helpful	Poor	(4)
22C	Poor	Yes	Poor	Yes	Not helpful	Poor	(5)
23C	Poor	Yes	Poor	No	Helpful	Fair	(3)
24C	Poor	Yes	Poor	No	Not helpful	Poor	(4)
25C	Poor	No	Good	Yes	Helpful	Fair	(2)
26C	Poor	No	Good	Yes	Not helpful	Fair	(3)
27C	Poor	No	Good	No	Helpful	Good	(1)
28C	Poor	No	Good	No	Not helpful	Fair	(2)
29C	Poor	No	Poor	Yes	Helpful	Fair	(3)
30C	Poor	No	Poor	Yes	Not helpful	Poor	(4)
31C	Poor	No	Poor	No	Helpful	Fair	(2)
32C	Poor	No	Poor	No	Not helpful	Fair	(3)

Relative Weights of Values

Education/School	Family Status	Psychological Evaluation	Drug Use	Social Assistance	Conclusion
Good = 0	Yes = 1	Good = 0	Yes = 1	Helpful = 0	Poor = 3.33–5.00
Poor = 1	No = 0	Poor = 1	No = 0	Not helpful = 1	Fair = 1.67–3.32
					Good = 0.00–1.66

Figure 10A–4. *concluded*

Diagnostic Assessment Evaluation—Reduced Decision Table

Rule	Psychological Evaluation	Mental/ Physical Disability	Drug Use	Extent of Factors	Conclusion	
1B	Good	Yes	Yes	Great extent	Poor	(3)
2B	Good	Yes	Yes	Little extent	Fair	(2)
3B	Good	Yes	No	Great extent	Fair	(2)
4B	Good	Yes	No	Little extent	Good	(1)
5B	Good	No	Yes	Great extent	Fair	(2)
6B	Good	No	Yes	Little extent	Good	(1)
7B	Good	No	No	—	Good	
8B	Poor	Yes	Yes	—	Poor	
9B	Poor	Yes	No	Great extent	Poor	(3)
10B	Poor	Yes	No	Little extent	Fair	(2)
11B	Poor	No	Yes	Great extent	Poor	(3)
12B	Poor	No	Yes	Little extent	Fair	(2)
13B	Poor	No	No	Great extent	Fair	(2)
14B	Poor	No	No	Little extent	Good	(1)

Relative Weights of Values

Psychological Evaluation	Mental/ Physical Disabilities	Drug Use	Extent of Factors	Conclusion
Good = 0 Poor = 1	Yes = 1 No = 0	Yes = 1 No = 0	Great extent = 1 Little extent = 0	Poor = 2.67–4.00 Fair = 1.33–2.66 Good = 0.00–1.32

stances of the crime and for the history, character, and condition of the respondent, is of the opinion that neither the public interest nor the ends of justice would be served by a placement (see 6, 7, and 8, which follow) and that probation supervision is not appropriate.

From the Final Recommendation decision table, the three combinations of values that yield a disposition of conditional discharge are

Present Offense Weight Evaluation = medium
Diagnostic Assessment Evaluation = good
Probation Investigation Evaluation = good

Present Offense Weight Evaluation = low
Diagnostic Assessment Evaluation = good
Probation Investigation Evaluation = fair

Present Offense Weight Evaluation = low
Diagnostic Assessment Evaluation = fair
Probation Investigation Evaluation = good

3,4,5. *Probation Supervision:* The court may order a period of probation if the court, having regard for the nature and circumstances of the crime and the history, character, and condition of the respondent, is of the opinion that

a. Placement of respondent is not or may not be necessary.
b. The respondent is in need of guidance, training, or other assistance that can be effectively administered through probation.

As shown in the Final Recommendation decision table in Figure 10A–4 there are 19 possible combinations that yield a disposition of probation supervision. Of these 19 outcomes, 6 are probation level 1, 7 are probation level 2, and 6 are probation level 3. The three levels indicate appropriate terms of sentencing. As an example, level 1 may correspond to 6 to 12 months, level 2 may be 12 to 18 months, and level 3 may be 18 to 24 months probation.

6,7,8. *Placement:* The court may place the respondent in his or her home or in the custody of a relative, other suitable private person, the commissioner of social services, or the division for youth.

There are five possible combinations that yield a disposition of placement. Of these five outcomes, three are placement level 1, one is placement level 2, and one is placement level 3. Figure 10A–4 shows the exact combinations needed for a placement recommendation. Unlike probation supervision levels, these three levels indicate *appropriate types* of placement. As an example, level 1 would correspond to non-secure placement, level 2 would be limited secure placement, and level 3 would correspond to restrictive placement for the convicted juvenile.

9. *Other Jurisdiction:* If the juvenile does not meet any of the conditions with regard to the Family Court Act, or fails to meet the requirements that constitute a Designated Felony Act, or is under 7 years of age or older than 16 years of age, he or she cannot be processed through Family Court and is referred to another jurisdiction.

Typical Situation Scenario

John Smith, age 14, has been convicted of robbery in the 2nd degree as defined under Article 160.10 of the New York State Penal Law, which states that

> A person is guilty of robbery in the 2nd degree when he forcibly steals property and when
>
> **1.** He is aided by another person actually present, or
> **2.** In the course of the commission of the crime or of immediate flight therefrom, he or another participant in the crime
> **a.** Causes physical injury to any person who is not a participant in the crime, or
> **b.** Displays what appears to be a pistol, revolver, rifle, shotgun, machine gun or other firearm.

As the respondent has committed a Designated Felony Act and is determined to be a juvenile delinquent, he has up to now been detained while waiting for a dispositional hearing, which must begin not more than 50 days after the fact-finding completion.

At the dispositional hearing, the presiding judge directs the probation service agency to summarize its investigation report. The case investigator states that John is presently a junior high school student and has had previous problems with irregular attendance. The investigator obtained this evidence from school attendance records. He adds that John lives with his mother and brother and that John's father died when he was 8 years old. His mother presently holds a clerical position, which pays slightly more than a minimum wage—an income not sufficient for her or the family. John's 17-year-old brother has been convicted of robbery to support his drug habit. John and his family live in a low-income, crime-ridden area of the city. Prior evaluations indicate that John has had no psychological problems.

The investigator recommends probation supervision because John has no prior court convictions or involvement. He feels John's actions were dictated by the financial difficulties of his family, as well as pressure from his brother to steal to support the brother's drug habit.

The judge then calls the preparer of the diagnostic report to come forward and present her assessment. She begins by stating that John's psychological and emotional well-being is not adequately being provided for in his present environment. She has reached this conclusion through several in-depth interviews with John and his mother. Although John has not been attending school on a regular basis, school reports show that he has been an average to above-average student when he has attended. She has concluded, therefore, that he does not possess any mental disability that would hinder his mental capacity and scholastic achievement.

The problem lies within the respondent's emotional and social environment, she states. Soon after the death of John's father, the family began to argue more frequently about finances. In addition, the family became bitter because of the change in its lifestyle. John's brother began to associate with the "wrong" crowd. Soon afterwards, he became involved with drugs. The pressures of crisis after crisis became unmanageable to John and his family. They sought social assistance but did not have the necessary resources to afford it. In her summary, she recommends that John be placed in the custody of his aunt and uncle so he can escape his present hostile and unsuitable environment.

In the victim impact statement, the victim of the crime, Mr. Joseph Doe, age 58, states that the respondent said, "Give me your wallet or else," as he was waiting for a subway train. When Mr. Doe complied with the respondent's request, the respondent then "pushed me and caused me to fall heavily on the platform, causing a bruise on my right hip and a sprain of my right ankle." He goes on to state that "my doctor bills were approximately $500" and that he is "now afraid to ride the subway because of these 'thugs'." Mr. Doe wishes to recover the money paid for his medical expenses as well as $5,000 in punitive damages from the respondent.

After reviewing the case and all supporting testimony and evidence given, the judge concludes that John's present offense risk to himself and the community is *medium*. This assessment is based on the fact that, although John committed a Designated Felony Act, he does not have two prior convictions where at least one was a felony. He also did not cause severe injury to the victim. The judge concludes that the victim's injury was not severe, since he did not suffer any broken bones during the robbery.

As for the probation investigation, the judge considers John's risk to be *fair*. Although the respondent showed poor school attendance before the act was committed, he comes from a broken family, that is fairly supportive in spite of its present financial difficulties. John has a good prior psychological evaluation and no prior drug or alcohol use; there is an uncertainty about obtaining social assistance for the family.

In considering the diagnostic assessment evaluation, the judge concludes that John represents a *good* risk. His current psychological state is good, he has no mental or physical disabilities, he is not a drug or alcohol abuser, and the factors contributing to the crime were very great at the time the robbery was committed.

Based on the results of the present offense charge weight, the probation investigation report, and the diagnostic assessment evaluation, the judge orders a disposition of probation for a period of six months. The terms of his probation are that

1. John return to school and attend regularly,
2. He visit with his probation officer every two weeks, and
3. He visit with a social service worker or psychologist regularly to help him cope with his situation.

The judge strongly suggests that other members of the family attend these meetings with the social worker or psychologist as well.

Test Case Validation

The following case comes from a real-life assault and robbery incident that occurred in the NYC area. The juvenile disposition decision in this case is used to validate the results obtained from the Juvenile Delinquent Disposition Advisory System.

A couple waiting for a train at the World Trade Center is accosted by a group of youths, including a 13-year-old boy, Ron J., who taunts them and shouts racial slurs. Two girls jump the woman and beat her while four boys, including Ron J., grab the man and hit him. Ron J., who had been arrested a few months earlier for another assault and robbery, grabs the wallet from the man's pocket as bystanders pull the other boys off. The woman is left bloody, with extensive cuts and bruises to her head and chest. After a trial, Ron J. is found guilty of 2nd degree robbery, two counts of 2nd degree assault, and 3rd degree assault. At dispositional sentencing, the youth consented to an 18-month placement in a youth home.[1]

The judge in Ron J.'s case reached his decision based on the following determinations:

- *The present offense weight evaluation was high.* Ron J. is 13 years old, the top adjudicated charge is a Designated Felony, Ron J. possesses two prior convictions (one of which was a felony), and he caused severe injury to the victim.
- *The probation investigation evaluation was poor.* Since Ron J. showed a poor personal history background through his prior behavior, the judge concluded that his psychological condition was poor. Ron J. was described as being truant from school and came from a family that was unable to meet his needs.
- *The diagnostic assessment evaluation was poor.* Ron J.'s current psychological evaluation showed that he is violent and volatile, as his actions have indicated. He possessed no noticeable mental or physical disabilities and there was no indication of drug use. Ron J.'s action(s) for which he has been convicted are largely attributable to these and other factors of his immediate environment.

This disposition outcome is consistent with the prototype system described here, which recommends placement level 2 as the appropriate disposition order and level.

---

[1]New York City Corporation Counsel, *New York Newsday* (October 28, 1990).

SYSTEM DOCUMENTATION

The dependency diagram in Figure 10A–5 shows the relationships among the three critical factors, the input questions, rules, values, and recommendations made by this system.

A sample consultation is shown in Figure 10A–6. A listing of the first of four knowledge base files for the Juvenile Delinquent Disposition Advisory System is given in Figure 10A–7. The other three knowledge bases can be examined by printing out the PROINV.KBS, DIAGASMT.KBS, and DISP.KBS files on the disk accompanying this book.

System Design Issues

Since the legal profession typically weighs evidence in favor of or against a respondent, this expert system also uses a weighing system to determine out-

Figure 10A–5. Juvenile Delinquent Disposition Advisory System: Dependency Diagram

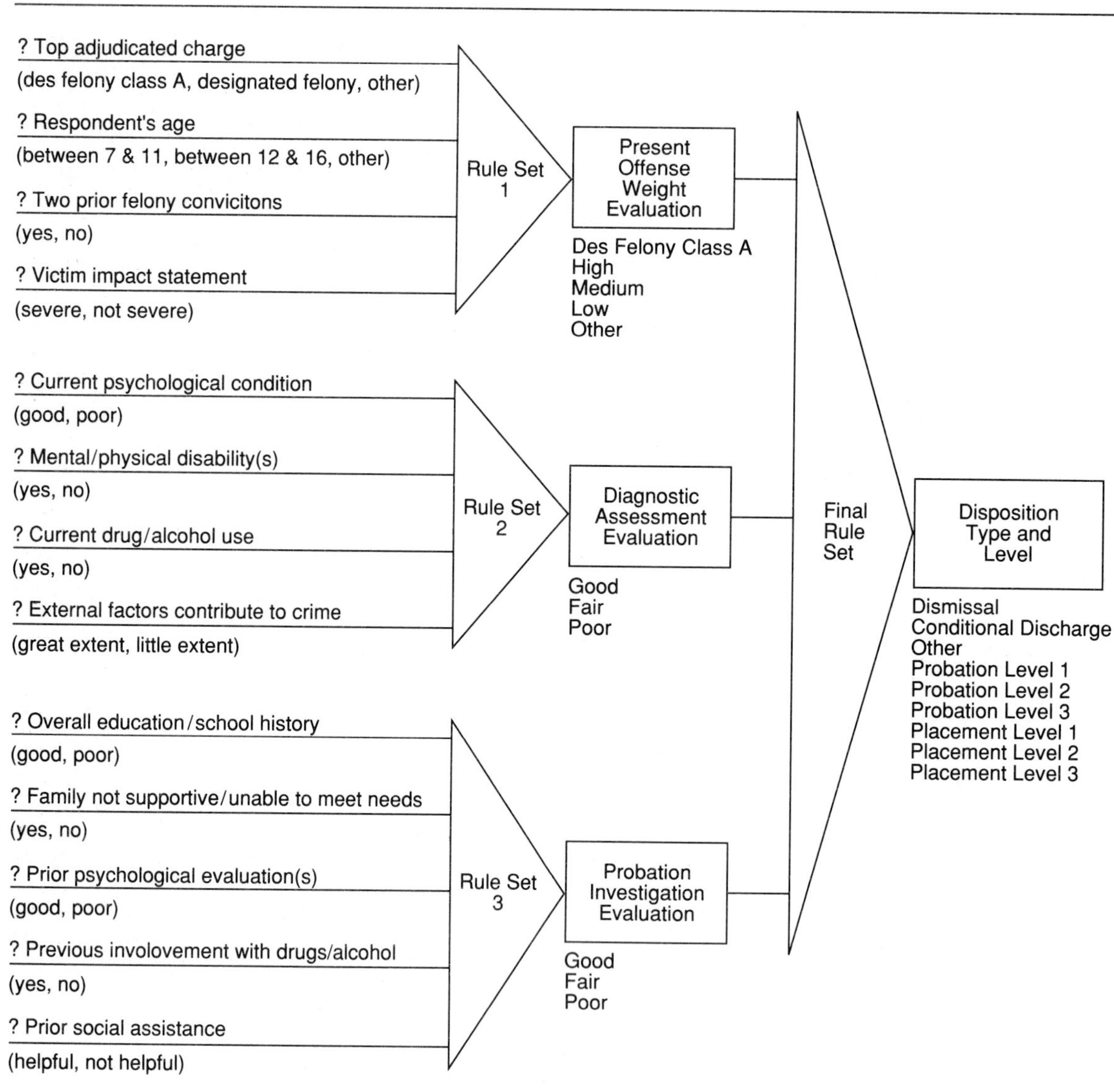

Figure 10A–6. Juvenile Delinquent Disposition Advisory System: Sample Consultation

```
                         Welcome to the

     ** JUVENILE DELINQUENT DISPOSITION ADVISORY SYSTEM **
                       Prototype Version

               Developed by Robert S. Pfeffer
           under the direction and supervision of
                       Dr. D.G. Dologite
```

Text only

```
                    PURPOSE OF THIS EXPERT SYSTEM

  This consultation assists a user to evaluate a juvenile delinquent who
has been convicted of a designated felony act.  It asks a series of
detailed questions about the juvenile, then recommends a dispositional
outcome which is appropriate for the information obtained during a Family
Court dispositional hearing.

                   PLEASE PRESS ANY KEY TO CONTINUE


               PRESENT OFFENSE WEIGHT RISK EVALUATION

  This section of the consultation classifies the top adjudicated charge
committed by the juvenile and categorizes the juvenile's age and
conviction record.  It also categorizes the extent of injury, economic
loss, or damage to the victim as described in a victim impact statement.

    PRESS ANY KEY TO BEGIN THE PRESENT OFFENSE WEIGHT RISK EVALUATION
```

Actual screen

```
                           INSTRUCTIONS
           Use the arrow keys to move the lightbar to a desired
           answer choice then press the Enter key.


 What is the age of the respondent?
  Between 7 and 11         Between 12 and 16 ◄     Other

 What is the classification of the Top Adjudicated Charge?
  Des Felony Class A       Designated Felony ◄     Other Felony

 Does the respondent have 2 or more total convictions where
 at least one was a felony finding?
  yes                      no ◄

 To what extent is the injury, economic loss or damage to the
 victim?
  severe                   not severe ◄
```

Actual screen

```
     Based on the responses given, the Present Offense Risk is MEDIUM
     because:

     1.    the respondent's age is Between 12 and 16;
     2.    the top adjudicated charge is a(n) Designated Felony;
     3.    no, the respondent does not have 2 or more total
             convictions where at least one was a felony finding; and
     4.    the injury, economic loss or damage inflicted by the respondent
             on the victim is not severe.


     PRESS ANY KEY TO GO ON TO THE PROBATION INVESTIGATION EVALUATION
```

Figure 10A–6. *continued*

Text only

```
                    PROBATION INVESTIGATION EVALUATION

   This section of the consultation evaluates the juvenile's family
background, educational/school history, previous substance abuse
record, prior personal history and/or psychological reports, and
prior effectiveness of social assistance administered to the
juvenile.

PLEASE PRESS ANY KEY TO BEGIN THE PROBATION INVESTIGATION EVALUATION
```

Text only

```
What is the history of the respondent's general overall school
attendance record and behavior?
 good                         poor ◂

Does the respondent come from a broken family which has not been
supportive or is unable to meet his/her physical or social needs?
 yes ◂                        no

After reviewing any previous psychiatric and/or general
personal history reports, what is the evaluation of the respondent's
prior psychological condition?
 good ◂                       poor

Has the respondent previously been involved with drugs/alcohol?
 yes                          no ◂

If social assistance was ever administered to the respondent
or his/her family concerning the above matters, what were the results?
(if never administered, assume that it could be 'helpful' to respondent)
 helpful ◂                    not helpful


Based on the responses, the Probation Investigation Evaluation is FAIR
  because:

  1.   the respondent's overall educational/school history is poor
  2.   yes, the respondent does live with a family which is
         broken or unable to meet his/her needs;
  3.   the respondent's prior psychological condition has determined
         to be good;
  4.   no, the respondent has not been previously involved with
         drugs
  5.   previously administered social assistance has been helpful
         to the respondent.

      PRESS ANY KEY TO GO ON TO THE DIAGNOSTIC ASSESSMENT EVALUATION


                    DIAGNOSTIC ASSESSMENT EVALUATION

  This section of the consultation evaluates the current physical,
emotional, and mental stability of the juvenile, as well as examines
possible involvement with drugs and/or alcohol. It also determines to
what extent, based on a clinical assessment, external factors have
contributed to the offense.

  PLEASE PRESS ANY KEY TO BEGIN THE DIAGNOSTIC ASSESSMENT EVALUATION
```

comes at the critical factor and final recommendation levels. Although the weights could have been built into the rules of the expert system, the developer chose to compute them manually. Essentially, these weights, as defined in the decision tables in Figure 10A–4, were used to plan the outcomes of the critical factor values and, ultimately, the final recommendation.

Text only

```
Based on current psychiatric reports, what is the
evaluation of the respondent's psychological condition?
 good ◄                     poor

Does the respondent exhibit any noticeable mental
disability(s) or signs of physical abuse?
 yes                        no ◄

Is the respondent currently involved with drugs/alcohol?
 yes                        no ◄

To what extent, based on the clinical assessment,
have external factors contributed to or caused the offense(s) the
respondent has committed?
 great extent ◄             little extent



Based on the responses, the Diagnostic Assessment is GOOD
because:

  1.   the current psychological evaluation of the respondent
         has been determined to be good;
  2.   no, the respondent does not possess noticeable
         mental disabilities and signs of physical abuse;
  3.   no, the respondent is not currently involved
         with drugs/alcohol;
  4.   based on the clinical assessment, external factors have,
         to a great extent, contributed to the offense(s)
         committed by the respondent.

       PRESS ANY KEY TO GO ON TO THE DISPOSITION DETERMINATION



                       DISPOSITION DETERMINATION

  The final section of the consultation presents the user with a
recommendation of disposition level for the juvenile convicted of a
designated felony act. It does this by evaluating the respondent risk
levels as determined in the present offense weight evaluation, probation
investigation evaluation, and diagnostic assessment evaluation.

  **  PLEASE PRESS ANY KEY TO OBTAIN THE DISPOSITION DETERMINATION **
```

In determining the final recommendation, the system ranks each disposition on a seriousness level; a dismissal is the lowest form of disposition and placement level 3 is the highest form. A recommendation of "other jurisdiction" does not have a corresponding value, since the juvenile would be referred to another court or government agency for disposition.

The system is structured into four distinct modules: one for each critical factor rule set and one for the final recommendation rule set. This enables inclusion of a detailed user interface and self-documenting explanation facility at the conclusion of each module. This also permits enhancing and enlarging the prototype in a more structured and logical fashion to facilitate modifications.

The method used for linking these four rule sets together include CHAINing, SAVEFACTS, and LOADFACTS facilities. The first rule set, PRESOFF.KBS, is chained to the second rule set, PROINV.KBS. PROINV.KBS is chained to the third rule set, DIAGASMT.KBS, which is chained to the final rule set, DISP.KBS. For the user to remain within the system, the final rule set chains back to the first

Figure 10A–6. *concluded*

Text only

```
              PLEASE NOTE EDUCATION/SCHOOL BACKGROUND

          Based on the response given for the juvenile's
          education/school history, it is strongly suggested
          that he or she receive special attention in this
          area for the duration of the sentence period or as
          a condition of discharge or dismissal.


              PLEASE PRESS ANY KEY TO CONTINUE.....



                    Based on the answers given,
              the recommended disposition level is:

                        PROBATION level 1

             This determination was reached because:

                  Present Offense Risk is MEDIUM,
           Probation Investigation Evaluation is FAIR,
                               and
            Diagnostic Assessment Evaluation is GOOD.

         PRESS ANY KEY TO OBTAIN THE INFORMATION SUMMARY
```

Actual screen

```
                          JUVENILE INFORMATION SUMMARY

   PRESENT OFFENSE   Respondent's Age:                 Between 12 and 16
        RISK         Top Adjudicated Charge:           Designated Felony
                     Prior or Concurrent Convictions
                      w/at least 1 felony finding:     no
                     Victim Impact Statement:          not severe

     PROBATION       Education/School History:         poor
   INVESTIGATION     Family Unable to Meet Needs:      yes
                     Prior Psychiatric Evaluation:     good
                     Prior Drug Abuse/Involvement:     no
                     Social Assistance Effectiveness:  helpful

     DIAGNOSTIC      Current Psychological Assessment: good
     ASSESSMENT      Mental/Physical Disability(s):    no
                     Current Drug Use/Involvement:     no
                     Factors Contributing to Act:      great extent

              PLEASE PRESS ANY KEY TO CONCLUDE THIS CONSULTATION
```

rule set. In this way, a user may do multiple consultations without ever leaving the VP-Expert program. Since the educational version of VP-Expert allows only three files to be chained, the last chain will not execute 100 percent of the time. This is not a problem in the full professional version of VP-Expert, which allows unlimited chaining.

In order to make a final recommendation of order and level of disposition, it is necessary to save the outcomes for each critical factor area. Therefore, the variables and outcomes for PRESOFF.KBS, PROINV.KBS, and DIAGASMT-.KBS are stored in temporary "holding" files named TEMP1, TEMP2, and TEMP3. To determine a final recommendation, these three files are loaded using the LOADFACTS command in the Actions Block of the DISP.KBS file.

Figure 10A–7. Juvenile Delinquent Disposition Advisory System: Printout of Knowledge Base File

> Note:
> Only one of four KBS files is shown here. It is PRESOFF.KBS. The other three are PROINV.KBS, DIAGASMT.KBS, and DISP.KBS and can be examined by printing them out from the disk accompanying this book. Instructions for printing KBS files are given in Figure 2-7.

```
! JUVENILE DELINQUENT PRESENT OFFENSE CHARGE WEIGHT & STARTING KBS
! Saved as PRESOFF.KBS
!Microcomputer Used:        Wang Microsystems PC 382
!Software Used:             VP-Expert, Educational Version 2.02
!KBS File Name:             PRESOFF.KBS
!Temporary File Access:     TEMP1
!Chained to:                PROINV.KBS
!***************************************************************************
EXECUTE;                             !start consultation immediately
bkcolor = 3;                         !set screen background color to light blue
runtime;                             !removes consultation windows during a run
endoff;                              !eliminate need to press END after a choice
!============================== Actions Block ==========================
ACTIONS
     wopen 1,1,1,20,77,3
     active 1
     display "

                              Welcome to the

           ** JUVENILE DELINQUENT DISPOSITION ADVISORY SYSTEM **
                             Prototype Version

                        Developed by Robert S. Pfeffer
                    under the direction and supervision of
                              Dr. D. G. Dologite
                        for further information, contact
                              Dr. D.G. Dologite
                          c/o Macmillan Publishing

                       PLEASE PRESS ANY KEY TO CONTINUE~

     "
     wclose 1
     wopen 1,1,1,20,77,3
     active 1
     display "

                         PURPOSE OF THIS EXPERT SYSTEM


   This consultation assists a user to evaluate a juvenile delinquent who
  has been convicted of a designated felony act.  It asks a series of
  detailed questions about the juvenile, then recommends a dispositional
  outcome which is appropriate for the information obtained during a Family
  Court dispositional hearing.

                        PLEASE PRESS ANY KEY TO CONTINUE~
      "
wclose 1
wopen 1,1,1,20,77,3
active 1
     display "

                    PRESENT OFFENSE WEIGHT RISK EVALUATION


   This section of the consultation classifies the top adjudicated charge
  committed by the juvenile and categorizes the juvenile's age and
  conviction record.  It also categorizes the extent of injury, economic
  loss, or damage to the victim as described in a victim impact statement.
PRESS ANY KEY TO BEGIN THE PRESENT OFFENSE WEIGHT RISK EVALUATION~
  "
 wclose 1                     !remove window 1
 wopen 1,1,1,5,77,2           !define instructions window 1
 active 1                     !activate window 1
 display "                              INSTRUCTIONS
```

Figure 10A–7. *continued*

```
     Use the arrow keys to move the lightbar to a desired
     answer choice then press the Enter key."
wopen 2,7,1,14,77,3          !define consultation window 2
active 2                     !activate window 2
find pres_off
find word
wclose 1                     !remove window 1
wclose 2                     !remove window 2
wopen 1,1,1,15,77,2          !define consultation window 1
active 1                     !activate window 1
display "
 Based on the responses given, the Present Offense Risk is {pres_off}
 because:

 1.   the respondent's age is {age};
 2.   the top adjudicated charge is a(n) {tac};
 3.   {two_prior}, the respondent {word} have 2 or more total
        convictions where at least one was a felony finding; and
 4.   the injury, economic loss or damage inflicted by the respondent
        on the victim is {vis}.


 PRESS ANY KEY TO GO ON TO THE PROBATION INVESTIGATION EVALUATION~
  "
wclose 1                     !remove window 1
SAVEFACTS temp1              !save all variable names and values
                             !in a temp text file called TEMP1
CHAIN proinv                 !link to another .KBS file called PROINV
;
!============================== Rules Block ==============================
RULE 1A
    if age = Other
    then pres_off = OTHER_JURISDICTION
    SAVEFACTS temp1
    CHAIN disp;
RULE 2A
     if age = Between_7_and_11 and
     tac = Des_Felony_Class_A then pres_off = DF_CLASS_A
     SAVEFACTS temp1
     CHAIN proinv;
RULE 3Aa
     if age = Between_12_and_16 and
     tac = Des_Felony_Class_A then pres_off = DF_CLASS_A
     SAVEFACTS temp1
     CHAIN proinv;
RULE 3A
     if age = Between_7_and_11 and
     tac = Designated_Felony and two_prior = yes and vis = severe
     then pres_off = HIGH;
RULE 4A
     if age = Between_7_and_11 and
     tac = Designated_Felony and two_prior = yes and vis = not_severe
     then pres_off = HIGH;
RULE 5A
     if age = Between_7_and_11 and
     tac = Designated_Felony and two_prior = no and vis = severe
     then pres_off = HIGH;
RULE 6A
     if age = Between_7_and_11 and
     tac = Designated_Felony and two_prior = no and vis = not_severe
     then pres_off = MEDIUM;
RULE 7A
     if age = Between_12_and_16 and tac = Designated_Felony and two_prior = yes
     and vis = severe then pres_off = HIGH;
RULE 8A
     if age = Between_12_and_16 and tac = Designated_Felony and two_prior = yes
     and vis = not_severe then pres_off = HIGH;
RULE 9A
     if age = Between_12_and_16 and tac = Designated_Felony and two_prior = no
     and vis = severe then pres_off = HIGH;
RULE 10A
     if age = Between_12_and_16 and tac = Designated_Felony and two_prior = no
     and vis = not_severe then pres_off = MEDIUM;
RULE 11A
     if age = Between_7_and_11 and tac = Other_Felony and
     two_prior = yes and vis = severe
     then pres_off = HIGH;
RULE 12A
     if age = Between_7_and_11 and tac = Other_Felony and
     two_prior = yes and vis = not_severe
     then pres_off = MEDIUM;
```

```
RULE 13A
     if age = Between_7_and_11 and tac = Other_Felony and
     two_prior = no and vis = severe
     then pres_off = MEDIUM;
RULE 14A
     if age = Between_7_and_11 and tac = Other_Felony and
     two_prior = no and vis = not_severe
     then pres_off = LOW;
RULE 15A
     if age = Between_12_and_16 and tac = Other_Felony and
     two_prior = yes and vis = severe
     then pres_off = HIGH;
RULE 16A
     if age = Between_12_and_16 and tac = Other_Felony and
     two_prior = yes and vis = not_severe
     then pres_off = HIGH;
RULE 17A
     if age = Between_12_and_16 and tac = Other_Felony and
     two_prior = no and vis = severe
     then pres_off = HIGH;
RULE 18A
     if age = Between_12_and_16 and tac = Other_Felony and
     two_prior = no and vis = not_severe
     then pres_off = MEDIUM;
RULE WORD1
     if two_prior = yes
     then word = does;
RULE WORD2
     if two_prior = no
     then word = does_not;

!================================= Questions Block ========================
ask age: "What is the age of the respondent?";
choices age: Between_7_and_11, Between_12_and_16, Other;

ask tac: "What is the classification of the Top Adjudicated Charge?";
choices tac: Des_Felony_Class_A, Designated_Felony, Other_Felony;

ask two_prior: "Does the respondent have 2 or more total convictions where
at least one was a felony finding?";
choices two_prior: yes, no;

ask vis: "To what extent is the injury, economic loss or damage to the
victim?";
choices vis: severe, not_severe;

plural: tac, age;
```

Another issue encountered during system design concerned the age and charge factors used in the first rule set, Present Offense Weight Evaluation. If a respondent is not between the ages of 7 and 16, he or she cannot be prosecuted in Family Court. In addition, if the respondent is convicted of a Designated Felony Class A act, he or she is automatically assigned to a restricted placement facility (placement level 3). In this case, there is no need to go through the PROINV.KBS and DIAGASMT.KBS portions of the consultation. Instead, the PRESOFF.KBS is chained directly to the DISP.KBS whenever a Designated Felony Class A occurs so that the user receives a final recommendation.

REFERENCES

Family Law of the State of New York (Family Court Act; Family Court Rules).

Juvenile Justice Case Processing: Volume I (Draft) (New York State Division of Criminal Justice Services, 1990 Albany, New York).

Juvenile Justice Information Services (New York City Mayor's Office).

Penal Law of the State of New York. Sachar, Emily. "Kid Crime: 'They Start With Gunpoint Robbery' A Surge of Violent Offenses by the Young Overloads the Juvenile Justice System." *New York Newsday* (October 28, 1990).

10**B**

Computer File Fixer Expert System

TECHNICAL PROFILE

Difficulty Level Advanced

Special Features This system illustrates the use of the MENU clause. It is used here to generate a menu of program names. Program names are contained in a dBASE database file. Another database file contains the names of the data files that each program accesses. Also used in this prototype is the WHILETRUE clause to create a program loop for a repetitive sequence in the knowledge base.

Files Used FIXER.KBS (KBS file) and FILES.DBF and PROGRAMS.DBF (dBASE database files)

To Run Load FIXER.KBS from the disk accompanying this book

OVERVIEW

As many independent programmers and other computer professionals know, Murphy's law definitely applies to computer systems: Whatever *can* go wrong, *will* go wrong. It is common for programmers to spend a considerable amount of time answering a client's questions and solving problems that occur after a new computer system is installed. Unfortunately, a programmer's time is limited. But every client wants an immediate solution to his or her problem.

The majority of problems encountered when running a computer system are of a recurring nature and relatively simple to fix. In many cases, once they are diagnosed, computer system problems can be corrected by the client organization itself. An expert system designed to make clients capable of handling some problems on their own goes a long way toward making the computer system more efficient. Also, reducing service calls allows independent programmers and consultants more time to seek new clients and generate new revenue.

STUDYING THE SITUATION

This prototype expert system diagnoses problems that occur while a client runs accounts receivable and billing computer systems. All problems relate to files, which can be either programs or data files.

These computer systems were developed by an independent programmer for various small businesses. The programs are written in Microsoft COBOL or BASIC and run on IBM-compatible microcomputers.

Although each client's system is different, all systems follow the same logical theme. They consist of a series of programs linked together by a Main Menu. Each program is essentially a stand-alone unit, but it shares common data files. The three different data file types used by programs are called indexed, random, and sequential. Errors in these data files are the concern of the proposed expert system.

The Microsoft COBOL compiler generates a file status code after each disk operation. This code is extremely useful in determining what kind of problem, if any, exists on the disk.

If the compiler generated an error message every time something went wrong, there would be no need for this system. Unfortunately, this is not the case. Errors are generated whenever a data file's index structure is damaged. But errors are not generated when the data file's record structure is damaged. Figure 10B–1 gives two examples of data file record structures. Instead, a corrupted record structure usually results in incorrect or garbled data retrieved on a disk read and a system crash on a disk write. The lack of any error or file identification makes finding a solution to this type of problem difficult.

A Typical Problem Scenario

In a typical problem scenario, the XYZ Company, a client of Carl Bacon, an independent programmer, is having a problem saving invoices. Whenever the data entry specialist types in an invoice and then tries to save the transaction, the system crashes. At 10 P.M. Mr. Bacon is called in to correct the problem.

First he tries to create and save a test invoice, which works fine. When he tries a second time, the error reoccurs. The error results in the message "Run Time Error Line 3042, Non-Numeric Data." Mr. Bacon tries to create a third test invoice, and a save action results in the message "Object Error." These messages, and the lack of any file name and error number, result in the determination that the problem is a "File in Error."

Next the programmer examines other programs in the system that use the same files as the invoice data entry program. He tries the customer file data entry program, and it works properly. The inventory file data entry program also works. He then tries a program that manipulates the open invoice file, a file containing the balance due on each invoice. This program gives similar strange error messages. Mr. Bacon concludes that the problem must be in this open invoice file. Since the open invoice file is indexed, the error could be either in its record structure or its index structure. Using information obtained earlier when deciding this is a "File in Error" problem, he concludes that the "Type of Error" must be in the file's record structure.

The "Type of Disk Access" is determined next with the knowledge that the invoice entry program is an online program, doing a relatively small amount of disk writing. The damaged file could be restored independently of the other system files and no backup disk is required.

The open invoice file is "recreated." Mr. Bacon runs the utility program, "Recreate open invoice file," to recreate this file using information from other files in the database. This is the solution to the problem, and the XYZ company is now able to enter the actual invoices without further problems.

Critical Factors

Four critical factors are evaluated in the Computer File Fixer Expert System to determine a final recommendation.

File in Error. This is the single most important critical factor. Determining the value of this factor involves a procedure that scans two databases of information. They are identified in Figure 10B–1. The "Programs" database is a control file that triggers a search into the "Files" database to learn the actual names of files involved in a problem.

Two related factors, identified in Figure 10B–2, are learned from a scan of the "Files" database:

- *Recreate.* This file contains a yes (Y) or no (N) value, which indicates if this file can be recreated from other files in the database.
- *Type of File.* File type can be either indexed, random, or sequential.

Figure 10B–1. Computer File Fixer Expert System: Structure and Content for Two Database Files

A. "Programs" Database File: Record Data Structure

Field Number	Field Name	Description	Size (in bytes)
1	Prog_Name	Program name	30
2	Key_Prog	Key program (Y = yes N = no)	1
3	Prog_Type	Program type: Batch read = BR Batch write = BW Online = OL	2
4	File_1	(Names of files	
...	...	used by the program	(12 × 5)
8	File_5	identified in the first field Prog_Name)	

"Programs" Database File: Record Data Content

Prog_Name	Key_ Prog	Prog_ Type	Cross Reference to Check in the "Files" Database File_1	File_2	File_3	File_4	File_5
Edit Inventory File	Y	OL	Inventory				
Edit Customer File	Y	OL	Customer				
Edit Invoices	N	OL	Invoice	Inventory	Customer		
Display Invoices	Y	BR	Invoice				
Print Invoices	N	BR	Invoice				
Print Invoice List	N	BR	Invoice				
Invoice Posting Process	N	BW	Invoice	Inventory	Customer	Open Invoice	Cust. Ledger
Invoice Costing/Profit	N	BR	Invoice	Inventory			
Edit A/R Transactions	N	OL	Transaction	Customer			
Display A/R Transactions	Y	BR	Transaction				
Print A/R Transaction List	N	BR	Transaction				
Post A/R Transactions	N	BW	Transaction	Customer	Open Invoice	Cust. Ledger	
Enter Payments	N	OL	Open Invoice	Transaction	Customer		
Print Statements	N	BR	Cust. Ledger	Customer			
Display Statements	Y	BR	Cust. Ledger	Customer			
End of Month Process	N	BW	Cust. Ledger				
Balance Report	N	BR	Open Invoice	Customer			
Customer Directory	N	BR	Customer				
Mailing Labels	N	BR	Customer				
Price List	N	BR	Inventory				
Cost Sheet	N	BR	Inventory				
Accrued Monthly Sales	Y	BR	Open Invoice				
Edit A/P Transactions	Y	OL	Payable				
Print A/P Transactions	N	BR	Payable				
A/P End of Month Process	N	BR	Payable				

Type of Data Access. This factor depends mainly on the program the user was running when the error occurred. A database search, as well as user input, is needed to establish this critical factor. It enables the system to decide if it is necessary to restore all files.

Type of Error. This critical factor is established entirely through user input and results in "Data structure error," "Index structure error," or "Not known."

Backup Quality. This critical factor is only looked at if the other factors indicate that a backup is necessary. Its value is determined entirely by user input and is either "Good" or "Not good."

Figure 10B–1. *continued*

B. "Files" Database File: Record Data Structure

Field Number	Field Name	Description	Size (in bytes)
1	File_Name		12
2	File_Type	INDEXED, RANDOM, SEQUENTIAL	10
3	Recreate	"Y" = file can be recreated "N" = file cannot be recreated	1
4 ... 9	Actual1 ... Actual6	(Names of all data files in a logical group)	(12 × 6)

"Files" Database File: Record Data Content

File_Name	File_Type	Re-create	Actual1	Actual2	Actual3	Actual4	Actual5	Actual6
			Actual Name of Data Files in Use					
Inventory	Indexed	N	AST001.*					
Customer	Indexed	N	AST002.*					
Invoice	Random	N	AST004.REL	AST005.REL	AST008.REL	AST009.REL	AST011.REL	AST012.REL
Transaction	Random	N	AST007.REL	AST010.REL	AST013.REL			
Cust. Ledger	Sequential	N	AST006.SEQ					
Payable	Sequential	N	AST016.REL					
Open Invoice	Indexed	Y	AST014.*					

Figure 10B–2. Computer File Fixer Expert System: Block Diagram of the Decision Situation

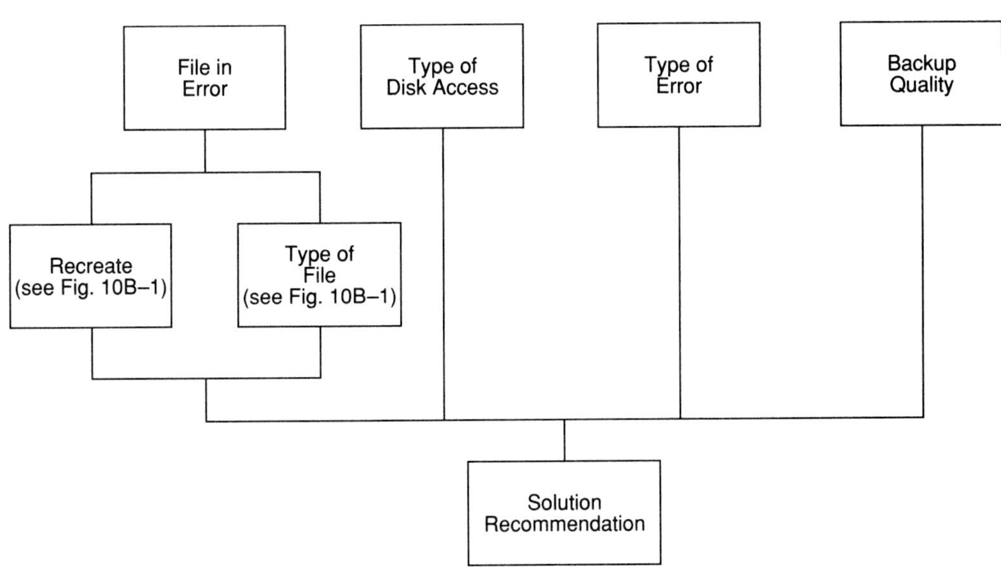

Questions Asked by the System

The sample consultation in Figure 10B–3 shows examples of the questions asked by the Computer File Fixer prototype system. In this case, a user has encountered an error in the "Edit A/R Transaction" program. (The A/R means

Figure 10B–3. Computer File Fixer Expert System: Sample Consultation

```
COMPUTER FILE FIXER EXPERT SYSTEM

Developed by Daniel Dubinsky
under the direction and supervision of
Dr. D.G. Dologite
```

Text only

```
Computer File Fixer Expert System

This expert system will help you to find
the solution to disk problems when using
the Accounts Receivable and Billing System.
The program asks you a series of questions
about the situation and recommends a
solution to your problem.

Press any key to start consultation
```

Actual screen

```
Computer File Fixer Expert System

Which program were you using when the error occurred?

Edit Inventory File    Edit Customer File     Edit Invoices
Display Invoices       Print Invoices         Print Invoice List
Invoice Posting Proc   Invoice Costing/Pror   Edit A/R Transaction ◂
Display A/R Transact   Print A/R Transactio   Post.A/R Transaction
Enter Payments         Print Statements       Display Statements
End of Month Process   Balance Report         Customer Directory
Mailing Labels         Price List             Cost Sheet
Accrued Monthly Sale   Edit A/P Transaction   Print A/P Transactio
A/P End of Month Pro

Use the arrow keys to highlight the desired choice and press enter.
```

accounts receivable.) After a series of questions about the nature of the problem, the system concludes that the user should zap (erase) the Transaction File and create a new one. The system instructs the user on how to zap the file.

The exact questions asked in each consultation depend on which program is being run when the problem occurs, as well as on which answers a user gives to earlier questions. The Questions Block of the program listing, at the end of this system discussion, identifies all possible questions contained in the system.

Recommendations Given by the System

Figure 10B–4 gives the reduced decision table for the final recommendations made by this system. Seven possible recommendations can be made.

1. *Rebuild the file:* This is displayed if the system decides that the error is in the file's index structure. It involves using a COBOL utility program to rebuild the index of a damaged file.
2. *Recreate the file:* This is displayed if the file can be recreated and the error is in the file's data structure. In some cases, a file can be completely recreated using bits of information found in other files in the system. This involves calling a utility program.

Actual screen

```
Computer File Fixer Expert System

Did you get a screen error message indicating filename and error no.?

 Yes                      No ◄

Is the program Edit Customer File working properly?

 Yes                      No                         Dont Know ◄

Is the program Display A/R Transactions working properly?
 Yes                      No ◄                       Dont Know

Use the arrow keys to highlight the desired choice and press enter.
```

Text only

```
Did the computer freeze up or crash?
 Yes                      No ◄

Did garbled or incorrect information appear?
 Yes ◄                    No

Do you have a good backup disk?
 Yes                      No ◄



Final Recommendation

You should zap the Transaction File.
Use the fixer program included with the package.

    At the C:\> prompt type FIXER.
    Enter your password.
    Select Zap Transaction file from the Main Menu.
    Note: Zap will erase the Transaction File and create
          a new one.  You will have to retype the information.

Press any key to continue.
```

Figure 10B–4. Compute File Fixer Expert System: Reduced Decision Table—Final Rule Set

Rule	Type_of_File	Type_of_Error	Type_of_Access	Backup_Quality	Re-creatable	Solution
1	Sequential	Index	—	—	—	Impossible
2	Random	Index	—	—	—	Impossible
3	—	—	Major	Good	—	Restore all
4	—	—	Major	Bad	—	Call
5	Indexed	Index	Minor	—	—	Rebuild
6	Indexed	Data	Minor	—	Yes	Recreate
7	Indexed	Data	Minor	Good	No	Restore
8	Indexed	Data	Minor	Bad	No	Call
9	Random	Data	Minor	Good	—	Restore
10	Random	Data	Minor	Bad	—	Zap
11	Sequential	Data	Minor	Good	—	Restore
12	Sequential	Data	Minor	Bad	—	Call

3. *Restore the file:* If a file is damaged beyond repair or if there is no way to accurately recreate the file from other files in the system, the only option is to restore the file from a backup disk. This solution uses the DOS COPY command.
4. *Restore all files:* If an error occurs during one of the disk writing operations, the only solution is to restore all files from backups and start over again.
5. *Zap file:* If a temporary file becomes corrupted and no backup is available, the file must be zapped (erased). The user then must reenter the information it contained. All temporary files in the system are random files that contain a list of invoices or transactions. They are used to store daily activity. At the end of each day a user runs a posting program that updates permanent files from these temporary files. Usually there is little more than a few hours work in this type of file.
6. *Impossible:* If certain critical factors conflict, then a correct recommendation cannot be made. The solution cannot be determined from the entered information.
7. *Call:* If a backup is necessary and no backup is available, the only solution is to call the programmer.

A final recommendation informs the user of what action is necessary to correct the problem. It also gives the *procedure* to follow to complete the corrective action. For example, if the final recommendation is "Restore all files," the system informs the user to

- Use the Restore choice from the Backup/Restore Menu.
- At the C:\ prompt type ASSIST.
- Select Backup\Restore Files from the Main Menu.
- Select Restore Data Files from the Backup/Restore Menu.
- Follow the directions on screen.

This step-by-step instruction is another feature of the system that makes it easier for a user to solve problems without assistance from the programmer.

SYSTEM DOCUMENTATION

The dependency diagram in Figure 10B–5 shows the relationships among the critical factors, input questions, rules, values, and recommendations for the prototype expert system. A complete listing of the knowledge base files appears in Figure 10B–6.

Design Considerations

Most of the Computer File Fixer knowledge base conforms nicely to the typical pattern of expert system design. Almost all of the critical factors could be established with decision tables and rule sets.

The only critical factor that was difficult to design was "File in Error." If the user does not know which file is causing the problem, its discovery becomes the responsibility of the expert system. This could not be accomplished through conventional means. The only way to determine the file in error without a direct screen message to a user is to examine other programs in the system, find those not working properly, and see which files are common among them. Each system contains about 40 programs, and each program can access up to six files. The number of rules required to check each program against others for matching files would quickly become unmanageable.

Figure 10B–5. Computer File Fixer Expert System: Dependency Diagram

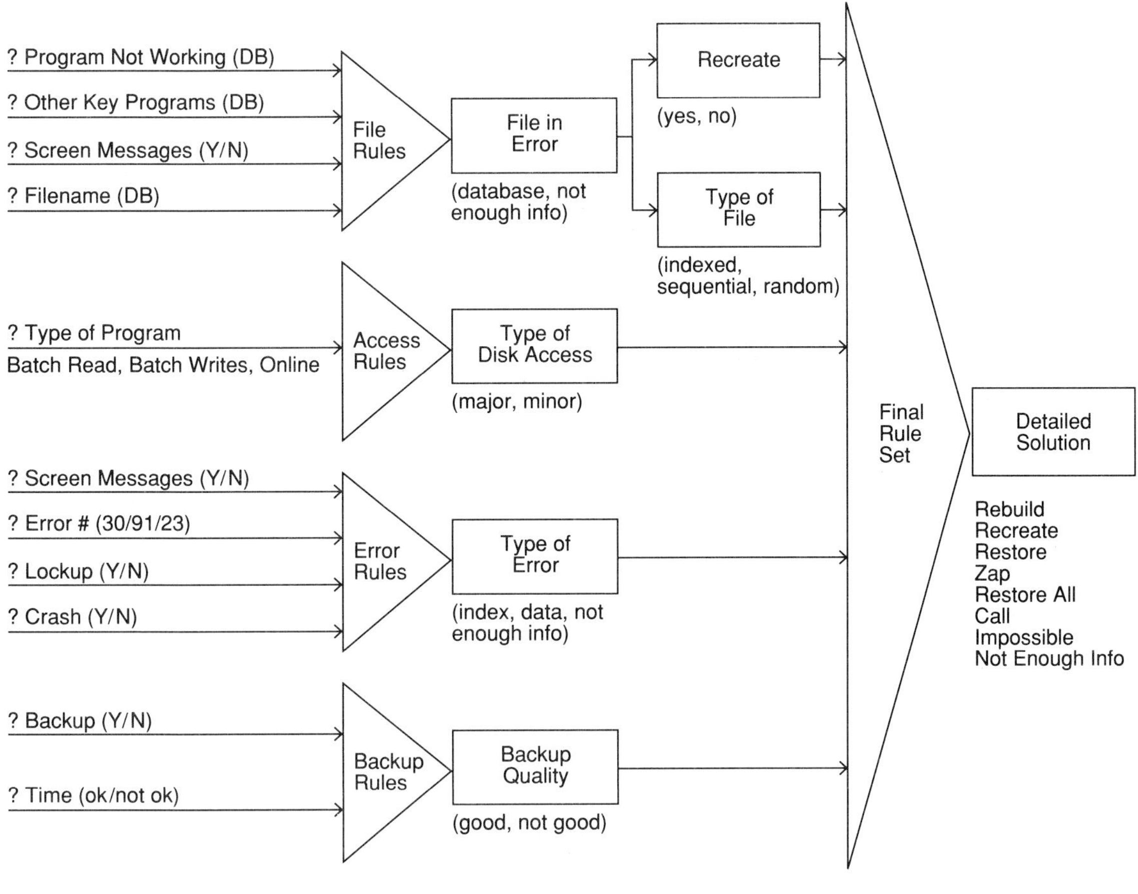

Figure 10B–6. Computer File Fixer Expert System: Printout of Knowledge Base File

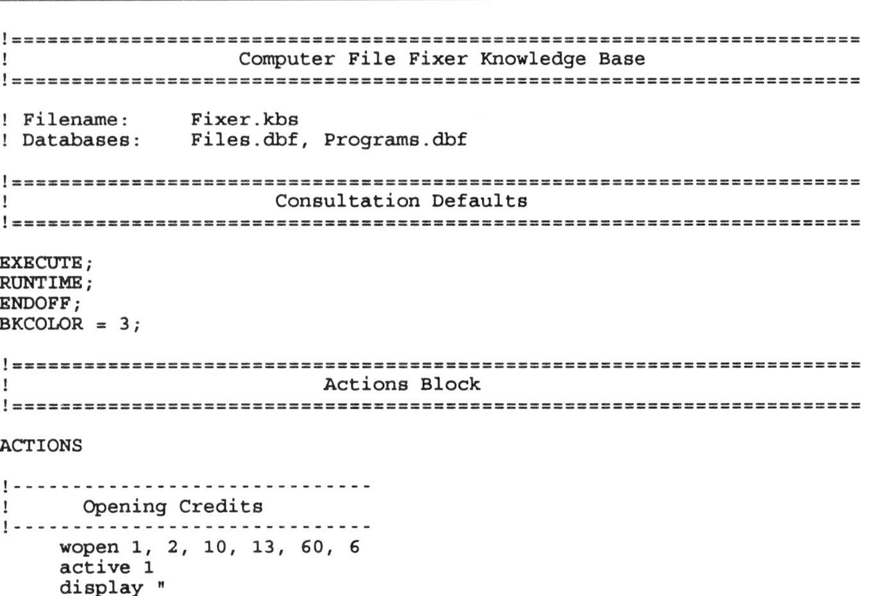

```
!=====================================================================
!                  Computer File Fixer Knowledge Base
!=====================================================================

! Filename:     Fixer.kbs
! Databases:    Files.dbf, Programs.dbf

!=====================================================================
!                        Consultation Defaults
!=====================================================================

EXECUTE;
RUNTIME;
ENDOFF;
BKCOLOR = 3;

!=====================================================================
!                            Actions Block
!=====================================================================

ACTIONS

!------------------------------
!     Opening Credits
!------------------------------
     wopen 1, 2, 10, 13, 60, 6
     active 1
     display "
```

Figure 10B–6. *continued*

```
          COMPUTER FILE FIXER EXPERT SYSTEM

             Developed by Daniel Dubinsky
        under the direction and supervision of
                  Dr. D.G. Dologite
           For further information, contact
                  Dr. D.G. Dologite
               c/o Macmillan Publishing


               Press any key to continue~"


!------------------------------
!       Introduction
!------------------------------

     wclose 1
     wopen 1, 2, 10, 13, 60, 6
     active 1
     display "

          Computer File Fixer Expert System

        This expert system will help you to find
        the solution to disk problems when using
        the Accounts Receivable and Billing System.
        The program asks you a series of questions
        about the situation and recommends a
        solution to your problem.


          Press any key to start consultation ~"


! --------------------------
! Set Up Consultation Screen
! --------------------------
     wclose 1
     wopen 2, 0, 20, 3, 40, 7
     wopen 3, 19, 0, 3, 79, 7
     wopen 4, 5, 1, 12, 77, 6
     active 2
     display "   Computer File Fixer Expert System"
     active 3
     display "    Use the arrow keys to highlight the desired choice and press
enter."
     active 4


! ---------------------------------------------------------
! Database Procedure with File Rules (below) to get Program
! Not Working, Program Type, File in Error, File Type
! ---------------------------------------------------------
     EOF = EOF
     FLAG = Y
     MENU program_not_working,EOF <>PROG_NAME,programs,prog_name
     FIND program_not_working
     MRESET program_not_working
     CLS
     GET program_not_working = prog_name, programs, ALL
     possible_file = (file_1)
     possible_file = (file_2)
     possible_file = (file_3)
     possible_file = (file_4)
     possible_file = (file_5)
     prog_type = (prog_type)
     CLOSE programs

     MENU name_of_file, possible_file = FILE_NAME, files, FILE_NAME
     RESET file_dummy

     COUNT possible_file, filecount
     FIND file_in_error
     WHILETRUE file_in_error = UNKNOWN OR file_in_error = not_yet THEN
          RESET key_prog_working
          GET EOF = PROG_NAME OR
                    flag = KEY_PROG AND
                    possible_file = FILE_1 AND
                    program_not_working <> PROG_NAME,
                                        programs,ALL
```

```
        file_1 = (FILE_1)
        prog_name = (PROG_NAME)
        FIND file_dummy
        file_in_error = (file_dummy)
        RESET file_dummy
    END
    MRESET files

    GET file_in_error = file_name, files, ALL
    Type_of_file = (file_type)
    recreateable = (recreate)
    file_to_restore = (actual1)
    file_to_restore = (actual2)
    file_to_restore = (actual3)
    file_to_restore = (actual4)
    file_to_restore = (actual5)
    file_to_restore = (actual6)
   CLOSE files
! -----------------------------------
! Transfer Control To rules Block
! -----------------------------------

    FIND solution

! -----------------------------------
! Reset Screen Windows
! -----------------------------------

    wclose 1
    wclose 3
    wclose 4
    wclose 2

! ------------------------------
! Get Text Associated with Solution
! ------------------------------
    wopen 1, 2, 5, 18, 70, 6
    active 1
    display "Final Recommendation"
    display " "
    Find Text
    Display " "
    Display "Press any key to continue. ~";

! =================================================================
!                               Rules Block
! =================================================================
! ------------------------------
! Rules for Solution Text
! ------------------------------

    RULE Text1
    IF solution = not_known
    THEN text = found
    DISPLAY "The information you have given is not sufficient to"
    DISPLAY "make a recommendation. Please check your information"
    DISPLAY "and try again.";

    RULE Text2
    IF solution = Impossible
    THEN text = found
    DISPLAY "The information you have given is conflicting. "
    DISPLAY "Please check your information and try again.";

    RULE Text3
    IF solution = Call
    THEN text = found
    DISPLAY "You have a real problem. You had better call the programmer.";

    RULE Text4
    IF solution = Restore_All
    THEN text = found
    DISPLAY "You should restore all of the files from backup."
    DISPLAY "Use the Restore choice from the Backup/Restore Menu."
    DISPLAY "                                         "
    DISPLAY "   At the C:\> prompt type ASSIST"
    DISPLAY "   Select Backup/Restore Files from the Main Menu"
    DISPLAY "   Select Restore Data Files from the Backup/Restore Menu"
    DISPLAY "   Follow the directions on screen";
```

Figure 10B–6. *continued*

```
    RULE Text5
    IF solution = Restore
    THEN Text = found
    DISPLAY "You should restore the {file_in_error} File."
    DISPLAY "Use the DOS copy command."
    DISPLAY " "
    DISPLAY "    At the C:\> prompt insert your latest backup disk in drive."
    DISPLAY "    Type Copy A:\<filename> C:\ASSIST once for each file listed."
    DISPLAY " "
    DISPLAY "File names:"
    DISPLAY "{file_to_restore}";

    RULE Text6
    IF solution = rebuild or
       solution = recreate
    THEN text = found

    DISPLAY "You should {Solution} the {file_in_error} File."
    DISPLAY "Use the fixer program included with the package."
    DISPLAY " "
    DISPLAY "    At the C:\> prompt type FIXER."
    DISPLAY "    Enter your password."
    DISPLAY "    Select {solution} {file_in_error} file from the Main Menu.";

    RULE Text7
    If solution = zap
    THEN text = found
    DISPLAY "You should zap the {file_in_error} File."
    DISPLAY "Use the fixer program included with the package."
    DISPLAY "    "
    DISPLAY "    At the C:\> prompt type FIXER."
    DISPLAY "    Enter your password."
    DISPLAY "    Select Zap {file_in_error} file from the Main Menu."
    DISPLAY "    Note: Zap will erase the {file_in_error} File and create"
    DISPLAY "          a new one. You will have to retype the information.";

! ---------------------------------
! Rules for "Not enough information"
! ---------------------------------

    RULE Stop1
    IF file_in_error = not_known
    THEN solution = not_known;

    RULE Stop2
    IF type_of_error = not_known
    THEN solution = not_known;


! ----------------------------------
! Final Rule Set: Solution to Problem
! ----------------------------------

    RULE Final1
    IF type_of_file = sequential AND
       type_of_error = index
    THEN solution = Impossible;

    RULE Final2
    IF type_of_file = random AND
       type_of_error = index
    THEN solution = Impossible;

    RULE Final3
    IF Type_of_Access = Major AND
       Backup_quality = Good
    THEN solution = Restore_all;

    RULE Final4
    IF Type_of_Access = Major AND
       Backup_quality = bad
    THEN solution = Call;

    RULE Final5
    IF Type_of_file = indexed AND
       Type_of_error = index  AND
       Type_of_access = minor
    THEN solution = Rebuild;
```

```
RULE Final6
IF Type_of_file = indexed AND
   Type_of_error = data AND
   Type_of_access = minor AND
   Recreateable = Y
THEN solution = Recreate;

RULE Final7
IF Type_of_file = indexed AND
   Type_of_error = data AND
   Type_of_access = minor AND
   Backup_quality = good AND
   Recreateable = N
THEN solution = Restore;

RULE Final8
IF Type_of_file = indexed AND
   Type_of_error = data AND
   Type_of_access = minor AND
   Backup_quality = bad AND
   Recreateable = N
THEN solution = Call;

RULE Final9
IF Type_of_file = random AND
   Type_of_error = Data AND
   Type_of_access = Minor AND
   Backup_quality = good
THEN solution = Restore;

RULE Final10
IF Type_of_file = random AND
   Type_of_error = Data AND
   Type_of_access = Minor AND
   Backup_quality = bad
THEN solution = Zap;

RULE Final11
IF Type_of_file = Sequential AND
   Type_of_error = data AND
   Type_of_access = minor AND
   Backup_quality = good

THEN solution = Restore;

Rule Final12
IF Type_of_file = Sequential AND
   Type_of_error = data AND
   Type_of_access = minor AND
   Backup_quality = bad
THEN solution = Call;


! -------------------------------------------------------
! Rule Set with Database Proc (above) to find File in Error
! -------------------------------------------------------

RULE File0
  IF prog_type = BW
  THEN file_in_error = all;

RULE File1
  IF filecount = 1
  THEN file_in_error = (FILE_1);

RULE File2
  IF screen_message = yes
  THEN find name_of_file
       file_in_error = (name_of_file);

RULE File3
  IF PROG_NAME = EOF
  THEN file_dummy = not_known;

RULE File4
  IF key_prog_working = no
  THEN file_dummy = (FILE_1);

RULE File5
  IF key_prog_working = yes
  OR key_prog_working = dont_know
  THEN file_dummy = not_yet;
```

Figure 10B–6. *continued*

```
! ---------------------
! Type of Error Rule Set
! ---------------------

    RULE Error1
      IF screen_message = no
      AND lockup = no
      AND bad_data = no
      THEN Type_of_error = not_known;

    RULE Error2
      IF screen_message = no
      AND lockup = yes
      THEN Type_of_error = data;

    RULE Error3
      IF screen_message = no
      AND bad_data = yes
      THEN Type_of_error = data;

    RULE Error4
      IF screen_message = yes
      AND error_number = 91
      THEN Type_of_error = index;

    RULE Error5
      IF screen_message = yes
      AND error_number = 30
      THEN type_of_error = data;

    RULE Error6
      IF screen_message = yes
      AND error_number = 23
      THEN type_of_error = data;

! ----------------------
! Type of Access Rule Set
! ----------------------

    RULE Access1
      IF prog_type = BW
      THEN type_of_access = major;

    RULE Access2
      IF prog_type = BR
      THEN type_of_access = minor;

   RULE Access3
      IF prog_type = OL
      THEN type_of_access = minor;


! ----------------------
! Backup Quality Rule Set
! ----------------------

    RULE Backup1
      IF Backup = Yes
      AND Time = OK
      THEN Backup_quality = good;

    RULE Backup2
      IF Backup = no
      THEN Backup_quality = bad;

    RULE Backup3
      IF Time = Not_ok
      THEN backup_quality = bad;
```

```
! ======================================================================
!                          Questions Block
! ======================================================================

    ASK program_not_working:
        "Which program were you using when the error occurred?
                                                              ";
    ASK key_prog_working:
        "Is the program {PROG_NAME} working properly?
                                                         ";
    CHOICES key_prog_working: Yes,No,Dont_Know;

    ASK screen_message:
    "Did you get a screen error message indicating filename and error no.?
                                                         ";
    CHOICES screen_message: Yes, No;

    ASK error_number:
    "Which error number did you see on the screen?
                                                        ";
    CHOICES error_number: 91, 30, 23;

    ASK name_of_file:
    "Which file was it?
                                                        ;
    ASK Lockup:
    "Did the computer freeze up or crash?
                                                        ";
    Choices lockup: Yes, No;

    ASK Bad_data:
    "Did garbled or incorrect information appear?
                                                        ";
    CHOICES Bad_data: Yes, No;

    ASK Backup:
    "Do you have a good backup disk?
                                                       ";
    CHOICES backup:Yes,No;

    ASK Time:
    "Remember, you will lose all work done since last backup was made.
    Is the amount of time since your last backup acceptable?
                                                        ";
    CHOICES time: Ok, Not_Ok;

    PLURAL: possible_file, file_to_restore;
```

The solution to this problem was to use program and file databases, as shown in Figure 10B–1, instead of rules. The databases are examined in a loop using the WHILETRUE statement, with the user being prompted for input when necessary. The loop is designed to search for a key program that uses the same file as the program that is creating the user's problem. Then, by asking the user whether the found program is working properly, the knowledge base can establish which file is causing the problem.

The databases also serve to make the expert system both easier to transfer to different clients and simpler to modify.

10C

Computer Job Scheduler Assistant

TECHNICAL PROFILE

Difficulty Level	Advanced
Special Features	This prototype system is designed to be used as a training tool. Its code illustrates the use of the WHILETRUE and WHENEVER keywords. A Help option is made available to users during the question and answer session.
Files Used	PROJECT.KBS (main KBS file), PROJECT2.KBS (linked KBS file), TEMP (temporary file to store consultation answers transferred between the two KBS files), and VALID.DBF (dBASE database file to hold consultation validation values).
To Run	Load PROJECT.KBS from the disk accompanying this book.

OVERVIEW

Note: This system deals with the technical area of computer job scheduling. It is necessary to include a certain amount of technical jargon to sufficiently describe the system. An effort has been made to clarify selected terms without overburdening the non-technical reader.

The Computer Job Scheduler Assistant prototype system helps schedule a computer maintenance job and verify that it ran successfully. This job, called the CXAJM81H production job, represents 1 of 10 production jobs that maintain a Patient Accounting Database and Reporting System (PADBARS) for a large hospital. The job is the final step in processing patient discharges. It assigns costs, generates revenue figures, and updates database information for all discharged patients. Scheduling the CXAJM81H job is done by a trained job scheduler.

New hires find the scheduling job difficult to learn. In addition, a supervisor does not always have time to fully explain the procedure or its complex processes and interrelationships with other sub-systems.

This prototype expert system is used as a training tool by new job schedulers. It provides guidelines for performing the computer job scheduling and verification task. It helps to maximize the learning experience for a new job scheduler and to free the supervisor's time for other work. The Computer Job Scheduler Assistant also can provide an automated, self-documenting double check of job accuracy for experienced schedulers.

STUDYING THE SITUATION

The initial task to be prototyped is scheduling the database maintenance process. As diagrammed in Figure 10C–1, it is supported by three general areas within the Management Information System/Cost Accounting Systems department: Applications Maintenance/Development, Hospital Facility Liaison, and General Ledger Services. The initial prototype has been narrowed to the Applications Maintenance/Development area. It is responsible for analyzing, coding, and implementing all changes to the PADBARS database. These changes include both routine maintenance and new development.

Figure 10C–1. Computer Job Scheduler Assistant: Block Diagram of Decision Situation

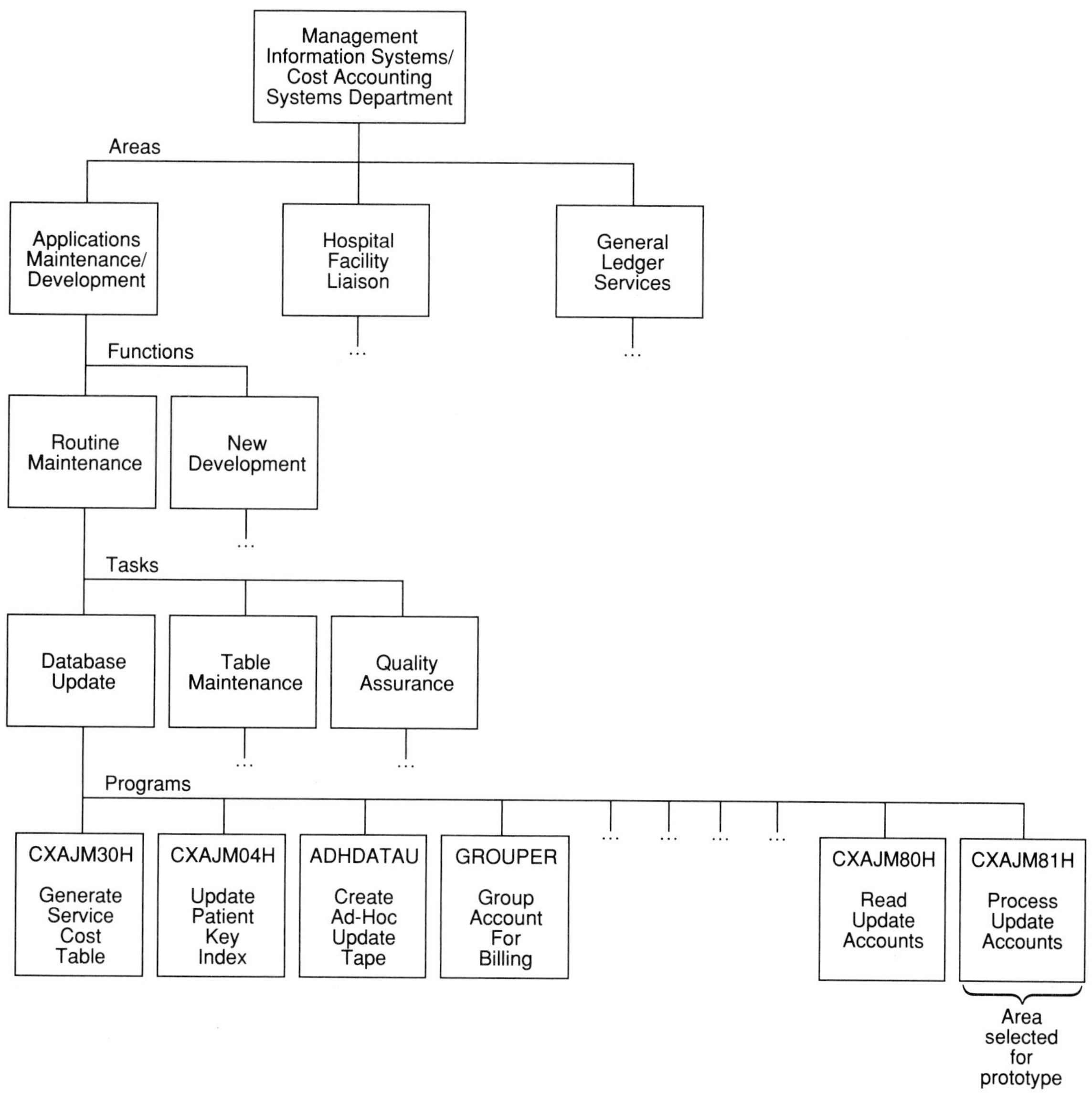

The prototype has further been narrowed to include only the routine maintenance tasks that the Applications Maintenance/Development area performs. Routine maintenance includes database updating, maintenance of tabular (table) data in relevant programs, and quality assurance. The routine maintenance task chosen to be prototyped is the database updating process. Database updating is performed by scheduling, running, and verifying 10 computer programs on a mainframe computer. One of the 10, the CXAJM81H program, was chosen to be the subject of this sample prototype. This program reads in raw patient information, applies costs, and generates patient revenue figures.

Critical Factors

The critical factors considered by the Computer Job Scheduler Assistant are examined in two groups: scheduling the update job and verifying the successful completion of the job. Figures 10C–2 and 10C–3 show diagrams of the two modules in this system and identify their critical factors. Figure 10C–4 shows the possible values, along with their explanations, for each of the critical factors in the two modules.

Scheduling. To properly schedule the CXAJM81H job, the first step is to track and verify the new input *tape*. Once the input tape is ready, all necessary *changes* are made to the revenue *rate* tables and to the program *code*.

Each step must be successfully completed before the CXAJM81H job can be scheduled. The true functionality of this prototype system is to help job schedulers to remember to perform all the necessary tasks, verify their completion, and prevent errors in the database updating process.

There are four critical factors for the scheduling module:

1. *Tape:* The CXAJM81H job requires an input tape, named the CX.CMNDLOS.PROD tape, that contains the raw patient data to be updated. The first step for a job scheduler is to determine that the input tape is current, that there are no write errors recorded, and that the block count is correct (that there are a reasonable number of records.)

Figure 10C–2. Computer Job Scheduler Assistant: Block Diagram for Scheduling and Verifying Modules

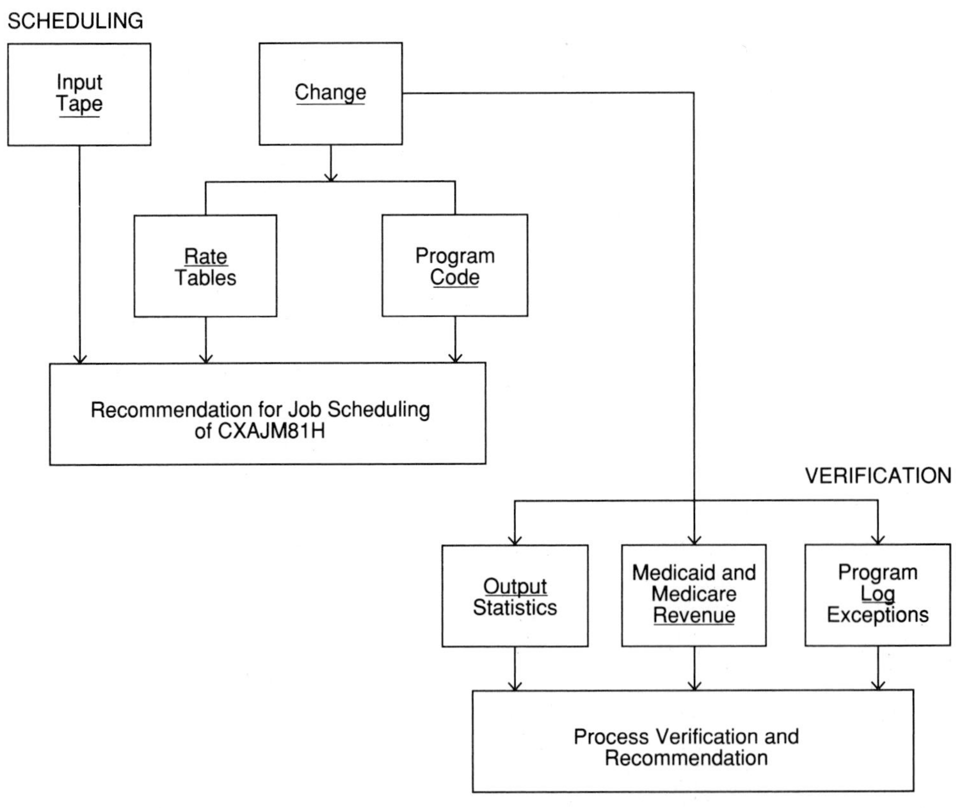

Figure 10C–3. Computer Job Scheduler Assistant: Dependency Diagram

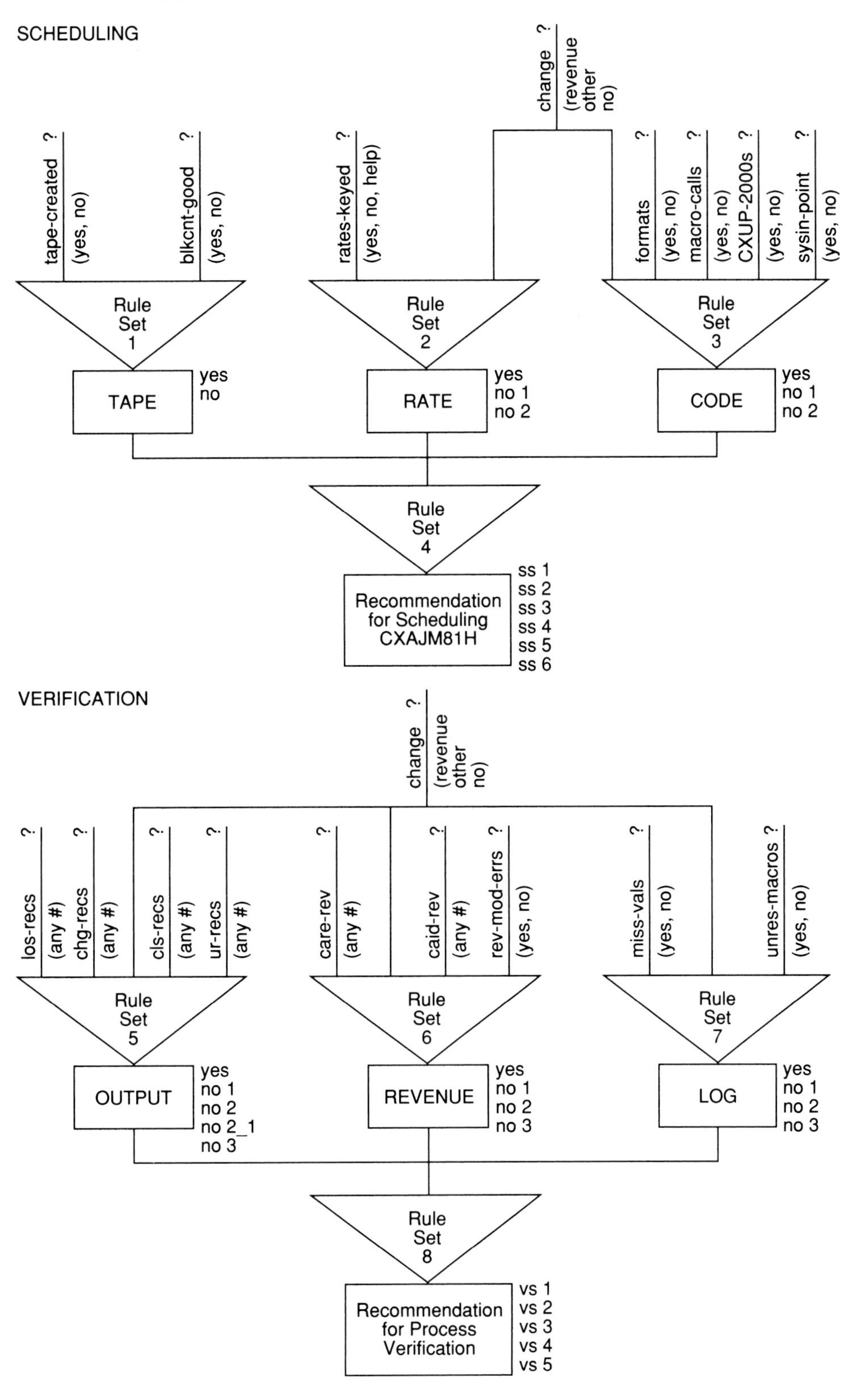

Figure 10C–4. Computer Job Scheduler Assistant: Explanation of Critical Factor Values

A. Module I—Scheduling

Critical Factor	Possible Values	Explanation
Tape	Yes	The input tape is ready for scheduling.
	No	The input tape is not ready for scheduling.
Change	Revenue	A new revenue scheme is active and changes need to be completed before scheduling CXAJM81H.
	Other	Some other change is occurring to the update process.
	No	No changes are occurring to the update process.
Rate	Yes	The revenue rate tables are ready for scheduling.
	No1	The revenue rate tables should not have been changed.
	No2	The revenue rate tables need to be changed.
Code	Yes	All program code is ready for scheduling.
	No1	The program code should not have been changed.
	No2	The program code needs to be changed.

B. Module II—Verification

Critical Factor	Possible Values	Explanation
Output	Yes	Record output is in valid range.
	No1	Record output is not in valid range due to a change in the data and not in the process.
	No2	Record output is not in valid range due to a change in the revenue module.
	No3	Record output is not in valid range due to a change in the revenue module and the data.
	No4	Record output is not in valid range due to an unspecified change to the process and/or data.
Revenue	Yes	Total revenue generated is in valid range.
	No1	Total revenue generated is not in valid range due to a change in the data and not the process.
	No2	Total revenue generated is not in valid range due to a change in the revenue module.
	No3	Total revenue generated is not in valid range due to a change in the process.
Log	Yes	There is no indication of any problems according to the log.
	No1	There is an indication of a problem in the log due to a change in the data.
	No2	There is an indication of a problem in the log due to a change in the revenue module.
	No3	There is an indication of a problem in the log due to a change in the process.

2. *Change:* The second step is to determine if any changes are required and what kind. There are many reasons why the CXAJM81H job may require changes. For example, a new revenue scheme requires new revenue rate tables and changes to the program code.
3. *Rate:* One of the functions of the CXAJM81H job is to generate billable revenue for patient discharges. The revenue generation task relies on many rate tables. If, for example, Medicare initiates a new rate scheme, the job scheduler needs to enter and verify the new rates in a table.
4. *Code:* The final step for a job scheduler is to determine and complete the necessary program module changes. The revenue-generating module usually requires most of the changes.

Verification. Once the job scheduler completes the scheduling and subsequent submission and completion of CXAJM81H, he or she needs to verify that it completed successfully. There are three critical factors that determine if the job completed successfully or requires changes and rescheduling:

1. *Output:* There are four program modules in CXAJM81H—patient records, charge records, classification records, and utilization review records—which produce individual output files. The number of records generated by each helps to determine if the process worked or possibly what went wrong.
2. *Revenue:* The revenue module reports how much money was generated for billing. The total dollars generated for each payor (Medicaid and Medicare) helps to determine if something is wrong with the revenue module or the revenue rate tables.
3. *Log:* Each program module generates a syntax log that shows the inner workings of the code during execution. The log is used to determine many kinds of problems and is the leading verification factor.

For each of the critical factors considered here, the prototype expert system asks users questions such as those shown in the sample consultation in Figure 10C–5.

Figure 10C–6 identifies the record structure and sample record content for the database file VALID.DBF. This file is designed to hold historical values to verify responses given by the user for Tape (the block count of the input tape), Output (the number of patient, charge, classification, and utilization records outputted), and Revenue (the amount of Medicare and Medicaid revenue generated). For the purpose of this prototype, all initial values are set to 1000. If the user inputs a value of at least 1000 for each of these factors, the system considers them to be acceptable.

Final Recommendations

The expert system makes two sets of recommendations, one for scheduling support and one for verification support. These are the possible recommendations for scheduling support (ss):

- *ss1:* All the scheduling critical factors are ready for submission of CXAJM81H. Schedule CXAJM81H.
- *ss2:* The code was changed when no change was required. Do not schedule CXAJM81H.
- *ss3:* The code required a change and the change was not completed. Do not schedule CXAJM81H.
- *ss4:* The revenue rate tables were changed when no rate change was required. Do not schedule CXAJM81H.

Figure 10C–5. Computer Job Scheduler Assistant: Sample Consultation

```
COMPUTER JOB SCHEDULER ASSISTANT

Developed by Jason Oliveira
under the direction and supervision of
Dr. D.G. Dologite
```

Text only

```
Computer Job Scheduler Assistant

This system is designed to be used as a training
tool for job schedulers. It helps to schedule
the CXAJM81H job. It then assists to verify
the completed job.

Please press any key to continue.


Has the CXAJM81H job been scheduled yet?
 yes                     no ◂

Has the CX.CMNDLOS.PROD tape been created successfully?
 yes ◂                   no                        help

What is the block count of the CX.CMNDLOS.PROD tape?
 1001

The block count is good.

Indicate what, if any, change is being made to the update
process.
 revenue                 other                     none
 help ◂
```

Text only

```
How to Determine A Change to CXAJM81H

Revenue: If it is a November process month,
a new Medicare revenue needs to be loaded. If
it is a February process month, a new Medicaid
revenue scheme needs to be loaded.

Other: Any changes to the process in general, such as
reading a new field or adding a new sort. Any
changes to the format of the CX.CMNDLOS.PROD(0+)
input tape, such as a new record length.

None: No changes are necessary.

Press any key to continue consultation.

Indicate what, if any, change is being made to the update
process.
 revenue ◂               other                     none
 help

Have the new revenue rate tables been keyed and verified?
 yes ◂                   no                        help

Have the formats for the new revenue scheme been coded?
 yes ◂                   no

Have the Macro calls for the new revenue scheme been
added?
 yes ◂                   no
```

```
Have the necessary changes been made to the CXUP2001 -
CXUP2004 Programs?
 yes ◄                    no

Have the SYSINs been repointed to the CX.PADBARS.NEWCODE
library?
 yes ◄                    no


    Recommendation for Scheduling of CXAJM81H

    Based on your responses during this consultation, it
    has been determined that the input tape is ready, the
    revenue rate tables are ready, and the code is ready.
    CXAJM81H is ready to be scheduled for submission.

    Press any key to continue consultation.



Is the scheduled CXAJM81H job completed?
 yes ◄                    no

Loading Verification Assistant...

Loading File...

Enter how many patient records have been outputted.
 1

Enter how many charge records have been outputted.
 1001

Enter how many classification records have been outputted.
 1001

Enter how many utilization review records have been outputted.
 1001

Enter the total dollar amount generated for Medicare.
 900

Enter the total dollar amount generated for Medicaid.
 1001

Are there any errors reported by the revenue module?
 no ◄                    yes

Are there any missing values other than Alternate Level of Care
days in the Log?
 no ◄                    yes

Are there any unresolved Macro variables (error 513) in the
Log?
 no ◄                    yes



   Problem with Changed Revenue Module

   Based on your responses during this consultation, a change
   was made to the revenue module, but indicators show that the
   changes did not work.  Please review the changes and correct.
   The CXAJM81H job has NOT completed successfully.


   Press any key to continue consultation.

Are you finished with the Verification Assistant?
 yes ◄                    no
```

Figure 10C–6. Computer Job Scheduler Assistant: Record Structure and Content of VALID.DBF dBASE Database File

VALID.DBF Database Record Structure

Field	Field Name	Type	Width
1	KEY	Character	10
2	VAL1	Numeric	7
3	VAL2	Numeric	7
4	VAL3	Numeric	7
5	VAL4	Numeric	7

VALID.DBF Database Record Content

Record Number	KEY	VAL1	VAL2	VAL3	VAL4
1	output	1000	1000	1000	1000
2	tape	1000			
3	revenue	1000	1000		

- *ss5:* The revenue rate tables required a new revenue scheme and one was not added. Do not schedule CXAJM81H.
- *ss6:* The input tape is not ready. Please check CXAJM80H for a successful completion. Do not schedule CXAJM81H.

The possible final recommendations for the verification support (vs) of the correctness of the CXAJM81H job are as follows:

- *vs1:* All the verification critical factors indicate a successful completion of CXAJM81H.
- *vs2:* No change was made to the process, but verification factors indicate that the process requires a change to accommodate a change in the data. Also check and verify the input tape and the CXAJM80H syntax log. CXAJM81H has not completed successfully.
- *vs3:* A change was made to the revenue module, but indicators show that the changes did not work. Review and correct the changes. CXAJM81H has not completed successfully.
- *vs4:* A change was made to the revenue module, but indicators show a process-wide problem. Review and verify the input data and the changed code. CXAJM81H has not completed successfully.
- *vs5:* The change made to the process is not working. Review the syntax log to determine where and what the problem is. CXAJM81H has not completed successfully.

Figure 10C–7 shows the reduced decision tables for the critical factors and final recommendation of the scheduling module of the Computer Job Scheduler Assistant. Although not shown here, similar decision tables exist for the verification module.

Figure 10C–7. Computer Job Scheduler Assistant: Reduced Decision Tables—Scheduling Module

Rule Set 1: To Determine TAPE Critical Factor

Rule	Tape_created		Blkcnt_good	Tape
R11	Yes	&*	Yes	Yes
R12	No	|	No	No

Rule Set 2: To Determine RATE Critical Factor

Rule	Change†		Rates_keyed	Rate
R21	<> Revenue	&	Yes	No1
R22	<> Revenue	&	No	Yes
R23	Revenue	&	Yes	Yes
R24	Revenue	&	No	No2

Rule Set 3: To Determine the CODE Critical Factor

Rule	Change†		Formats		Macro_calls		cxup2000s		sysin_point	Code
R31	None	&	Yes	|	Yes	|	Yes	|	Yes	No1
R32	None	&	No	&	No	&	No	&	No	Yes
R33	Other	&	No	&	No	&	Yes	&	Yes	Yes
R34	Other	&	Yes	|	Yes		—		—	No1
R35	Other	&	—	|	—		No	|	No	No2
R36	Revenue	&	Yes	&	Yes	&	Yes	&	Yes	Yes
R37	Revenue	&	No	|	No	|	No	|	No	No2

Rule Set 4: To Determine Scheduling Support Recommendation

Rule	Tape	Rate	Code	SSUPPORT Value‡
R41	Yes	Yes	Yes	ss1
R42	—	—	No1	ss2
R43	—	—	No2	ss3
R44	—	No1	—	ss4
R45	—	No2	—	ss5
R46	No	—	—	ss6

*Logic operator key: | = OR; & = AND; <> = NOT; — = not in rule.

†The value of the critical factor Change is determined by a single user question. Change is also one of the variables used to determine the final value of the critical factors Rate and Code, as well as the values of each of the verification critical factors.

‡SSUPPORT is a plural variable and can be assigned more than one value during a consultation.

Typical Scenario

Job scheduler Carol Robinson is preparing to submit the CXAJM81H job to the computer department. It is the last step in the processing of data before writing it to the final patient discharge database file. It summarizes charges, generates revenue, and prepares utilization review and classification data. There have been a number of jobs and steps prior to this point that have taken two weeks to complete.

All processing is done on an IBM mainframe computer. Carol is connected to the mainframe through a terminal emulator board in her personal computer (PC) and is able to switch from the PC native mode to the mainframe mode by pressing the shift key.

Carol first needs to determine if the input source of information is ready for processing. The raw input data is recorded on a tape that was created by a previous program. She goes into the tape management system and queries it for the most recent copy of the tape. She then checks that the creation date is from the current month, that the block count is in a reasonable range, and that there are no write errors recorded for the tape. In this case, the most current tape is for the correct month, but it has a low block count. Carol, therefore, needs to check and/or re-run the previous program to properly create the tape. The next day the input tape is re-created and ready for processing.

She next needs to check if the process requires a change. A change can be in response to new revenue schemes, new data formats, or other improvements in the process. For example, the CXAJM81H job accesses Medicare and Medicaid revenue rate tables, which change and need to be updated every January and October. Because she is processing October discharges, Carol needs to key in the changed rates and verify the numbers with the reimbursement staff.

Since the new revenue rates necessitate a change to the program code, the code is copied to a test library and modified. The formats used for revenue generation are changed, as well as the macro calls that generate different revenue schemes. Other necessary changes, other than to the revenue module, are also made. All references to programs are done through the SYSIN Job Control Statement so "pointers" must be changed to direct the programs to the test library. These types of rate and program changes are the cause of 99 percent of all processing problems later in the job run.

A file called PARMFILE contains variables used by the entire database maintenance process. It includes information such as the discharge month, indicators of what data to archive, whether this is a first run or re-run, and so forth. The values of these variables are crucial. One mistake in a deletion indicator can wipe out three months of discharges and necessitate a reconstruction of the database. Carol needs to carefully keep track of what she is loading, what she is deleting, and whether it is a re-run or not.

After Carol completes these activities, she schedules the job. It completes without any program syntax errors.

Carol now must determine if the job processed correctly. She first checks the output record counts for the patient, charge, classification, and utilization review file modules created by CXAJM81H. She then examines the revenue module results. She checks the total dollars generated by the Medicare and Medicaid revenue schemes and looks for any reported errors. She finally checks the program log for any missing values or unresolved macro variables. Such conditions indicate a definite problem with CXAJM81H.

Unfortunately, Carol finds that zero dollars were generated for the Medicaid revenue scheme. She reviews the changed code and discovers that she misspelled the name of the new revenue rate table. She corrects the table name, re-schedules the CXAJM81H program, verifies the new output, and determines that it is now successfully completed.

SYSTEM DOCUMENTATION

A partial printout of the scheduling module of the Computer Job Scheduler Assistant is given in Figure 10C–8. The other verification module, PROJECT2.KBS, can be printed out from the disk accompanying this book.

In the sample consultation shown in Figure 10C–5, the scheduling module finds that the CXAJM81H database update program is ready to be run. After the job is completed, answers given in the verification consultation indicate that the job did *not* run correctly due to an error in changes made to the revenue module. In this case, the user should find and correct the error(s) and then re-run the program and check the new results.

Figure 10C–8. Computer Job Scheduler Assistant: Selections from Knowledge Base File

Note: Only selections from the main file, PROJECT.KBS, are given here. Other segments of this file can be examined further, along with the chained file PROJECT2.KBS, by printing them out from the disk accompanying this book.

```
! KBS Name    : The Computer Job Scheduler Assistant (Scheduling Support)
! Filename    : PROJECT.KBS
! Description: An expert system to be used as a tool for training new CXAJM81H job
                schedulers.
! Hardware    : IBM PC/XT DOS 3.3
! Shell       : VP-Expert educational version
! Files used  : PROJECT.KBS (Main KBS file: CXAJM81H Job Scheduling Consultation)
!               PROJECT2.KBS (Chained KBS file: CXAJM81H Job Verification
!                 Consultation)
!               VALID.DBF (dBASE file for database link: Consultation Validation
!                 Values)
ENDOFF;
EXECUTE;
RUNTIME;
BKCOLOR = 3;

ACTIONS
    WOPEN 1,1,1,20,77,3                      !Defines opening credit window
    ACTIVE 1
    DISPLAY "

                     COMPUTER JOB SCHEDULER ASSISTANT

                        Developed by Jason Oliveira
                    under the direction and supervision of
                              Dr. D.G. Dologite
                       For further information, contact
                              Dr. D.G. Dologite
                          c/o Macmillan Publishing


                   PRESS ANY KEY TO BEGIN CONSULTATION~
     "
     WCLOSE 1
     WOPEN 1,3,10,13,60,7                     !Defines opening window 1
     ACTIVE 1
     DISPLAY "

              Computer Job Scheduler Assistant

    This system is designed to be used as a training
    tool for job schedulers.  It helps to schedule
    the CXAJM81H job.  It then assists to verify
    the completed job.
```

Figure 10C–8. *continued*

```
          Please press any key to continue.~
     "
  WCLOSE 1
  WOPEN 2,1,1,5,77,2                     !Defines instructions window 2
  ACTIVE 2
  DISPLAY "                            Instructions
       Use the arrow keys to move the lightbar to a desired
       answer choice then press the Enter key."
  WOPEN 3,7,1,14,77,3                    !Defines consultation window 3
  ACTIVE 3

  FIND done_yet                          !Find Is CXAJM81H Scheduled yet?

WHILETRUE done_yet = no THEN
  RESET done
  RESET finish
  FIND ssupport                          !Find CXAJM81H Scheduling Support
  ACTIVE 2
  ACTIVE 3
  FIND done                              !Find Is CXAJM81H Completed yet?
END
DISPLAY "Exiting the consultation ...." ;

! %%%%%%%%%%%%%%%%%%%%%%%%%%%%%% Rules %%%%%%%%%%%%%%%%%%%%%%%%%%%%%%%%%%

! *****  Rule Set 4 to Determine Scheduling Suppport *****

RULE r4_1
IF   tape     = yes    AND
     rate     = yes    AND
     code     = yes
THEN ssupport = ss1
     ind      = ss1
     SAVEFACTS temp;

RULE r4_6
IF   tape     = no
THEN ssupport = ss6
     ind      = no;

RULE r4_4
IF   rate     = no1
THEN ssupport = ss4
     ind      = no;

RULE r4_5
IF   rate     = no2
THEN ssupport = ss5
     ind      = no;

RULE r4_2
IF   code     = no1
THEN ssupport = ss2
     ind      = no;

RULE r4_3
IF   code     = no2
THEN ssupport = ss3
     ind      = no;

!***** Rule Set 1 to Determine TAPE Critical Factor and Help ********
RULE tape_help
IF tape_created = help
THEN tape = help
     whiletrue tape_created = help THEN
      RESET tape_created
      find tape_created
     end
     reset tape;

RULE tape_valid
IF     tape_created = yes  AND
       blkcnt_good  >= 0
THEN   tape =  check_valid
       search_key = tape
       get search_key = key, valid, all
       close valid
       reset tape;
```

```
RULE r1_1
IF   tape_created =  yes      AND
     blkcnt_good  >= (val1)
THEN tape         =  yes
     display "The block count is good."
     display "  "
BECAUSE
"The tape is of a current creation with no write errors and
the block count is within a normal range

";

RULE r1_2
IF   tape_created =  no       OR
     blkcnt_good  <= (val1)
THEN tape         =  no
     display "The input tape is not ready!!  /Q if you wish to quit."
     display "  "
BECAUSE
"Either the tape is not of a good current creation or
the block count falls below the acceptable range

";

!***** Rule Set 2 to Determine RATE Critical Factor and Help ******
RULE rate2_help
IF   change         =  none  AND
     rates_keyed2   =  help
THEN rate           =  help
     whiletrue rates_keyed2 = help THEN
      RESET rates_keyed2
      find rates_keyed2
     end
     reset rate ;

RULE r2_1
IF   change         <> revenue AND
     rates_keyed2   =  yes
THEN rate           =  no1
     display "The rate tables are in err!  /Q if you wish to quit."
     display "  ";

RULE r2_2
IF   change         <> revenue AND
     rates_keyed2   =  no
THEN rate           =  yes;

RULE rate_help
IF   change         = revenue  AND
     rates_keyed    =  help
THEN rate           =  help
      whiletrue rates_keyed  = help THEN
      RESET rates_keyed
      find rates_keyed
     end
     reset rate ;

RULE r2_3
IF   change         =  revenue  AND
     rates_keyed    =  yes
THEN rate           =  yes;

RULE r2_4
IF   change         =  revenue  AND
     rates_keyed    =  no
THEN rate           =  no2
     display "The rate tables are not ready!  /Q if you wish to quit."
     display "  " ;


!*****  Done With Scheduling Support Consultation Rules *********
RULE done_yet_yes
IF   ask_done_yet = yes
THEN done_yet = yes
     savefacts temp
     display "Loading Verification Assistant ....."
     chain project2;
```

Figure 10C–8. *continued*

```
RULE done_yet_no
IF   ask_done_yet = no
THEN done_yet = no;

RULE done_yes
IF   ind         = ss1 AND
     ask_done = yes
THEN  done = yes
      display "Loading Verification Assistant...."
      savefacts temp
      chain project2 ;

RULE done_no
IF   ind         = ss1 AND
     ask_done = no
THEN done=no
     WHILETRUE ask_done = no THEN
      reset ask_done
      find ask_done
     END
      display "Loading Verification Assistant...."
      savefacts temp
      chain project2 ;

RULE done_no_no
IF   finish = no
THEN  done = no
      done_yet = no
      reset ssupport
      reset tape
      reset rate
      reset code
      reset tape_created
      reset blkcnt_good
      reset rates_keyed
      reset rates_keyed2
      reset change_any
      reset change
      reset macro_calls
      reset cxup2000s
      reset sysin_point
      reset formats
      reset formats2
      reset macro_calls2
      reset cxup2000s2
      reset sysin_point2
      reset ask_done_yet
      reset ask_done
      reset finish
      DISPLAY " ***** New Consultation *****

"
ELSE  done=yes
      done_yet = yes;

!*********  WHENEVER Help Rules **********
WHENEVER
      tape_created
IF    tape_created = help
THEN  COLOR=14
      WOPEN 4,5,5,16,70,1
      ACTIVE 4
      DISPLAY "
  OSTIQ  Tape Management System Query

  From Option 6 of ISPF or TSO
  ( <shift><shift> to get into MainFrame Mode. )

   - Type OSTIQ <enter>
   - Type MASTER <enter>
   - Type CX.CMNDLOS.PROD(0) <enter>
   - Read the screen to check that the creation date
     (CRTDATE) is in the current month.
   - Write down the block count (BLKCNT) for the
     next consultation question.

   Press any key to continue consultation.~"
```

```
        WCLOSE 4
        ACTIVE 2
        ACTIVE 3
        COLOR = 0
        ;

WHENEVER
        change_any
IF      change_any = help
THEN    COLOR=14
        CLOSE 3
        CLOSE 2
        WOPEN 4,5,5,18,70,1
        ACTIVE 4
        DISPLAY "
 How to Determine A Change to CXAJM81H

 Revenue: If it is a November process month,
 a new Medicare revenue needs to be loaded.  If
 it is a February process month, a new Medicaid
 revenue scheme needs to be loaded.

 Other: Any changes to the process in general, such as
 reading a new field or adding a new sort.  Any
 changes to the format of the CX.CMNDLOS.PROD(0+)
 input tape, such as a new record length.

 None: No changes are neccessary.

 Press any key to continue consultation.~"

        WCLOSE 4
        COLOR = 0
        ACTIVE 2
        ACTIVE 3;
```

Design Considerations

There were several design issues considered in the development of the Computer Job Scheduler Assistant. A first attempt was to make both scheduling and verification one logical knowledge base. Because the critical factors did not combine in a manageable way, however, it was decided to chain two KBS files together.

In this system, a recommendation can contain multiple values. A first attempt made the recommendation variables plural. This made it difficult to display the multiple recommendation text in any aesthetic or coherent way. So the final prototype is designed to fire WHENEVER clauses when the recommendation variable is set to a value. The WHENEVER clauses display the recommendation in a window at the exact moment the user answers the set of questions that support that recommendation. The WHENEVER clauses then reset the recommendation variable and the consultation continues to satisfy other conditions that could lead to additional recommendations. One result of this was that the final rule set had to be reordered so that certain questions were not asked too early.

Since the purpose of this prototype is to train a new job scheduler, it was imperative to include a help facility. This was done by adding a Help option to the answer choices of questions as appropriate. WHILETRUE and WHENEVER clauses were used. When the user selects the Help option to a question, a WHENEVER clause displays the help text in a window. But VP-Expert does not allow a consultation to re-evaluate the rule that fires a WHENEVER clause. The system, therefore, has separate rules to handle each help option. They provide a program loop to enable a user to query the help text multiple times.

The following segment of code from the KBS file demonstrates how the Help option is programmed.

```
RULE tape_help
IF tape_created = help
THEN tape = help
     WHILETRUE tape_created = help THEN
       RESET tape_created
       FIND tape_created
     END
     RESET tape;

WHENEVER
     tape_created
IF   tape_created = help
THEN COLOR = 14
     WOPEN 4,5,5,16,70,1
     ACTIVE 4
DISPLAY "

           (help message)

WCLOSE 4
```

Future Development

The prototype is currently run on a personal computer. A PC-to-mainframe emulator would allow a job scheduler to hit a "hot key" and switch from the PC mode to the mainframe mode. In this way, the scheduler can answer system questions on the PC and, when given an action, hit a key to carry out the appropriate action on the mainframe.

Another goal is to migrate this prototype expert system to an IBM mainframe. Once this is accomplished, a more elaborate system could be developed to track input/output tapes, submit production jobs in proper sequence, monitor and check the completion of jobs, and determine corrective actions—all on an automatic basis.

Additionally, the Computer Job Scheduler Assistant prototype can be expanded to include the entire routine database update process.

GLOSSARY

ACTIONS *See* General Keywords Summary, Chapter 7.

Actions Block A basic element of a knowledge base file that sets the agenda for a consultation. It tells the inference engine what it needs to FIND, and in what order, during a consultation. The keyword ACTIONS identifies the beginning of the Actions Block.

ACTIVE *See* General Keywords Summary, Chapter 7.

ALL *See* Database Keywords Summary, Chapter 7.

artificial intelligence The capability of a device, such as a computer, to perform functions or tasks that would be regarded as intelligent if they were observed in humans.

ASK *See* General Keywords Summary, Chapter 7.

AUTOQUERY *See* General Keywords Summary, Chapter 7.

backward chaining A problem-solving method used by an inference engine to manipulate rules during a consultation session. Backward chaining starts by identifying a "goal variable." It then works through the rules until it can assign a value to the goal variable. Rules in the rule base are not processed in a purely sequential order, but rather are selected based on their relevance to the problem at hand.

BCALL *See* General Keywords Summary, Chapter 7.

BECAUSE Used optionally to offer an explanation of the premise, conclusion, and alternate conclusion of a RULE.

BKCOLOR *See* General Keywords Summary, Chapter 7.

BUTTON *See* Graphics Keywords Summary, Chapter 7.

CALL *See* General Keywords Summary, Chapter 7.

CCALL *See* General Keywords Summary, Chapter 7.

chaining Linking two or more knowledge bases for use in a single consultation. Chaining encourages the modular development of very large knowledge-based systems by designing smaller independent subsets of the whole KBS. Chaining is accomplished with the CHAIN, SAVEFACTS, and LOADFACTS keywords.

CHOICES *See* General Keywords Summary, Chapter 7.

CLOSE *See* Database Keywords Summary, Chapter 7.

CLS *See* General Keywords Summary, Chapter 7.

COLOR *See* General Keywords Summary, Chapter 7.

COLUMN *See* Spreadsheet Keywords Summary, Chapter 7.

conditions Factors from a dependency diagram that are mapped onto a decision table. The number of conditions and their possible values help determine the number of rows necessary in a decision table.

confidence factor A number attached to a value that indicates the developer/expert's or user's degree of certainty in the value. In VP-Expert, zero indicates no confidence and 100 indicates total confidence or trust in the value.

Consult Menu A menu that appears on the bottom of the screen in VP-Expert when "Consult" is chosen from the Main Menu. Among the options on the Consult Menu, "Go" starts the consultation, "Variable" gives the current value of a variable, and "Edit" switches to the VP-Expert Editor.

DBFORM *See* Graphics Keywords Summary, Chapter 7.

debugging Correcting errors in a file.

decision table A table that shows the interrelationships of values to the outcome of any intermediate phase or final recommendation of a knowledge-based system.

demon A technique for using forward chaining in a backward chaining knowledge base. The WHENEVER rule acts as a demon in VP-Expert: it watches the variable(s) referenced by its IF condition(s) and executes each time the condition(s) evaluates as true. This causes the inference engine to jump out of its backward chaining search strategy and, instead, leap forward to execute the appropriate WHENEVER rule, wherever it appears in the knowledge base.

dependency diagram A diagram that indicates the relationships, or dependencies, among critical factors, input questions, rules, values, and recommendations made by a knowledge-based system.

DISPLAY *See* General Keywords Summary, Chapter 7.

Dynamic Image A predefined graphic object in VP-Expert that is dynamically linked to the value of a specified variable. Dynamic Images include a gauge, button, formfield, meter, and time-series graph.

Editor A term to reference the crude word processor that is built into software, such as in an expert system shell; also called Editor and debugger.

EJECT *See* General Keywords Summary, Chapter 7.

ELLIPSE *See* Graphics Keywords Summary, Chapter 7.

ELSE Used optionally to identify the beginning of an alternative conclusion of a RULE.

END *See* General Keywords Summary, Chapter 7.

ENDOFF *See* General Keywords Summary, Chapter 7.

EXECUTE *See* General Keywords Summary, Chapter 7.

expert system A computer system designed to replicate functions performed by a human being. It is used to capture, magnify, and distribute access to judgment; also called knowledge-based system.

explanation facility The component of a knowledge-based system that stores a history file during a user consultation of the rules that contribute to a conclusion.

FILL *See* Graphics Keywords Summary, Chapter 7.

FIND *See* General Keywords Summary, Chapter 7.

FORMAT *See* General Keywords Summary, Chapter 7.

FORMFIELD *See* Graphics Keywords Summary, Chapter 7.

GBCOLOR *See* Graphics Keywords Summary, Chapter 7.

GCLS *See* Graphics Keywords Summary, Chapter 7.

GCOLOR *See* Graphics Keywords Summary, Chapter 7.

GDISPLAY *See* Graphics Keywords Summary, Chapter 7.

GET *See* Database Keywords Summary, Chapter 7.

GLOCATE *See* Graphics Keywords Summary, Chapter 7.

GMODE *See* Graphics Keywords Summary, Chapter 7.

Go Menu A menu of options available during a consultation and accessed by pressing the slash (/) key. Go Menu options include "Why?" to show why a question is being asked and "Slow" and "Fast" to slow down or speed up a consultation.

graphics tree A graphics illustration of the search path followed by the inference engine to reach a conclusion. A graphics tree represents a consultation as recorded by the Trace command and is viewed by choosing the Graphics command on the Tree Menu.

HGAUGE *See* Graphics Keywords Summary, Chapter 7.

HOTREGION *See* Graphics Keywords Summary, Chapter 7.

How? A command on the Go Menu used to describe how a value was assigned to a variable selected from a list of choices.

hypertext Text that is contained in an external text file and automatically appears in a pop-up window during a VP-Expert consultation when a user clicks on a "hot" word, or hyperword, or button.

HYPERTEXT *See* Graphics Keywords Summary, Chapter 7.

hyperword A "hot" word embedded in hypertext that causes the current text on the screen to be replaced with new text related to the hyperword. Hyperwords are displayed in uppercase letters.

icon A graphic image used to communicate information to a user.

IF Identifies the beginning of a RULE condition(s).

indifference symbol A mark, such as a hyphen, used in a decision table to indicate that the condition does not have any bearing on the evaluation. Its effect is to collapse two or more rules into a single rule.

indirect addressing A technique where a variable name is used as an indirect way of addressing its value. This technique is useful, for example, to display the results of a consultation.

Induce Menu A menu that appears on the bottom of the screen in VP-Expert when "Induce" is chosen from the Main Menu to create a knowledge base from an induction table. Among the options on the Induce Menu, "Create" invokes the Editor to allow a user to enter a table file.

induction system An expert system optimized to take a file of examples and produce a working knowledge base from the file without any programming.

inference engine The program in a knowledge-based system that handles the logic processing and makes it work.

integrated systems Enhanced knowledge-based systems that are linked to other systems, such as spreadsheets or databases. Such linkages enable building knowledge-based systems that add value to already developed computer-based files and systems.

keywords Words used in the construction of a knowledge base. They include the words that begin every line (clause or statement), special words used in rule construction, and other words reserved for special use in the knowledge base.

knowledge base A collection of information, or expert knowledge, in a knowledge-based system about some specific area or field.

knowledge-based system A computer system designed to capture, magnify, and distribute access to judgment. It has three main parts: the knowledge base, an inference engine, and an explanation facility; also called expert system.

knowledge domain The area of expertise under study in a knowledge-based system development project.

knowledge engineer A computer specialist with skills to mine heuristics from human experts and transfer them to a computerized knowledge base.

LBUTTON *See* Graphics Keywords Summary, Chapter 7.

LINETO *See* Graphics Keywords Summary, Chapter 7.

loop processing Repetitively executing a series of commands inside a WHILEKNOWN-END loop until some exit condition is reached; also called iterative processing.

Main Menu The opening menu that appears at the bottom of the screen in VP-Expert when the program begins. Among the options on the Main Menu, "Edit" opens the Editor, "Consult" begins a consultation, and "FileName" is used to select a knowledge base file.

MENU *See* Database Keywords Summary, Chapter 7.

MENU_SIZE *See* Database Keywords Summary, Chapter 7.

METER *See* Graphics Keywords Summary, Chapter 7.

MOUSEOFF *See* Graphics Keywords Summary, Chapter 7.

MOUSEON *See* Graphics Keywords Summary, Chapter 7.

MOVETO *See* Graphics Keywords Summary, Chapter 7.

MRESET *See* Database Keywords Summary, Chapter 7.

NAMED *See* Spreadsheet Keywords Summary, Chapter 7.

PDISPLAY *See* General Keywords Summary, Chapter 7.

PLURAL *See* General Keywords Summary, Chapter 7.

POP *See* General Keywords Summary, Chapter 7.

PRINTOFF *See* General Keywords Summary, Chapter 7.

PRINTON *See* General Keywords Summary, Chapter 7.

prototype A small developmental test version of a larger computer system. Prototypes are useful to test the feasibility and soundness of larger systems before expensive development efforts begin.

PSET *See* Graphics Keywords Summary, Chapter 7.

PUT *See* Database Keywords Summary, Chapter 7.

PWKS *See* Spreadsheet Keywords Summary, Chapter 7.

Questions Block A basic element of a knowledge base file that contains all the questions a user may be asked during a consultation.

RECEIVE *See* General Keywords Summary, Chapter 7.

RECORD_NUM *See* Database Keywords Summary, Chapter 7.

RECTANGLE *See* Graphics Keywords Summary, Chapter 7.

remark Any text, or comment, preceded by an exclamation point in a VP-Expert knowledge base file to document what is going on in the knowledge base; also called in-program documentation or internal documentation.

RESET *See* General Keywords Summary, Chapter 7.

ROW *See* Spreadsheet Keywords Summary, Chapter 7.

RULE *See* General Keywords Summary, Chapter 7.

Rule A command on the Consult Menu used to examine any rules in the currently active knowledge base.

Rules Block A basic element of a VP-Expert knowledge base file that, along with the Questions Block, contains the expertise used to solve the problem of a consultation. Control typically is passed to the Rules Block when the FIND keyword is encountered in the Actions Block. Once the value of the FIND variable is known, control is passed back to the Actions Block.

RUNTIME *See* General Keywords Summary, Chapter 7.

Set Menu A menu that appears on the bottom of the screen in VP-Expert when "Set" is chosen from the Consult Menu. Among the options on the Set Menu, "Trace" causes VP-Expert to "record" the next consultation so that it can be viewed as a text or graphic tree and "Slow" slows down the activity in the Rules and Values windows to view the execution of a knowledge base.

shell packages Expert system software that contains an inference engine but no knowledge base. The knowledge base can be entered by a knowledge engineer or, in some cases, directly by a user.

SHIP *See* General Keywords Summary, Chapter 7.

Slow A command on the Set Menu used to slow down the execution of the knowledge base so that the developer can more easily follow the activity in the Rules and Facts windows.

SmartForm A form that appears on screen as it might on a paper form. Unlike a paper form, if certain information is entered, it can offer advice to the user, remove irrelevant items, add new items, and maintain consistency between the items on the form.

SORT *See* General Keywords Summary, Chapter 7.

stack A term used to describe how PLURAL variables are stored in memory. The POP keyword is used to obtain the top value from the stack, causing the next-to-the-top value to move to the top of the stack.

static range A rectangular block of one or more spreadsheet cells that is treated as a unit. The block is referenced by naming the cell coordinates of the two most distant cells in the range.

subscript A bracketed number assigned to a dimensioned variable that corresponds to a position in a column, row, or range in a spreadsheet.

text tree A text illustration of the search path followed by the inference engine to reach a conclusion. A text tree represents the consultation as recorded by the Trace command and is viewed by choosing the Text command on the Tree Menu.

THEN Identifies the beginning of a RULE conclusion.

TMODE *See* Graphics Keywords Summary, Chapter 7.

Trace A command on the Set Menu used to record the path of the inference engine during the next consultation. The path is stored in a file that can be viewed using the Text or Graphics commands on the Tree Menu.

TRACK *See* Graphics Keywords Summary, Chapter 7.

Tree Menu A menu that appears on the bottom of the screen in VP-Expert when "Tree" is chosen from the Main Menu to view the file created by the last execution of the Trace command. Among the options on the Tree Menu, "Text" displays a text tree of the Trace file and "Graphics" displays a graphic representation of the Trace file.

truth threshold A number supplied by the developer to determine the minimum confidence factor required for a rule to be considered true.

TRUTHTHRESH *See* General Keywords Summary, Chapter 7.

update To edit, change, or revise an existing file or record in a file.

user interface All the parts a user actually sees and interfaces with when running a knowledge-based system in a consultation session. At a minimum, the user interface consists of the opening and closing messages and the questions posed during the consultation session.

Variable A command on the Consult Menu used to examine the value(s) and confidence factors assigned to any variable selected from a list of choices.

VGAUGE *See* Graphics Keywords Summary, Chapter 7.

WFORMAT *See* Spreadsheet Keywords Summary, Chapter 7.

WhatIf A command on the Consult Menu used to determine how a change in a variable's value could affect the solution arrived at in the last consultation.

WHILEKNOWN *See* General Keywords Summary, Chapter 7.

Why? A command on the Go Menu that allows a user, or developer, to stop a consultation anywhere and ask why a question is being asked.

Windows Menu A menu that appears on the bottom of the screen in VP-Expert when "Windows" is chosen from the Set Menu to change the size and location of the windows that appear during a consultation. Among the options on the Windows Menu, "Consult," "Rules," and "Values" allow the respective windows to be moved or re-sized.

WKS *See* Spreadsheet Keywords Summary, Chapter 7.

WOPEN *See* General Keywords Summary, Chapter 7.

working memory Temporary storage in the computer's memory to hold the paths and intermediate conclusions of the inference engine during a consultation. This information is useful for developing and debugging a knowledge-based system and is displayed in the Rules and Facts windows on a consultation screen. Working memory is sometimes called cache.

INDEX

GUIDE TO USING THE M.1 DISK ACCOMPANYING THIS TEXT

The instructions for running the runtime and educational development versions of VP-Expert are found in Chapter 7, "Installation."

The M.1 program can be run from a diskette drive or, if preferred, it can be installed to a hard disk. To install to a hard disk, insert the M.1 disk in diskette drive A and at the C: prompt type

```
C:\>MKDIR M1
C:\>CD \M1
C:\M1>COPY A:*.* C:
```

When the files have copied successfully, remove the M.1 disk from drive A.

The instructions for running the educational development version of M.1 are as follows:

1. Load the M.1 expert system shell program and related M.1 data from the C:>, A:>, or other DOS prompt by typing "start" and pressing the Enter key.
2. The M1> prompt appears on the screen. To load the desired system file, type

   M1> load file_name.extension
   Example:
   M1> load career.rev

   where file_name.extension represents the full DOS name of the M.1 file you wish to run (Note: lowercase letters must be used at all times while M.1 is running.) Press the Enter key. Loading the file can take from one to five minutes.
3. Once the file is finished loading, the M1> prompt reappears. Type "go" and press the Enter key.
4. Follow the instructions on the screen to run the knowledge-based system consultation. The prompt that appears on screen during the consultation is the >> prompt.

Special functions available while running a consultation:

- To go back to the M> prompt while a consultation is in session, type "abort" at the >> prompt and press the Enter key.
- To exit M.1 and go back to DOS, type "exit" or "quit" at the M1> prompt or >> prompt and press the Enter key.
- To print out a consultation's reasoning steps, turn the printer on. Before typing "go", type "log printer" and press the Enter key. Then type "trace on" and press the Enter key. Typing "go" starts the consultation, which prints out as it appears on the screen. (To turn the trace function off, type "trace off" and press the Enter key.)

Note: If too many systems are loaded in a single session of M.1, the memory in your computer (RAM) may fill up, resulting in an error message ("Error 275"). In order to clear the memory, "quit" M.1 and begin again with Step 1.